Laura,

Congratulations the contest, I hope you enjoy this book!

Brendan Hughes

THE
Wandering
INVESTOR

BRENDAN HUGHES

First Printing, 2020
BookBaby
7905 N. Crescent Blvd.
Pennsauken, NJ 08110

This is a personal book. Any views or opinions represented in this book are personal and belong solely to the book owner and do not represent those of people, institutions, or organizations that the owner may or may not be associated with in professional or personal capacity, unless explicitly stated.

ABOUT THE AUTHOR

Brendan Hughes is an investment advisor for Lafayette Investments, where he personally manages a portion of the approximately $500 million in assets under management and assists in the investment decision making process for the equity portfolio.

Previously, he served as a senior analyst for Primatics Financial, where he operated in a lead role on the largest whole-book loan implementation in company history for a top 10 U.S. bank with more than $300 billion in assets.

Brendan is a Chartered Financial Analyst (CFA). As a 2012 James Madison University graduate who received a BBA in finance and accounting,

Brendan remains active within the JMU community, serving as an associate member of the College of Business Board of Advisors and formerly serving as Madison Network Committee Chair for the GOLD Network Board, which represents the young alumni of the university. Brendan serves as a Board Member for the Maryland Chapter of the Cystic Fibrosis Foundation (CFF) in addition to serving as Tomorrow's Leaders Co-Chairman for the Maryland Chapter of the CFF. He served as a member of the 2019 Maryland's Finest Committee for the Cystic Fibrosis Foundation in addition to having served on the 2018 Maryland's Finest Nominating Committee and was an honoree of the 2017 Maryland's Finest program (a select group of individuals who have demonstrated leadership in the community and excelled in their profession). Brendan was awarded the Tomorrow's Leaders Award by the CFF for his contributions to the Foundation. Brendan serves as a Board Member for CanEducate, a registered Canadian charitable organization that raises money to provide scholarships for students in developing countries. Brendan is a Board Member for ZERV Inc., an innovative Canadian technology start-up. Brendan is on the Member Engagement Committee for CFA Society Washington D.C.

Brendan will be donating a portion of the proceeds from the sales of *The Wandering Investor* to James Madison University, the Cystic Fibrosis Foundation Maryland Chapter, and CanEducate. If you would like to support these organizations, please visit these links: https://www.jmu.edu/give/, https://www.cff.org/Maryland/, https://www.canadahelps.org/en/dn/4977.

Feel free to contact Brendan at Hughes2525@gmail.com.

TABLE OF CONTENTS

INTRODUCTION

This book takes the reader on a unique journey around the world in a discussion about various economies, my personal adventures along the way, business outlooks and observations for each country, lists of recommended activities in each country with a focus on outdoor adventure experiences, and lessons learned in terms of both travel and business. Given my experience as an investment advisor and what I would consider to be a deep knowledge base when it comes to global adventure excursions, I believe this writing provides a much different perspective than your average travel or investment book. It reads like a thriller in detailing extreme activities such as skydiving over Queenstown, New Zealand, while weaving in the details mentioned above.

I will cover my travels across 17 countries spread out across six continents. As of the time of this writing, I had visited 28 countries. This book is the culmination of five years of work and thousands of hours of research in terms of country-specific macroeconomic data, information about local laws and regulations, historical facts about specific countries, and recommendations for mostly adventure-related activities to do while in a country. I have learned a lot through the years by studying individual businesses and macroeconomic developments, but I learned more through the process of writing this book than anything else.

If you have examined my personal background, you may have wondered how I have fit this work into my schedule along with regular work as an investment advisor, extensive philanthropic involvement, and past experience studying for the CFA Exam. The truth is that I have spent years often waking up at 3:30 a.m. during the week and countless hours on the weekends to create a writing piece that I am proud to present. In addition, almost all of these trips were done over holidays to limit the amount of work missed.

I think it is important to note that many adventure activities discussed in this book present inherent risks that should be considered. I still enjoy activities such as scuba diving, but I will no longer partake in activities such as skydiving because I now manage millions of dollars for clients and it would not be responsible for me to be participating in such high-risk adventures while being entrusted with an individual's life savings. If you decide to go skydiving, abseiling, or participate in any other activity that presents elevated risks, please make sure to conduct your due diligence in regard to risks related to the activity in aggregate as well as on the company that is providing the services.

I hope you enjoy this book and find it helpful in terms of country-specific information, investment perspectives, and travel recommendations. I have documented my travels over the years on my Instagram account: @ the_wandering_investor. Additionally, I have provided travel advice and recommendations on my The Wandering Investor Facebook page. Without further ado, here is my take on the world.

New Zealand

Introduction

The door swung open and a violent rush of cool air poured in. I watched two tandems vanish in front of me. I looked down to check my gear one last time before putting my life in the hands of a man I had met just an hour prior. The group was surprisingly calm given the severity of the situation.

Upon receiving a tap on the shoulder from the daredevil attached to my back, I knew it was my time. From our seated position, we navigated our way toward the open door by dragging our butts across the floor most likely similar to how a penguin would move along the ground on its stomach. As I sat in the doorway of the tiny airplane, my feet dangled over the edge as the sobering breeze hit me harder than a Randy Johnson fastball. Those few brief seconds of looking out over the snow-covered mountains from 12,000 feet were among the most surreal of my life. Fear might have overwhelmed me in that moment, but the picturesque snowcapped mountain background diverted my attention.

Then I was nudged out of the small airplane, and we performed a perfectly executed backflip before locking into our free fall position and plummeted toward the ground at a speed nearing 200 miles per hour. I have no words to describe that 60-second free fall other than the pinnacle of exhilaration and feeling as though I was floating on top of the world. I posed for pictures from the in-air photographer and took in the stunning view of the area around Queenstown, New Zealand. I still replay in my head the series of events, as it does not get much better than that free fall.

I was then abruptly yanked as the parachute opened and filled, a huge relief, and that's where the real adventure began. I doubt whether the plane should have gone out that day given the high winds that threw us around like an older brother does to a younger sibling. There were moments during the ensuing minutes where I was not certain if we were going to land safely, much less land anywhere close to our intended target. The reportedly 1,000 jumps done by each NZONE Tandem Master did not quell the doubts I had during that descent. I became a bit nauseous as we were jostled left, then right, then down 30 feet (similar sequences would be replayed). Much to my surprise, we were suddenly just 1,000 feet from the ground and rapidly closing in on our desired destination. I readied my feet before making what turned out to be a smooth landing, all things considered. Looking up at the sky, I realized that my life had just changed forever. This officially spawned my interest in adventure travel that would continue for years to come.

My mother and I had flown to New Zealand seeking some travel adventures, and we were not disappointed. It turned out to be a destination of a lifetime. I also wanted to check out the business climate to evaluate any investment opportunities the small country might have to offer.

My interest in international travel began two years before when I studied abroad in Antwerp, Belgium, in Summer 2010. The cultural differences in countries all over Europe fascinated me, and I quickly learned to appreciate simple things that I had at home in Arlington, Virginia. Things I had never reflected on before such as air conditioning on the metro I now perceived as a luxury.

The trip to New Zealand and Australia further fueled my pursuit of outdoor adventure in terms of physical and cultural ambitions abroad. I want to thank my former girlfriend for criticizing me the year of my Australia and New Zealand trip, 2012, for not being brave enough to try activities such as skydiving. It seems rather silly at this time and we are still friends, but when she broke up with me not long before my trip Down Under, I made it a personal mission to attempt the most daring sports possible just because she said that I wouldn't. Little did I know that these aspirations, combined with my thirst for worldwide cultural and financial knowledge, would lay the groundwork for the writing of this book.

In planning a trip upon my graduation from James Madison University, my mother, who is close to 30 years my senior, and I needed to agree on a location that interested us both. I had initially wanted to venture to China, but my mom preferred a primarily English-speaking country. She also opposed the extreme pollution in China's larger cities. Despite the New Zealand/Australia trip being a pricier option, we agreed that it would be an outstanding opportunity. I wanted to travel across the world because I was unsure as to when I would be able to get two consecutive weeks off work again. Additionally, these countries stood in stark contrast to many European countries in that they offered a plethora of outdoor options that I had never been exposed to. After conducting my research, I found that this excursion was surely an outdoor adventurer's dream and would test the boundaries of what I thought I could do at the time.

As we boarded the airplane in Los Angeles, anticipation coursed through my body. 14 hours later, after crossing the Pacific Ocean in the dark, lights suddenly appeared. My six-foot-four frame felt quite sore from the 6,482-mile flight to Auckland. I looked forward to stretching my legs and the adventures that lay ahead.

The two major islands, North Island and South Island, are separated by the Cook Strait, which measures approximately 14 miles at the narrowest section. New Zealand has a total land area of 103,500 square miles, of which 9,300 are along the coast. The South Island contains the majority of the country's land mass and is more mountainous than its northern counterpart, with 18 peaks over 9,800 feet.

The country is subject to high levels of volcanic activity and we were diverted from the Christchurch airport while we were there due to several earthquakes in the area. Many scientists believe the country is long overdue for a major earthquake, assessing a high probability of the Alpine Fault rupturing in the next 50 years, which could cause catastrophic damage to the country. In fact, in 2016 the Christchurch area was hit with a 7.8-magnitude tremblor that left two people dead, followed by a 6.2-magnitude aftershock.

Economy

Auckland is the financial capital of the country and located on the North Island. Upon arrival at the Auckland Airport, one of my first observations was the extent to which the country was attempting to protect the agriculture industry. I saw numerous signs reminding those entering the country that attempting to bring in fruit such as oranges or bananas would result in hefty fines. If you don't believe it, check the Internet for horror stories citing $400 fines for fruit that was forgotten in carry-ons.

This fabulous country consisting of nearly 4.5 million people as of 2016 is a parliamentary democracy and has been one of the most economically successful countries in the Asia-Pacific region. Extensive deregulation and privatization that occurred in the 1980s and 1990s proved to be a turning point for the country's economy. The World Bank gives the country high marks in terms of ease of doing business, starting a business, registering property, and obtaining credit, which were all ranked number one in 2015. In fact, with no minimum capital required, it can take as little as one day to start a business there. Compare this to 35 days in Libya, along with a minimum capital requirement amounting to a whopping 33.18% of income per capita as of 2015.

New Zealand has the lowest subsidies among all Organization for Economic Cooperation and Development (OECD) countries; it removed all farming subsidies more than three decades ago, which provided a huge tailwind for the agriculture industry (maybe the United States should take note). The country had a 2016 average tariff rate of 1.4%, compared to 1.5% for the United States, along with low barriers for nontariff goods. The overall tax burden in 2016 amounted to 32.1% of total domestic income, compared to 25.4% in the United States.

New Zealand receives high marks for transparency and places a heavy emphasis on providing a judicial system that is free of corruption. According to *The World Factbook*, the country has managed to keep public debt to 33.5% of GDP as of mid-2016 which is relatively low compared to many other developed nations.

The service sector of the New Zealand economy accounted for 63% of GDP in 2013. Major contributors include rental, hiring, and real estate services (13.3% of 2015 GDP), manufacturing (10.1% of GDP), and agriculture, forestry, and fishing (6.2% of GDP). The World Bank ranks New Zealand 8th out of 120 countries in terms of natural capital per capita, which is only behind petroleum-exporting countries. The country has access to plentiful clean water and productive soil, along with a moderate climate that is suited for agriculture and humans, substantial petroleum and mineral reserves, and an impressive expanse of biodiversity.

As of mid-2016, and relative to other developed countries, New Zealand had achieved an impressive 3.5% trailing GDP growth rate. New Zealand has kept unemployment low at 5.1% as of 2016. In the financial sector, it operates the New Zealand Exchange, NZX, and recognizes the New Zealand dollar as the formal currency.

As previously mentioned, tourism is a major strength of the New Zealand economy due to the beautiful scenery and wealth of outdoor options. Barring temporary setbacks from environmental disasters such as earthquakes, I would expect this industry to continue to perform well for years to come.

According to the OECD, New Zealand ranked in the top 25 out of 70 countries in reading, science, and math as of 2016. I would like to see the country place a stronger emphasis on education, which further benefits the economy over the long run. The country does currently have a large housing bubble in progress, and it is only a matter of time before it implodes. While this development would be a short-term setback for the economy, I do not see it leading to destruction of the long-term fundamentals put in place by pro-business government policies, vast natural resource deposits, and a diverse economy that has allowed the country to deal relatively well with recessions.

New Zealand pulled out of the 2008 global recession quickly compared to many other OECD countries, achieving 1.7% growth in 2010 and 2% in 2011. I would attribute this success to a balanced economy that is not dependent on any one resource or service. Additionally, while I have highlighted the growing dangers brewing in the local residential real estate market later in this chapter, the New Zealand and Australian banks remain well capitalized for the most part. Basel III (regulated by the Reserve Bank of New Zealand) requires a minimum total capital ratio of 8% along with an additional 2.5% buffer.

A wildcard for the country will always be the high risk of a catastrophic earthquake taking place, but just like any other high-risk location, both the residents and the government can't do anything to avoid such a situation given the current technological environment.

Adventure

One of our first observations while in Auckland was the relatively high price of food in the city. While we were in the business district and more touristy areas, my mom and I found it normal to pay the equivalent of $25 per person for a lunch that was not even anything special. New Zealand was likely the most expensive country I have visited in my travels around the world. It is important to note the currency exchange rate fluctuations that have occurred between the U.S. and New Zealand in recent years. As of 2017, the U.S. dollar had appreciated significantly against the New Zealand dollar compared to a few years prior, making the country much more accessible to Americans. We spent the majority of our two days in Auckland touring the city and went on an all-day excursion the second day.

Prior to setting out for our tour, we went to the top of the Auckland Sky Tower. This soaring spire, measuring more than 1,076 feet in height, provides fantastic views of the Auckland region and is the tallest man-made structure in the Southern Hemisphere. In hindsight I probably should have done the SkyJump, which is a base jump via wire from atop the tower. While terrifying, it would have been another exciting adventure to add to the list during this trip.

After we joined our tour, we went through the nearby suburb of Ponsonby, a trendy area packed with boutique fashion stores. We continued over the Harbour Bridge to the North Shore before reaching the summit of Mount Victoria, which provided for stunning views of Auckland across Waitemata Harbour. The day-long trip made for quite an experience considering we went from a downtown financial district to a harbor area before venturing close to 25 miles outside the city to visit Waitakere Ranges, the area's largest regional park. This diverse landscape in such close proximity, along with the financial presence in Auckland, make it a popular tourist destination. New Zealand's international visitors increased 10.6% to 3.3 million for the year ended June 2016.

Upon continuing our tour to a rainforest region located in a regional park, the extreme swing in weather certainly lived up to the billing as it went from being a sunny day to pouring rain within minutes. No wonder the Maoris, New Zealand's indigenous people, dubbed the island *Aotearoa*, land of the long white cloud. The locals attribute the wide-ranging weather to the lack of a surrounding land mass to protect the island country from winds sweeping across the Southern Pacific Ocean.

Weather in New Zealand is notoriously unpredictable, as we found it to be a running joke that weathermen didn't even attempt to make forecasts due to the sometimes hourly swings. The mean temperatures in the south are about 11 degrees cooler than that of the North Island (48 and 59 degrees Fahrenheit, respectively). If you are visiting both the North and the South Island, be prepared with various sets of attire. I brought clothes varying from shorts and a t-shirt to pants and sweatshirts which I would deem to be appropriate given the temperature ranges and unpredictability of the weather patterns.

At the Arataki Centre we were pleased with the views from our perch that allowed us to look out over the Tasman Sea and Pacific Ocean. Another highlight from the day was walking through the rainforest where we got acquainted with the kauri trees and took pictures next to a beautiful waterfall.

We capped off the adventurous day with a brief tour of a couple of beaches in the area. What was interesting about the west coast beaches was that they had black sand. I had never seen black sand before and was enthralled by the vast expanse of the rainforest in the background, along with the waves crashing into the shore. We met a family from Chicago and learned that we had nearly identical trips planned, as we would see them in two other cities during our stay in New Zealand.

The following day we left early in the morning for Rotorua. The car ride along the way was amazing and reminded me of southern Ireland because we could easily find ourselves gazing for hours at the sprawling green coun-tryside. Our tour stopped at the famous Waitomo Glowworm Caves. There we took a leisurely boat ride through the caves, where we saw thousands of tiny glowworms, a species endemic to New Zealand, illuminating our surroundings. This silent boat ride provided for a relaxing opportunity to witness a unique experience.

When we arrived in Rotorua, home to 65,000 Kiwis, a nickname for New Zealanders, I really started to pick up the intensity in regard to the activities we had planned. I began by "zorbing" on the outskirts of the town. This inter-esting sport, founded in New Zealand in the mid-1990s, consists of entering a large plastic ball, an orb, and rolling down a slope. I opted for the wet version of the zorb, where I crawled into a ball half filled with water. I then zigzagged down a large hill in this absurd-looking device while getting quite dizzy along the way. I had never heard of zorbing prior to arriving in New Zealand, but I could not pass up the opportunity to experience this intriguing pastime.

Afterward, my mom and I rode a gondola up Mount Ngongotaha, which provided majestic views of Rotorua and the surrounding lake. We took several runs down the side of the mountain via a luge. I opted for the advanced track each time, which was a route that virtually went straight downhill for approximately six-tenths of a mile. I had to wear a helmet as the advanced track allowed for riders to tear down the mountain at speeds up to 30 miles per hour. It was exhilarating while looking out over beautiful Lake Rotorua.

Once our adrenaline levels returned to normal, we took a brief tour of the town. Rotorua is known for its geothermal activity and features geysers in the area. We saw abandoned houses deemed uninhabitable due to the presence of scorching geothermal steam rising from the ground.

The following day we awoke early to set out for a day-long whitewater rafting trip on the Kaituna River. I had done research the day before and was fascinated by the opportunity to navigate through Class V rapids and encounter the highest commercially rafted waterfall in the world at roughly 23 feet. I somehow managed to withhold all of this information from my mom in advance of the activity with the exception of the fact that the rafting excursion in the area sounded like a promising adventure. The ride down the Kaituna was undoubtedly one of the highlights of the trip and one of the most challenging rafting I have done (behind the Zambezi River and with the rapids in the Colorado River notching third place). Given my weight, I sat at the front of the boat and had to quickly learn to work with the group to steer the boat through vicious rapids that threatened to capsize the boat on several occasions.

The climax of the journey came when we arrived at the 23-foot waterfall. Leading up to the plunge our tour guide assured us that there was little risk of overturning, as a mere one raft a month flipped into the freezing cold water, which I was later told on an adventure to Canada that this was not true. Stay tuned for commentary in that chapter. We later encountered a tourist who had broken his foot on the ride and required medical attention.

Being the lead man aboard, I was tasked with steadying the raft prior to the waterfall. As soon as we started to go over the waterfall, I peered over the edge and knew we were doomed when our weight shifted sideways. The next feeling I had was one of bone chilling water and a sense of panic. Upon being sucked to the bottom of the river by the overwhelming current, I gasped for air as I was stuck under the raft. I used my strength to force my way to freedom after a few moments, but it did provide for quite a thrill. While I know after the fact my mom had a great time on the trip, she was not happy with me at that moment. Both of our bodies ached by the end of the excursion, and we couldn't help but laugh at the events that unfolded on the Kaituna. While I am not your average traveler, that day I wouldn't have done anything differently. Amazing.

Once we had changed into dry clothes and stopped shivering, we attended a *hangi* feast in Tamaki Maori Village. *Hangi* is a method of cooking using heated rocks buried in a pit oven. Prior to dining, we witnessed a *haka* song and dance by a Rangiatea cultural group, and demonstrations of daily activities that took place in a pre-European Maori village.

New Zealand was one of the last major land masses settled by humans. The Maori, the indigenous Polynesian people of New Zealand, arrived about 800 years ago, between 1250 and 1300. They resided there for several centuries in relative isolation and developed their own language and rituals prior to the arrival of Europeans in the 17th century, which brought tremendous change to their lives. The evening concluded with a succulent meal consisting of slow-cooked meats and vegetables.

The following day, the flight into Queenstown was incredible in and of itself. The ride provides spectacular views of snow-covered mountain ranges.

Queenstown is a small town, with only 13,000 year-round residents as of the time of this writing. It sits at just over 1,000 feet above sea level. The city is primarily a resort town and known by many as the adventure capital of the world. Popular adventure sports include skydiving, bungy jumping, whitewater rafting, skiing, jet boating, and paragliding.

I was eager to get moving upon arrival. After dropping our belongings off at the hotel, we proceeded to the gondola located just a few minutes outside of central Queenstown. The gondola carried us up Bob's Peak to the Skyline complex, which provided for unparalleled views of the majestic Southern Alps, which include The Remarkables and Coronet Peak, and across Lake Wakatipu to Cecil and Walter Peaks. As far as I am concerned, Queenstown gives Patagonia a run for its money when it comes to being named the most beautiful place on planet earth.

The next adventure in our queue was jet boating. We opted for the Skippers Canyon Jet over the more popular Shotover Jet due to longer duration, cheaper price, and what appeared to be a more cultural experience. The bus ride to Skippers Canyon along the notorious Skippers Canyon Road was probably worth the money alone. The winding road had no guardrails and was just feet from precipitous cliffs that plunged several thousand feet. Along the way we learned the history of the mining area and saw several sites where *The Lord of the Rings* trilogy was filmed, including the Gates of Mordor. My mom shielded her eyes for most of the journey, as she was not reassured by the driver traveling at such high rates of speed along the gravel road.

The entire group enjoyed the jet boat ride. Many times I heard gasps of oohs and aahs, as our boat driver navigated the waters of Skippers Canyon with such precision, at times coming within feet of the surrounding walls while racing along at speeds of up to 50 miles per hour. Our driver showed off his talents on a few occasions by executing full 360-degree spins on a dime. He noted a few locations along the river where additional scenes from *The Lord of the Rings* had been filmed.

Next on our list was an unforgettable journey to Milford Sound. Located within the World Heritage Fiordland National Park, the fiord has been called the eighth Wonder of the World, and some believe it to be the most beautiful place on earth. We hopped aboard our Red Boat vessel for a spectacular cruise that allowed for majestic views of Mitre Peak (an iconic mountain standing at 5,500 feet), rock walls ascending to 4,000 feet from the sea, and several waterfalls, including the impressive 495-foot Stirling Falls. No words written here will do that two-hour boat ride justice. I stood on the roof deck of the ship for the duration of the journey, hanging out with a newfound friend from Germany. We came so close to a few of the waterfalls that we were rather drenched by the end of the ride, but we did not mind it one bit. The boat turned around upon reaching the Tasman Sea, which appeared to be choppy, and we returned along roughly the same route. I would have explored the open waters if we had more time in the country.

Additional Activities and Recommendations

My skydiving experience in Queenstown was truly exceptional but there are several other popular locations to do so in New Zealand which include Taupo, Wanaka, Bay of Islands, Abel Tasman, Franz Josef, and Fox Glacier. Keep in mind that weather conditions in New Zealand are unpredictable. If you are set on doing a skydive while in the country, I would recommend scheduling it toward the front end of your trip in case it must be rescheduled. Additionally, be prepared for a good deal of wind while in the air. After my parachute was launched, we were blown around quite a bit which may make some people nauseous.

The exciting luge experience can be done in both Rotorua and Queenstown. If you are traveling to both locations, I would recommend doing the luge in Rotorua just given the amount of other opportunities available in Queenstown relative to Rotorua.

There are various rivers that provide for high quality rafting in New Zealand. Some of the most highly regarded for experienced rafters include The Rangitikei, The Rangitata, The Mohaka, The Shotover, and The Wairoa. We opted to do the Kaituna River, as it has what is claimed to be the world's highest commercial waterfall that is available for rafting at 23 feet high. It is an amazing time and recommended for any adventurer staying in Rotorua.

In regard to the Milford Sound experience, note that this is a long day if you are doing it as a day trip from Queenstown. One of our biggest regrets was not splurging for the flight back to Queenstown which allows for landing on a glacier. This would have been an amazing experience that is offered few and far between globally. There are other experiences offered at Milford Sound such as helicopter tours and kayaking. Some tourists also choose to visit Doubtful Sound via a three-hour boat cruise.

There are various locations to bungy jump in New Zealand. The world's first commercial bungy jump was in Queenstown, which remains a popular attraction today. Queenstown remains the premier destination in New Zealand to try this adventure sport. Other locations include Auckland and Great Lake Taupo.

The SkyJump which was mentioned earlier in the writing is located in Auckland and is New Zealand's highest jump and the only Base Jump by wire. Plunge 630 feet from the famous Sky Tower at over 50 miles per hour! This activity is reserved for only the most adventurous. If the SkyJump is too extreme, you can also walk around the observation deck atop the Sky Tower. The SkyWalk is also offered where individuals walk around the outside of the top of the structure.

Regularly hailed as one of the best treks on earth, the Routeburn Track is one to consider. This three-day, 20-mile trek is located on the South Island at the base of New Zealand's Southern Alps. There are various other hikes and treks available in New Zealand to explore the incredible scenery. If you are interested in the Routeburn Track which provides beautiful mountain views as well as glimpses of the beach, make sure to book in advance, as there are only a limited number of people allowed on this trek.

Based in Auckland, there are canyoning tours that run to the west coast of New Zealand near Piha in the Waitakere Ranges Rainforest. Here you will have the opportunity to abseil down huge waterfalls, navigate canyons, and leap into pools of water. Canyoning is also offered in Coromandel, Nelson, Canterbury and Wanaka.

Fox Glacier and Franz Josef Glacier are the two most accessible glaciers. Adventure seekers can have the chance to experience the glaciers for all levels of ability. Strap on your crampons for traction to enjoy the once in a lifetime excursion!

Business Outlook

My long-term outlook for the business prospects of New Zealand is largely positive. The privatization policies by the government in recent years have been a boon for the economy, and I expect this to continue into the future. The health of the economy will be aided by the rich natural resources that the country possesses. Lenient requirements for starting a business in the country should continue to encourage innovation and lead to greater GDP growth.

While New Zealand has a lot of positive momentum in regard to the economy, aided by the various expansionary policies highlighted above, housing affordability in the country is a grave concern. Auckland has one of the least affordable housing markets in the world at eight times the average income as of 2014. The government increased the loan-to-value (LTV) ratio for property investors to a 30% deposit in 2015, and recent legislation requires overseas real estate buyers to register with the Inland Revenue Department. Despite these efforts to slow the cost of housing, prices have continued to increase, rising 74% from 2006 to 2016, and may continue to do so until migration declines—which could be aided by improvement in overseas labor markets—unemployment rises, land-use restriction subsides, or interest rates increase.

It is worth noting that only 3% of houses sold between January and March 2016 were purchased by investors outside of New Zealand. A combination of prolonged low global interest rates, excessive home prices, and potential reliance on housing price increases raises several disturbing red flags. What would the impact on the economy be if there was a substantial decline in the price of homes, much like we witnessed in many U.S. markets between 2007 and 2009? What if unemployment skyrocketed above 11% as it did in Ireland in 2009, leading to a 35% decline in the real estate market? These are questions that we do not have answers to.

Some would argue that "negative gearing," when interest payments exceed investment income, has further exacerbated the house price inflation. This approach is favorable in New Zealand because investment property deductions can be taken against personal income tax. Put in simpler terms, people are buying properties with the expectation of a short-term loss (which is partially subsidized by the government), ultimately leading to price appreciation that could be flipped for a quick profit. Investors speculating with a negative gearing strategy often choose interest-only loans due to the fact that they increase the tax-deductible expenses on the investment property. Loan practices such as this resulted in many U.S. banks getting into financial difficulty in 2008, particularly to borrowers that were speculating on several properties and putting little money down.

It is worth noting that negative gearing is not a new concept; for example, the U.S. government shares in investment losses on real estate as well as various other investments. However, during an extreme run-up in house prices a taxation policy such as this, combined with easy credit, can lead to a perfect financial storm. What about individuals who are priced out of the housing market due to stratospheric prices? Where are they going to get yield in a world of 0% interest rates? New Zealand's Official Cash Rate (equivalent to the prime rate in the U.S.) was 2% at the time of this writing. This could lead to stretching for yield by bidding up the prices of equity investments, which could potentially lead to a similar doomsday scenario witnessed in the U.S. in 2008-2009 with the simultaneous crash of equity and housing prices.

A nosedive in New Zealand home prices could result in a further outsized impact to the nation's economy, given that the banks keep residential loans on their balance sheets, and these loans constitute 55% of the banking system's assets as of mid-2016. This impact could come as a result of increased mortgage rates leading to an uptick in default rates. One concession that New Zealand does currently have going for itself is that fixed-rate mortgage loan-to-value (LTV) rates are close to the upper boundary of 80%, which would lessen the potential impact of rising rates.

The relatively conservative LTV rules for New Zealand and Australian banks, which are closely connected, provide a certain margin of safety for the industry when it comes to a potential short opportunity. I would argue that the risk in both the New Zealand and Australian banking sectors has risen over the past few years despite these factors due to similar warning signs seen in the United States' housing bubble in 2008.

For example, Bendigo Bank, a regional bank in Australia, recently announced a new program called Homesafe, which they describe as "an innovative approach to help elderly customers to access equity in their homes." In essence this program allows homeowners to sell a percentage of the future sales proceeds of their home in return for an immediate cash payment. Any time various banks begin introducing self-proclaimed "innovative" loan practices that are based upon factors such as recognition of future home appreciation, this is a concern for me.

With the New Zealand and Australian banking sectors being so intertwined and having similar characteristics, I looked into a potential bet against the banking sector in these countries. I found a short sale of Commonwealth Bank of Australia to be intriguing. The Australian banking sector has more options and is of larger scale which makes it more attractive from an investment perspective. I should preface this conversation with my personal belief that in aggregate, shorting stocks is incredibly stupid. The most an individual can make on a short sale is doubling your money and the liability is unlimited. This would be the equivalent of walking into a casino and being told that the best you could do was double your money and the worst-case scenario is going bankrupt. Would you take that bet?! It is probably better to consider options strategies to take advantage of potential price declines.

The Australian banks have been the most profitable in the world, regularly recording high-teens return on equity in years around the time of visit. With Commonwealth, the largest bank in Australia, trading at over two times price to book value, I think the firm is potentially significantly over-valued if real estate default rates start to be realized at a higher rate. A rise in unemployment or mortgage rates could lead to a significant uptick in default rates in the residential loan portfolio and provide substantial downside in the share price.

Given the relative ease of doing business in New Zealand and the fact that tourism appears poised to be a growth industry for years to come with several tailwinds, prospective investors may want to look at this space. Because the World Bank considers New Zealand the easiest country to start a business, this could have the adverse impact (from an investor's point of view) of bringing in a wealth of competition but if the tourism industry continues to grow at a healthy rate of close to 10% a year for the foreseeable future, there should be plenty of opportunities to go around. Direct investment in the country is probably best accessed through outright purchase of a company or simply starting a new entity given the lack of stock brokers' offering direct access to the New Zealand market, which is also why I covered the Australian housing market above.

In recent years the New Zealand technology industry has seen an influx of investment that topped $1 billion in 2017. The local industry has begun to carve out a competitive advantage in that they are becoming known for the openness and transparency that many other regions around the world are struggling with. Additionally, the close proximity to the Asian market makes the country attractive for technology investment because of the relative ease of enticing Asian investors. Technology investors may want to consider taking a closer look at New Zealand.

The New Zealand agriculture industry would be appealing to prospective investors. To give you an idea of how protected the agriculture industry is, when we were visiting and passing through a small town all farming production had stopped at the moment because a single fly had been found on one of the fruits! This extreme level of agricultural scrutiny has allowed the New Zealand industry to flourish over time due to the highly regarded nature of the products. The country has managed to build a competitive advantage in primary production and distribution infrastructure and is the world's largest dairy and sheep meat exporter. Investors interested in the agriculture space may want to look into direct investments in a New Zealand agricultural opportunity, an outright purchase of a company, or simply starting a new firm given the ease of doing so in New Zealand.

Updates Since Visit

Despite downbeat confidence among consumers and businesses, the New Zealand economy continues to chug along into 2019 with 2.5% annual GDP growth expected. The Reserve Bank of New Zealand has been cautious with interest rate hikes, holding the Official Cash Rate at 1.75% for a prolonged period due to fears that a further rise in the rate would lead to an overheated economy. The recent moderation of the Chinese economy is a worry for New Zealand given that China is their number one trade partner. Having said that, products sold to China such as butter and cheese should be relatively insulated from economic gyrations.

In 2018, the World Bank ranked New Zealand 1st out of 190 countries globally in terms of ease of doing business. The report specifically highlighted recent improvements to starting a business, dealing with construction permits, and registering property. New Zealand holds the shortest time to start a business, with that time being one day. New Zealand has long been a model economy when it comes to cultivating a business-friendly environment so to see continued positive commentary on these areas is refreshing.

I had previously commented on hoping to see improvements in the New Zealand education system. The 2017 World Economic Forum's Global Human Capital Report ranked New Zealand 7th out of 130 countries for preparing individuals for the future of work. Additionally, a 2017 report ranked New Zealand's education system as number seven on the World Economic Forum's Competitiveness Rankings. These are encouraging signs for the future of the country.

One of the long-term challenges that New Zealand faces is an aging population. According to FP Analytics, "Today, more than 700,000 people age 65 and older make up more than 15 percent of the country's population of 4.7 million. By 2032, New Zealand will become a super-aged society, when the percentage of people age 65 and older exceeds 21 percent." New Zealand should consider easing immigration requirements or it could risk ending up like modern-day Japan. Recent law changes which have restricted pathways to long-term residency under the skilled migrant category are not a good sign. The government should consider these powerful underlying demographic trends when laying the groundwork for future immigration laws. They need to be mindful not only of the aging population but also that there are still just 4.8 million people living in the entire country in 2019 and any disruptions to the economy or elsewhere could potentially lead to severe labor shortages in certain areas. I would be more worried about thoughtfully growing the population base for the long-term while maintaining the natural beauty of New Zealand (which is a boon for tourism) than looking for ways to restrict immigration.

My commentary in regard to the housing markets in New Zealand and Australia is ever relevant in 2019. While not a crash or housing crisis by any means, 2018 marked the first time in many years that housing prices in Australia declined in value which could start to give property speculators pause. The pause in speculation appears not to have happened yet, as 2018 reports show that 40% of Australian mortgages are interest-only. The problem with interest-only loans for mortgages is that homeowners will go underwater when the price of homes declines. I think what I underestimated in my initial report on the housing markets in New Zealand and Australia was the extent to which the housing bubbles have been propped up by easy credit. I believe the ultimate demise of this madness will be when lenders have a more skeptical eye when it comes to issuing mortgages. The halt or significant retrenchment in lenient property loans will have catastrophic effects for the New Zealand and Australian markets especially considering the 2018 numbers show Australian household debt reached a record level of

190% of household disposable income. For New Zealand households, this ratio stood at 168% which was above the pre-financial crisis levels of 159% (as of 2018). Much like many other areas in the world, the rising debt levels in New Zealand remain a long-term concern. The IMF has gone as far as suggesting that the Reserve Bank of New Zealand adopt a debt-to-income limit to reduce the growing risks related to consumer debt.

After the outbreak of COVID-19, the world was likely thrust into a global recession (that can't be confirmed as of the time of this writing). This dramatic economic shock has some predicting that Australian home prices could plunge by 40%. It took years to play out, but my thoughts concerning the Australian and New Zealand housing bubble appear to have come to fruition. In a little over a month between February and March 2020, the share price of Commonwealth Bank of Australia was roughly chopped in half.

Zorbing in Rotorua

Right before our raft flipped over!

Skydiving in Queenstown

Australia

Introduction

We arrived in Sydney, Australia, looking forward to the adventures that awaited in the second half of our trip Down Under. Sydney is the oldest and largest city in Australia. Located on the east coast of Australia, this capital of New South Wales surrounds the world's largest natural harbor.

Given that we only had a limited amount of time in beautiful Sydney, I opted out of the planned morning walking tour in favor of the famous Sydney Harbour Bridge Climb. My mom chose not to participate in this excursion, as she did with the skydiving, due to fear of heights. Upon getting equipped with our safety gear, the tour group proceeded outside onto the platform located at the bottom of the bridge. Over the course of the next hour or so, we proceeded up the bridge via the railing while being safely attached via safety belt. Our tour guide explained the history of the Sydney Harbour Bridge, which opened in 1932. The summit of the Sydney Harbour Bridge is 440 feet and provides panoramic views of the spectacular Sydney Harbour area and the city itself. I would recommend this activity for all travelers and do not think it was particularly frightening, although I may not be the best reference for that department. Adventurers can join the likes of many other celebrities who have done the tour, ranging from Ben Stiller to Heidi Klum.

Australia is the world's smallest continent and 6th largest country measured by total area. The country has over 16,000 miles of coastline. Australia lays claim to the world's largest coral reef, Great Barrier Reef, which stretches for over 1,400 miles. There is a diverse set of landscapes within the country, with mountain ranges in the southeast and southwest, tropical rain-forests in the northeast, and desert covering the interior. The dry desert land referred to as the outback makes up the large majority of land area in Australia. Australia is the second driest continent on planet earth behind Antarctica with average annual rainfall less than 24 inches per year. In comparison, Cleveland, Ohio, gets 38 inches of rain in an average year. The continent maintains one of the lowest population densities in the world with a population of approximately 24.1 million as of 2016. The outback covers a vast expanse of the land, and 85.8% of the country's population resides in urban areas. The climate varies throughout the country, as the northern section of the country is tropical, the southwestern portion considered to have a Mediterranean climate, and the southeastern piece being temperate in nature.

Being home to a wide array of habitats, Australia is labeled as a diverse country when it comes to flora and fauna, with a large portion being unique to the country. The greatest number of different reptile species reside in Australia, currently numbering 869. Australia is famous for being home to countless deadly animal species. In fact, 21 of the world's 25 most deadly snakes can be found in the country. Protection of the environment has become a major political issue in recent years due to factors such as the carbon dioxide emission per capita being among the highest in the world. An estimated 10% of Australian mammal species have been lost in the past 225 years. Additionally, the Great Barrier Reef, which is a global tourist attraction, has shrunk by more than half over the past 27 years and could halve again by 2022 if trends continue with the damage being attributed to tropical cyclones, starfish feeding, and increased $CO2$ levels caused by man-made chemicals.

Prior to British settlement in the late 18th century, the country was inhabited by indigenous Australians. The British initially used Australia as a penal colony, with the first ship full of convicts setting sail for Australia in 1787. There was a gold rush in the country in the early 1850s which brought more European settlers. Australia still uses the same territory system that was set up in the early days, with six recognized states: New South Wales, Queensland, South Australia, Tasmania, Victoria, and Western Australia.

There are two major territories, the Australian Capital Territory and the Northern Territory. It is interesting to note that federal legislation can only override state legislation in areas highlighted by Section 51 of the Australian Constitution. Each state and territory claims its own parliament. The government is set up as a federal parliamentary constitutional monarchy.

Australia does not have an official language, but English has always been considered the unofficial language of the country, being spoken as the only language by 72.7% of homes. The country has no state religion and the majority of residents consider themselves to be Christian. However, Australia does have one of the lowest levels of religious participation in the world.

Economy

Australia has an extremely high adult literacy rate, estimated to be around 99%. The long-term picture for the education system may not be as rosy due to the fact that the country ranked 22nd out of 37 OECD countries in terms of total education investment as a percentage of GDP as of 2015.

The Australian economy prides itself in going nearly 25 years without a recession as of the time of this writing, which is longer than any other developed country. The deregulation of financial and labor markets since the 1980s have been positive developments for the economy, which was growing at a 3.1% annual rate as of mid-2016. Australia is one of the wealthiest nations in the Asia-Pacific region as of 2016, as the country has seen more than two decades of economic expansion. Much like neighboring New Zealand, Australia maintains one of the most transparent and efficient business environments. The country enacts business-friendly policies such as being able to start a company in as little as two days. Australia has few limits on foreign investment and low non-tariff barriers which have been positive signs over the long-term for successful economies. The top income tax rate is high at 45%, which could limit incentive to innovate. It is worth noting that the overall tax burden as of 2016 is a reasonable 27.5% of GDP. As of March 2016, Australia had a low unemployment rate of 5.7%. The Australian dollar is the currency used in the country, and the Australia Securities Exchange (ASX) is the largest stock exchange in the South Pacific. The Australian dollar has appreciated in recent years, rising from roughly on parity with the U.S. dollar toward the beginning of 2013 to trading at a 25% premium by the beginning of 2017.

Services account for 58% of GDP followed by construction (9%), manufacturing (7%), mining (7%), and retail trade (5%). The mining boom that had been a tailwind for the Australian economy for years, began to see signs of weakness starting in 2015 due to a global collapse in commodity prices. Slowing demand in China, which purchased 54% of Australia's resource exports in 2015, led to a free fall in the price of several raw materials including coal, nickel, iron ore, and zinc. It will be interesting to see how the economy fares over the next couple years as Australia looks for new levers to trigger economic growth. Australia is rich in natural resources and is a major exporter of products such as wheat and wool, minerals including iron ore and gold, and energy such as coal and liquefied natural gas.

A potential concern in regard to the economy would be if a slowdown in the real estate market were to occur. This adverse development combined with the ongoing lag in mining would almost certainly cripple the economy at least in the near term. As discussed in the chapter on New Zealand, both the Australian and New Zealand residential housing markets are among the most expensive in the world. While public debt figures for the country are not alarming, Australian households have more debt in relation to the size of the economy than any other country in the world with $2 trillion household debt compared to $1.6 trillion GDP in 2016. Australia's banks have assets of more than $4.1 trillion and nearly $2.6 trillion in loans outstanding compared to GDP of only $1.6 trillion as of 2016. Then factor in that four banks control the large majority of the assets and one can see how an implosion of the real estate market could quickly take down the entire economy. Again, there is no imminent trigger on the horizon and there will not be until unemployment rises, lenders tighten lending standards, land use restriction subsides, or interest rates increase. It is worth noting that as of early 2016, for the first time in 25 years more Australians have migrated to New Zealand than the other way around for ten consecutive months which could prove to be an ominous signal for the economy. However one looks at the property bubble in Australia, it does not have a happy ending. I advise Australian residents to fasten their seatbelts for when the next recession comes to fruition.

Adventure

My mother and I took a tour of Sydney and it did not take long for me to realize that it was my favorite city in the world in terms of where I would like to live outside of the United States. I could see myself calling Sydney home at some point in the future. We stopped at the Sydney Opera House which is recognized as one of the 20th century's most distinctive buildings and it was named a UNESCO World Heritage Site in 2007. The area outside of the opera house provides for stunning views of the Sydney Harbour and the iconic bridge in the background. The tour took us through trendy city areas such as Paddington where we saw beautiful Victorian terraces. We stopped at the Sydney Tower which is the second tallest observation tower in the Southern Hemisphere at 1,014 feet. We did not feel the need to go up to the observation deck since we had gone to the top of Auckland's Sky Tower just days prior, but it was a sight to see. One of my personal favorite destinations on the afternoon tour was Bondi Beach. This popular beach located four miles outside of the Sydney central business district is known as a great surfing destination. If we had more time to spend in this amazing city, I would have taken a lesson, as I have not attempted the sport as of the time of this writing (I later took a surfing lesson in Chile which is documented in this book). I found it to be entertaining that our bus driver had the impression that everyone in the United States owned several weapons and that he was terrified to visit the country. He had this perception due to the intense media focus on shootings in the U.S. He was surprised to hear that not one of my friends owned any form of firearm.

The following day we took a cruise out on the Sydney Harbour which ended at the Taronga Zoo. I am not usually a huge fan of zoos since most of them are largely the same, but I believe that the zoo in Sydney is among the best in the world. The San Diego Zoo is another highly rated zoo that I did not find to be as enticing as the Sydney zoo, although there is a bias here given that I am more familiar with some of the local animals from the United States. I later visited the world-renowned Singapore Zoo which I discuss in the coming chapters. One of the highlights from our zoo experience was the section where the kangaroos roamed freely in a grassy area. I hung out here for probably 30 minutes just petting ten kangaroos in unison, as they had surrounded me and were eager to receive attention. I had heard that the species was usually angry and even violent at times but found from my personal experience that this was the furthest thing from the truth. Do note that this encounter was in a controlled zoo environment and wild kangaroos can still be aggressive at times. I had capitalized on an opportunity to take a picture with a koala. This native herbivore requires an immense amount of sleep, usually between 18 and 22 hours a day! While they are awake, they do tend to be grouchy and eat for a large majority of the time that they are not sleeping. Despite the common belief that koalas are a form of bear, they are actually marsupials and their correct name is koala.

That evening we went to a restaurant where we would indulge in local delicacies to see what Australia had to offer. The kangaroo exceeded every expectation that I had and was nothing short of impeccable. I found that it tasted much like a very tender steak which was probably not what I expected either. The next time I am at a local Ruth Chris devouring a filet mignon, I will think to myself, "wow tastes just like kangaroo." The saltwater crocodile was adequate and somewhat comparable to chicken. I am glad that I tried crocodile but I will not be ordering this on a regular basis in the future.

Despite my wish that we could remain in Sydney for several more days, it was now time to proceed to Cairns. Cairns is located on the east coast of Far North Queensland and is a popular tourist destination due to the tropical climate and access to the Great Barrier Reef: one of the seven natural wonders of the world.

The highlight of our time in Cairns was our cruise to the Great Barrier Reef. This day-long journey was one of the most thrilling of my lifetime. While weather conditions were far from optimal, it was pouring rain during our entire stay in Cairns, I was just excited to find out that our boat was indeed going out on the choppy waters. If you have seen the movie *The Perfect Storm*, it is not too far a stretch to say that certain scenes from the movie were comparable to what we experienced that day in the Coral Sea. The boat ride out to the Outer Barrier Reef which was a few hours in duration was highlighted by several people aboard getting seasick due to the massive waves, with several vomiting at various points. Fortunately for me, I am largely immune to seasickness and thought that the adverse weather conditions provided an additional opportunity for adventure.

It was an exhilarating feeling upon arriving at the world's largest coral reef system. Here we were, looking out over the turbulent waters of the Coral Sea with the Great Barrier Reef looming beneath the surface. The Great Barrier Reef, a UNESCO World Heritage Site, is the world's largest coral reef system and can be seen from outer space and is the largest single structure made by living organisms. Chills were running down my spine, as I was getting ready to scuba dive at the most iconic location on planet earth.

Despite not being PADI scuba certified at the time (I would later go on to get certified prior to my trip to Southeast Asia), I was allowed to take part in the activity as long as I was able to pass a series of brief tests prior to entering the Coral Sea. Fortunately, I had taken a scuba diving class at James Madison University, so I was confident in my abilities and easily passed. Half of the group, including my mom, failed the scuba test and were not allowed to dive at the Great Barrier Reef. My mom opted for an alternate option that I would describe as getting dressed in a space suit complete with a helmet which allows individuals to sit about 20 feet under the water on the sea floor to observe the aquatic life. It is surreal to think that my first open water scuba diving experience was at that location.

Even though the weather conditions were borderline hurricane worthy above the surface, once you went down below none of that seemed to matter. Visibility was not as good as it would be on a bright sunny day, but it was still impressive, and the group had an opportunity to see an array of spectacular aquatic animals that day. Some of the highlights included seeing the clownfish which rose to fame because of the movie *Finding Nemo* along with the sea turtles that prodded along through the water at their own pace. My love for scuba diving spawned that day at the Great Barrier Reef, as it was a euphoric feeling perusing the depths of the Coral Sea.

Our experience in Australia was a very positive one. While I would recommend visiting New Zealand in favor of Australia if given the option between the two, Sydney is still my number one location on earth in terms of places to live outside of the United States. We did find Australia to be a bit more affordable than New Zealand so travelers on a budget may find the former to be a more viable option.

Additional Activities and Recommendations

If we had more than a week to visit the country, I would have enjoyed seeing Melbourne. Located near the southeastern tip of the country, it is Australia's second most populous city and considered the nation's cultural capital. At some point down the line I will make a return trip to the country to visit the west coast along with the outback. This would include a tour of locations such as Perth (capital of Western Australia) and Ayers Rock (a large sandstone formation standing at 1,142 feet high located near Alice Springs). Given the size of Australia, it is difficult to cover everything in one trip unless the traveler has about a month at their disposal.

Surfing enthusiasts come from around the world to enjoy the great waves that Australia has to offer. Popular surfing locations include Noosa

(Queensland), Northern Beaches (New South Whales), Margaret River (Western Australia), North Coast (New South Whales), Bells Beach (Melbourne), and Snapper Rocks (Gold Coast). Australian beaches have a reputation for having a high density of sharks such as the Great White Shark. While individuals should be cognizant of this potential threat, it should be noted that the likelihood of a death from a shark attack is still extremely low.

Sydney offers a helicopter tour where individuals can enjoy stunning panoramic views of the Sydney Harbour with highlights including the Sydney Harbour Bridge, Sydney Opera House, and Bondi Beach.

The Sydney Tower Eye allows individuals to enjoy spectacular views of the city from Sydney's tallest structure where the Observation Deck sits 820 feet above the ground. Adventure seekers can opt for the SKYWALK experience where the individual takes a 45-minute guided SKYWALK tour around the outside of the top of the tower.

Gordon Dam which is located in Tasmania claims to be the highest commercial abseil in the world, this intimidating descent comes in at a staggering 460 feet!

Aerobatics is offered at various locations throughout Australia. Have the opportunity to ride along with a stunt pilot where they will perform various exhilarating plane maneuvers. A much more expensive option is to navigate your own stunt plane under the direction of an experienced pilot. An activity reserved for only the most adventurous. Thrill seekers can find skydiving available at various locations if they want to experience the fall from a plane.

Cairns offers bungy jumping that gets the adrenaline pumping with a 164-foot jump that AJ Hackett operates and is reserved only for the most adventurous.

Darwin City offers the Cage of Death dive that allows you to share the underwater environment with a massive saltwater crocodile! Get 360-degree views from the enclosure as an on-site photographer captures pictures of the crocodiles outside the enclosure.

Arguably the world's most famous scenic coastal driving route, experience the diverse landscapes of the Great Ocean Road. The road extends from Torquay in the east to Warrnambool in the west with the area between Lorne and Apollo Bay being the most attractive from a scenic perspective. There are several different itineraries and driving locations offered to experience the cliffs, beaches, and rainforests along the way. Adventurers doing a multi-day self-drive along the Great Ocean Road can also plan to do excursions such as cycling, canoeing, and beach walking along the way.

Ayers Rock, also known as Uluru, is one of Australia's most recognizable natural landmarks; this rock formation stands at 1,142 feet high with a total circumference of 5.8 miles. Given that this is off the beaten path, there are various multi-day itineraries offered at this location. These mostly include various desert-related tours.

Regularly rated as one of the top ten treks in the world, the Overland Track is a 40-mile journey through the Cradle Mountain-Lake St. Clair National Park which provides spectacular views of the surrounding mountains, lakes, and extensive forests in the area. Be prepared to book well in advance given the limited availability of this activity. Prospective trekkers will have the option to travel with a guide or do a self-guided trek. Those choosing to do a self-guided trek should ensure that the adventure is thoroughly planned, as there have been perilous excursions due to lack of adequate planning.

Business Outlook

My long-term business outlook for Australia is largely positive but does come with a few caveats. Pro-business policies are expected to continue into the future and encourage innovation, foreign investment, and transparency. The rich collection of natural resources at the country's expense will be a positive over the long haul. It will be interesting to see how Australia adapts to a potentially prolonged economic malaise in China. With such a heavy reliance on the country for the purchase of exports, Australia may have to alter trade patterns or search for new areas for economic growth. Additionally, the country will have to focus on alternative areas of investment in the event that the mining slump continues for years. Many small towns that were booming as recently as the end of 2014 when the prices of commodities were soaring, have been abandoned along with mines in the area. A collapse in the inflated residential real estate market in the near term could prove to be disastrous for the Australian economy when combined with the developments in the mining sector, reliance on construction (contributing 9% of GDP), and slowdown in the Chinese economy. Despite these apprehensions, Australia continues to be one of the most successful economies globally and has a bright future ahead.

Tourism presents an interesting investment opportunity given the close proximity to the growing Asian tourism markets. As of 2017, Australia was the 7th largest tourism market in the world, and the number of international visitors should only accelerate in future years. One of the interesting underlying macroeconomic trends to monitor over the coming years will be the rise of the middle class in China and other countries such as India. As this shift takes place, more consumers will have money to spend on luxuries such as travel. Investors may want to explore the tourism infrastructure markets. As of the beginning of 2017, the occupancy rates for luxury and business hotels in the major Australian cities such as Sydney, Melbourne, Brisbane, and Perth were about 90%. This indicates that there is room for growth in infrastructure in the luxury tourism sector in the country which will only be exacerbated by the growing number of outbound travelers in several key Asian markets. The local cruise market which has seen growth of more than six-fold in the past decade ending 2017 will see limited growth relative to the potential if the country does not solve the port infrastructure issue. The height of the Sydney Harbour Bridge currently places a limit on the number of cruise ships able to enter the Sydney port at one time but if the local government places emphasis on workarounds in this area, Australia will reap the benefit of millions of additional dollars being spent on everything that comes with a growing cruise industry which includes money spent on hotels, car rentals, restaurants, etc.

There is money to be made in Australia pertaining to the consumer shipping industry. Australia has been notorious for seeing much longer and higher shipping costs relative to other developed countries such as the United States because of the geography of the country, with the major cities being spread out mostly along the coastline and being placed far apart. Amazon announced their entry plans into the Australian market in 2017 which may seem surprising given the developed market potential, but this market has been a difficult one to crack for most operating retailers given the logistical challenges.

Another potential area of interest is secondary education. According to the 2017 OECD numbers, the average annual university tuition fee charged by an Australian public school at the bachelor level was less than 60% of the United States counterpart. Australia should leverage its geographic location by continuing to focus on attracting students from the Asia-Pacific region. They can boast about the impressive ease of doing business climate in the country along with an enticing student loan program known as Higher Education Loan Program (HELP) which bases the loan repayment amount on the percent of income earned post-graduation instead of on the amount borrowed. If this sounds like it could potentially be taking advantage of the government in the event that the graduate goes on to earn a low salary, that's because it is. Prospective investors could leverage these competitive advantages and look into private for-profit secondary education investment opportunities which could be attractive. Is there any better business situation to be in than when the consumer has zero incentive to look for lower cost options? If citizens take advantage of the HELP program, then they do not have any reason to seek lower cost options. Despite the negative public media attention on the sector in recent years, a for-profit school that focuses on doing what is best for the future of its students at an attractive price could benefit the investor along with the student. Of course, this investment opportunity depends on changes to the current legislative environment in Australia. The for-profit education sector would have to receive loans from the government to make the opportunity enticing given the competition they have from local public institutions that receive government loans on what some would consider to be the most generous college loan program in the world. If the for-profit institutions can prove that their programs are benefitting graduates and more broadly the economy as a whole, then I would think there is a chance for this to occur down the line. The recent developments in the United States pertaining to the challenge of federal loans provided to for-profit schools may prove to be an ominous sign for the sector as a whole but any government that is willing to lend students money with complete disregard as to repayment on the basis of the loan amount should at least be willing to consider a well thought out loan program to for-profit schools that benefits the local economy.

Updates Since Visit

As of early 2019, Australia had gone a staggering 27 years without a technical recession. While much smaller than the U.S. economy, the longest economic expansion in United States history is ten years as of the time of this writing (this number continues to lengthen as the current U.S. expansion goes on). I touched on some of these points earlier, but most experts would attribute this incredible phenomenon to Australia's natural resources, prudent fiscal management, and net immigration. Australia was at the right place at the right time when it comes to geographic location in that they are located near China and have benefited from the prolonged Chinese infrastructure boom. Australia had low debt levels going into the 2008 global financial crisis, which enabled the country to react quickly with fiscal stimulus and mitigated the economic impacts compared to many other countries. Australia has seen net immigration for many years which has boosted GDP growth. As of 2018, the immigrant share of Australia's population growth was high at 22.2%. The immigration growth could be jeopardized by 2018 government reforms which toughened requirements for prospective Australian visa applicants.

I won't further discuss the Australian housing market since I have covered this topic extensively in the New Zealand chapter along with previous commentary in this chapter. The other major concern for the Australian economy going forward is the reliance on the Chinese economy. As of early 2019, a third of Australia's exports are shipped to China. The picture for Australia would not be pretty if China had a major financial crisis and had to halt or scale back many large-scale physical infrastructure projects. Having said that, over time the dependence on the Chinese economy will likely lessen with other large countries such as India in desperate need of physical infrastructure to catch up with the exploding population growth.

I have written about my bearish stance concerning overall profits in the e-commerce business (which you will read about in my India chapter) so it may have come as a surprise that I wrote positively on the potential for consumer shipping for Australia in this chapter. I think this has more to do with the demographics of Australia than anything. Over 85% of the country lives in urban areas, and if the larger players in the consumer shipping industry were to focus all of their energy on these markets, I could see a relatively clear path to a profitable business. Amazon has been investing in Australia in recent years and early 2019 reports have analysts expecting the company to dominate the retail landscape in the country within a few years.

As for an update on the Great Barrier Reef, a 2018 report released by The Reef & Rainforest Research Centre said that the reef was showing better-than-expected signs of recovery after a mass coral bleaching event in 2016 and 2017. Major coral bleaching on the Great Barrier Reef occurred in 1998, 2002, and 2016-2017 and has been attributed to water temperatures and other stressors being too extreme which upsets the relationship between the coral and algae. The 2018 report attributed the improved conditions to relatively mild 2017–2018 summer conditions along with increased cooperation between science and government experts, which has helped with the reef recovery.

As my writing was coming off the press, bushfires were raging across Australia, already having burned over 12 million acres with the haze visible in New Zealand which is located more than 1,000 miles away. I will leave the climate change discussion for someone else to research and write about, but this event will be a major drag on economic growth. Tourism and consumer spending should be particularly vulnerable, with the potential for spillover into the housing market if there is a lasting impact on overall consumer confidence. These fires made me think more about country diversification in terms of where economic growth comes from. In Australia, Sydney accounts for nearly half of the economic growth of the country with Sydney and Melbourne making up nearly two-thirds of the entire economy. It would be catastrophic for the Australian economy if these fires were to severely threaten Sydney.

My final update is in regard to the overall Australian economy following the global outbreak of COVID-19. It looks like Australia will finally have its first recession in 29 years. My fears about the Australian reliance on Chinese growth came to fruition and the looming data should show economic catastrophe for Australia. Australia is in a much more precarious situation than many other countries following the COVID-19 pandemic because a lot of the trajectory of their economic recovery will depend on how demand in China recovers and that is completely out of their control. This is what I had warned about.

I also had sounded the alarm about the stratospheric household debt levels in Australia and New Zealand. The Australian banks were relatively well capitalized heading into this crisis, but it may not be enough to stave off a financial crisis for Australia. Australia had overextended borrowers, and the economy has now come to a halt, which will send shockwaves through the financial system. All of my worst fears about the Australian economy that I had written about ultimately became reality. We will see how this ultimately plays out but it could take years for Australia to recover if there is a deep financial crisis combined with an ongoing demand shock from China.

Found some friends at the zoo!

Sydney Harbour Bridge

Bondi Beach

Belize

Introduction

The day was finally here: Black Hole Drop. I had been mentally preparing myself for this activity for months by looking at pictures, watching videos, and reading reviews from those that were brave enough to partake in the rappelling/abseiling excursion. On our ride to the destination, we noticed children hacking away at the grass with machetes that nearly dwarfed the size of their bodies in fields along the side of the road. This continues to be perfectly legal for people to do in Belize during the day, but Chapter 102 of the Laws of Belize prohibits carrying articles with blades and offensive weapons between the hours of 8 p.m. and 5 a.m. (this law had long been overlooked but the government has been trying to reinforce efforts recently due to an uptick in knife attacks across the country).

We arrived at the location where we would be signing the necessary documentation in order to take part in the adventures for the day. My palms were sweating profusely as I signed a waiver saying that the company was not liable in the event that death did occur during the relatively dangerous excursion that was set to take place in a few hours. At this point, all I could think about was the man at our lodge the night before telling my friend Greg and I about how terrifying the Black Hole Drop experience is and that the government of Belize had covered up tourist deaths in the past from activities such as this. Upon signing our lives away, we set out in jeeps with massive tires to the rainforest.

We arrived at the forest entry point and the tour guides briefed us on safety measures for the hike up to the top of the sinkhole (natural sinkholes are created by the natural process of erosion, the collapse of a cave roof, or gradual removal of bedrock material by flowing water). The hike was going to be approximately two hours in duration and strenuous in terms of difficulty. The guides were to lead the rest of the group carrying machetes and were prepared to protect us from aggressive snakes located along the trail if necessary. At least nine poisonous snakes have been identified in the country, with the most notable being the fer-de-lance. This coral snake is considered to be the most dangerous snake in Central America. This large, deadly predator is feared throughout Central America and for good reason. Some reports from Costa Rica have estimated that roughly 50% of snakebites in the country are from this venomous snake.

After being told of all of the ways that we could be potentially killed over the ensuing six or so hours, the group set out on a hike that I would quickly realize would be the most challenging of my life up to that point. As sweat poured down my face, we trekked onward along the narrow path that would eventually lead to the summit overlooking the sinkhole. The weather in subtropical Belize averages about 77 degrees in November through January so it is much warmer than the northeast U.S. at this time of year. The ground was uneven at times and I found myself stumbling at several points along the journey but fortunately did not suffer any injuries. I was constantly on the lookout for any snakes hanging in the trees, as the branches often overlay directly across the path on which we were walking. Both Greg and I agreed that the hike in and of itself was a tremendous experience. We were looking for an activity that was both challenging and rewarding and this two hour hike certainly fit the bill. One of the guides even allowed us to take pictures with a machete posing in the midst of the beautiful lush forest scenery.

We were finally here: the edge of the Actun Loch Tunich sinkhole, which is located 310 feet above the rainforest floor. Companies operating abseiling from Table Mountain in South Africa advertise their location as being the highest commercial abseil in the world at 367 feet (although this is refuted by

Gordon Dam in Tasmania). This would put Black Hole Drop close to being the highest commercial abseiling location in the world.

Reality was starting to set in as I was staring out over the steep drop directly in front of me located in the foothills of the Maya Mountains. I am usually able to hold my poker face in these situations, but I would be withholding the truth if I said I was not nauseous and nervous. I can only imagine what my face looked like as I was attempting to mentally envision myself barreling over the edge of the steep cliff.

After watching some of my near fearless companions go before me, it was time to prove myself. I was placed in a harness that was attached to a tree at the top of the mountain. Despite what some others may tell you, just getting started when rappelling is not easy. It is against human nature, for those with a wish to continue living, to throw yourself backward over the edge of a high cliff. I was literally dangling over the edge of the 310-foot cliff for about 30 seconds as I attempted to properly shift my weight backward! At this point I was frustrated, as I was looking down at a potentially lethal drop below and had not made any progress in route to safety. I finally was able to figure it out and proceeded on my way down to the rainforest floor. The first ten feet or so consisted of rappelling along the initial cliff wall. The rest of the trip down was pure abseiling and required little effort other than manually moving along the rope. I tried to take in the stunning views along the way but realized that I was going at a pretty rapid pace considering I was dangling from a rope. The next 200 feet after the rappelling portion provided amazing vantage points of the mountainous area above the rainforest canopy. Upon reaching the forest canopy and realizing that I was now only about 100 feet above the ground, I was slightly relieved that if anything were to happen at this point, I may only be impaled as opposed to imminent death higher up. It was a feeling of sheer personal accomplishment upon touching the ground of the rainforest floor that day. Both Greg and I had bright smiles on our faces, as we knew that we had just overcome fear and reached another fantastic milestone in our lives. We ate lunch right there in the sinkhole, just taking in the scenery and reflecting on the events that had just unfolded.

Despite the climax being behind us, the adventure was far from over. Now we had to actually get out of the sinkhole that we had just descended into, which required a fairly rigorous trek uphill. We arrived at a 50-foot ladder which we had to carefully navigate one at a time. For those that have a fear of heights, this activity by itself would have been too much to handle, as you could look down at the steep drop below with the sprawling mountains in the background. Once the group had achieved this climb, we continued on the less arduous adventure back to the starting point, as most of the walk back was downhill.

I arranged for a trip to Belize with my college friend and fellow fraternity brother, Greg Di Chiara, for eight days in November 2014. We decided on Belize because it offered the opportunity to experience life in a remote jungle as well as on a tropical island while being relatively close at approximately 6.5 hours from Washington D.C. The trip was also affordable, costing $2,550 which included international airfare, accommodations, and various excursions. Additionally, neither Greg nor I had been to any countries in Central America and were excited to see it for ourselves. Getting around Belize is relatively easier than some other countries since the official language of the country is English making Belize the only country in Central America that can make this claim.

The government of Belize is arranged as a parliamentary constitutional monarchy that is modeled after the British parliamentary system. I found it interesting to learn that the Queen of Belize, Queen Elizabeth II, lives in the United Kingdom and has a representative present in Belize. Belize is still a relatively new country, as it achieved independence in 1981 when the UK agreed to protect the country from invasion by Guatemala (Guatemala recognized Belizean independence in 1991). The country consists of 8,867 square miles of land with more than 70% being covered by forest on the eastern coast of Central America and is bordered by Mexico to the north, Guatemala in the south and west, and the Caribbean Sea to the east. As of 2015, the country had a population of approximately 360,000 but did lay claim to one of the highest population growth rates in the Western Hemisphere at 1.87% (for 2018).

Economy

The Belizean economy is based on the export of crude oil and petroleum (there was a commercial oil discovery in 2005), agriculture (citrus, sugar, bananas), and tourism. Like any other country that relies heavily on oil production, the Belizean economy has suffered in recent years from low crude oil prices, but they have managed to weather the storm better than most of their Central American counterparts. The country has seen a large economic shift over the two previous decades with agriculture and tourism now being the primary sources of both income and employment. According to the Belize Tourism Board, there are few reliable estimates, but they believe tourism contributes anywhere from 18–25% of GDP and accounted for 28% of employment as of 2013. Belize received 1.3 million tourists in 2015 with roughly 60% coming from the United States. The economic growth rate of the country is volatile, as Belize largely depends on imports and exports and has exposure to natural disasters such as hurricanes, tropical storms, flooding, and drought. According to the World Bank, the economy in 2015 decelerated to 0.9% GDP growth which was down from 4.1% in 2014.

The top income tax rate is 25% while corporate tax rates vary. Profits on petroleum are taxed at a rather unreasonable rate of 40%. The country has additional taxes on certain goods and services with the overall tax burden amounting to approximately 23% of domestic income.

Starting a business in the country is still difficult, as it costs about half the level of annual income to do so. Additionally, getting the necessary permits to start a business takes more than 70 days on average. If Belize wants to get serious about creating a more competitive landscape for entrepreneurs, they will have to change some of these laws to make them more business friendly. The country has a poor reputation for enforcement of the commercial code which can hinder entrepreneurial activity. The government continues to maintain price controls on products such as sugar, rice, and flour. It has been proven throughout history that price controls ultimately fail because producers in pursuit of profits do not have the incentive that those operating in free markets do. Why would it make any sense for rice to continue to be sold for $2 per pound if supply has diminished and demand has increased? Just ask any Russian citizen that is not brainwashed by the local government how this has worked for their country over the years. Belize has an average tariff rate of 10% which is high compared to 2.96% in the United States in 2014. According to the Central Bank of Belize, unemployment in 2015 was 9.97%, as defined by those actively looking for a job.

Belize is not known as being a large player in the financial industry which made the country more resilient in the aftermath of the global banking crisis in 2008–2009. The country continues to peg the Belizean dollar to the U.S. dollar. Belize does have a substantial offshore financial sector and the government continues to encourage growth of these offshore activities which are vulnerable to corrupt activities such as money laundering.

The school system remains a serious challenge for Belize. All children in the country are required to attend primary school until age 14; primary education is free, and is technically funded by the government. However, families are still responsible for costs such as transportation, schoolbooks, uniforms, etc. and it is difficult for poorer families to finance. This has caused a massive attrition rate after primary school where less than 40% of students attend secondary school at all as of 2014. The government will have to go back to the drawing board in this category, as the lack of schooling coupled with restrictive business laws is crippling innovation within the country. Improvements in education could lead to progress in reducing the historically high poverty rate which was 45% in 2014.

Adventure

I was a bit surprised that our travel company, Adventure Life, routed us through El Salvador on our way to Belize City. El Salvador remains on the travel warning list provided by the United States Department of State due to what they consider to be crime and violence levels that are critically high, with San Salvador posting the third highest murder rate in the world in 2015. Conditions have deteriorated since we traveled through the country but luckily we did not leave the airport.

We arrived in Belize City near sunset and my first observation was that the planes were manually towed to their respective destinations upon arrival which I had not seen before. Ground tugs provide for more efficient fuel consumption as well as more precise parking. From here, we had an hour and a half long journey to our accommodation at Pook's Hill Lodge. I will never forget the amount of foot activity that we witnessed as we were passing through the local villages at nighttime. Unlike most cities in the United States, most people here walked everywhere due to closer proximity of destinations and for economic purposes. We were aware that our final destination was in a remote location in the jungle but perhaps we underestimated the reclusiveness. I would estimate that it was 30 to 40 minutes removed from any sort of mainstream roadway and we had to drive along various substandard unpaved trails to reach the seemingly elusive Pook's Hill.

We finally arrived at the lodge sometime in the middle of the night. It was a sight to see, as there was a clearing in the middle of the remote jungle located in the foothills of the Maya Mountains where about 12 cabanas with thatched roofing seemed to appear out of thin air. Greg and I were greeted by a member of the staff and told about the lodge itself along with a few precautions that had to be taken. At the time, I thought that the warning in regard to checking our beds and pillows for tarantulas, wolf spiders, and scorpions was a joke. We would quickly come to realize just how serious the staff member had been, as we were confronted with two large wolf spiders in our cabana on the very first night! Although I am not scared by many things in life, I am terrified of spiders. Both Greg and I were too petrified to go anywhere near these highly poisonous creatures and stayed awake until we could not keep our eyes open any longer. We finally closed our eyes around 3:30 a.m.

with the spiders looming by our feet (there was some form of deadly spider in our cabana each night).

The following day we arose and did not have time to think about how exhausted we were because of the activities that were planned. After the drive over to Jaguar Paw, the first item on the agenda was zip-lining which was a first for both Greg and me. We were fitted with our necessary gear and did a short hike up to the canopy site where five platforms were situated where we would be partaking in the adventure activity. The highlight of the excursion was the platform that allowed us to hurdle 125 feet in the air across a river to the destination on the opposite side. The longest distance that was travelled during this activity was 700 feet which is quite impressive (Jaguar Paw is usually ranked as one of the top zip-line destinations globally). Both Greg and I enjoyed the zip-line, but I must say that it ranked low on my personal fear index and would not be sufficient for any true adventure seeker. I was a bit surprised that the company did not offer action photographs for sale upon completion of the excursion. I captured few pictures from this entire trip because of the presence of water, caves, cliffs, etc. along the way and would have gladly paid $20-30 for a fine memory. Other countries that I have visited such as New Zealand were quick to capitalize on opportunities such as this.

The afternoon activity of choice was cave tubing at Caves Branch River. This seven-mile "River of Caves" provides a look at the centuries-old passage-ways that were inhabited by the Mayans and used for rituals at the time. Mayans often considered caves to be among the holiest places on earth and part of an underworld that they considered to be separate from ordinary time. The Mayan people often believed that gods were present in the caving systems and priests were often summoned to these locations.

The group applied helmets equipped with flashlights since we would be passing through sections of caves where little light could be seen. Upon entrance into the water, the guides hooked the group of tubes together so that we would not go drifting aimlessly down the waterway. For the most part, they would be responsible for leading the way and pulling the group of tubes along so very little effort was exerted from the rest of us. We waded through the river in our tubes over the course of the next hour on this leisurely ride which provided great views of the ancient caves filled with interesting rock formations. Since we were visiting the country at a time when it was not the height of the tourist season, the activity on the river that day was relatively tempered. There were a few times when the cave did get relatively loud with other groups being nearby but overall it was a relaxing and serene experience and would be recommended for a family activity. The group exited the river after about an hour and we then made our journey back to Pook's Hill which took around 40 minutes.

That evening Greg and I became friendly with some of the others staying at the lodge. It was mostly families staying here but everyone was welcoming and with no television or computer available at the location, we had little choice but to converse with one another and create our own fun. We ended up playing card games with our new friends for hours that night, as we were both enjoying their company and also terrified of the thought of going back to our cabana to attempt to sleep while being surrounded by enormous poisonous spiders. We were delighted with the fact that the beers (the local beer in Belize is Belikin which is a solid option) only cost $2–$3 despite the lodge having a monopoly on the product. I would be lying if I said that we did not consume several Belikin's prior to retiring for the evening, hoping to partially assuage both of our arachnophobias.

The excursion for the following day consisted of delving deep into the Mayan underworld by exploring the Actun Tunichil Muknal cave. The cave, also known as "ATM", is a famous Mayan archaeological site where tourists can view ancient remnants of skeletons, ceramics, and stoneware. There are over 1,400 documented artifacts in what is thought to be a bloodletting center where the Mayans made sacrifices to please the gods. By examining the artifacts, experts estimate that the cave was in use from 1–1000 CE. It is one of the most popular Mayan burial sites in Western Belize. It was only discovered in 1989 and has been open to the public since 1998.

In order to get to the ATM cave, we had to hike approximately 45 minutes through the Tapir Mountain Nature Reserve. It was an enjoyable trip, as we waded through three streams along the way, getting up to waist deep at times, and had the luxury of spotting a few large poisonous snakes in our passing.

We finally arrived at the entrance to the cave, where the group would swim through a body of water in order to proceed. The first portion of the three-hour long cave expedition was mostly wet, as we were navigated through various passageways via water which was much too deep to stand at certain points.

The second part of the adventure was the chamber where artifacts can be viewed from the Ancient Maya. We had to remove our shoes at this point, as the country wants to be as respectful as possible to this historical site. The group proceeded to climb various ladders and delve deeper into the dark abyss with our flashlights as we worked our way into the back chamber where the majority of the artifacts were located. The ATM cave is often referred to as the "Cave of the Crystal Maiden" because of the presence of the skeleton located here which is believed to be a teenage girl who was a sacrificial victim. It was interesting and rather eerie to view these ancient skeletons, some of which belonged to children less than five years old. We were able to view various clay pots and knives that were believed to be involved in the process of sacrifice to the gods. After taking this rather remarkable scene in, we exited the chamber the same way in which we had entered and worked our way back toward the front of the cave.

It is widely debated as to what caused the collapse of the Mayan Empire that ruled Central America for over 1,200 years. One of the most dominant civilizations in the ancient Americas fell apart relatively quickly around 950 CE. Researchers debate to this day scenarios such as warfare, famine, environmental change, etc. that could have caused the demise of the Mayan civilization that looked poised to become a powerful empire for years to come.

The entire ATM cave was extremely interesting and enjoyable. I do want to emphasize that there is a minimum level of fitness required in order to partake in this activity for those that are potentially interested. While not as difficult as the hike for Black Hole Drop, it could be a bit challenging for those that do not participate in any physical activity. There were only a few points where I would imagine the narrow passageways being an issue for those with claustrophobia. Overall, I think this experience is an absolute can't-miss for any adventurer heading to Belize and in search of an enjoyable hike that also allows for an intriguing look into the Mayan culture.

After dinner that evening, we spent more time with the rest of the people staying at Pook's Hill Lodge. Certainly the most horrifying event of the night occurred at the dinner table. A tarantula that was close to a foot in diameter crawled under the table where Greg and I were eating. I am not sure who noticed it first, but when I looked under the table it was almost directly at my feet! I jumped out of my seat and alerted the staff. The locals were so used to seeing these creatures that they were not phased in the least. The owner of the lodge scared the spider out of the dining area so we could resume our meal in peace. Our delicious dinners served at Pook's Hill (every meal that we had here was top notch) usually consisted of some form of chicken served with rice, salad, and fried plantains which are very popular in Belize. Upon conclusion of our meal, the owner of Pook's Hill "entertained" the entire group by allowing the large tarantula that was present during dinner climb all the way up his arm. This was rather difficult for me to watch given my strong distaste for all forms of spiders.

The morning following Black Hole Drop we set out for the airport in Belize City. We stopped at the Belize Zoo and Tropical Education Center, which is located approximately 29 miles west of Belize City. The zoo is home to over 175 animals with the native jaguar considered to be the centerpiece by most. Greg and I received a glimpse of how fierce of a predator the animal is when it growled loudly and readied for attack mode when we were eyeing the animal directly outside of its cage. Even though there was a barrier between the jaguar and us, it was a bit startling. I would not want to come into contact with one of those in the wild!

We took a tiny plane from Belize City to Ambergris Caye, the largest island in Belize measuring 25 miles end to end, since it is only a 15-minute flight. This short flight provided the most spectacular views of the trip as we made our way out to the island located in the Caribbean Sea known for some of the best scuba diving in the world. Upon arrival at our hotel, which was located very close to the water, it was clear that there were few others staying there. Despite the supposed Belize tourist high season beginning in late November, the entire island was empty. This does not bode well for a location that thrives on tourist spending much the same as a location such as Ocean City, Maryland. Greg and I then rented wave runners and went out on the beautiful water. We raced each other along the coastline for about an hour, often picking up speed before crashing into waves created by nearby boats. We then enjoyed a few cocktails by the water in a completely worry-free afternoon. As we found was the case all over Belize, the workers at this restaurant were overly kind. They were appreciative of our business and I would consider them to be among the nicest people as a whole that I have come across in my travels. This should provide a tailwind for the tourism industry over the long haul as more people come to appreciate the great natural treasures that the country has to offer. Greg and I were very relieved in knowing that we would not have to stay awake all night in fear that a large spider would bite us.

The following day, we set out on a snorkeling excursion in Shark Ray Alley. It is no secret where this body of water gets its name: there was a plethora of sizeable nurse sharks and sting rays located in the area. While I am not a huge fan of snorkeling, it gives me a headache because of the bobbing along at the surface, I would highly recommend the activity here. We docked in the middle of the channel and the group of excited tourists jumped into the water with our fins and masks on. Almost immediately I was surrounded by about ten nurse sharks that extended up to 12 feet in length. Fortunately, the nurse shark is docile in nature and usually only bites when provoked by actions such as touching of the mouth. As far as safety, I would say that the seven-foot stingrays would have been the larger concern. A few times I felt the tails of the rays brushing along my legs (I did think of Steve Irwin a time or two while I was in the water). Overall, this was an absolutely incredible experience, and I agree with the assessment that Ambergris Caye is one of the most desirable diving destinations (I found it to be much better than the Great Barrier Reef).

In wanting to take full advantage of the world-class aquatic life, I went scuba diving the next two days. This was undoubtedly one of the great experiences of my lifetime. There is nothing quite like the rush of being 60 feet below the surface, completely vulnerable in the underwater world. Nothing else matters when you are down there except for the tremendous appreciation for the environment that you are temporarily infringing upon. Other than the sharks and sting rays noted above, there were several sea turtles and manta rays as well. If we had more time on the island, I would have made the two-hour trip out to the Great Blue Hole, which is regularly ranked a top 10 diving destination in the world. However, I found the local reef diving to be utterly fantastic and highly recommend it to all of my adventurers reading this.

The entire tourism industry at Ambergris Caye is built around scuba diving. The island provides easy access to the Belize Barrier Reef which is the second largest coral reef system globally behind the Great Barrier Reef. I do want to note that the beautiful island really does not have any beaches and most visitors spend the majority of their time out on the water doing various activities, scuba being the most popular. For those with a passion for diving, Ambergris Caye is an unbelievable vacation destination and offers a wide array of aquatic life accessible just a few minutes off the shore. However, there is not too much to do on the island in terms of alternate activities. We did rent a go-kart one day, the main form of island transportation, to tour the rest of the island but activities such as this can only consume so much time. I was perfectly content spending the majority of my time out on the Caribbean and could have done this for weeks longer, but I do realize that not everyone shares this same sentiment.

While Ambergris Caye was largely quiet at night while we were there, we did have a memorable evening. The locals told us that we had to go see the World Famous Chicken Drop, as it was the most popular nightly attraction on the island. Greg and I did not gather too many additional details but decided to attend to check out the scene. Upon arrival, we were surprised to see a large crowd of people, as all of the other bars and restaurants were sparsely populated. We navigated our way inside the bar to purchase a number on which you basically place a wager. What we were about to witness would have violated several animal laws in the United States and aggravated every animal rights activist, but it was an intriguing sight. There was a large gathering around a ring outside of people that had undoubtedly been drinking for a few hours. A DJ was located by the ring that was in charge of playing music and commentating for the event. The premise of this unbelievable spectacle was that different members of the crowd would take turns placing a live chicken inside the ring. The wagers placed were on which number the chicken would lay its waste on! I could not believe what I was seeing, as the crowd was screaming at the top of their lungs as the chickens danced around in the ring while a DJ was hyping the audience. It would often take several chickens in order for a winner to be selected, as many simply did not have to go to the bathroom at the time they were placed in the ring. Unfortunately, neither Greg nor I had the luxury of a chicken laying their droppings on one of our lucky numbers, but we did come away with a memory that we will surely never forget. I do want to note that it did not appear that the venue was being harmful to the animals in any way.

Additional Activities and Recommendations

Cave kayaking is an activity available at Nohoc Chen Park. Venture into the dark cave system where you will get to see a total of six caves on the Caves Branch River. You will get to see various rock formations along the way along with a waterfall. This can be combined with the zip-line excursion.

Waterfall rappelling is an adventure activity that can be found at Bocawina Rainforest. Rappel 100 feet down the Bocawine Falls and swim in the emerald pools below. This can also be combined with a zip-line activity.

Xunantunich temples and jungle pontoon waterfall tour is found at San Ignacio. View the Mayan Temples of Xunantunich which lies in a region dating to around 1,000 BCE. You will have the opportunity to climb onto one of Belize's tallest Mayan Temples called El Castillo, which rises to about 130 feet. Then you will proceed to the Vaca Plateau Forest Reserve, where you will board a jungle pontoon to explore the area. There is optional cliff jumping along the way. A horseback riding tour to Xunantunich is also possible at this location.

For those not overly interested in scuba diving, deep sea fishing is available at Ambergris Caye. The barrier reef lies less than ½ mile from shore where you will be able to find billfish, wahoo, dorado, kingfish, grouper, snapper, and shark. Other popular locations include Turneffe Atoll and Lighthouse Reef.

I found Belize to be a great travel option for any outdoor adventurer, particularly for those on a budget. I think it is important to emphasize the lack of offerings the country has in terms of activities outside of those that I discussed above. If you are not interested in visiting Mayan ruins, scuba diving, rappelling or abseiling, hiking, zip-lining, or nature watching then this trip is not for you. If I had a second opportunity to plan this extreme adventure, I would definitely not stay at Pook's Hill Lodge despite the amazingly authentic jungle experience equipped with an overly kind staff. I am not exaggerating when I say that three hours may have been the maximum amount of sleep that I received any night at the location due to concerns over poisonous spiders and other deadly creatures in our cabana. While this made for a hilarious story looking back, it was nothing short of miserable at the time. Additionally, if we had one more day in the jungle, I would have liked to take a day trip over to Tikal. Tikal is the ruins of an ancient Mayan city located in Guatemala. It would have been interesting to see this major site of

Mayan civilization consisting of more than two dozen major pyramids that flourished between 600 BCE and 900 CE. Tikal National Park was declared a UNESCO World Heritage Site in 1979.

Business Outlook

My expectations for the Belizean economy over the long-term remain tempered at this time. It is always a risky proposition to maintain such a heavy reliance on tourism for the well-being of an economy. While Belize is considered a low terror threat relative to other locations around the world, the country is subject to various natural disasters given the location in the Caribbean which could negatively impact tourism as well as agriculture. Various storm systems over the past 15 years including Tropical Storm Arthur, Tropical Depression #16, and Hurricane Richard have resulted in substantial flood damage to the banana, rice, sugarcane, and corn harvests. I would need to see the local government pass laws that are more favorable for entrepreneurship in order to get excited about the country's future prospects. While manufacturing production has increased significantly since 2000, it still only amounted to 8.7% of GDP in 2014. The United States has seen a decline in manufacturing in recent years but that has been due to a shift toward services and human capital businesses. This has not been the case for Belize with the exception of tourism and the trend toward manufacturing and human capital projects could be accelerated in the country if the people were more incentivized and had less restrictions to do so. The economy remains too focused on such a limited number of offerings: tourism, oil, and agriculture. Just within the agriculture segment, sugar and molasses accounts for roughly 30% of the country's exports. There have been reported sugar shortages within the country in the past (using 2011 as an example) which came as a result of the price fixing put in place by the Belizean government. Companies were smuggling sugar outside of the country instead of supplying the agreed-upon amount to local producers. If demand outside of the country was outstripping the set price in place by the price-control, then why would any company want to distribute the product locally? I hope that the local government does their homework on basic economics and looks at various real-world examples to conclude that policies such as this do not work.

Having said all of that, the government has introduced legislation in the past to encourage foreign investment in Belize. For example, the Fiscal Incentives Act of 1990 introduced tax holidays for international investors looking to start a company in Belize. The standard tax holiday is up to five years but in cases where a company is engaged in agriculture, agro-industrial products, mariculture, etc., and the operation is strictly for export and highly labor intensive, the tax holiday may be for a maximum period of 25 years. Tax efficient investors looking for exposure to the agriculture sector may want to take a look here.

The International Business Companies (IBC) Act allows international investors to establish offshore companies in Belize. These entities are not allowed to own an interest in real property in Belize or to conduct business in banking or insurance with Belizean residents. However, they benefit from tax exemptions on all income with dividends paid to persons resident in Belize or elsewhere: interest, rent, royalties, and compensation paid to persons who are not residents of Belize; and capital gains realized on shares, debt obligations, or other securities of an IBC by persons who do not reside in Belize. Maybe Lafayette Investments, my investment management company, should relocate to Belize!

Real estate investors might want to take a look at locations such as Ambergris Caye. I would expect tourism in Belize only to get more popular in future years, as the country is two hours from Miami and is the only country in Central America that can claim to have English as the official language. I would expect retirees to see an increasing interest in Belize property due to the incentives offered by the Qualified Retired Persons (QRP) Program. Anyone over the age of 45 is eligible to apply for this program that allows for individuals to not be taxed on their international income or on capital gains. Unlike Belizean residents, participants are allowed to maintain an international bank account in Belize, and an offshore international business corporation. While you won't be able to work for a company with offices in Belize, individuals could work for an American based company online and enjoy the generous incentives offered by this program. It doesn't really make sense to me why the local government would do this given that the economy would be better off having more workers and dollars flowing to companies that are based domestically, but investors can reap the rewards. Real estate investors should take necessary precautions regarding natural disasters and do extensive research on insurance-related products given the high risk of hurricane-related damage in the area.

Updates Since Visit

The Belizean near to intermediate term economic outlook as of early 2019 looks solid but the IMF has called attention to potential risks. The IMF has warned against the risks that have arisen concerning the Belizean debt levels and the current account deficit. A 2018 report by the IMF claims that contested legacy claims are estimated to be around 5.5% of GDP and could lead to large public and external financing needs on top of the mounting debt levels. Given that Belize's 2016–2017 debt restructuring marked the third such episode in a ten-year period, the IMF has reason to be wary of the country's finances.

According to the 2019 Ease of Doing Business report produced by the World Bank, Belize clocked in at a country worst 125th out of 190 global economies. Belize's ranking has plummeted in recent years since appearing on the list of ranked countries at 56 in 2006. This is not a good trend for Belize.

I continue to believe that investment in Belize in aggregate is a risky proposition. Look at what happened to the economy in 2016 when growth dropped to -0.8% from 2.9% in 2015 which was attributable to a steep decline in the primary sector resulting from flooding and disease in the agricultural sector. The growth in the tourism sector has been able to offset periodic weak-ness in areas such as agriculture but the overall economy remains undiversified and overly reliant on factors that are completely out of their control. This reality combined with high debt levels, a country that has a history of fiscal defaults and reorganizations, and the ever-present risk of natural disasters and you can see why many prospective investors would be hesitant.

According to 2018 reports, tourism is believed to make a total contribution of over 45% of country GDP. To put it simply, the importance of the sector can't be overstated. With the success of this sector also comes risk. Belize is always one major hurricane away from ravaging the entire economy given the outsized reliance on the tourism sector. The risks that the IMF have warned about when it comes to debt levels could become an immediate catastrophic development if this were to occur.

The issues that I discussed earlier in regard to education in Belize continue to be a major impediment for the economy. Unemployment in the country averaged 11.56% from 1993 to 2017 and this figure remains elevated. The driving force behind the consistently high unemployment is the shortage of skilled labor which is a direct result of the poor education system. Belize can continue to try and attract immigrant workers to fill some of these skilled labor positions, but the real long-term solution is to fix the problems in the education sector with a particular focus on secondary education.

While not much has been written about how the Belizean economy is responding to the COVID-19 crisis, I think we can arrive at some conclusions ourselves. I had previously written and warned about the undiversified nature of Belize's economy and the reliance on tourism and oil. With tourism having halted across the globe at least for the foreseeable future and oil prices having plunged following a feud between Russia and Saudi Arabia, I think it is safe to say that the Belizean economy will be pummeled. This is another lesson for many other countries that are overly reliant on tourism and oil revenues when thinking about total contributions to country GDP. Belize must focus on their education system and train locals to be productive in areas outside of the tourism and oil industries. Incentives should be provided to start businesses in other sectors of the local economy.

Scuba diving at Ambergris Caye

Survived the abseiling at Black Hole Drop!

World Famous Chicken Drop

Morocco

Introduction

We arrived in Marrakech around 12:30 p.m. local time. Despite having conducted research regarding Moroccan pricing prior to arriving in the country, we quickly received our first insights into how to negotiate in the country and just how much services really did cost. We paid 250 dirham, $25 USD, for a ride from the airport to our riad which is the Moroccan equivalent of a hostel. Only later did we realize how much we overpaid for this ride, as we negotiated a $10 fare to the airport upon departure from the country. I would consider myself to be a well-travelled individual, but immediate culture shock set in when we were weaving through the crowded city streets in that taxicab ride. I would be withholding the truth if I did not admit to being nervous during those first 20 minutes. Our driver was navigating his way through the narrow streets of Marrakech with reckless abandon (it was unanimous consensus that Morocco is home to some of the worst drivers in the world). Our taxi pulled up to a fork in the road of the crowded market and the driver yelled in Arabic to a young boy in a straw hat. At this point, we did not have the slightest inkling as what to expect, but the boy did direct us to our riad which would have been impossible to find given the location off the side of the road in an alley. We were later informed by the workers at our riad that the boy was not an authorized guide and could be arrested for the services that he provided us in exchange for compensation.

My close friend from high school, Joe Meringolo, had been living in Spain for the past four years and was scheduled to return to the United

States in the summer of 2016. I had always wanted to visit him prior to his departure, so this was my last opportunity to do so. We ended up deciding on spending the majority of our time in Morocco because of the close proximity to Madrid, strength of the U.S. dollar against the Moroccan dirham (which was approximately $1 USD per 10 Moroccan dirham at the time of our visit), wide geographic diversification within the country, and the fact that neither of us had stepped foot in Africa. Even better deals could be found in Morocco at our time of visit due to public perception of a high terrorism threat mostly derived from overall instability in the North African region (a fresh squeezed orange juice at the local market could be purchased for the equivalent of $0.40). Countries such as the United Kingdom had labelled Morocco as having a heightened threat of terrorism due to an increasing number of Moroccans becoming sympathetic with extremist groups. Along our journey, we encountered fewer than ten Americans total, and it was clear that the negative media publicity was having a profound impact on the tourism industry in the country. According to the World Bank, Morocco had approximately ten million tourists visit the country in 2014. Judging by our personal experience, I would estimate that the actual 2016 number would be quite a bit lower, as we were the only guests at our hotel the entire week.

In conducting research on Morocco, I found that the country offered a variety of activities due to the fact that an individual could travel to the desert, mountains, and beach all within a day's time. Additionally, Morocco is a fine economic case study considering the relative success it has endured compared to other North African countries in recent memory. Morocco achieved GDP growth of 4.5% in 2015 compared to 1.2% in Tunisia and 3.7% in Algeria. Countries in the region such as Libya do not have reliable economic statistics due to a current lack of government presence.

Morocco is a constitutional monarchy with an elected parliament and is officially known as the Kingdom of Morocco. The King of Morocco holds a great amount of legislative and executive powers. As of the time of this writing, Morocco is home to approximately 35 million people. It is one of only three countries to have both Mediterranean and Atlantic coastlines.

The capital of Morocco is Rabat and the largest city in the country is Casablanca. Morocco continues to claim the territory known as Western Sahara to be part of its Southern Provinces. This has been an ongoing conflict since Morocco annexed the territory in 1975 and the Polisario Front still refuses to recognize the land ownership by Morocco. The Sahrawi Arab Democratic Republic is governed by the Polisario Front, which still controls around 20% of the Western Sahara and the whole area is deemed unsafe to visit due to ongoing conflicts in the region.

Economy

At the time of writing, Morocco laid claim to the 5th largest African country in terms of GDP and was considered the most successful in the North African territory. As of 2014, services accounted for approximately 53% of GDP with industry and agriculture adding 22% and 12%, respectively. The major resources the country has to offer are phosphate, agriculture, and tourism. Morocco holds approximately 75% of the world's phosphate reserves and is currently the world's third largest producer. Agriculture represents around 40% of the country's workforce and includes barley, wheat, olives, wine grapes, and citrus fruits. As previously discussed, from our experience exploring the country, the Moroccan tourism industry seems to have been noticeably diminished. It is difficult to overstate the negative public perception of the North African region in the U.S. leading up to our trip. I did not speak to a single individual that wasn't gravely concerned about our travel plans, as they viewed the ISIS terror threat to be extremely high in the country. I think this concern could be viewed as a positive for local safety and was assisted by the various police checkpoints that we noticed throughout the country. Morocco has attracted a number of large auto and aerospace investors in recent years including Bombardier, Delphi, and Eaton Corporation. The country now projects $10 billion in auto industry exports by 2020, which would account for 20% of GDP. Morocco attracted more foreign investments than most during the 2008 financial crisis by branding itself as a conveniently located export base for Europe, Africa, and the Middle East.

Morocco benefits from its geographic location, which it has taken advantage of in recent years by increasing the focus on industries such as automobile and aeronautics. Morocco has business-friendly policies in place such as the ease of starting a new business. According to the World Bank, it only takes 11 business days to open a business as of 2015 and has relatively less government bureaucracy involved in the process compared to other North African countries such as Egypt (although there have been documented issues regarding lost registration papers and other delays). Additionally, Moroccan business formation only requires minimum capital of $1,000, of which only 25% must be paid prior to incorporation, which opens the entrepreneurial dream to almost any aspiring male citizen. Morocco encourages foreign investment by not subjecting outside investors wishing to start a business within the country to higher capital requirements in most industries and does not require foreigners to form a joint venture unlike other countries such as Algeria, Libya, and Saudi Arabia. Despite these policies that are favorable to foreign business, Morocco does have a high corporate tax rate of about 30%, which could deter some potential investors.

Adventure

Upon settling into our riad, we confirmed our bookings for the following day with our tour operators. This process took over an hour due to the fact that the workers at our riad barely spoke English (Moroccan Arabic is the official language of the country with French being an unofficial second language and used for business, government, and diplomacy) and even the individuals speaking on the phone at the tourism companies were not very proficient in the English language. We then proceeded to the plaza area where we enjoyed a fabulous Moroccan lunch overlooking the market. The meal consisted of four dishes including couscous, tagine, and an array of local juices all for a great price of $35 for us both including tip.

As is often written about the country, the Moroccan people are extremely persistent in regard to selling goods and services to tourists. It was not uncommon for Joe and me to be walking down the street and to have a stranger whisper into our ear asking if we would like to purchase drugs ranging from marijuana to heroin. I would avoid eye contact with these people and had no issue declining the offers but could see how the relentless sales efforts deter some from visiting.

After concluding our delicious meal, it was late afternoon and we were in search of a location that provided alcohol. We knew that this task would be a challenge considering that 99% of the Moroccan population adheres to Islam but I think we still overestimated the number of locations that would serve alcohol. I would have thought a beer would be a bit easier to acquire given Morocco's history of relative tourism success, with tourism contributing 6.5% contribution to GDP in 2015. However, with Ramadan overlapping with the first several days of our trip, this provided an additional challenge in this regard. It was strange visiting bars and restaurants during the day only to find several patrons not eating or consuming any beverages at all due to religious obligations. We resorted to calling it an early night because of our looming 3:00 a.m. wake-up call so that we could make our sunrise hot air balloon ride which cost about $200 per person.

I awoke just prior to 3:00 a.m. the next morning. The series of events that followed will be permanently ingrained in my memory. The kind man working at our riad had breakfast prepared for us promptly at 3:30 a.m. Since Ramadan was going on and he was set to be awake all night eating food and consuming fluids anyways, this was not out of the ordinary for him. To Joe and me, the meal preparation at this hour was an extraordinary aberration. Additionally, starting somewhere around the 3:00 a.m. hour, a voice could be heard over the city megaphones speaking Arabic. We are still unsure as to the exact wording of the citations, but we inferred that the message meant it was time to eat and pray. We left our hotel around 4:00 a.m., it was still dark out at this time, and passed several thousand people gathered in the streets praying which was an incredible sight to witness.

Our vehicle continued onward to approximately an hour outside of Marrakech in the middle of the desert. Our hot air balloon flight was delayed due to high winds in the area. The group was concerned, with me being the most anxious for the flight, that the ride may be cancelled altogether for the day. We ate breakfast prior to the excursion in an effort to wait for the winds to regress enough to ensure a safe trip. Joe and I bonded with other members in our group during this time, so we did not mind the wait. Our new friend Becky who currently resides in London was also traveling throughout Morocco and shared stories of her adventures around the northern portion of the country. After about an hour and a half of waiting, one of the two hot air balloon operators determined that he was ready to take off despite the tourist consensus that the wind had actually increased during the waiting time. Joe and I were quick to jump at the "opportunity" given the hesitancy of the seemingly less experienced and confident operator of the second balloon. Prior to departure, the group was informed that the takeoff and landing would be a bit turbulent (we would later realize that the latter would be quite the understatement).

Despite the warnings, the takeoff went relatively smoothly all things considered. Upon ascension over the desert, we took in the magnificent views that lay beneath us. Here we were, looking out over the sprawling desert area that stretched as far as the human eye could see. We elevated to a maximum height of approximately 3,000 feet and were well above the clouds at this point. Everyone in the balloon was taking in the views and snapping pictures for the duration of the hour-long journey over the desert. Toward the latter half of the ride, we flew over a couple small villages where count-less children pointed up in the sky at our unusual method of transportation. Our pilot informed us that we would be taking the more adventurous route over the mountains which heightened the excitement amongst the group. We gathered speed during this last part of the ride and then descended rather rapidly once the mountains were in arrears. The pilot then warned us that the landing would be a bumpy one given the windy conditions and that we would have to hang on to the side of the balloon and crouch down in a squatting position to minimize chance of injury. It is safe to say that we significantly underestimated the turbulence that was set to ensue. Our balloon crashed into the rocky ground in an uncomfortable fashion only to continue to bounce along an additional five or six times. This made even the worst plane landings look incredibly smooth but both Joe and I agreed that this only added to the overall experience. Our crash landing from above had drawn quite the commotion amongst the local children in the area, as about 20 children had run from a nearby village to survey the scene. One of the tour operators informed us that the children referred to us as the people who fell from the sky which we found to be amusing.

The following morning we were escorted from our riad to a bus at 7:00 a.m. where we would embark on an eight hour excursion to a section of the Sahara known as Zagora which is located approximately 30 miles from the border of Algeria. Along our expedition, we passed through the Atlas Mountains, which stretch 1,600 miles through Morocco, Algeria, and Tunisia and provided several desirable photography vantage points from elevations reaching higher than 13,000 feet, which I often found to look similar to the Grand Canyon. Again, our driver persisted with irresponsible carelessness often exceeding the speed limit by 20 to 30 miles per hour, accelerating into hairpin turns on mountain cliffs at several thousand feet of elevation, and constantly passing vehicles despite the looming threat of oncoming traffic. Joe and I became friends with Cam and Sarah, who were from Canada, on the bus ride. They had quit their jobs back home a few months prior and were traveling around Europe since that time. I was interested in hearing about their adventures in places such as Croatia that I would like to see for myself.

After passing through the mountains, we went through stretches of desert and even areas where there was a great bit of vegetation which mostly consisted of red acacia trees, date palms, and doum palms. I found this to be interesting considering that the Sahara overall averages only 0-25 millimeters of rain per year (our hot air balloon operator informed us that it hadn't rained in the Marrakech area in three months). We finally arrived at our destination which was miles from any form of civilization in the Zagora around 6:00 p.m.

What happened upon arrival at the camel site in the middle of the Zagora was clearly a case of major cultural differences and the only point on the trip during which I felt uncomfortable other than upon initial arrival in Marrakech. We had been traveling on the bus for the duration of the day with a group of about 15. Upon exiting the bus, without explanation or introduction to our new tour guides who would lead us further into the desert on camels, the group split in two. In American culture, it would have been standard procedure to provide a formal introduction and explain the plan going forward just to make the group comfortable with the situation. I watched as our group of six which was led by our two new tour guides wandered what seemed to be aimlessly in the opposite direction of the rest of the group. The entire experience turned out to be incredible but I would be lying if at this point there weren't thoughts of potential kidnap, or worse, going through the back of my head, particularly after the lady at the Philadelphia airport told me of a story of a similar African tour where this did occur. In hindsight and considering the tourist murders that occurred at the foothills of Mount Toubkal in December 2018, this activity was one of my biggest travel regrets. Anyone with ill intentions could have kidnapped or murdered our group in the middle of the night, as there was nobody nearby to deter such actions. We had a great time on our desert adventure, but the reward was not worth the risk.

Here we were, looking out at the wide open Sahara. The Sahara is the largest hot desert on planet earth at 3.6 million square miles and consumes most of North Africa, covering large portions of Algeria, Chad, Egypt, Libya, Mali, Mauritania, Morocco, Niger, Western Sahara, Sudan, and Tunisia. The group quickly got to see why the Sahara Desert has a reputation for being one of the harshest climates, as the temperature at this point reached 130 degrees Fahrenheit, which was an experience in and of itself. In fact, it was so hot that the orange color of my Berkshire Hathaway hat was melted, and I was forced to leave it behind in the desert! The color was completely distorted and unrecognizable after the camel journey was over.

Our camels were roped together and led by the guides out front of the pack. Our guides assisted the group in mounting the camels, which nobody had a great difficulty in doing. We ventured deeper into the desert for about two hours via camel. I was in awe at the sprawling desert scenery which included sand dunes and mountains in the distance. We took turns taking camel "selfies" and some entertaining videos of this once in a lifetime experience. Upon arrival at our campsite, which I was slightly relieved actually existed, we rehydrated and nursed our new sunburn wounds from the scorching heat. The group then took in the most beautiful sunset I have ever witnessed. The view of the sun setting over the Sahara Desert sand dunes near our campsite simply can't be put into words.

Joe and I then proceeded into the large tent where we would be eating dinner (at this point there were about 30 travelers gathered at the campsite). We further connected with our new Spanish friends Laura, Foix, Georgina, and Guillermo over the delicious Moroccan meal. Our small group then split off into an unoccupied area of the desert where we learned to play Moroccan melodies on the drums and other percussion instruments led by our guide Hassan (it became clear early on that I did not possess any musical talent). The stars that night were the clearest I had ever seen with not a single cloud in the sky. We lay there in the sand looking up as we saw countless shooting stars, just watching in admiration.

Our new Spanish friends resided from the Barcelona area. They became upset with some of the other Catalan, an ethnic group with origins in Catalonia who form a nationality in northern Spain, members in the group when they became disrespectful to the tour guides by chanting loudly during their musical performance. They explained that instances such as this were the reason that the Catalan people sometimes had a poor reputation amongst others in Spain. Joe and I found our Catalan friends to be welcoming and it gave me an opportunity to practice my long-lost Spanish listening skills. Hassan discussed the meaning of the Berber, sometimes referred to as the mountain people, population with the group. Berber can refer to any of the descendants of the pre-Arab inhabitants of North Africa. They live in scattered communities across Morocco, Algeria, Tunisia, Libya, Egypt, Mali, Niger, and Mauretania. The Berbers speak Amazigh languages and their population was reduced to fluctuating sizes in the 20th century after the French distinguished between the Arab majority and the Berbers of the mountains. The Berber influence in Morocco declined over time due to the forbiddance of Berber studies in school after the monarchy felt endangered by the role that Berber officers played in the attempted assassinations of the king during would-be coups in 1971–1972. Today, the Berber people travel down from the mountains surrounding cities such as Marrakech and supply food to local markets.

Our new friend Foix was asking Hassan about being a tour guide in Morocco, as it was her career goal to be a guide in an undetermined location. Hassan informed her that it is illegal for a woman to possess this occupation in the country. Policies such as this inhibit the country from reaching full economic growth potential, as placing such restrictive measures on roughly half the population will curtail labor force participation and in turn diminish total GDP productivity. The discrepancy between men and women outside during the day was immediately noticeable when we were walking around the streets. The lack of women around was likely even more pronounced given that Ramadan was in full swing, as many were likely at home preparing food that could be consumed during the evening hours, but it was clear that Morocco has a long way to go in terms of placing both genders on equal footing.

We retired to our tent around 1:00 a.m. after sharing stories for several hours. It was a bit difficult arising at 5:00 the following morning so that we could catch the desert sunrise and begin our journey back to Marrakech. We stopped at a UNESCO World Heritage Site called Aït Benhaddou on our way back. There are still a limited number of families that live in this mud town built along the side of a hill. This fortified city has provided the scenery for films such as *Gladiator*, *Kingdom of Heaven*, *Prince of Persia*, and *The Mummy*. We took in some of the most breathtaking views of the trip from the top of the city. The view was similar to what I would expect to see in a *Star Wars* movie on the planet Tatooine with the desert stretching for miles in every direction and dotted with small huts made from mud that could withstand the intense climate.

Our new bus driver had even less regard for human life than our fearless leader on the way to the Zagora. Since our journey continued up until close to sunset, we received a glimpse into what happens when everyone in a country is rushing to get somewhere at the same time due to Ramadan. This was the religious equivalent to when Domino's Pizza guaranteed all deliveries within 30 minutes or less. We saw several automobile accidents on our return trip and witnessed drivers speeding up to 100 miles per hour swerving into oncoming traffic to try and ensure timely arrival prior to sunset! Prior to this experience, I thought that nearly everything in life had a price. Now I can safely say that there is no premium that could be high enough to entice me to insure any form of automobile in Morocco. Thankfully our only collision on this expedition occurred when a scooter ran into the side of our bus and did not result in any injuries.

Joe and I made arrangements with our new Spanish friends to meet up later that night and go out in Marrakech. Despite being exhausted from the long journey, we did want to wish our friends farewell, as they would be continuing on to Fes which is located in northern Morocco the following day. Our fine evening consisted of delicious pizza and much needed cocktails on the top of a four story lounge. It was refreshing to be in this club-like atmosphere with dance style music and beverages after settling for early retirements the preceding evenings. The most eye-opening part of the night occurred when Joe and I were walking Laura and Georgina back to their riad. It was 2:30 a.m. and the streets were more crowded than we had seen for the duration of our trip up to that point. It was the night before Eid al-Fitr which marks the end of Ramadan, so the entire town of Marrakech was out and about and all of the stores were open despite it being deep into the night. This is another experience that I will surely never forget.

The following morning, we awoke around 6:00 a.m. so that we could travel to the bus station to attempt to catch a ride to Essaouira, a coastal beach town located a few hours to the west of Marrakech. The bus operators had told us a few days prior to arrive at the bus station the day of Eid al-Fitr to see if they would be operating on the holiday. This made absolutely no sense at all to me given the fact that all other bus and train operators I had ever worked with offered tickets well in advance. It turned out that the buses were not operating on the holiday, so Joe and I resorted to cab negotiations which was an adventure in and of itself. We agreed upon a price with our initial driver and he assured us that we would receive a direct route to Essaouira. After a couple minutes of driving, we were handed off to one of his taxi counterparts and were again told that we would be receiving a ride to the beach. While Joe and I were getting angry by this point, we received another valuable lesson on how individuals negotiate and swindle in countries such as Morocco. Our initial driver informed the second man that our agreed upon price was about $30 lower than what it actually was, knowing that he would expect a kickback from us in return. We gladly handed over a few bucks to him for saving us money on the overall exchange. Joe and I agreed to pay the second driver half the money up front and half upon arrival in Essaouira. Again, we drove just a few minutes before stopping at our initial bus station and were passed on to a third driver. At this point, Joe and I were screaming at both men demanding that we head to the coast immediately. We were worried that half of our money would never be seen again and were somewhat surprised when the third man finally made good on his word. He claimed the ride required police authorization which I found to be strange. While authorizations such as this may help reduce some security concerns in a country such as Morocco, it leads to inefficiencies and constrains overall productivity. Upon arriving at what looked more like a drug dealing compound than a police station, the man sprinted off and again we thought that we had been robbed of half of our money. It was a relieving feeling when our driver returned, and we finally were heading toward Essaouira. The taxi fiasco made me think about what a tremendous opportunity there is for on-demand rides from companies such as Uber and Lyft. Given that Morocco is still largely a cash society, these companies would have to consider accepting cash such as how they operate in countries such as India, but this service would be filling a huge gap in the Moroccan transportation system.

Along our drive to Essaouira, I looked out the window to the right and thought I must have been imagining the present sight or dreaming. The driver asked if we would like to pull over to take a few pictures. Sure enough, there were about 15 goats sitting up in a tree right along the highway! This native goat species is adept at climbing the argan trees and are not afraid to scamper out onto branches up to 30 feet high in pursuit of the fruit produced by the rare tree. Almost equally as surprising as seeing several goats hanging out in a tree is the high demand for the waste that these goats produce. The sought-after goat droppings are used to produce argan oil which is one of the most desired cosmetic liquids in the world.

The ride up to Essaouira was nothing short of breathtaking. The landscape reminded me of the Greek islands in a way, with the light-colored buildings and beautiful beach in the backdrop. The weather here was considerably cooler than it had been in Marrakech, around 75 degrees Fahrenheit, and there was an enjoyable beach breeze passing through. This town was much smaller than Marrakech and had far less traffic along the walkways. The result of this was that we were not solicited by nearly as many people for products or services as we wandered around for the majority of the day. Joe and I enjoyed a delicious Moroccan meal on the rooftop of a local restaurant. Like most of the locations that we visited, the server was overly accommodating and extremely delighted when we informed him that it was our favorite meal thus far in Morocco.

The following morning we arose early in hot pursuit of a kitesurfing lesson. Some refer to Essaouira as the windy city due to its high winds in the months of June to September which makes for ideal kitesurfing conditions. Joe and I strolled down to the beach on this glamorous morning and were easily able to secure a four hour lesson which cost $130 each. I had heard that kitesurfing was difficult, but perhaps I underestimated the demand of the initial phase. We reviewed the basics of the sport with our instructor for about an hour on the beach. Here we would practice the different kite positions and how to get the kite in the air and keep it upward while allowing it to turn at our discretion. It is vital to understand which direction to turn the kite, how to apply and release tension, what to do in the event of an emergency, etc. Given the extreme winds present on the beach, one hardly had to apply any pressure at all to elevate the kite to the desired position. It took me a few attempts to use the correct hand when directing the kite to the 12:00 position. Once Joe and I had what our instructor deemed an adequate understanding on the beach, we proceeded to the water where we would practice further. This proved to be a much more arduous task, as waves would crash into our bodies at the very instant that we were attempting to redirect the kite above. Overall, it was a tremendous experience and we were both glad that we were given a chance to try this extreme sport in the most demanding of environments. Joe and I both wish to build on this initial kitesurfing experience in the future.

We traveled back to Marrakech that afternoon via bus, which was only $8 each for a two hour ride. Joe and I had decided the day prior that we were going to make our last night in Marrakech a memorable one. We had arranged for an evening dinner reservation at Palais Jad Mahal. Not only was this lounge known for its exquisite food, but it also provided entertainment in the form of Moroccan belly dancers and an assortment of performers. This upscale establishment was located in what was referred to as "new Marrakech." The area consisted of numerous brand new five-star gated hotels that looked like they belonged in Beverly Hills. The hotels, restaurants and prestigious nightclubs in this neighborhood would be hurt if the Moroccan tourism industry suffers further setbacks in the coming years due to terror-related fears or other developments.

Upon arrival at Palais Jad Mahal, Joe and I headed to the back of the venue to the bar for a few drinks prior to our much-anticipated meal and show in the main room. The drink prices here were several multiples of the other venues we had been to but still similar to what one would expect to pay at a comparable location in Washington D.C. We would soon come to a consensus that the elevated prices were well worth the unforgettable experience. The bar area was comparable to an upscale lounge in the United States with a Moroccan twist. I found it interesting that the bartender removed our drink menus after we had ordered two glasses of Johnnie Walker Black. This practice may be the cultural norm in Morocco but can curtail the number of drinks ordered by the customer, and possibly intentionally so given the overwhelming Muslim presence in the country.

When it was nearing show time in the main room, we were seated by the hostess in the viewing area. Joe and I opted to split the Moroccan and Thai samplers, which we would soon realize entailed a portion of practically every food product ever created from both cultures. This dinner was nothing short of heavenly and certainly our favorite meal while in the country. Despite the superb food, the real highlight was the performance on display in front of us. The show started with two men entering a glass area that could be seen from the dining room. The individuals began juggling sticks of fire in an effort that reminded me of Cirque du Soleil in Las Vegas. It became evident early on that we were in the minority in that we were not regular attendees of the venue. I was actively taking videos and pictures while most of the crowd acted as if this amazing cultural display was just another Thursday night. After this impressive performance came the beautiful Moroccan belly dancers. They danced to the beat of the Moroccan percussion and made sure to get the audience involved in the well-orchestrated routine. Our food consumption completely halted during this time period, as it was difficult to take our eyes off the beautiful women shaking their hips just a few feet from our table. Sufficiently full after dessert and still in awe of what we had just witnessed, Joe and I departed for our riad close to midnight.

Additional Activities and Recommendations

There are some quality rock climbing opportunities in Morocco. Todra Gorge is located on the eastern side of the High Atlas Mountains which is accessible from Marrakech. There are nearly 400 different climbing routes in the Todra Gorge with rock walls reaching as high as nearly 1,000 feet. September to November and February through May are the best months for climbing. Depending on the rock climbing route that is chosen, you can stay at a hotel or camp. There is a climbing choice for everyone here so don't worry if it is your first time.

Canyoning is an activity that is available in the Middle-Atlas region. This adventure activity is suitable for all parties. Enjoy trekking through the Atlas Mountains, abseiling from waterfalls, and even cliff jumping.

Sandboarding at Merzouga is a popular attraction. Race down the highest dunes in the country at speeds of up to 50 miles per hour! Sandboarding excursions are often combined with camel trekking and camping in the Merzouga dunes.

There are various cooking classes offered in Marrakech where individuals can learn how to make some of Morocco's finest meals.

Adventurers may want to look into climbing Mount Toubkal in the Atlas Mountains. Get a chance to reach the highest peak in North Africa. You will spend a night at Toubkal Refuge. Around eight hours of walking can be expected on the hike up to the top. Take in the views of the fantastic surrounding scenery.

Not many think to go snow skiing in Morocco but there are surprisingly quite a few destinations that will get thrill seekers excited about with relatively limited crowds. Various tours are offered in the High Atlas for experienced skiers. Morocco's most noteworthy ski resort is Oukaimeden which is 50 miles east of Marrakech. This mountain tops out at over 10,000 feet.

Mountain biking in the High Atlas Mountains is an activity worth consideration. The High Atlas Mountains can offer an adventurous ride even for the most experienced mountain bikers. There are various other routes for all types of riders in Morocco. Two popular mountain biking routes are Oued Amizmiz and Azegour. Other than the High Atlas, biking can be done in the northern and western side of the Middle Atlas as well. Do note that the High Atlas climbs along many of the mountainous routes can be dangerous even for the most experienced riders.

Business Outlook

I am optimistic on the business prospects of Morocco as a whole. Phosphate is a key ingredient in fertilizer, which will become increasingly important in the future as the global population is projected to reach close to ten billion people by 2050 with a decreasing amount of arable land available for farming which will only make fertilizer products more valuable. Holding 75% of the global phosphate reserves will prove to be an enormous advantage in the future due to the macroeconomic factors mentioned above. A potential concern that could arise from these conditions is an invasion by another country short of fertilizer to extract the sought-after natural resource.

A high-quality potential investment idea came to my attention on the way to Morocco. This came in the form of traveling to the country from Spain via Ryanair, Europe's lowest fare and lowest cost carrier. I had traveled on Ryanair years earlier when I was studying abroad in Europe. My experience at that time with the Irish carrier was nothing short of horrible. Up until recently, Ryanair only operated out of smaller airports that turned out to be nowhere near where the passenger was trying to get to. For example, when I had booked a flight to what I thought was London I was routed to the Stansted airport instead. Only upon arrival did I realize that Stansted was over an hour from London. I viewed this as deceptive selling practices. Additionally, we had to stay overnight in a Belgium airport operated by Ryanair that did not have any janitors. There was vomit on the floor and garbage everywhere! These scarring experiences were in addition to the downright dismal customer service offered by the company.

Fast forward to my trip to Morocco, and I could tell some things were starting to change at Ryanair. Ryanair now operated out of primary airports and we were able to take a flight out of Madrid's main airport which made the experience far more enjoyable. Ryanair had placed an increased emphasis on the customer experience through their "Always Getting Better" plan created in 2014. The carrier focused on areas such as relaxing its hardline cabin baggage allowance, reducing penalties for failing to print out boarding passes and introducing allocated seating. While the experience was still far from luxurious, it was noticeably better than in years prior. Ryanair's reputation is still far from stellar and they do get in the news from time to time for the wrong reasons. For example, in 2017, they had a very public dispute with their pilots in regard to compensation. Ryanair ultimately relented and agreed to pay the pilots a 20% premium to competitors but the whole ordeal did dent the reputation of the company.

Why did I find Ryanair to be interesting from an investment perspective given that airlines have had a long history of being terrible investments? Ryanair is different in that it has consistently shown that it can achieve high return on invested capital employed with annual numbers showing above 15% except in recessionary years. Ryanair has managed to run a low-cost operation profitably which has been elusive for many other European carriers. What is even more remarkable is that Ryanair has achieved this by offering average fares that are nearly 230% cheaper than all other competitors. These incredibly low prices leave many consumers with no other choice but to fly with the Irish carrier. The fact that their average plane fare is around 40 euros and they are able to make a high profit margin on the sale is admirable. I am not sure how they do it, but they simply just get the job done. Part of the explanation is that they charge for anything that is in addition to the flight itself, with the plane ride serving as a flying 7-11 offering everything from snacks to cologne.

I continue to love the story. Ryanair will grow through expansion into new airports and routes along with further upside in ancillaries. Ryanair expects to have more than a staggering 200 million yearly passengers by

2024. The company has been marketing themselves as more of a technology company that happens to sell airlines and be the Amazon of the air. Recent initiatives such as serving as the short haul carrier that connects long haul flights to other carriers provides additional growth potential. Ryanair has been able to gain additional market share as other European carriers have failed in recent years which can be at least partially attributable to the fare war that Ryanair continues to wage and win. I would suggest reading the biographies written about CEO Michael O'Leary, as they provide for great life lessons on how to build a successful enterprise.

Given the location of the country along with the relatively low industrial wages compared to neighboring European countries such as Spain and France, I would expect the Moroccan industrial sector to continue to thrive. The aeronautics industry may especially be appealing given the fact that global passenger miles flown are expected to continue to increase on a torrid pace in the coming years. As of 2015, the demand for global air travel was projected to double by 2035, providing a low runway for industry growth. It could be wise to invest in an airplane manufacturing facility in Morocco and export the planes to European, other African, and Asian countries. In addition to the growing automobile manufacturing sector present within the country, Morocco does have an expanding textile and leather industry as well.

There is large potential for ridesharing in Morocco. This investment opportunity does not come without political caveats, however. Uber launched in Morocco in 2015 only to be banned by the local authorities one month later. Uber has faced an uphill battle ever since, with taxi drivers continuing to protest and make the business environment difficult for the company to operate. If Uber and other ridesharing companies can overcome these political challenges, there is a lot of room for growth. Given the extreme difficulties that Joe and I faced in regard to transportation while in Morocco, I am confident that many individuals would pay up for the much-improved experience.

Updates Since Visit

As of early 2019, the economic outlook for the Moroccan economy looks solid, with 2.9% projected GDP growth in 2019 followed by 3.7% in 2020. The Moroccan High Commissioner for Planning highlighted industrial activities including the automotive, aeronautics, and electronics industries as contributing to Morocco's economic growth. As I touched on earlier, the automotive and aeronautics industries should continue to see tailwinds for many years benefitting from the country's geographic location, relatively low labor costs compared to European counterparts, and historical stability relative to North African neighbors.

According to the 2019 World Bank Ease of Doing Business rankings, Morocco ranked 60th out of 190 global economies, which is a record for the country and significantly better than the 90 average between 2008 and 2018. Morocco ranked third in Africa in terms of ease of doing business, and the recent report highlighted that the country has made it easier to start a business by reducing registration fees, easier to register property by streamlining procedures, and easier to resolve insolvency. The report also noted that Morocco made exporting and importing easier by implementing a paperless customs clearance system and improving infrastructure at the port of Tangier. It is these types of improvements and long-term relative stability in terms of economic structure and ease of doing business that should continue to attract foreign investment in Morocco.

Over 12 million tourists visited Morocco in 2018 which was up 8% from 2017. Tourism remains a significant economic driver for the Moroccan economy and it is critical that the country maintains a reputation as being a safe tourist destination. The horrific December 2018 terrorist attack of the two Scandinavian hikers put a negative global spotlight on the Moroccan tourism industry and the sector will likely suffer at least in the near term. The U.S. Department of State has maintained a Level 1 Travel Advisory for Morocco, which is a positive sign, but the country can't remain complacent in its efforts to thwart the ever-present risk of terrorism. The UK government has stated, "authorities have warned of an increased threat linked to the number of Moroccans sympathetic or belonging to Daesh [formerly referred to as ISIL] and other extremist groups, and regularly report the disruption of terrorist cells across the country." There has always been a threat of terrorism in the country and Morocco has a strong track record of preserving safety so let's hope that this can continue into the future.

I had previously written about the potential ridesharing opportunity in Morocco. In February 2018, Uber announced that it would be suspending operations in the country after two years of service in Morocco. Uber cited a lack of any constructive progress on the regulations pertaining to the industry as the reason for halting the service. Despite posting solid numbers in the Ease of Doing Business rankings, it is anti-capitalist measures such as in the transportation sector that provide an opportunity for future improvement and increased foreign investment.

As for Ryanair, the company faced a great deal of turbulence (pun intended) in 2018, which was attributable to rising oil prices and pilot strikes that disrupted flight schedules and eventually increased input costs. The rising oil prices lead to the failure of an array of European airlines and in my opinion has only widened the moat of Ryanair. The union presence and possibility of strikes is something to consider when thinking about European aviation (when was the last time there was a large scale strike in the U.S. aviation sector?) but I think this concern is more than offset by the extreme input cost advantages that Ryanair maintains. Ryanair commands 15% market share in Europe and has robust growth opportunities over the long haul. Ryanair went on to rebound strongly in the ladder half of 2019 as some of the concerns around the European macroeconomic backdrop and airfare pricing subsided. The rebound for Ryanair was put on hold following the COVID-19 outbreak. Widespread aviation bankruptcies across the globe are imminent and it is unclear as to how this will play out. It could ultimately lead to higher pricing in the future for a carrier such as Ryanair if they survive because a lot of industry supply will be taken out. Having said that, this unprecedented crisis has really shined the light on potential issues related to businesses that have a high amount of fixed costs. Few could have predicted a scenario where virtually every flight on the planet was suspended for a period of months, but businesses with higher proportions of fixed costs have higher risks related to crisis situations because it is much more difficult for them to respond to these adverse scenarios.

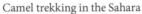

Camel trekking in the Sahara

The hot air balloon adventure

Kitesurfing at Essaouira

I wasn't lying about the goats!

Incredible sunset over the Sahara

Atlas Mountains

Iceland

Introduction

We were picked up in a "Super Jeep", which had four-foot tires with each costing approximately 1,000 euros, in the morning to set out for an unforgettable tour that included Geysir, Gullfoss, Langjökull, and Thingvellir National Park. In driving to our first destination, Gullfoss, we engaged in conversation with our tour guide and learned some interesting information. Iceland has less than 1,000 police officers in the country and does not have an army, air force, or navy. Despite Iceland's abundant energy resources, hydroelectric and geothermal, they do not export energy. Renewable energy provides close to 85% of the country's primary energy consumption and despite lack of energy exportation, Iceland is the world's largest electricity producer per capita. Iceland votes annually on which names are legal to name children in the country. Our tour guide told us that the Icelandic equivalent of "Air Chicken" was deemed legal that year yet names such as "Aaron" were not. I think this unusual naming could be due to the fact that the naming committee for the whole country consists of only three individuals who have all of the authority. The main exports of the country are aluminum (currently three plants in operation with the country placing 11th worldwide in aluminum production), fish, and prosthetic limbs. If you are wondering what ties prosthetic limbs have to Iceland, the Reykjavik-based company Ossur is at the forefront of innovative technology in this industry creating "brain controlled" bionic limbs for amputees.

As an investor, I was interested in the foreign land ownership laws in Iceland. As of 2013, those who are not registered residents of Iceland are not able to acquire land or property unless "shown to support their legal right to residence or employment in the country." Laws such as this wouldn't be considered expansionary and limit potential growth avenues for an economy with few natural resources, limited to energy production, cement manufacturing, and aluminum smelting, and reliant on tourism and fishing. I later tried to visit the Iceland stock exchange, ICEX, and was informed that outside guests were not welcome to visit. Again, it is my opinion that a country such as Iceland should not only open their economy to outside investment but also should be bending over backwards to attract potential foreign interest.

We arrived at Gullfoss, "Golden Falls", and walked up to the best viewing location available. Gullfoss, a waterfall location in southwest Iceland, is one of the most beautiful sights in the country, if not the world. Despite the cool temperatures and the snowfall that continued to blanket the area, the water continued to thunder down the initial "staircase" before vertically plummeting the final 105 feet. If you are visiting Iceland, this is a must-see.

Our group continued our journey out to Langjökull. We proceeded despite the heavy snow and treacherous road conditions. After a few hours, we finally arrived at the second largest glacier in Europe, Langjökull, where we would be snowmobiling. Driving over this 31 mile-long glacier during a blizzard was one of the great adventures of my lifetime. We each operated our own snowmobile and raced along the glacier at speeds up to 50 miles per hour. The only comparison I can make in regard to the conditions that were present that day would be to the movie *Vertical Limit*. In my opinion, this made the experience all the more memorable. Just prior to pulling back into our ending location, my brother tipped his snowmobile over, and it landed on top of him. Luckily, the snow braced the impact, and he was not hurt at all. Once our friend Sam and I confirmed that he was indeed safe, we started laughing hysterically.

While we were out snowmobiling, several feet of snow had accumulated. Not long after we departed in route to Geysir, we got stuck in about three feet of snow. After approximately 45 minutes of digging out the tires and attempting to push forward, our guide finally consented to allow for the only other remaining jeep, which was smaller than ours, to attempt to tow us. At this point our tour guide was visibly upset and informed us that this situation had occurred only one other time. The result of that one other occurrence was that the axles of both vehicles broke. At this point, we were coming to the realization that we may be sleeping in central Iceland during a blizzard (I thought I was lucky that I hadn't eaten my sandwich yet). Fortunately, that would not be the case, as the tow was successful, and we did eventually make our way slowly to Geysir.

Geysir, a geyser located in southwest Iceland on the slopes of Laugar-fjall hill, is the original geyser after which all others in the world are named. We had the pleasure of seeing an impressive geyser eruption multiple times with it erupting about every five minutes. We proceeded on to Thingvellir National Park, where Silfra is located, where we would conclude our tour. It was dark by this time, so we could not see much, but we did get to learn more about how this park came to be in 1928, when legislation was passed to protect this national shrine. The foundation of the Icelandic parliament is believed to have led to the formation of Iceland as a nation.

My brother Connor, our friend Sam, and I purchased roundtrip tickets to Reykjavik, Iceland where we spent five days exploring the country departing on December 18, 2015. We made the last-minute arrangements when offered roundtrip airfare and hotel for $750 each. Many tourists are deterred from traveling to Iceland in the winter due to the short days (on December 19, which was the first full day of our trip, the sun rose at 11:21 a.m. and set at 3:29 p.m.) and the perception of frigid temperatures. The average low temperature in Reykjavik during December 2014 was 31 degrees Fahrenheit with a high of 46 degrees. This is comparable to a December in New York City which sees average lows of 25 degrees Fahrenheit and a high of 64 degrees. Traveling to Iceland during the winter is also enticing due to the wide array of winter sports available. Other than magnificent winter sports, local prices are more reasonable than in the past due to the Global Financial Crisis in 2008. As it currently stands as of this writing, one U.S. dollar translates to approximately 130 Icelandic króna. The relative affordability of visiting Iceland seems to have contributed to a tourism boom in recent years. "More tourists visited Iceland in 2008-2016, than over the 60 preceding years" and "In the 50 years from 1950-2000, only four million foreign tourists visited Iceland - in total. Then something happened. Since 2010, tourist numbers have surged. Again, four million new tourists visited Iceland, but this time it only took the three years between 2014-2016" and "Tourist arrivals in Iceland have increased fivefold since 2010 to 2.2 million in 2017."

Economy

The devastating financial crisis brought the default of all three of the country's major privately owned commercial banks, which were saddled with $85 billion in debt. The financial collapse that occurred in Iceland in 2008 led to a severe economic depression that lasted through 2010. Leading up to the banking collapse, the three largest banks in the country, Kaupthing, Landsbanki and Glitnir, had been growing at a rapid pace by accessing easy credit in international markets. Prior to the collapse, these banks had ballooned to ten times the size of the domestic Iceland economy. Lenient credit terms allowed for purchase of an increasing amount of overseas real estate and investment in foreign companies. The Icelandic banks were offering international investors higher interest rates than could be received in their own domestic countries to achieve further growth. Iceland was offering interest rates as high as 15%, which encouraged "carry trade" where investors borrow in a lower interest rate currency and use the proceeds to buy higher interest rate currencies. As would happen in America, a housing bubble was fueled by lenient lending in some cases requiring no down payment for the purchase of a home. Homeowners assumed that their homes would continue to increase in value which resulted in overconsumption of other luxury items. Between 2003 and 2004, the Iceland stock market skyrocketed an astounding 900%. When the international crisis hit in 2008 (which saw the Icelandic stock exchange fall by more than 90% and put 25% of homeowners into default), trust in the Icelandic financial system began to wane, a common event called contagion where exogenous shocks produce an impact on an economy which spreads to other countries, and the Icelandic króna depreciated rapidly. The depreciation of the local currency naturally led to difficulties for the major banks to repay short-term debt that was borrowed when the economy was promising, and terms were generous. The Icelandic government attempted to stabilize the situation by initiating capital controls, limits on people taking money out of the financial system, on the króna reaching a debt agreement with the IMF and Scandinavia (with $2.1 billion coming from the IMF and $2.5 billion from Scandinavia), and guaranteeing all domestic deposits at Icelandic banks. Iceland is only now beginning to unwind the capital controls that were imposed all the way back in 2008. Time will tell if the Iceland governments plan to have creditors renounce approximately $6.8 billion in claims in exchange for the right to shift money out of the country is successful.

While we have yet to see the full impact of the unwinding of the capital controls, the Icelandic economy has performed relatively well since the financial crisis compared to countries such as Ireland and Greece. Iceland's economy is set to grow in the 4% range for 2015 with a lower unemployment rate than the U.S. and European Union. Implementing capital controls for such an extended period of time (Iceland only initially planned to have them in place for six months) has had negative impacts on the economy as well. New investment in the country has been pressured, as investors are hesitant to invest in a country where it is unclear when they will be able to withdraw capital. Icelandic companies have faced increased borrowing costs, as higher interest rates will compensate for increased risk.

Adventure

We arrived at the Reykjavik airport around 5:00 a.m. local time. This is the only international airport I have been to that did not check customs upon entry into the country. Upon conducting online research, there was apparently a fork in the airport where individuals can choose to declare items. Many people online noted the relaxed policies at this airport and said that nobody asked them a single question when they went down the aisle for no items to declare. In speaking with a native Icelander on the bus to our hotel, I learned that few people in the country practice any religion with the majority of citizens being atheist. Upon conducting further research, I found a 2012 poll that ranked Iceland among the top ten atheist populations in the world with the majority of the citizens considered Lutheran even though most of these declared Lutherans do not regularly practice the religion. Lutheran is the official religion of the country. My new friend confirmed the prior research that I had done in regard to the makeup of the economy. She informed me that her family, like many others at the time, started a tourism company in 2009 as the industry had begun to take off. I found it interesting that Icelandic children are required to learn two languages: English and Danish. Given the long-term economic outlook, Icelanders would be much better served learning Chinese or Spanish as opposed to Danish.

Reykjavik has a population figure of approximately 200,000 people with only around 330,000 in the entire country. Reykjavik is the northernmost capital city for any independent nation. It is fairly well spread out and spans approximately 106 square miles with the entire country of Iceland encompassing 40,000 square miles which is about the size of Ohio. Despite not having slept in about 24 hours, we decided to go on a tour of the town since we were so excited to be there. One of our first observations was how late everything in the city opened. It was largely impossible to acquire a coffee prior to 9:00 a.m. We went to the top of Hallgrímskirkja, a 244 foot-tall Lutheran church that provides fabulous views of Reykjavik. While at the top of the church enjoying the views of the city, a Ukranian man informed us of

how the Russians had forced him from his hometown by demanding excessive bribes. After explaining his situation in Ukraine, he pleaded that we ask
President Obama to invade Russia. Despite being sympathetic toward this
man that I had known for only a few brief moments, I was not going to be
the person to inform him that an average U.S. citizen is unable to walk up to
the White House and notify the president that they thought it was a prudent
time to invade another country. He may have been under the impression that
this was possible since anyone could do exactly that in Iceland! The president
of the country lives in a home with no security and an average citizen can
knock on his door at their own discretion.

At around 12:30 p.m., we departed for the Blue Lagoon which is located
about 50 minutes outside of Reykjavik. The Blue Lagoon, which was opened
to the public in 1992, is a man-made lagoon that is heated by water output
from a nearby geothermal power plant named Svartsengi. The temperature
in the lagoon averages 98–104 degrees Fahrenheit. National Geographic
has named this spectacle one of the 25 Wonders of the World citing, "the
steaming turquoise pools of Iceland's Blue Lagoon, trapped in volcanic rock
represent an otherworldly vision."

If you have done independent research on the Blue Lagoon, you may
have heard horror stories about the required public showering prior to entering the geothermal spa. Within the past year, the Blue Lagoon has installed
private showers so one can choose to rinse off in there if uncomfortable
in doing so in the presence of complete strangers. We waded around the
lagoon, took pictures, purchased a cocktail from the bar in the lagoon, and
just enjoyed the overwhelmingly relaxing atmosphere for a couple of hours.
The lagoon has steam rooms, offers in-water massages, and has several other
amenities designed for the pinnacle of comfort.

In arriving back to our hotel, we took a brief nap as we had not slept in
36 hours at this point. We had heard only great things about Saturday nights
out on the town in Reykjavik and the experience didn't disappoint. At around
12:30 a.m. (people do not go out until very late in Reykjavik. The crowds were

still relatively thin at this hour), we set out for the night. We briefly went to a small microbrewery before venturing to The English Pub. The live music here was great (they even played "Sweet Home Alabama". I doubt anyone else in the pub knew where Alabama was) and the crowd was vibrant. There was a wheel behind the bar where a patron could request a spin for $16 to earn a chance to win prizes ranging from a shot to eight beers. I am not sure why the show *Bar Rescue* has not caught on to this concept for locations where this would not be considered gambling, as it surely was a huge money maker and required no overhead cost.

At 2:00 a.m., we went across the street to a club called Austur, which catered to a younger crowd looking to dance the rest of the night away. We quickly realized that it was going to take some time to get in, as the VIP line, which consisted of people that were friendly with the bouncer was actually longer than the regular line. While in line, we became friendly with a few local Icelanders named Arthur who was from Poland and Brian from Kenya. They were overly welcoming, and we thoroughly enjoyed exchanging stories about our respective hometowns. Despite the variety of countries being represented, they all spoke English with relative ease. We finally entered the club at around 2:30 a.m., and it was worth the wait. With our group now having grown to five, we proceeded straight to the dancefloor where we would spend the next several hours not worrying about anything else other than the music in the present. Despite the official closing time of Austur being at 4:30 a.m., the club operators simply locked the doors at this time and kept the venue open as long as people wanted to stay. When we left at 5:00 a.m., the party showed no sign of slowing down.

7:45 a.m. That is when my first alarm went off. At about 8:05 a.m. I heard my brother shouting to disarm my alarm, as I had somehow managed to sleep through two of the loudest alarms known to man for the previous 20 minutes. I quickly gathered my belongings and raced to the lobby in time to catch my shuttle to Silfra. I had booked my snorkeling trip to Silfra through a separate tour operator, so I had to leave a few minutes earlier than Sam and Connor. As we learned was typical of the Iceland tourism industry, the logistics operations did not make any sense. I was shuttled to a separate location where I would wait for 20 minutes until a van carrying my brother and Sam would arrive and pick me up. A talented logistics specialist could surely improve operating margins at Icelandic tour companies by 20% with fairly minimal effort.

The Silfra fissure, located in Thingvellir National Park, is consistently voted one of the top ten dive and snorkel sites in the world. The underwater visibility at this site is phenomenal, usually up to 150 meters (492 feet). Despite the lack of aquatic life at this site, there are tremendous views of what I would consider to be the equivalent of an underwater Grand Canyon. Silfra is located between the North American and European continents where the tectonic plates meet and drift apart at approximately two centimeters per year. This makes it the only location in the world where one can dive or snorkel between two continental plates.

Prior to entering the 34 degree Fahrenheit water at Silfra (water temperature consistently ranges between 34 and 36 degrees Fahrenheit throughout the year), we changed into a "teddy bear suit", which makes an individual feel as though they are wrapped in a blanket, along with a dry suit. The dry suit was so tight that it felt as though a person was lightly choking you throughout the experience. We entered the water and took in the spectacular views below. We continued to drift downstream in this freshwater paradise for close to 40 minutes. The rock formations were stunning with the climax occurring at Silfra Cathedral, 328 feet long, where it is possible to see end-to-end. Anyone claiming that the water at Silfra is "not that cold" is lying. While the dry suit did a good job keeping us warm for the first 20 minutes, the experience after that was unlike any I had ever felt before. I lost feeling in my toes, fingers, and face for the second half of the snorkel experience due to the extremely cold water. Despite the frigid temperature, I would recommend this excursion for any adventurer that would like to experience such an unparalleled underwater treasure. As I had read online prior to making the trip to Silfra, I was happy with my decision to snorkel instead of scuba dive at this location even though I am a scuba diving enthusiast. Snorkeling was half the price of diving through most operators and provided very similar views of the rock formations from the surface.

That evening we had a fine meal at 3 Frakkar, which was recommended to me prior to arriving in Iceland as well as by the hotel receptionist. Here we would try three food items that were new to us: whale pepper steak, shark, and smoked puffin breast. We were all in agreement that the whale filet was one of the best food products we had ever consumed. This tender, thinly sliced piece of meat was incredibly delicious. I would have expected there to be a lot of fat on whale as blubber constitutes a large portion of their body-weight, but this was not the case at all. As tasty as the whale was, the shark was equally as horrible (we later discovered that this was Greenland shark. It is fermented for several months prior to consumption and those eating it for the first time are often told to pinch their nose to the high ammonia content). We should have known what we were in for when the shark was served with three shots of brennivín, a local form of schnapps, to wash it down. There were mixed reviews on the puffin, but I found it be pretty good.

Connor and Sam decided not to partake in the final adventure, so I hopped on a bus to head down to the southern tip of Iceland to go glacier hiking and ice climbing with about 20 strangers. I would soon make friends with a school teacher who lives in Washington D.C. and was originally from Argentina. We arrived at the Sólheimajökull glacier after approximately two and a half hours. This spectacular glacier, which advances from Myrdalsjokull glacier, is an 11 kilometer-long outlet glacier that has shifted in recent years due to climate change. It is possible that it will not even exist in the next 100 years due to temperature increases.

The group was equipped with crampons, spikes placed on our feet to dig into the glacier, and an ice axe which was much too short for my 6'4" frame for optimal performance in navigating the glacier. We spent the next few hours hiking up the glacier and enjoying majestic views of the glacier itself and the nearby shoreline. At times the walkway was narrow and there were cliffs on either side of the single file line where a slight misstep would have resulted in a fall several hundred feet to a perilous death. As is usually the case when I go on excursions such as this, nobody seemed to be phased in the least.

After hiking up the glacier, it was time to test our ice climbing abilities. We alternated climbing up a naturally formed ice wall that was situated along the hiking path. I will be the first to admit that this was by far the most difficult sport I have ever attempted. I scaled the ice wall by digging the front spikes of my crampons into the wall and hacking away with my two ice axes, sometimes taking three or four digs before reaching the necessary support to move upward. I had read various online forums citing blood rushing to the hands and a feeling of nausea after completing a climb but figured that this would not happen to me. Immediately upon finishing my climb, I felt the symptoms that I had read about online and could not speak for five minutes. Clearly, I had expended more energy than necessary in climbing the wall due to the vicious swings to carve out the ice along the way. Despite this feeling, it was a wild experience, and I am glad that I tried it. I now have more respect for those who ascend difficult waterfalls. My Argentinian friend was able to capture some classic action shots of the ice climb, which I was thankful for.

On the drive home we stopped at Skógafoss waterfall. Some would consider this 200-foot waterfall to be the premier attraction in Iceland, as you can hike up to the top and enjoy a fabulous view of the waterfall. Unfortunately, we did not have time to do so since we spent the majority of the day hiking Sólheimajökull, and I was so exhausted at this point that I am not sure I could have hiked further anyway. We then continued onward two more hours to Reykjavik to end a phenomenal day of adventure.

Additional Activities and Recommendations

The Northern Lights is one of the most popular tourist attractions in Iceland. Popularly done as a cruise, enjoy the Northern Lights from one of the best vantage points on earth. It is highly recommended to plan this for the first day of the trip, as weather often does not allow for the Northern Lights to be seen and may need to be rescheduled for another day. We tried to see the Northern Lights each day during our stay, but weather conditions did not cooperate.

Whale watching can be done at Faxaflói Bay which is near Reykjavik. Cruise around in search of humpback and minke whales during this excursion. A biologist on board will discuss more about these interesting animals. Participants can choose between a 2.5 hour high-speed boat and the full-length 3.5 hour tour.

The mountain helicopter tour is done outside of Reykjavik. Take a helicopter tour to a nearby mountain summit from Reykjavik. Upon landing, take in the majestic views of the surrounding scenery.

The South Iceland glaciers, waterfalls, and beaches tour is done in South Iceland. Visit the town of Vik in South Iceland and see the Sólheimajökull and Mýrdalsjökull glaciers. Walk along the intriguing black sand beaches of Vik. Visit the Skogafoss and Seljalandsfoss waterfalls. You will have the chance to walk behind the Skogafoss waterfall for spectacular views.

Horse riding can be done just outside of Reykjavik. Hop aboard the Icelandic horse for a ride in the countryside. The Icelandic horses are small, and this should be taken into consideration for larger individuals.

Volcano hiking tours can be found two hours from Reykjavik. Take a trip down to Fimmvorduhals Volcano via 4X4 jeep and stop at Seljalandsfoss Waterfall along the way. Commence on the ten mile-long route by this active volcano which exploded in 2010.

Iceland is a premiere destination for any outdoor adventurer. There may not be any other international location where you could claim to do all the activities described above for a total trip cost of $2,000. Despite my overwhelmingly positive review of Iceland, I would not recommend visiting if you are not interested in the outdoors. Reykjavik is indeed fun to visit, but I would not say that it is any more special than other European cities. I touched on it briefly above, but food and everyday items are still expensive in Iceland despite the currency depreciation in recent years. We resorted to eating at Subway on multiple occasions due to the high price of meals. I have not had the pleasure of visiting Iceland in the summer, but the winter timeframe was more appealing to me due to the adventurous sporting options along with cheaper rates. If you are interested in visiting Iceland, I would recommend doing so in the next few years, as there is a lot of construction going on in regard to tourism and I wouldn't be surprised if prices were to rise substantially in the near future.

Business Outlook

I am not bullish on the Iceland economy over the long haul. The lack of natural resources combined with a reliance on a few industries, tourism and fishing, can be a devastating combination. A single volcano eruption or terrorist attack could cripple the tourism overnight and take the entire Iceland economy with it. I was discouraged by the lack of enthusiasm for foreign investment in the country. I view Iceland's taxation policies as a mixed bag. Their 20% corporate tax rate, one of the lowest in the world, encourages economic expansion. The same can be said for the 20% tax rate on capital gains. On the other hand, the 24.5% standard VAT leads to higher costs of goods and can ultimately hinder tourism. We noticed a strong work ethic during our brief stay in Iceland which was greater than most other European countries I have encountered. Most of our tour guides worked 12 hours a day, seven days a week. Our hotel receptionists often worked through the night to accommodate guests (since tourism is such a large part of the economy, I consider this more representative of the overall economy than most other countries).

If you are a foreign expert looking to do business in Iceland, a special tax deduction allows that only 75% of income is considered taxable for the first three years of employment. Iceland is providing heavy incentives to encourage investment outside of the capital area, which include the authorization to fix an income tax rate ceiling of only 15% for ten years, fully depreciate real estate and equipment, and reduce the rate of property tax and the general social security charge by 50%. Looking to invest in the film production industry? According to the Icelandic Film Centre, "Producers can apply for reimbursements from the State Treasury of 25% of the costs incurred in the production of films and television programs in Iceland."

Given the tourism boom in recent years, Iceland has been struggling to keep up with the rapid growth in terms of infrastructure with new hotels and other building related to tourism. Infrastructure companies should be lining up to offer contracts to Iceland in anticipation of the tourism boom continuing for years to come.

The majority of current United States investment in Iceland lies in the aluminum sector. You may ask yourself why it would be cheaper to operate an aluminum company in Iceland compared to the United States. The answer lies in the cost of electricity, with the resource being much cheaper in Iceland than the United States. As long as the discrepancy in energy costs continues, I would expect Iceland to continue to attract investment in this industry.

Updates Since Visit

Have you noticed that 80% of your Instagram friends have gone to Iceland in the past three years? You are not the only one. An early 2019 report said that the Iceland tourism boom may finally be over after eight years of robust growth. International visitors to Iceland skyrocketed 39% in 2016 followed up by a 24% increase in 2017. However, 2018 only posted a 5.5% increase and the sector looks poised to slow further in 2019. Icelandic airlines have kept airfares extremely cheap (this is why I decided to go to Iceland) but many of these rates are not sustainable for the long-term, as we have seen numerous European airlines go bankrupt in the last few years due to rising oil prices and unsustainable business models. Given the high price of everyday items such as food in Iceland, this will likely lead to further declines in growth in the tourism sector and have an outsized impact on the overall economy given that tourism accounts for 8.6% of GDP as of 2018. The rate of finished hotels in Iceland has not increased at a pace fast enough to keep up with demand which has increased prices and likely contributed to slowing tourism numbers. Additionally, among a certain segment of the travel population it perhaps ironically makes it less desirable to go to a location if you believe that all of your peers have recently been there. This is where I think Iceland is at this point in time when it comes to tourism.

As for the capital controls enacted during the financial crisis, Iceland finally lifted the last remaining in 2017. The capital controls helped stabilize an economy where the combined assets of the country's three largest banks were 14 times the size of overall economic output but would you invest in a country that has a history of disallowing foreign removal of capital for nine years? That is the million-dollar question.

The Icelandic currency remains an issue for the country. Iceland is the smallest economy in the world to have its own floating currency and the króna has a history of instability. Since the last capital controls were removed in 2017, the króna has been devalued with pension funds and investors moving money to other countries in search of a more stable currency. Iceland has considered it in the past, but it needs to peg its currency to that of a more stable currency. It is outlandish for a country of this size with only three main products in the entire economy, fish, tourism, and geothermal electricity, to have a floating currency. This is just asking for disaster and Iceland may well get it in the form of a cooling tourism sector.

The long-term outlook for the Iceland economy does not look good given the lack of diversification. Technology has become more important for the Iceland economy over the last several years but the road to diversification is not happening fast enough. The rise of data centers in Iceland brings up an issue addressed by a 2018 Wall Street Journal (WSJ) article. Iceland's Nordic climate and the geothermal steam rising from the fault line provide two necessities for computers: cooling and electricity. The WSJ reports that by 2030 Iceland data centers could use more electricity than all of China did in 2018 which could hurt the environmental image the country has built that has helped fuel the tourism explosion.

As my writing was coming to a conclusion, all of my fears about the Icelandic economy looked to be coming to fruition. As stated by Bloomberg,

"Icelanders in shock as tourism collapse halts economic miracle." This is the problem with having an undiversified economy. The bankruptcy of WOW Air roiled tourism traffic to Iceland in 2019, with estimates pegging the total impact on overall Icelandic GDP to be 1.4% for the year. Talk about lack of diversification.

The spread of COVID-19 only exacerbated the difficulties mentioned above pertaining to the collapse in Icelandic tourism. As I said would be the case, given Iceland's outsized reliance on tourism, this has caused a complete implosion of the local economy. It is believed that Iceland will endure the worst recession since World War II. It will be far more difficult for Iceland to emerge from this recession than most other countries because it is unclear when tourism will recover. In response to the economic woes resulting from the COVID-19 fallout, Iceland's central bank cut interest rates to all-time lows. Low interest rates may help spur growth, but it could also lead to issues such as the depreciation of the local currency. Further destabilization of the króna could present more problems, as previously discussed. If Iceland has to resort to capital controls for the second time in 12 years, I would not be able to comprehend why any human or organization on this planet would ever remotely consider placing a single dollar of investment in the country.

Hallgrímskirkja church

Blue Lagoon

Silfra

Gullfoss

Geysir

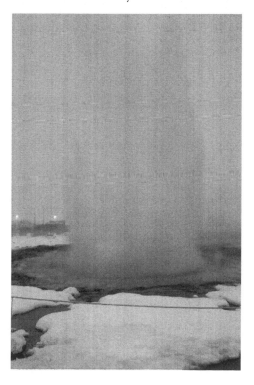

Sólheimajökull

Peru

Introduction

My brother Connor and I had booked a sandboarding, the snowboarding equivalent of sand dunes, excursion in the afternoon several weeks in advance. I found it to be a little strange that nobody we had talked to within the country had heard of a sandboarding operation that was in close proximity to Lima. We were told that the closest sandboarding location was approximately four hours from Lima. Not thinking too much of it considering I had a similar experience when arranging a hot air balloon tour in Morocco, Connor and I set out for our tour.

We were the only two people going on the sandboarding adventure that day, as our guide promptly picked us up from the hotel. In driving to the far end of Lima, we were given the opportunity to see the sheer poverty that covers a good portion of the city. Crumbling unfinished homes stretched for miles on end as we looked out from the road bordering the Pacific Ocean. The waves near our hotel in the Miraflores District seemed to be prime surfing material, as they broke very far out and came slowly rolling in. The waves at this end of Lima were big, about 12 feet high, and came crashing down on the beach with ferocity. It is worth noting that the water temperature is not far from the air temperature in the city, which is cool (average water temperature of 66 degrees Fahrenheit).

Upon arrival at the alleged sandboarding shop located in a slum, we met the men who, we were told, would be teaching us how to sandboard that afternoon. Despite already being a bit hesitant of this whole operation, the two men were nice, and we set out for the sand dunes upon being fitted for our necessary gear. As we shifted off the main coastal road inland toward what was becoming clear were the largest sand dunes I had ever seen by far, with some around 700 feet, it was now apparent that we were with an illegal company. Now about 20 minutes off the main road in the sand, our driver signaled for an extremely peculiar man to unlock a gate so that we could proceed to the enormous dunes. I can only imagine what this man was doing out here in the middle of nowhere with five tenacious guard dogs by his side but I would presume that it was something drug-related. Both Connor and I also noticed the several signs displayed in the area noting that this was private property.

I will be honest, at this point I did have slight doubts as to whether we would arrive back in Lima safely ever again but was reassured a bit by the genuineness that I sensed in our guides' character. Now in full off-road mode in the SUV, we barreled ahead navigating the otherworldly sand dunes. Without any warning, our driver sped sideways along a dune that I would estimate to have been close to 100 feet high only to come crashing down at the bottom of the hill! Clearly noticing that Connor and I were quite anxious at this point, he joked that he didn't even have a valid license. To this day I really think he was telling the truth on that one.

Finally reaching the dune that our two fearless leaders had elected would be the one that we would be riding down (and slightly relieved that we weren't just heading to a black market for human organs), we looked out in awe and hesitation over the 700-foot dune. Neither Connor nor I had ever tried sand-boarding in our lives and had little to no experience in winter sports either so we knew this would be a challenge. We actually turned out to be pretty decent at the sport all things considered. In taking turns heading down the daunting sand dune, we temporarily forgot all of our fears and simply lived in the moment. Flying down those dunes that day was an incredible adventure that I would recommend to all of my fellow thrill seekers. The sport was easier to pick up than I was expecting, as I had failed to successfully ski on another occasion but was able to adequately sandboard down an enormous dune with relative ease. That is not to say that everything went perfect, as I did take a few painful spills that would leave my body in regret the following day.

Thoroughly content with our sandboarding adventure and now realizing that we were going to get back several hours later than our parents were expecting us, we informed the guides that we needed to head home. With darkness rapidly approaching at this point, large clouds of fog suddenly blanketed the area which provided for a terrifying scenario given that we were winding our way through 700-foot sand dunes and could not see further than five feet in front of us. To add to the anxiety, our driver admitted that he had become lost and was trying to find his way. Knowing that there would not be any help on the way considering the men were operating an illegal company, we drove around for close to 40 minutes trying to find the correct path. One of our guides informed Connor and I that on another occasion they had to drive through the night when a similar development had occurred. Again, this was no reassurance and we both had our doubts that we would ever return from the South American sand dunes alive. Fortunately, the fog did clear a bit and we finally came upon a developed road after the extensive search. Reaching our hotel back in Lima that evening provided for a great feeling of relief.

In attempting to reach a consensus for a family trip idea for fall 2016, we were contemplating various locations to arrive at an agreement that would satisfy all members. My parents had initially set their sights on Alaska given the outdoor options available as well as remaining a domestic location that differs greatly from the rest of the United States. From the start of the search, I voiced my desire to go overseas given my love for learning from different cultures. My brother had wanted to see Machu Picchu for himself since he was a child and I knew that Peru was not an unreasonably far international destination, at about 7.5 hours from Washington D.C., by plane. There was also the incentive that no member of the family with the exception of my brother had ever stepped foot in South America. My father had received positive feedback on visiting Peru from a couple of his clients in recent years, so the final decision was made after a few months of consideration.

Our Peruvian adventure was organized through a company called Belmond, which operates luxury hotels, train services, and river cruises throughout the world. Contrary to some of my other trips, Belmond handled every step of the entire process from the moment we landed in the country. Upon arrival in Lima, we were met by a Belmond employee who walked us to our nearby hotel and the service was seamless throughout the entirety of the trip. The Belmond tour guides were all top notch, and I feel comfortable going on record saying that everyone in the family would happily recommend the company to other travelers.

Peru is located in western South America and bordered to the north by Ecuador and Colombia, to the east by Brazil, southeast by Bolivia, and west by the Pacific Ocean. It is a geographically diverse country with the Andes Mountains located in the north to southeast, the Amazon rainforest in the east, and the Pacific coastal region in the west.

Peru is a representative democratic republic that is separated into 25 regions. It is worth noting that voting in Peru is required by law for citizens aged 18 to 70 and is punishable by fine in the event that an individual fails to comply, as is the case in some other South American countries as well as places like Australia. Peru has opened up to the outside world in recent years and has become an active member in various trade organizations such as APEC (Asia-Pacific Economic Cooperation) and WTO (World Trade Organization).

There is evidence of human existence in Peru dating back to 9,000 BCE. The oldest known complex society that formed in Peru was the Norte Chico civilization between 3,000 and 1,800 BCE. There were several other pre-Incan civilizations that existed prior to the 15th century but the Incas are much more widely well known today. The Incas began to make their mark on the country during the 15th century and over the course of 100 years formed the largest empire in pre-Columbian America. Known for their social prowess and peaceful assimilation tactics, the Incas came to control most of the Andean region from 1438 to 1533. As socially adept as the Incas were, they were perhaps the least effective group of people in the history of the world in terms of fighting ability. When the Spaniards arrived in 1532, it did not take long to dispel the successful yet short dominance of the Inca Empire. It is nothing short of baffling to read about examples such as Francisco Pizarro's conquest that entailed a group of 200 men defeating a massive army of 35,000 Incas largely due to the fear that the Incas had of the horses that the Spaniards were armed with. Outside of the Spaniards using modern day weapons such as bombs, there is no way that they should have been able to come close to winning a battle such as this due to the extreme numbers advantage that the Incas possessed.

The Spanish conquest started the spread of Christianity in South America that remains to this day. Many people in the 1500s were forced to convert to Catholicism. As we witnessed around the Cusco area, many structures with religious meaning created by the Incas were destroyed by the Spaniards in the 1500s in order to expedite the shift to Catholicism.

There were numerous wars in South America during the early 19th century where countries claimed their independence. Peru declared independence in 1821 following a collapse of the Peruvian oligarchy in support of the Spanish leadership. Peru has had their share of political issues over the years since declaring independence but seems to be moving in the right direction. I am still cautious in regard to the long-term political outlook considering events such as the 1992 Fujimori's Auto-Coup in which President Alberto Fujimori dissolved the Congress of Peru and rewrote the Constitution. What is going to prevent another leader from doing this in the future? I guess you could say this about any country, but I would put a country where this has actually occurred as being at higher risk for political catastrophe in the future.

Economy

Not that Peru has had much in the form of economic competition when compared to its South American counterparts as of late, but the country has been a star performer in recent years. The Peruvian economy expanded

3.7% year over year in the second quarter of 2016, which looked like a raging success compared to the dismal economic outputs of Brazil and Venezuela. Peru has the 7th largest economy in Latin America. The services sector accounts for nearly 60% of country GDP, which is primarily made up of telecommunications and financial services. I found it interesting that some areas of Cusco operated on 4G data while most were on 3G. Countries such as Brazil still have areas where 2G is being used. Mining is important to the Peruvian economy, with the country being the number five player worldwide in gold. Peru has made great progress in recent years in the agriculture industry. They decided to specialize in products that command higher international prices such as avocados, chocolate, coffee, artichokes, etc. Fishing is a major industry in the country, as it borders the Pacific Ocean. Peru has established itself as one of the most unique tourism destinations in recent years which has led to dramatic increases in tourist arrivals, attracting over four million visitors in 2015.

The Peruvian economy has grown every year since 2000, following a 30-year period where the currency was changed on three occasions. The Peruvian economy in recent years has allowed for relatively stable inflation and several budget surpluses which has enabled an increase in expenditures on the public sector. There has been a progressive appreciation of the currency, sol, in recent years.

The overall tax burden in Peru amounts to only 16.8% of total domestic income as of the time of this writing. The government has kept public debt low, at around 24.8% of total domestic output. The Peruvian government has abolished many barriers that used to exist in regard to starting a company. There is now zero capital requirement to start a business, which can be accomplished relatively easily. Although I do not agree with the state controls in place for domestic food and fuel prices, it was a positive development to see the government refrain from propping up commodity prices during the widely reported commodity downturn. I would still like to see the government push further toward economic freedom by removing restrictions such as the inability to import a used car.

As noted by our tour guide and various online sources, corruption remains a serious problem in Peru. The influence of drug traffickers has been on the rise. There are frequent corruption scandals within the government which is widely distrusted. These points, along with the country's history of political instability, would be far and away my largest concern in regard to making an investment in Peru.

Adventure

The first destination of the trip was the Sacred Valley of the Incas which is reached from Cusco. Our drive from Cusco to the valley was nothing short of spectacular. We were given the opportunity to capture unbelievable vantage points overlooking the impressive town on the ride in. There were several police checkpoints along the way, which I had also encountered in my travels throughout Morocco. The checkpoints assist authorities in tracking who is in the country and also can help minimize threats due to terrorism. I asked our tour guide various questions along the ride while taking in the scenery. We were informed that the Incas of Peru were the first to grow potatoes between 8,000 and 5,000 BCE and today there are upwards of 4,000 different types of potatoes grown in the country. Roman Catholicism is considered to be the main religion in Peru, and unlike countries such as Iceland where few regularly practice any religion, most citizens in the country practice the religion regularly. This participation could be impacted by the government requirement to include religious education in all school curriculums through the secondary level. Peru requires 12 years of schooling which should be a long-term positive for the country if citizens believe in the benefits provided by the education system. Our guide explained that the Peruvian presidential elections take place every five years and the campaigning only lasted about six months. I thought it was interesting that a president is not allowed to get re-elected immediately following their first term but can choose to run again after another president's reign.

The Sacred Valley stretches close to 40 miles and is an area of fertile farmland that was home to Spanish colonial villages. Upon arriving at the Belmond Hotel Rio Sagrado, we were pleasantly surprised with the hotel amenities and landscape. Walking around the grounds, one could gaze off into the distance overlooking the Urubamba River with the majestic mountains located in the background. The grass was as green as the Ireland countryside and lively flowers decorated the stone walls.

We did not have much time to settle in, as we were quickly shuttled over to the nearby town of Urubamba which would be the launching point for an ATV excursion. I had prior vehicle experience, having done a self-tour in Greece, but the rest of the group took a few minutes to get acquainted with the ATVs. Over the next couple hours we crossed the farming communities of Rumichaca, Palcaraqui and Pumahuanca and took in the surreal scenery that the Sacred Valley has to offer. Speeding along dirt and uneven gravel, I couldn't help but smile, thinking that I was living a fairy tale taking place in a location that at times resembled the South Island of New Zealand. Everyone in the group had a fabulous time, and we took turns snapping pictures upon reaching an optimal photography location with snow-covered mountains in the background while being covered in dirt by this point. As we would find throughout the duration of our time in Peru, our excursion operator was overly kind and helpful. In fact, I found the people working in the Peruvian tourism industry to be the nicest I have encountered globally which should certainly provide a long-term tailwind for the economy.

The following day, our adventures continued with a ride down the Urubamba River. Normally this would be deemed whitewater rafting, but with the "rapids" on this particular river being so tame at this time of the year I refrain from even using that term here. My brother and I volunteered to be situated at the head of the raft and lead the group in rowing. The first 1.5 hours of the ride did not encounter any waves or water disturbances at all and we were required to self-propel the raft a bit at times due to the virtually stagnant current. Nonetheless it was an enjoyable ride and put everyone in a fabulous mood. That was until the last 30 minutes of the trip. Our guide warned us that we would soon be encountering what he deemed to be the first of a set of three "rapids." With my mother and I having previously gone on a class V whitewater rafting trip in New Zealand in which we flipped over the highest waterfall in the world that is available for commercial rafting, we were prepared for much greater challenges than the minuscule wakes that the Urubamba River had to offer. Immediately upon reaching the first rapid, my brother Connor flew off the left side of the raft and took his girlfriend Meghan and my dad with him when the weight shifted considerably. My brother's miscue at the front of the raft cost my dad and Meghan their dryness. My mom, the tour guide, and I remained in the raft as we had promptly shifted our weight to the interior of the raft once the water became a bit unstable. If I had a picture of my dad and Meghan's faces while they were lying in the shallow water, I could undoubtedly sell it for millions. They all raced back to the raft as if a Great White Shark were biting at their heels and we struggled to pull them back aboard. Fortunately, nobody in the group was injured on the shallow rocks in the river and the experience provided for the highlight of the day. I think I can still hear an echo of my mother and me laughing at that string of events.

For most normal families, a rafting trip would be sufficient in regard to vacation activity for the day. The Hughes family had planned a horseback riding adventure for the afternoon around the Sacred Valley. None of us had ever ridden a horse, so we were excited to see what the experience had to offer. The Peruvian Paso horses that we were set to ride appeared to be small, considering the relative giants that were about to climb aboard for what we envisioned to just be a leisurely stroll. My horse looked more like a pony with me on it, as my feet left dangling could nearly reach the ground. Getting acquainted with the serene animals took but just a few moments, as they all followed each other, and we really did not have to do much at all in terms of providing personal direction. Our tour guide led us on our two-hour journey of the beautiful Urubamba area and surrounding farmlands. My horse, being the elder statesman of the group, consistently nipped at the heels of the lead horse without any provocation from me to increase speed. We were all surprised at the rate of speed that we reached on the horses, at times galloping through small towns and villages in which locals had no choice but to move aside or risk being stampeded by a series of what I would deem to be mini horses. We saw various produce being grown in the area such as fresh strawberries, avocados, and corn (all of which we would try while in the Sacred Valley). Our overly friendly guide would inform the group that there is virtually zero crime in the Sacred Valley area due to the fact that all the local people know each other. The horseback ride was an overall success despite being sore by the conclusion of the ride. I am glad that we opted in for the adventure, but it might be safe to say that was my first and last horseback ride.

The following day we were scheduled for three of the lesser advertised attractions in the Sacred Valley area: a visit to a nearby salt mine, a location where weaving techniques are taught, and Moray, which is an Inca ruin. The day started off just like the previous two, calm and relaxing prior to beginning our adventure activities. This day in particular turned out to bear possibly the most traumatic experience of my life, beginning not long after we set out for the surrounding hills where the salt mine was located. In navigating the treacherous gravel road that bordered a cliff that was almost entirely absent any form of guardrail, we traded turns passing a group of ATVs that were operating at a high rate of speed given the dangerous conditions. Looking out over the majestic mountains and admiring the steep drop of several thousand feet back into the Sacred Valley just feet away, my father noted that he wished we had done our ATV excursion in this particular location instead of around the less adventurous Urubamba area. My mom disagreed given her fear of heights and warned that she did not believe this area was safe for this sort of activity. Just a few moments later, my mother's conviction was spelled out right before us in the form of tragedy. As the group of ATV riders had just passed us around a corner, I noticed a woman screaming and crying loudly upon approach. Our vehicle promptly stopped, and we exited really not knowing what to expect at this point. The American woman was screaming "He's dead! He's dead!" I looked over the side of the cliff and saw an ATV located approximately 300 feet down and somehow still sitting upright.

My stomach immediately dropped, and I felt as if I were going to vomit any second. While I pray that the unfortunate rider survived, I realize that the odds may not have been in his favor given the steep fall and lack of any emergency vehicles in the area over the next few hours. It was unsettling to find out that I could not find any trace of this accident having been reported to any news outlets online, and it goes to show that these types of incidents do go unnoticed to the outside world more often than some would hope to believe. Keep in mind that there is a dark side to participating in activities that are inherently high risk in nature and accidents do unfortunately happen. This particular incident could have been prevented with the implementation of guardrails along the road. Our guide would inform us that the budget for guardrails is funded by the local governments and most choose to spend the small amount of money that they do have in town as opposed to along roads that are mostly used by tourists.

Despite being very shaken up from the series of events, we had to make the most of our day while in the beautiful country. We entered the salt mine area that provided for fabulous views of the surrounding mountainous area. Our guide informed us that the salt mines were historically community property but a cooperative, an entity that is owned and run jointly by the members, was formed to regulate the production of salt about 30 years ago. The cooperative takes the salt from the individual families and acts as a middleman by taking a percentage of the profits when selling to the end consumer. The salt mine workers use wood to compact the salt by laying it on top of the salt, which takes approximately three days and this process is repeated over the course of a month. We watched as the men carried the heavy bags of salt to the top of the hill, dripping in sweat but never losing focus and not stopping to complain about the arduous working conditions. The men working here earn the equivalent of only a few hundred dollars a year for their hard, manual labor that is done without the help of any modern agricultural tools. As we witnessed all over the country, the Peruvians are a hardworking group of people, which seems to be embedded within their culture. I am optimistic about the labor output of Peru, particularly if more individuals earn access to modern tools widely available in other countries. We purchased a few bags of pink salt prior to leaving the mine. The pink salt is the "luxurious" form of the mineral, and is relatively expensive outside of Peru, which exports the commodity to other countries.

Continuing onto the surrounding foothills of the Sacred Valley, our guide explained that during the late 1980s to early 1990s there weren't many schools in the countryside due to terrorism threats from the Shining Path. This terrorist organization sought to replace the government with what they deemed to be a "New Democracy." In reality, they were trying to implement a dictatorship with the goal of arriving at worldwide communism and inducing violence against government officials, trade union leaders, etc. in an attempt to sway public opinion. The threat from the Shining Path is largely contained today, but they do operate in certain areas as more of a narcotics organization, serving as bodyguards for drug lords. The diminished influence of the terrorist organization since the early 1990s has allowed for tourism to flourish within the country and also for a re-emphasis on education in the countryside.

We then reached an Inca ruin called Moray which is situated to the west of a village called Maras. The interesting spectacle is best viewed from above, as it appears to be a seemingly random series of steps located far out in the countryside. The steps form circular depressions in the middle of which the largest is 98 feet deep. Scientists today believe that Moray was used as a form of laboratory for testing the growing conditions of various types of corn products judging by the traces left behind of the agricultural commodity. Scientists have found that the variance in temperature and pressure between the different steps is actually quite profound and provided the Incas with a range of testing conditions in one location. If you make it to Peru, I would advise visiting this gem, as it provides for an interesting history in addition to unforgettable views of the Sacred Valley area.

Our picnic lunch that followed the visit to Moray was the surprise of the day. Normally when you think of a picnic, it means consuming peanut butter and jelly sandwiches while sitting on a blanket in the wilderness. Much to our delight, Belmond had a fancy display of tables and unbelievable food waiting for us in an area that provided outstanding views of the countryside. We proceeded to eat everything from alpaca, a domesticated South American species that resembles a llama, to local chicken throughout the course of the meal. If I ever have another picnic that remotely resembles this flawless setting, I will be a fortunate man.

Looking out over the sprawling countryside, our guide explained that while the Incas were in power, the government distributed the land to residents similar to communism. In exchange for the land provided by the government, taxes were paid by the people in the form of labor or food production. I also inquired about foreign investment in land within the country and was delighted to hear that it was possible to purchase land in Peru.

We concluded our day-long journey in the town of Chinchero. On our way to the town, we noticed several stones in the middle of the roadways and were informed that there had been a strike in the Sacred Valley about five days prior to our arrival where the workers blocked the road access. I am not sure what we would have done if this occurred just a few days later!

Chinchero is a small, Andean Indian village located in the plains of Anta. Here we learned about the traditional pre-Hispanic weaving techniques used when the Andean weavers put their skills on display in the pleasant courtyard before us. The women explained that some of their pieces took a year to complete and I would later find that these items would only sell for $300. Can you imagine working tirelessly on a single project for a year only to receive $300?! Neither can I. Yet the Andean women did so without complaint. In fact, one of the nice ladies went as far as to say that she was "addicted" to weaving. This may be the first and last time I ever hear someone make such a statement in my life, yet it again showed the undying work ethic amongst the Peruvian people that I was quickly falling in love with. We opted to purchase various blankets and products from the women as a token of gratitude for maintaining the pre-Hispanic culture in modern times despite the lack of monetary benefit.

We were pretty sad to leave our fine hotel in the Sacred Valley, but we knew that even greater adventures lay ahead in the coming days. Prior to departing Belmond Hotel Rio Sagrado, we had to say goodbye to our two alpaca friends that we had fed the previous couple days. The alpacas were overly friendly and had even waited outside of our villa waiting for us to give them some attention the day prior. We were hesitant to say goodbye to these interesting animals that reside mostly in high altitudes.

The train ride to the base of Machu Picchu was just an hour and a half and provided for fine scenery along the way. The train ran parallel to a good portion of the Inca Trail which was the 26-mile path used by the Incas to reach Machu Picchu. Most people that hike the Inca Trail today take four days to complete the rewarding journey that is easily the most famous trek in South America and regularly rated in the top five in the world. If I was traveling alone, I would have taken on this challenge. If you are interested in hiking the Inca Trail, I would advise booking at least six months in advance as there is limited availability and spots fill up quickly. I foresee limitations along many of the Machu Picchu hiking trails getting more stringent in future years and would advise adventure seekers to visit sooner rather than later. Our guide informed us of a government-sponsored race that occurs along the Inca Trail every five years. I would imagine this would be dangerous given the uneven grounds on which the trail lies that is largely undisturbed and eroding since the time of the Incas.

The next step in the road to Machu Picchu was to take a bus from the nearby town up to the top of Machu Picchu. Even though it was not peak season, there was still an extensive line and I thought it was certainly a positive that we were not visiting during peak tourism numbers which is usually in June and July. The bus ride up to Machu Picchu that lasted 20 minutes was nothing short of breathtaking. As we navigated the 19 switchbacks to the top of the mountain along the dirt roads that were again largely unshielded by guardrails, we peered out over the landscape in awe.

That afternoon we did a tour of Machu Picchu. There is nothing that I can write here that will come close to capturing the feeling that an individual receives upon entrance into the area. Here we were, looking out over one of the New Seven Wonders of the World that was declared a UNESCO World Heritage Site in 1983. The ancient marvel, which was believed to be built around 1450, sits approximately 8,000 feet above sea level. It was originally believed that Machu Picchu was used as a royal palace during the winter months. The theory has evolved over the years and it is now more widely accepted that Machu Picchu served as a form of university where various experts within the Incan Empire gathered to test their beliefs and collaborate. It was estimated that fewer than 1,000 people lived here and the city was suddenly abandoned around 1572. It remains a mystery why the Incas fled the village leaving behind clothes, pottery, tools, etc. The two main theories that stand today to explain the vanishing act of the Incas in the late 1500s are war and disease. If a war did in fact cause the evacuation, it is likely that it was a civil war due to the location of the establishment. Machu Picchu then lay idle for over 300 years until it was rediscovered in the early 1900s.

We walked around Machu Picchu for the majority of the afternoon, taking several pictures and learning more about the famous historical site. I found it interesting that despite being relatively advanced in respect to many social categories, there was not any evidence of furniture found at Machu Picchu. Even those in high stature slept on the bare ground. It was noticeable how prominent the trapezoid figure was in the Inca construction. Prior to retiring for the afternoon, I made sure to head to the top of the surrounding staircase where the Machu Picchu "postcard" pictures are taken. I did not want to pass up this opportunity given that the weather was beautiful not knowing what the following day would bring (especially considering that the area sees 71 inches of rain in the 100 rainy days per year). It would turn out that our weather during the majority of our stay in Peru was amazing.

That night we stayed at the only hotel situated next to Machu Picchu which has just 31 rooms. While expensive, the stay avoids the need to travel back down to the nearby town via bus and wait in the extensive lines. It has the added benefit of providing first access to Machu Picchu in the mornings before the outside tourists can come in. We took full advantage of our accommodation by being the first people in line to enter Machu Picchu. Individuals who do not stay at the hotel next to Machu Picchu have the option of hiking to the top of the mountain starting at 5:00 a.m. if they so choose. We watched as a few daring individuals had sprinted up the steep slope and arrived close to 5:40 a.m., which was before the first bus load reached the area around 6:00 a.m. They were perplexed as they stood there gasping for air wondering how they failed to be the first in line. I couldn't help but laugh as I sat there and calmly pointed to the nearby hotel. I was the first person to enter Machu Picchu that day and ran full speed to my predetermined photograph location for the sunrise over the mountains. It was an otherworldly feeling being the only person, with the exception of a few guards, overlooking one of the most famous historical sights on earth for close to five minutes before others arrived. I captured the moment with a few pictures while aggressively gasping for air and nearly vomiting, given the impact that the high altitude surely had on my sprint. Would I have done it any differently in hindsight? Absolutely not. I probably won't ever have another opportunity to be alone with one of the Seven Wonders of the World.

Our real Machu Picchu adventure began later that morning. My brother, father, and I opted for the hike up Huayna Picchu, which is the large mountain that sits behind Machu Picchu and provides spectacular views of the site given the 1,180-foot height advantage. My mom and Meghan decided not to join out of fear that the daunting mountain imposes upon physical examination. From a distance, it does not look as though this mountain can be climbed without being attached to a rope, given the nearly vertical slope that must be ascended. I would only later find out after doing some research that some refer to the hike up Huayna Picchu as the "hike of death" and it is regularly rated as one of the five most dangerous on earth! A couple websites claim that upwards of 20 people have died attempting the trek in recent years, but it is difficult to verify given the lack of disclosure that can occur at times.

The hike to the top of Huayna Picchu was not a walk in the park and not for the faint of heart, either. I managed to do fine and was thrilled with the hike of a lifetime, but my brother did say that there were a few moments when he seriously doubted whether he would be able to finish the hike due to exhaustion. I tried to take in the views of Machu Picchu and the surrounding jungle area during the steep climb up the mountain. There were no railings along the entire trail, but there were ropes in certain areas, which helped with balance. The path was largely unchanged from the Inca period and was unstable along the way, which could be a cause for concern given the nearby cliffs. The climax of the hike occurs close to the summit of the mountain where the hiker encounters the "death stairs." The stairs reach an angle of 60 degrees at some points and virtually require individuals to crawl, given the steepness and the fact that a small misstep could result in fatality.

It took us approximately 40 minutes to reach the top of Huayna Picchu, and it was a rewarding feeling reaching the top of the mountain. Possibly the greatest pictures I have captured in my lifetime were taken at the rock situated at the summit. The Incas used this location to provide sacrifices to the gods, but now it simply serves as one of the great sightseeing locations in the world. While atop the mountain, a woman did have vertigo, so I would advise against making this climb if an individual has a fear of heights or any form of health condition. I pray that this person made the trek down on her own accord, as the online community presents horror stories of similar situations that have occurred along this intimidating trail. Fortunately, the trail is limited to only 400 people per day so traffic is pretty tame on Huayna Picchu. We were lucky that the rain held off while we were on the trail, as a storm came in just a few hours later. Hiking this trail under slippery conditions would be nothing short of a death sentence. The hike down the mountain was much easier than going up with the exception of the initial descent and tight squeeze through a small cave. I know this whole description of the hike up Huayna Picchu may sound like something out of a science fiction novel, but I am not sure that I am creative enough to invent this material.

The next destination on our list was Cusco. Cusco, the 7th largest city in Peru with a population of 312,140 people, is located in southeastern Peru and sits at an elevation of over 11,000 feet which poses challenges for some travelers. The city was declared a World Heritage Site by UNESCO in 1983 and has become a major tourist destination (the most significant in Peru). Cusco served as the capital of the Inca Empire through 1532, at which time the Spaniards began to arrive and challenge the group's regional dominance. A major earthquake damaged more than half of the city's buildings in 1950, and the threat of earthquakes in the country is ever present.

One of the first observations that we had upon arrival in Cusco was the extreme amount of unfinished buildings in the area. While driving through the town, I found that virtually the only buildings that appeared to be fully completed from the outside were hotels and restaurants. Our tour guide would later inform us that Peruvian residents are exempt from property taxes if their home is deemed to be "under construction!" This insane tax exemption is also present in countries such as Greece and places a large incentive for people never to fully finish their homes which considerably takes away from the potential that an area has in terms of appearance. If anything, a resident should receive a tax break for finishing a construction project in a timely manner.

The next day and a half was spent in Cusco. Our morning tour on the first day took us to the outskirts of the city. Here we found the archaeological site Saksaywaman, which was located on a steep hill overlooking Cusco. Many once believed that Saksaywaman was used as a fortress for the Incas, but that thinking has evolved to the present-day theory that the Incas used it as a religious gathering area. The Incas used their renowned stone-building techniques to complete the religious site.

The rest of the group wanted to go shopping, so we stopped at a nearby store. I was uninterested in making any purchases, but I did get another lesson on Peruvian sales tactics. As I was perusing the store, a woman offered to give me a presentation on the various product offerings (as we had seen on other occasions). I did not personally feel any more inclined to buy an item after learning more about the origin, but I do think that this is a fine strategy as I did see it have a positive impact on other individuals. I found that the Peruvian people were not overly aggressive in their sales approach, which was in line with their overall demeanor and made me more comfortable when walking into a store.

In the afternoon, we made our way around the inner city of Cusco. The highlight was probably the Cusco Cathedral which was completed in 1654 and designated as a UNESCO World Heritage Site in 1983. We walked around the impressive structure perusing the 400 paintings of the classical Cusqueña schools. While visiting churches is not exactly my idea of a perfect day, this particular one was impressive, and my dad agreed that it stands in the class of those found in Italy.

We set out for Lima the following day via airplane. Lima is the capital of Peru and also the largest city in the country. As of 2016, approximately ten million people live in Lima which represents roughly a third of the country (which had 31 million people as of 2016). The urban area of Lima covers roughly 310 square miles of mostly flat terrain along the coast. Lima is the world's second largest desert city after Cairo, Egypt. Weather in Lima between April and December tends to be mostly overcast. Despite the cloudy conditions, the city receives less than an inch of rainfall per year which is surprising. Lima serves as the financial center of the country and accounts for more than two-thirds of Peru's industrial production.

That evening, we ate dinner at a renowned restaurant called Huaca Pucllana, which is situated next to ancient ruins and provides for an interesting upscale atmosphere. We met my good friend Joe Meringolo at the restaurant. Joe had joined me on my adventures through Morocco and had been living in Lima for a few months at the time of our visit. I tried a wide array of food items here that I had never eaten before. Joe and I delved into guinea pig, baby goat, and cow hearts. I think the guinea pig would have been tasty if it had not come in fried form. I found the baby goat to be delicious and would recommend it to other individuals. I did not find the cow hearts to be appetizing, as they were chewy and had a strange flavor. All of the locals raved about the alcoholic beverage pisco sours, so I felt obligated to try one here. I was not a fan of this drink but did find that Peru had a surprisingly excellent selection of craft beers available. I found beers such as Lima Pale Ale and Cusqueña Roja to be enjoyable.

I spent the rest of the evening hanging out at a couple bars with Joe and discussing topics such as this book, the Peruvian economy, and some things that Joe had been working on himself. The area close to the water does provide for some fine views of the city at night. I was fortunate to have Joe with me to arrange for a cab ride back to my hotel, as it would have been extremely difficult to describe to a Spanish-speaking driver where to go. I must note the horrible traffic that we witnessed throughout the night and for the duration of our stay in Lima. I have no doubt that the traffic here rivals that of New York City or any other major city in the world. Combine this with the fact that the local drivers do not pay attention to any rules, and you have a recipe for disaster. Fortunately, the city is working on constructing the first underground subway, but this is long overdue, and I wonder how much of an impact it will have on the city given the current overcapacity. Regardless, this is a step in the right direction, and Joe did note other observations in regard to government investments in infrastructure, which should aid long-term economic growth.

The following morning, we took a tour of Lima. Our once-again magnificent guide was flush with valuable information as we took in the best sights that the bustling city had to offer. In passing the Presidential Palace, which was very large and impressive, we were informed that the newly elected president had chosen not to move into the building at that point due to what he claimed to be a termite problem. Could you imagine a United States president refusing to move into the White House due to such a factor?! As we were perusing the city, I did notice that there were more people selling goods and services on the city streets than I was used to. Our guide told us that Peru does not have a welfare system (and welfare has failed in South America in general) and that Lima frowns upon begging for money. Maybe the United States should wake up and take note of this. There were even people out on the streets in wheelchairs doing anything they could to make an impact on both their personal lives and society. We tried to walk inside the Bolsa de Valores de Lima, the stock exchange of Peru, but it was under construction for a few days. I viewed it as a positive that it was usually open to visitors, though, as this was yet another sign that foreign investment was being encouraged within the country. The area where the stock exchange was located reminded me a lot of Wall Street, with little car activity in the direct area and various businessmen walking the streets in fashionable suits.

Along the tour, our lovely guide explained that electronics and other imports are expensive due to excessive customs fees, which is also the case in countries such as Brazil. I told her that I believe the United States should adopt Peru's welfare practices and that Peru should lower customs fees on imported goods to stay competitive with other countries. It does not make any sense to encourage citizens to travel abroad to illegally purchase electronics in bulk only to bring them back in the country to resell. Free markets always win in the long-term; this has been proven out over an extensive history (ironically a global trade war that started with the U.S. and China broke out a few years later).

A contentious issue within Peru is that abortions are currently illegal, and it is a felony for both the mother and the physician that performs an abortion. Naturally, this law has led to an extensive black market for abortions that are expensive. An issue that is always being debated in the United States as well, our country should take a closer look at countries like Peru and the impact that illegality has had on overall society.

Despite the ever-present intense traffic in Lima, we all thoroughly enjoyed the tour, and I would advise a visit here for both educational and sightseeing purposes. Lima also hosts a great deal of impressive musical performances given the large population that resides in the city.

Additional Activities and Recommendations

The legitimate sandboarding experience can be found at Huacachina, which is four hours from Lima. Truly an exhilarating experience, as you will glide down this 1,640-foot sand dune. This is often combined with the sand buggy excursion.

The Nazca Lines air tour is located in Paracas which is a day trip from Lima. Take a 1.5-hour flight above this UNESCO World Heritage Site that consists of 300 massive geometric figures. These mysterious drawings are believed to date as far back as 400 CE. There have been various rumors connecting the Nazca Lines to alien activity over the years. If you have never heard of Nazca, look at some of the pictures. It is interesting and curious as to why these symbols were drawn here. While this is one of the more popular attractions in Peru, the safety ratings for the flights done here are low. There have been a high number of accidents and tragedies here, so consider this before booking your flight.

Bungy jumping is a popular activity in the Cusco area. At roughly 400 feet, this intimidating bungy jump is the highest in Latin America. This area also has one of the highest slingshot experiences, both of which are reserved only for the most adventurous.

A unique extreme camping experience can be found in the Sacred Valley. Ever wanted to sleep on the side of a mountain suspended over a beautiful valley? Skylodge Adventure Suites in the Sacred Valley allows for just that with a unique camping experience. Stay in a transparent luxury capsule that dangles 1,200 feet above the valley floor! To reach the capsule, adventurers much either climb Via Ferrata or hike a trail through zip-lines. This option will set adventure seekers back around $400 per night.

Surfing can be done at various locations throughout the country. Surf lessons are available in Lima in addition to other popular locations such as Máncora, Chicama, Punta Hermosa, and Pico Alto. The Pacific coast of Peru is considered to have consistently high-quality waves.

Business Outlook

In order for me to get really bullish in regard to Peru's long-term prospects, I need to see further improvements in regard to government corruption. While I do think there are potential investment opportunities such as purchasing a parcel of land in the Cusco area, I would still not have enough assurance at this time that the Peruvian government wouldn't simply confiscate the land for their own benefit. I would advise placing an increased emphasis on manufacturing, given the wealth of cheap labor available. There is currently no car manufacturing done in the country, and I think this could be an opportunity given the close proximity to the United States. There is still a lot to like about what the local government has done in recent years with respect to opening to the outside world.

Additionally, the Peruvians are a hardworking group of people that will serve the country well in the long haul. The economic growth trajectory would further accelerate if they could use this dedication more efficiently. There have been signs that the government has been working to focus on efficiency with the recent investments in infrastructure (examples include underground rail system and added bus lanes). The wealth of natural resources that the country possesses is a long-term positive. Peru has the potential for a bright future; it is really just up to the government to steer it in the right direction and look out for the good of the people.

I see a potential investment opportunity for land in the Cusco area, given the current construction of an international airport and the array of tourism options. This does come with caveats in the form of continued political stability and earthquake protection in a country that has been marred by corruption in the past.

Investors looking at the infrastructure space may find Peru to be of interest. If Peru wants to take the next step in terms of economic advancement, they will have to dramatically improve their local infrastructure. It is estimated that communications problems account for nearly 23% of the country poverty rate. From what I saw and heard from discussions that I had with my tour guides and some locals, the government has been placing an increased emphasis on infrastructure investment in recent years. The underground rail system will be a significant investment, estimated to be a $5 billion project, but innovative private companies with alternate cost-effective solutions to help alleviate the extreme level of traffic congestion in Lima could benefit immensely. There are three regional airport concessions that are up for grabs in addition to the major railway project.

There seems to be an opportunity regarding study abroad programs in Peru. Many American universities still do not offer study abroad programs to Peru despite the relatively close proximity to the U.S. and the broad appeal of the country. Private companies such as EdOdyssey have taken advantage of this by providing what I would describe as an all-inclusive experience in that they offer short and long-term programs complete with everything from volunteering opportunities, tours and excursions, and connections with local businesses where students can ultimately land a job abroad. I studied abroad in Antwerp, Belgium, and thoroughly enjoyed the experience, but innovative programs such as what EdOdyssey is offering are much more enticing from a resume perspective in that students can come out of the program saying that they have accomplishments such as publishing an article with a local publication. The opportunity to acquire a full-time job in countries such as Peru is particularly alluring to some as well. I would expect to see increased investment in international education in this country in the coming years provided that Peru remains relatively safe and does not suffer from some of the political issues that have plagued the country in the past.

Much like what I experienced in my adventures across Southern Africa, Peru is still stuck in the stone ages in terms of phone and smartphone usage. As of 2015, only 28% of Peruvian locals had access to a smartphone which was the lowest penetration among six Latin American markets studied. American-based cellular tower companies such as SBA Communications have taken note of the enormous growth potential in the country and entered the market in recent years. If the political environment in Peru remains stable, expect more foreign companies to be placing large investments in this area.

Updates Since Visit

Peru is set to grow 3.8% in 2019, which would make it one of the fastest growing economies in South America. This strong economic performance continues the country's recent track record that has been boosted by private investment and consumption.

Even though Peru dropped ten positions in the "Doing Business Report 2019" published by the World Bank, they still produced a solid ranking of 68th out of 190 global economies, which puts them in a similar category as Morocco. The report highlighted strong performance for registering property, getting credit, and protecting minority investors while underperforming in paying taxes and trading across borders. When it comes to paying taxes, it takes more than 30 weeks to complete a corporate tax audit compared to less than 22 weeks in the region. To climb the business rankings, Peru should look at making processes such as this more efficient and less costly to companies. This would only further encourage more foreign investment and lead to an increase in the number of start-ups in Peru.

Despite the recent strong economic performance, Peru has continued to be ravaged by a string of political scandals. In early 2019, Peru's attorney general resigned amid accusations that he hindered a corruption probe involving the Brazilian construction company Odebrecht. Peruvians have felt that the corruption has been so bad that the citizens overwhelmingly approved a government overhaul that among other things would fire all members of Congress by 2021. Voters also approved a voting measure that would ban consecutive re-election in Congress. As I have seen in my travels around the globe, in addition to my extensive studies of various economies, it is a tall task to rid a country of corruption after it has been so ingrained in the culture for long periods of time. How Peru addresses the corruption and manages the government will go a long way in determining the future success of the country over the coming years.

As I previously discussed, Peru has to continue an infrastructure push if they are to take the next step in terms of economic advancement. They have long lagged behind their neighbors in this segment. Unfortunately, infrastructure investment has struggled due to ongoing corruption scandals which has hampered the country's ability to address an estimated $160 billion infrastructure gap. As of late 2018, Peru was set to launch over 40 public-private partnerships related to infrastructure totaling $6 billion, which is a step in the right direction. If they are to build on successes such as these, they will have to reassure investors more than anything that corruption is being held in check and that infrastructure projects are looking out for the benefit of shareholders.

In response to the COVID-19 crisis, the Peruvian government was aggressive in taking economic reforms. The government created an economic stimulus package that was the equivalent of 12% of GDP and interest rates were slashed to historic lows of 0.25%. These bold economic measures were in contrast to Latin American counterparts such as Brazil and Mexico that were hesitant to provide large economic stimulus packages. Peru had a lot more fiscal flexibility to respond coming into the crisis because their public debt to GDP of 26.9% was one of the lowest in Latin America. Given the quick and aggressive measures taken to combat the economic slowdown, the relatively good financial condition of the country heading into the crisis, and a local economy that has more diversification than many others in the region, I would expect Peru to recover more quickly than many others in Latin America. Having said that, Peru is the world's number two copper producer which had a significant impact on the local economy because demand for the resource plummeted in the wake of the global economic slowdown.

Horse trek excursion

Moray

Very first person to enter the Machu Picchu grounds (picture taken by a guard)

View atop Huayna Picchu overlooking Machu Picchu

Sandboarding down a 700-foot sand dune outside of Lima

South Africa

Introduction

My girlfriend, Paula, our tour guide, and I drove to Simon's Town where we would be kayaking in False Bay. The 45-minute drive from Cape Town to Simon's Town is a scenic drive much like virtually every other in the Cape Town area. I had never been kayaking before, so I found the activity to be quite difficult. We paddled along the inlet for approximately two hours and covered 3.5 miles on a densely foggy journey. It provided for a particularly ominous atmosphere similar to what you would expect near Halloween at a haunted forest, especially considering the fact that False Bay is home to great white sharks. While most of the reported shark attacks occur on beaches that are a little ways from Simon's Town, I could not help but think at times that there could be a shark lurking right beneath the surface. The simple fact that an individual can also book a shark cage diving trip in Simon's Town is a potential warning sign. Fortunately, many of the nearby beaches have shark spotters that communicate with individuals on the beaches and warn surfers of sharks in the area. Sometimes the surfers refuse to get out of the water even after being notified of a nearby Great White Shark!

We eventually reached Boulders Beach, which is home to 3,000 African penguins. The penguins were swimming right beneath our kayak as we were watching in awe. Paula and I couldn't get enough of watching these interesting animals swimming around in the water and then drying off on shore by flapping their wings. Do note that tourists can't get nearly as close to the animals if viewing from the shore. If you want the close-up shots, then I would opt for the kayak trip.

From Simon's Town we continued on to Cape Point. Cape Point is also located within Table Mountain National Park and this section covers the southern tip of the Cape Peninsula. Cape Point is at the southwestern tip of the African continent and provides extraordinary views of the cape. I was blown away by the scenery that we experienced here. I would compare the backdrop to a combination of the Cliffs of Moher, located in Ireland, on one side and somewhat similar to the Greek Island landscape on the other side. Sitting atop the lighthouse at the top of the area, one could sit there for hours digesting the panoramic views. We encountered baboons along our walk up to Cape Point. As long as an individual is not carrying food, it is unlikely that he will be harassed.

Next on our schedule for this busy day was a visit to a nearby ostrich farm. Here we were able to learn more about the second fastest land animal in Africa behind the cheetah and feed some of the ostriches. While we were observing the animals, there were a couple times where an ostrich excreted only to have another ostrich eat the feces! I certainly didn't know I would be witnessing that when I went to the ostrich farm. This can be viewed as partly attributable to the fact that they have small brains. If you were wondering where the derogatory term "bird brain" came from, then here is your answer. It was an enjoyable activity feeding the ostriches. They all huddled over when it was evident that we were going to provide food. The animals ate out of our palms in what I would describe as an aggressive pecking motion. Paula and I laughed as they gobbled up all the food.

On our way back to Cape Town, we stopped at a couple wineries in the Constantia region. We had a fabulous experience at the beautiful venues. I could imagine one visiting Cape Town and just spending weeks visiting all the local vineyards.

That evening we went to the widely renowned La Colombe Restaurant for dinner. Located 30 minutes outside the city on the Silvermist Wine Estate, the restaurant provides views overlooking Cape Town. In 2016, TripAdvisor ranked the restaurant as the best restaurant in Africa and top 20 in the world. Our experience here was nothing short of amazing and it was by far the nicest restaurant I have ever been to. The meal consisted of about ten smaller portions that were delivered over the course of three hours. In the middle of the meal, we were taken to an "Enchanted Forest," where we were served food and delicious beers in an elaborately decorated room similar to what you would expect to find in a Dr. Seuss book. If you are looking for a high-end restaurant for a special occasion, La Colombe Restaurant is just the place for you. Be prepared to make reservations well in advance, as I confirmed the booking about a month and a half prior to our reservation and some of the dates were already unavailable.

My girlfriend Paula and I departed for Southern Africa on June 29, 2017. Two common routes to get to this part of the world are through airports in western Africa such as Ghana and Senegal or London. I decided to opt for the London route given my preference for taking British Airways as long as we could and because Paula had not been to London before. We did a long layover in London and explored the city for the day, which I would recommend considering if you decide to make a trip to South Africa. Be forewarned that this is quite a journey. Flight time from Washington D.C. to London is about seven to eight hours in addition to the 11 to 12-hour flight from London to Cape Town.

We made our trip during the winter months for countries located in Southern Africa. If you are considering travel to countries such as South Africa, Botswana, Zimbabwe, and Namibia, I would recommend visiting during their winter months as well. What you will find is that crowds will be smaller for the most part and prices will be more affordable overall, particularly in South Africa. Weather in Cape Town while we were there was mostly in the 50s and 60s, which is not overly warm, but if you are planning to participate in various outdoor activities such as what we did, then this is perfect. I could not imagine doing the Table Mountain hike or visiting Cape Point with the summer heat and larger crowds. While we were lucky with the lack of rain during our time in Cape Town, it is worth noting that there is always a higher risk of rain during this time of the year, but I believe this could be largely overstated given the advantages in temperature, prices, and amount of people visiting. Prices will be higher along with more tourists in countries such as Botswana, Zimbabwe, and Zambia during the winter months, as this is the dry season and animals are much more active during this time of the year. If you decide to visit various countries such as this itinerary, bring a variety of clothing as the weather varies substantially from Cape Town to Zimbabwe.

The Republic of South Africa is the southernmost country on the African continent that has 1,739 miles of coastline with the Atlantic and Indian Oceans. South Africa is bordered to the north by Namibia, Botswana, and Zimbabwe and to the east by Mozambique and Swaziland. It is a geographically diverse country consisting of mountainous areas, indigenous forests, coastal strips, and vast rolling flat regions. South Africa would be classified as having a temperate climate for the most part but keep in mind that this varies greatly from the subtropical climate in the east to the extreme desert conditions in the northwest. The country is roughly the size of Colombia or Mali and one-eighth the size of the United States. South Africa is the 25th largest country on earth by land area and home to over 55 million people as of 2017, making it 25th largest by population. 64% of the population in the country resides in urban areas, and the median age is only 26 years. It is interesting to note that South Africa does not have a legally defined capital city.

South Africa is a diverse country with 80% being of Sub-Saharan African ancestry, which is divided among various ethnic groups and languages. There are 11 official languages in the country (Afrikaans, English, Ndebele, Northern Sotho, Sotho, Swazi, Tsonga, Tswana, Venda, Xhosa and Zulu). In recent years English has been promoted as the main language to be used by the government.

South Africa is classified as a democracy which is comprised of a parliamentary republic with nine provinces. It is worth noting that the president serves as both head of state and head of government which differs from most traditional democracies. The president is elected to a term of five years and may not serve more than two terms in office.

Dutch influence is still apparent in the country today, as they colonized the Cape Town area in the 1650s. The attempted eastward expansion by the Dutch colonists in the following years led to several wars which played out over decades. The instability in the region opened the door for the British who came into the area in the late 1700s. Great Britain formally ceded the Cape after the end of the Napoleonic Wars, which led to British immigrants arriving in South Africa in 1818. Many Dutch settlers fled the area that was now under formal British control. Hostility between the British and the local indigenous people intensified after the discovery of diamonds and gold in the latter part of the 1800s. South Africa did not become fully sovereign from British rule until 1931, when the United Kingdom passed the Statute of Westminster which abolished the last powers of British Government.

Economy

South Africa is Africa's second largest economy behind Nigeria. The country is a large producer and exporter of gold and platinum. The country accounts for a startling 35% of the continent's total GDP. The top industries in South Africa are mining, agriculture, manufacturing, tourism, fishing, finance, and real estate. Mining propelled the country to the status of an advanced economy but low commodity prices in recent years have hurt South Africa. Mining's contribution to GDP fell from 21% in 1970 to 6% in 2011, but still represented 60% of country exports. Agriculture accounts for a comparatively low, relative to some other African nations, contribution to employment and overall GDP. Only 13% of the land in the country can be used for crop production, and South Africa accounted for 42% of Africa's total maize trade. Manufacturing accounts for 12% of GDP, and products such as automobiles are manufactured here. The reason that manufacturing is not a larger part of the economy is that wages in South Africa are higher than in many other emerging countries. Tourism in South Africa has been booming in recent years. In 2016 more than ten million international tourists arrived in the country which was 13% more than in 2015, which easily outpaced the global tourism growth.

Unfortunately, South Africa has been rife with corruption since Jacob Zuma was elected president in 2009. There have been numerous political scandals ranging from the use of taxpayer funds to renovate the president's home to Zuma undermining the countries legislative powers by shaking up the Cabinet in the middle of the night. The political uncertainties have staved off foreign investment and led to a dramatic weakening of the currency.

South Africa continues to face other issues such as high levels of crime. Cities such as Cape Town still rank near the top on the lists for highest homicides globally and overall murders have been increasing. Johannesburg has a reputation for being unsafe and locals often joke that the only reason an individual would travel there is if he wanted to get robbed. South Africa has one of the world's worst education systems. As of early 2017, South Africa ranked 75th out of 76 mainly rich countries in terms of quality of the education system. Keep in mind that the condition of education varies considerably and the experiences that students have in certain private schools can be of high quality (and even in certain public schools). Interestingly enough, it doesn't appear that the amount of dollar investment in public education has been the issue. In South Africa public spending on education is 6.4% of GDP as of 2017 compared to 4.8% in EU countries. They need to resolve this crisis and figure out how to more effectively allocate their public funds in this area if they are ever going to take the next step in terms of global stature. As you will see in the Botswana chapter, they face a similar issue pertaining to the allocation of education funds.

Along with many other African countries, South Africa faces an ongoing battle with HIV/AIDS. According to a 2012 UNAIDS World AIDS Day Report, it is estimated that 17.3% of the general population (ages 15-49) lives with HIV. South Africa and other countries on the continent will have to continue to deal with this issue and more effectively allocate medical resources going forward.

Much like other African nations, there is a shortage of water in the country. While we were in South Africa, the country was experiencing a drought and doing what they could to conserve water. I have long predicted that the next global war will be over clean drinking water. Even though most in the United States take it for granted, there is a large population of the world that battles every day to just get enough water to safely drink.

Political policies seem to have stalled much of the progress that was made in the country in the 1990s. Unemployment hit a 12-year high in 2016 reaching over 27%. Real GDP growth has come to a halt and South Africa remains one of the most unequal nations in the world.

If South Africa is going to get back to the glory days of the late 1990s then the government will have to instill confidence to spur foreign investment. The government could consider lowering the corporate tax rate from 28% to 20% or lower to encourage more companies to relocate to the country. The government could also make it easier to start a business in the country. For example, it should be a priority to reduce the average time to start a business from 43 days to 15 to provide a relative advantage over other Sub-Saharan countries. The South African government needs to do a better job of simply enforcing the laws that it does have. We were informed that citizens often blow off parking tickets when they receive them. How is the government supposed to raise steady revenue and instill confidence if it can't uphold the standard rule of law? Public school funds need to be more effectively allocated which could go a long way to reducing the widespread inequality that currently exists. It would be worthwhile to consider paying teachers on more of an incentivized basis so that they would work more closely with the students to achieve a common goal.

Adventure

Upon landing in Cape Town, we were retrieved by the local travel agency: Ilios Travel. We did not have much time to spare, as Paula and I would be heading off to an afternoon tour of the beautiful South African wineries in just a few short hours. Upon checking into Four Rosmead Guest House, we quickly showered and then were off for our first adventure. There are several wine areas in South Africa but on this particular day we headed to Stellenbosch which is about 45 minutes outside of Cape Town. Driving through the city, I noticed that I did not see any individuals begging for money on the side of the road as I would expect to see in the U.S. Our guide, Avril, informed us that it is illegal to beg for money in South Africa. Much like most countries in South America, there is no welfare in South Africa, so you tend to see people doing whatever they can to make money and contribute to the local economy. I think our country would be much better off if policies such as these were adopted.

Taking in the scenery, Paula and I looked out over the beautiful Cape Town coastline that leaves onlookers in awe. I had only been in the city for a couple of hours at this point, but I already knew that it was my favorite larger city I had ever visited (it is difficult to compare a place such as Cape Town to small cities like Queenstown, New Zealand). Cape Town is an absolute spectacle, with mountains behind the city giving way to buildings that border a magnificent coastline with beaches and coastal views. It was interesting that our tour guide, Avril, took the time to talk about the slums along the way. Much like cities such as Lima, there are several districts in Cape Town that are comprised of extremely poor individuals. There are often fire issues in these areas, as houses are close together and largely unregulated. It is worth noting that there are virtually zero requirements for subsidized housing in the city. The government has made it a priority to provide a house for everyone in the city.

We went to three wineries that afternoon in the Stellenbosch region. The scenery was nothing short of stunning along the way, with sprawling vineyards seemingly at every turn, again with the beautiful mountain landscape as a backdrop and the atmosphere at each location was very relaxed. I am not too experienced in the field of wine and vineyards, but Paula confirmed that this experience was superior to that of the Napa region in California. This excursion combined with the fact that high-quality wines could be purchased for the equivalent of $4 made it truly a winning combination. Head to South Africa fast while the local currency is still weak! The afternoon was full of visiting local vineyards, drinking wine along with pairings such as chocolate, and taking in some of the most beautiful scenery in the world. The mountainous backdrop provides breathtaking photos at several of the wineries and other areas in the region. If you are visiting Cape Town, a full-day or half-day wine tour is an activity that simply can't be passed on.

Table Mountain is a short drive outside the city and forms part of Table Mountain National Park. It is recognized as one of the New 7 Wonders of Nature. Overlooking Cape Town, it provides unparalleled views of the area and draws tourists from around the world. The top of the mountain can be reached by walking or cableway. Conditions for our hike up the mountain were perfect that day. Upon our ascent to the top, which took about 45 minutes, the skies were clear and the temperature was in the low 60s. We stopped at several points along the way to take pictures and digest the otherworldly scenery. I could not believe how few people were on the trail with us. We are talking about a hike that provides some of the most generous vantage points in the world and we probably did not come across more than 150 people on our way up. I would rate the hike difficulty as between easy and moderate. Individuals are more than likely to stop at various points along the route to catch their breath and just enjoy the view. We did the standard hike up, which I thought was great in terms of timing and what we were able to see. Paula and I took pictures at the top of the mountain overlooking Cape Town and the rest of the majestic coastal landscape. I am glad that we took our pictures quickly because the clouds rolled in over the course of just a few minutes. As they say locally, the city is capable of having four seasons in a single day. It was a prudent decision to opt for the cableway down, as we were a bit tired at this point and a hike down the mountain would not have provided any views that we hadn't already seen.

Our wonderful tour guide, Avril, then took us around Cape Town to show us more of the city. I continued to fall more in love with Cape Town along our journey as I remained ever inquisitive about local customs, the economy, etc. We drove past the Cape Town Stadium which was built for the 2010 FIFA World Cup hosted by South Africa. Avril informed us of how important the stadium and other developments in city surrounding the World Cup were for the future of Cape Town. However, there were various issues with workers going on strike while building the stadium for the World Cup and the stadium was finished just one month before the event. Certainly a potential cautionary tale for capital projects in the country. The World Cup provided a global spotlight on cities such as Cape Town and boosted tourism and economic development. Unlike in countries such as Brazil that seemed to have largely wasted their investments related to the World Cup, South Africa has used most of them to their advantage.

I couldn't help but notice how few people were walking around during the day. We were informed that most people were taking part in religious practices since it was Sunday. Unlike the modern-day U.S., most individuals in South Africa take part in some form of religion. Various religions are practiced in the country, which is reinforced by the constitution and guarantees religious freedom, but Christianity does make up the majority of the population.

Paula and I delved further into the local culture upon visiting the Iziko South African Museum. It was a moving experience learning more about apartheid, which was a system of racial segregation and discrimination that only ended in 1991. Much like in the United States until the 1960s, there was segregation of public facilities, housing, and employment opportunities. Avril told us stories about families who were separated simply because of the color of their skin. Nelson Mandela, who is widely praised across the country to this day, helped bring an end to apartheid. Mandela was imprisoned for 27 years for his actions relating to protests pertaining to the racial divide and the oppressive regimes that were running South Africa. Mandela was released from prison in 1990 and became the first black president of the country in 1994. We did not have time during our visit, but it is popular to take a day trip to visit Robben Island, which is where Mandela spent 18 of his 27 years in prison and is recognized as a UNESCO World Heritage Site. If you are considering this activity, do monitor weather closely much the same as you would for the hike up Table Mountain.

That afternoon we also went to Cheetah Outreach, which is located about 20 minutes outside of Cape Town. Here we learned more about the species and were given the opportunity to pet a fully-grown cheetah. The fastest land animal on the planet is now on the endangered list, and it is estimated that there are only 7,100 cheetahs left in the wild as of 2017. I was a little nervous when we walked into the area where the cheetah was. While there were individuals in the enclosed area who were quite familiar with this particular cheetah, I did keep thinking about all of the chase scenes that I had seen on Animal Planet over the years in which the cheetah ended up scarfing down another large animal. Paula and I caressed the beautiful cat while he was fed and somewhat distracted by one of his human friends that work with him on a daily basis. This would be our only encounter that we had with a cheetah on the trip.

That evening, Paula and I went down to the Cape Town waterfront area for dinner. This is a nice area complete with a mall, various restaurants with outdoor seating, and attractions such as a Ferris wheel. I could not believe how packed the mall was on a Sunday night. This experience reminded me of malls in the United States in the 1990s and early 2000s. The mall even had CD stores, which I hadn't seen in the U.S. in years! I didn't want to break the news to the locals, but I think I can predict how the mall landscape in the country will play out over the coming years as more people get accustomed to the convenience of online shopping and the shift will only be expedited with an improving economic backdrop.

We arose the following day at 5:00 a.m. and set out for Gansbaai, which is located about two hours southeast of Cape Town along the coast. Gansbaai is a small fishing town most popularly known for its proximity to the most famous region in the world to come into contact with great white sharks. Only about a 15 to 20-minute boat ride from Gansbaai, there is a shallow channel popularly known as "Shark Alley," which has been well documented by Discovery Channel as having the highest density of great white sharks in the world. Dyer Island is the largest group of islands in this area where 60,000 Cape fur seals can be found during the winter months. The great white sharks frequent these waters during the winter and hunt the seals.

Ever in search of an adventure, I had booked a day trip with Marine Dynamics to cage dive with the great white sharks. I had done extensive research in regard to the safety of the activity and regarding shark attacks in the country in general prior to opting for the activity. Despite the fact that the media often portrays the risk of entering the South Africa waters as resulting in imminent death, there was only an average of 1.13 reported deaths per year in all of South Africa between 2010 and 2017 from shark attacks. Additionally, I could not find a single instance where a cage diver was killed. There were a couple cases over the years where a shark did breach a cage, but these instances did not result in the death of any divers. Contrary to popular belief, activities such as swimming in South African beaches and cage diving with sharks is very low risk relative to almost any other activity besides sitting stationary in a chair.

Despite this, I was still nervous given that great white sharks are the most physically imposing species on earth for many individuals. We hopped aboard *Slashfin*, the name of the boat, and departed on the brief 15 to 20-minute ride. The water was pretty choppy, and I would not recommend this activity if you are prone to getting seasick. We were again presented with magnificent views of the coastal landscape, but this time we were looking from an aquatic vantage point. We took pictures as we approached Geyser Rock where a large amount of seals were located and making their distinctive noises which are important for enabling individual recognition. Dropping anchor not too far from the island, the crew deployed chum and other tactics that are commonly used to draw the sharks into the area. We sat there for three hours and disappointingly did not see a single Great White Shark. They informed us that this was a rare occurrence and was due to what they believe was unique development in recent months of orcas in the area hunting the great white sharks. They had found four great white sharks over the past few months that were killed by what they believed to be a pair of orcas working together to hunt the sharks. This was surprising to me, as I would not have envisioned the Great White Shark to be so vulnerable to any other animal. I later watched a documentary about orcas that had attacked great white sharks off the coast of California, which had the same result. The great white sharks immediately left the area, and scientists speculate that the reason is that they smelled the death of their own species in the water! If the great white sharks do not come back in numbers to Gansbaai, then companies such as Marine Dynamics will go bankrupt and the South African tourism industry as a whole will take a hit. We were told that there had been great white sightings in False Bay, which is located closer to Cape Town. If you are considering a shark cage diving trip, I would highly recommend reaching out to local companies in advance to make sure that there have been shark sightings in recent days.

We made the most of the rest of our day thanks to our amazing tour guide. She took us back to Cape Town along the scenic Clarence Drive, which I would recommend if you decide to visit Cape Town. Along the drive, we saw several baboons on the side of the road, which we would become accustomed to along our journey. Avril informed us that if homeowners in the area did not lock their doors and close their windows, baboons were known to let themselves in and open cabinets to get to the food. Wouldn't that be entertaining to see! We stopped at Stony Point Nature Reserve along the drive. This area is home to the African penguin and is worth a visit. Paula and I couldn't get enough taking pictures of the adorable penguins located in this coastal reserve. I had only found out about a week before the trip that penguins even existed in Africa.

I had arranged in advance for us to eat dinner at City Grill that evening. Eager to taste an array of new foods, City Grill offers options such as zebra, ostrich, warthog, and biltong. Paula and I started with an appetizer of biltong, which I would compare to a high-quality beef jerky in the U.S. This was delicious and I could have gone on eating this for hours had it not been for the zebra and ostrich filet that would arrive in the near future. I had previously read online that zebra was comparable to horse and found that most people did not have very positive reviews of the product. Paula and I agreed that zebra was delicious, and I would compare it to more of a pork or steak than horse. The ostrich filet, which was comparable to a steak, was tasty as well. I would have liked to try warthog, but, unfortunately, it was unavailable at the time. Warthog is often considered the locals meat of choice for special occasions and is a delicacy along with ostrich. Zebra is not consumed as often as these options. I washed the meal down with a Green Room IPA, which was one of the few beers that I enjoyed on our trip. As I had found in Morocco, most African beers are similar to products such as Bud Light and offer little in the way of Belgian style and more bitter-tasting IPAs. I think this is going to change over the coming years, as African beer palettes get more adventurous and they follow in the footsteps of the craft beer craze that has taken hold in the U.S. over the past decade. Again, the total price of the meal was extremely cheap by U.S. standards. The total cost of the meal was $75 for what I estimate would have cost $250 in Washington, DC.

Additional Activities and Recommendations

In addition to our activities in South Africa, it is popular to visit Kruger National Park, a four-hour drive from Johannesburg, and the many other attractive safari options in the country.

While it is not of particular interest to me, Johannesburg is still popular to visit even though it can be unsafe at times.

If you are an adventurer looking for something special, then consider hiking the Drakensberg Grand Traverse. This famous hike can take up to two weeks but can be rewarding with the views provided of the Drakensberg Mountain range and various cliffs and valleys along the way. If considering this option, it is highly recommended that the activity be arranged through a local guide, as it can be unsafe if not planned appropriately due to lack of water, thieves, etc.

Another option would be to rent a car and drive the Garden Route, which is the road that extends along the coast between Port Elizabeth and Cape Town. We traveled a portion of the Garden Route on our way back from Gansbaai to Cape Town and I can say from the expedited version that the views are nothing short of spectacular.

Surfing is popular in South Africa. There are various surfing locations across South Africa, but Jeffrey's Bay is often considered to be the best surfing destination in the world. Rides here can be up to 900 feet long!

Canyoning at Plettenberg Bay is also a popular attraction. Activities at this location range from cliff jumping to zip-lining. Swim through the river and enjoy the wildlife along the way. If you are looking into canyoning, also known as kloofing, also consider Suicide Gorge near Cape Town if you are adventurous. The highest required jump is around 50 feet, so make sure you are ready prior to committing to this one.

Whale watching at Hermanus is another option to consider. Get up close and personal with the Southern Right Whales that come to Hermanus annually to breed. This can be done as a day trip from Cape Town. Visitors can consider stopping in Hermanus on the way back from Gansbaai if interested in doing a Great White Shark tour at that location.

Sandboarding can be done right around the Cape Town area. Cape Town has two popular sites that are both under an hour's drive from the city, Betty's Bay and Atlantis. Having done sandboarding myself, it is not overly difficult to pick up as a beginner. It's much easier than snowboarding or skiing and can be done successfully with limited training.

The more adventurous may want to consider bungy jumping at Tsitsikamma National Park. This is the highest commercially-operated bungy jump from a bridge in the world.

Business Outlook

Despite the seemingly endless mountain of issues facing the country, I am optimistic about the prospects over the long haul. Disregarding the current government, which is universally despised after speaking with the local people, South Africa is a country that has everything. The beautiful landscape will always make it a premier tourism destination as long as individuals can be somewhat assured as to their safety while in South Africa. The expansive coastline will continue to provide opportunities for fishing. The coastline can also be used to take advantage of the global increase in cruise tourism. The diverse landscape can be used creatively as a competitive advantage. For example, varying elevations even within a single winery allow for both red and white wines to be grown even though they require different altitudes for optimal taste. South Africa is blessed with various natural resources with gold and platinum being the most prominent. It is worth noting that South Africa does not suffer from the major natural disasters that many other countries suffer from such as earthquakes, hurricanes, tornadoes, etc.

The real estate market in South Africa is an industry that is worth monitoring. Only about 3% of all real estate in the country is currently owned by foreigners, which is interesting considering the lack of restrictions for outside investors. Upon conducting research on local apartments and condos, I found high-end properties with 24-hour security in nice areas with superb views of the beach and mountains for $200,000. I would estimate that similar properties in the Washington D.C. area would be well over $1 million and likely in the neighborhood of $1.5-$2 million. This does come with caveats, however. While upholding public contracts such as real estate has not been a large issue in South Africa in the past, one has to be a bit wary given the widespread corruption that has occurred in the country in recent years. This is a potential development that would need to be monitored closely.

Additionally, I found a publicly traded South African-based telecommunications company to be interesting. MTN Group Limited operates in over 21 countries with 225 million subscribers as of June 2016. MTN owns a 29% interest in IHS Holding Limited, which has over 23,000 cellular towers in the African mobile market. After witnessing first-hand the dismal state of mobile technology in countries such as Botswana and Zimbabwe that are still operating on 2G, it is easy to see how there is potential opportunity in the world's fastest growing mobile market. Africa still has a relatively low mobile penetration rate and the use of Internet on mobile devices is predicted to increase 20-fold in the next five years starting in 2017. As of 2017, South Africa only had a 33% smartphone penetration rate, which provides huge upside along with other countries in which MTN operates, such as Nigeria with an astoundingly low 10 to 20% penetration. Given the capital-intensive nature of the cellular tower business and heavy government regulations that exist, it is difficult to amass such an expansive portfolio of assets. MTN could be one of the prime beneficiaries of the mobile data explosion on the African continent.

I believe there is a large opportunity in regard to the travel sector of the South African economy and Africa overall. As more people around the world come to appreciate the many jewels that the continent has to offer, there will be a higher demand for good quality affordable and safe air transportation in Africa. In conducting extensive research regarding airlines operating in Southern Africa, the only local airline I was comfortable allowing my girlfriend to travel on was South African Airways. If a company could model Ryanair's low-cost, no-frills model with a pristine safety record that is audited by the U.S. and UK and effectively compete with the state-run loss making South African Airways and other African carriers, there is serious money to be made here. The other huge opportunity I foresee related to travel is in the cruise industry. As of 2016, Africa accounted for a tiny 0.6% of the global cruise market. The global cruise market has been surging in recent years, but there were still only 24.73 million passengers in 2016, which provides incredible growth potential given the global population of 7.5 billion as of 2017 along with macro trends such as the growing middle class, shift from investment in brands to spending on experiences (particularly with the millennial population), the rise of the river cruise, which provides shorter trips and more opportunities for additional passengers, and increased interest in cruises in general. South Africa can offer attractive cruise itineraries to surrounding locations such as Madagascar, Namibia, and Mozambique.

As I mentioned previously, I think there is an opportunity pertaining to the rise of more premium drinks in the African beer and liquor space. Companies such as Diageo PLC, the owner of brands such as Johnnie Walker and Guinness, should continue to benefit over the coming years as they upsell consumers in developing countries that are just starting to scratch the surface on interest in higher quality alcohol products that provide higher margins than lower end brands.

Updates Since Visit

Since our visit to South Africa, the country could largely be described as a disaster in terms of political and economic performance. The country entered recession in the second quarter of 2018 for the first time since 2009. The World Bank is only projecting 1.3% GDP growth for 2019, which is especially disappointing given the weak comparison in 2018. The World Bank report noted high levels of unemployment, mining production challenges, low business confidence, political uncertainty, and slow growth in household credit.

In February 2018, Jacob Zuma was essentially forced to resign as South Africa's president. Given Zuma's dismal track record as president, this ushered in a sense of hope among the South African community. Unfortunately, the early returns from Cyril Ramaphosa have not exactly brought a sense of sweeping political certainty to South Africa. For example, the African National Congress (ANC) passed an amendment to the South African Constitution allowing the seizure of white-owned farmland without compensation. Did they not learn anything from Zimbabwe when they did exactly this several years ago and it caused all of the farmers to flee to surrounding countries such as Zambia, Botswana, and South Africa? Not only does such political policy drive out all of the hardworking farmers, but it also creates immense uncertainty pertaining to home ownership in general. I had previously written about the potential for investment in the South African real estate market but how could a prospective investor have much confidence in this sector if they know the government is willing to seize land from citizens?

In 2018, the World Bank named South Africa as the nation with the highest inequality on earth. The 2018 unemployment rate averaged over 27%, which was near a 15-year high. The high rate of inequality and extreme unemployment is a direct result of having one of the worst education systems in the world. The issues are said to lie in the state-run schools, which further exacerbates the income inequality because the private school children are receiving a much better education, in aggregate. Similar to Botswana, South Africa needs to provide substantial improvements to the education system which will in turn increase the number of qualified skilled workers and decrease inequality.

Despite the ongoing economic and political turmoil in South Africa, the tourism sector has continued to perform well. The number of overseas tourist arrivals is projected to grow over 7% in 2019 with the largest contributor being the relaxation of visa rules. Given that we have seen a lot of isolationist political policies globally over the past few years, it is refreshing to see South Africa ease visa rules.

Foreign investors with an ownership stake in MTN Group Limited have been hurt by the weakness in the South African rand. Having previously faced a string of political headaches in Nigeria, MTN has had recent issues in Uganda where the country recently deported four top MTN executives citing "national security" concerns. This cautionary tale makes me wonder whether a corporate model of operating across various African countries even works.

It seems like there is always going to be a raft of unexpected political developments and trying to manage this across various countries is a losing battle.

Despite the mostly negative update commentary, South Africa is still the second largest economy in Africa in terms of GDP in 2019. They have their work cut out for them in terms of improvements in education and political stability but the foundations in terms of natural beauty, expansive coastline, diverse landscape, and plethora of natural resources are in place. I hope that South Africa can get back on track, but the jury is still out. While it seems as though many of Ramaphosa's policies regarding corruption have had good intent, critics have complained that the economic reform agenda has been painfully slow which has led South Africa to the brink of junk status for the debt of the country.

I provided some commentary about the growth of the global cruise industry in this chapter and other chapters. The future trends and growth trajectory of the industry had supported this research up until the outbreak of COVID-19. The cruise industry had been resilient in the face of various health-related outbreaks in the past, but never before had the entire global industry been shut down for several months. With no revenue coming in the door and the cruise operators having a high level of fixed costs and debt coming due, the future of the industry is in question. To make matters worse, the major cruise operators have ships on order for several more years because there are only a few shipyards in the world that produce cruise ships that are up to the standards of the cruise titans. Despite headlines calling cruises "floating prisons," people will cruise again in the future but it will be a long, arduous path to recovery.

Following the outbreak of COVID-19, South Africa is in trouble. The country already had a 29% unemployment rate in 2019 and a weak economy coming into the crisis. South Africa's finances were not in good shape prior to the outbreak which makes their situation all the more difficult. As of the time of this writing, South Africa had no investment grade credit ratings for the first time since 1994 and the local currency reached an all-time low relative to the U.S. dollar.

I had included previous data that stated that South Africa had the highest reported inequality on earth as of 2018, which will only exacerbate the economic issues. In the section about the economy, I noted that the top South African industries are mining, agriculture, manufacturing, tourism, fishing, finance, and real estate. All of these sectors will be hit hard by the economic fallout of COVD-19. Following what I think will wind up being the single most devastating global economic event in modern history, countries should go back and re-think the industries that the government incentivizes and promotes. When almost every business in the world was either dramatically curtailed or put on pause altogether, people still have to eat, drink, and the majority of people in the world still use the Internet. Going forward, I would recommend more of a focus being placed on utilities because we have seen what can happen if the entire global economy comes to a virtual standstill.

The beautiful South African wineries

Cape Point

Our best attempt at cage diving with great white sharks

The ominous kayak experience

Penguins!

The "Enchanted Forest" at La Colombe Restaurant

Botswana

Introduction

F lying over Botswana in route to the airport located in Kasane, located in the northeastern corner of Botswana, I could only spot one dirt road the entire way. Excitement started to build as I looked down over the green grasslands that seemed to extend in perpetuity. When we landed in Kasane, our plane which held about 30 people or so was easily the largest at the airport. I could see this changing in the coming years as the tourism further ramps up which will likely be accelerated with the newly finished terminal.

Upon landing, we had about an hour drive to Camp Kuzuma which is where Paula and I would be staying the next three nights. Within the first few miles of the journey, I noticed something interesting along the road. Trucks were lined up for several miles right there on the shoulder, which would never be allowed in countries like the United States. We were informed that the trucks were waiting to be shipped by boat upstream to countries like Kenya and Tanzania. The truck drivers have to sit there all day for what can be over a month's time just to ensure that they do not lose their position in queue. If you can think of a larger waste of time in this world, then please let me know. It quickly became evident how poor the roads were in the country. There were potholes everywhere and the driver had to frequently stop to avoid disaster on our way to Camp Kuzuma. Imagine what it would be like if they had more than one road in the area to maintain. The entire experience became more surreal when we started to see animals such as zebras and elephants roaming in the complete wild along the side of the road. Here we were, completely disconnected from the outside world on a one lane dirt road in Botswana with rolling grasslands to either side containing animals that most are only fortunate enough to encounter at the zoo.

The Republic of Botswana is a landlocked country in Southern Africa bordered by South Africa, Namibia, Zambia, and Zimbabwe (working around the clock from the south starting west). Botswana is the 48th largest country in the world by land size, which is similar to France or Madagascar. Despite the land mass of Botswana, the country had fewer than 2.5 million people as of 2017 making it one of the more sparsely populated countries on earth. The Kalahari Desert covers 70% of the land in this mostly flat, rolling country. One of the world's largest inland deltas, Okavango Delta, lies in the northwest part of the country. The Chobe River is in the north of Botswana and divides the country from Namibia.

The government of Botswana is a representative democratic republic in which the President is both the head of state and the head of government as in South Africa. The Botswana constitution is the rule of law in the country. Botswana has often been considered the least corrupt country in Africa and regularly ranks highly in annual democracy indices by African standards.

It is believed that the first humans, the Bushmen, came to Botswana more than 100,000 years ago. The country remained under tribal rule until Europeans came to the area in the 1700s. Christian missionaries that were sent from Europe spread to countries such as Botswana in the 1800s. In fact, the Christian influence in Botswana had a lasting impact and by 1880 every major village was represented by a missionary. The Christian movement was recognized by King Khama III who reigned from 1875-1923. The influence exists today as around 70% of the population identifies themselves as Christians. Battles were fought in the late 19th century between Tswana inhabitants and Ndebele tribes while the country remained under British rule. Botswana did not achieve full independence from the United Kingdom until 1966.

The Tswana ethnic group makes up the majority of the population in the country. The white population existing in Botswana accounts for only about

7% of the total. Due to deteriorating economic conditions in recent years, Zimbabweans have come to Botswana in large numbers given the relative economic stability existing in the country. The official language of Botswana is English, but Setswana is also frequently spoken.

The Botswana Defence Force was formed in 1977 and still exists today. The President is commander-in-chief of the Defence Force. As Paula and I found out when we were on our game drives and came across several men carrying assault rifles, the armed forces have become increasingly focused on tasks such as anti-poaching given how important the fauna is to the Botswana economy. We were informed that if individuals are found to be poaching in Botswana, they are immediately shot to death! No need to go through the court system for these matters. I guess just hope that the Defence Force doesn't mistake you for a poacher.

Economy

Education expenditure in Botswana ranks among the highest in the world at 9% of GDP and includes free primary education. Unlike countries such as South Africa, Botswana has been moving in the right direction in recent years in regard to their education system. However, the country has yet to create a skilled workforce and needs to take the next step. The country still relies heavily on the harvesting of diamonds and tourism. It would go a long way if the education system worked to prioritize making Botswana the specialist at a few service-oriented professions. Unemployment has remained high into 2017 at around 18% and inequality is among the highest in the world.

Botswana has been a consistent success story over the years since it gained independence from the United Kingdom in 1966. At the time, Botswana was one of the poorest countries in Africa with a gross GDP per capita at only $70. Real GDP has increased by an average of 5% per year over the past decade as of 2016. Countries like the United States would kill for even a 3% average. The country has consistently rung up a current account surplus while most developed nations around the world have seen deteriorating trends in recent years. Diamond mining has fueled much of the economic expansion in Botswana and accounts for 25% of the total GDP, 85% of export earnings, and one-third of government revenues. Botswana operates a joint venture with the global diamond player De Beers. The diamonds are harvested in Botswana and then shipped on to the diamond district in Antwerp, which I have visited, for distribution. While the diamond industry has been a tremendous boon to the Botswana economy, the future of the diamond revenues is uncertain. The diamond output is already well past the peak at this point, and nobody knows when the deposits will be fully exhausted.

Behind diamonds, tourism is the second largest industry in Botswana, accounting for 12.7% of GDP as of 2016. The country has traditionally focused on high-end tourism but is now conducting due diligence on expanding into the mid-range tourism. The government's undying focus on protecting the wildlife and the strict regulations of accommodation within the country seems to be paying off. *The New York Times* ranked Botswana as the world's fifth most desirable location to visit in 2017. Botswana maintains an elephant population that is believed to be over 130,000, making it the largest in Africa and the highest density elephant population in the world. The country is home to all of the big five found in Africa (lion, elephant, buffalo, rhino, and leopard). If you want to find the black rhino, then head across the border to Zambia or Zimbabwe as we did. As Paula and I found out, Botswana also provides the opportunity to experience animals in their natural wild habitat that few other locations offer. Unlike visiting Kruger National Park in South Africa, an individual can stay at a lodge located outside of a national park or tag along with a guide looking for animals in completely unfenced areas. The rolling grasslands outside of the national parks are also regulated by the Botswana Defence Force. Tourist arrivals for the country surpassed two million in 2016. This is remarkable considering that the entire country has only 2.3 million people as of this writing. Tourists seemed to have flocked to the country for the above reasons as well as the reputation for being the safest country in Africa to visit.

Botswana has one of the highest HIV/AIDS rates in the world at around 22% of the population as of 2016. The country faces an uphill battle in this regard, and this healthcare crisis has the potential to stunt future economic growth. The government will have to continually work to educate the population and invest in treatments and facilities to mitigate the problems it faces here.

The government of Botswana has really done all they can do—and then some. Unfortunately, they just weren't given a very strong hand to play with. It is critical that the government continue to make it a priority to diversify the revenue streams of the country. As stated previously, this should all start with the education system which should prioritize making Botswana a leader in a couple service-oriented industries that do not depend on the amount of resources left in the ground (as is the case with diamonds). While most likely not a long-term solution, the government could offer incentives to start certain service or manufacturing oriented businesses which could assist in expediting the transition away from the reliance on revenue from diamonds.

Adventure

Upon arrival at Camp Kuzuma, we took another 10 to 15-minute ride on a safari vehicle through the bush to get to our lodge. When we reached the camp, it quickly became clear that this was by far the nicest hotel accommodation I had ever stayed at in my life. Paula and I were informed that we would be the only guests staying at Kuzuma for the next three nights, as there are only five tents available at the site in total. This could be alarming to some at first but any anxiety was at least partially assuaged by the fact that this meant a staff of 10-12 people was waiting on just Paula and me to prepare food, take us on game drives, provide cocktails, and do whatever we wanted at any time of day. Did I say that the dollar was strong against the currencies in Southern Africa? An accommodation such as this could very well cost $10,000 a night in countries such as the United States and can be had for about $500 a night in Botswana.

Paula and I perused our decadent tent that was located in the wild without any boundaries or fences as you would find in most countries. Fortunately, this tent was zipped up and had a mosquito net to protect against animals such as spiders coming in at night. I guess I should inform my friends in Belize that this is how camping should be done! Out front of the main lodge area was a watering hole where elephants came to drink water. If you are interested in seeing what the place looks like, then check out www.earthcam.come/world/botswana/chobe?cam=campkuzuma, which provides a live feed of the watering hole. Here we were, 50 miles from any other form of civilization at a luxury camping site in the middle of Botswana operating on 2G wireless. Certainly does not get much more surreal than that.

After settling in, we set out for the first game drive of the trip on the Camp Kuzuma grounds. That evening, we were able to spot animals such as elephants, giraffes, vultures, and baboons. After parking our safari vehicle in the middle of a clearing, we were provided with a generous spread of food and drink laid on top of the vehicle as we took in a sunset that was nothing short of incredible. Looking out over the grasslands, there were three giraffes that could be seen roaming the area that now had a sunset which was causing the sky to turn the combination of a beautiful red, pink, and orange hue. I hope that everyone can experience this once in their lifetime for themselves, as there is no substitute for a safari experience in a completely wild atmosphere.

The next day we went on three game drives on the grounds and were fed way too much food in between. I think it is important to note what I would consider to be desert-like weather variations that occur in Botswana. The temperature was in the 50s (Fahrenheit) every morning when we woke up only to reach the high 70s by the afternoon. One of my personal highlights was sitting there watching a giraffe up close. It is so interesting to watch these animals, as they are inquisitive and will intently try and figure out the purpose of a visitor's stay. As the giraffe continued to chew unlocking its jaw in a sideways motion that is interesting, Paula and I couldn't help but laugh and stare in awe. We were informed by two guides that if the giraffe lies down for longer than two minutes, they will have a stroke and die. Could you imagine standing up every minute of every day for the remainder of your life?! Another highlight of the day came when a group of elephants came to the watering hole right outside of our lodge. While the staff at Camp Kuzuma may be used to seeing this on a regular basis, to anyone from the United States or other developed countries, this is an incredible sight to see. Paula and I sat there looking on from the outdoor lobby area as the elephants consumed a portion of the 140–235 liters per day of water that adult African elephants require. After Paula had gone back to the room, one of the elephants came over about 20 feet from where I was sitting, just trying to figure out what I was doing there. Don't mind me, just taking in some of the coolest scenery of my lifetime! Apparently, the wildlife team at Walt Disney also agrees, as the guests that stayed at the lodge before us were two employees of the company that were filming an elephant documentary that is scheduled to be released in 2020 (Disneynature's Elephant was released on April 3, 2020).

The following day, we set out for a full day at Chobe National Park. Chobe is the third largest game park in the country and the most biologically diverse. We encountered far more wildlife here, as the reputation for this being the best time of year to visit Botswana for the wildlife rang true. May to September is considered the dry season and far superior for game viewing. Upon speaking with the locals, it seems like fauna activity really starts to pick up in the late June and early July timeframe. That day at Chobe we saw hundreds and hundreds of animals which included lions, hippos, buffalo, giraffe, elephants, crocodiles, hyenas, antelope, water buffalo, zebra, warthog, baboons, and impala.

I would highly recommend a visit to Chobe National Park, as it is an absolute spectacle. It is a combination of the rolling grasslands that we had back at Camp Kuzuma along with a river that provides for lush vegetation and an amazing view. It was shocking as to the sheer volume of animals that we encountered along our game drive. We would come across ten giraffes at a time just roaming the area. Unlike back at Kuzuma, there were zebras everywhere. The highlight of the day came when we encountered a pride of lions eating a recently killed giraffe. As we were sitting there watching the incredible scene unfold, the large male lion started to walk over toward our vehicle. He came within ten feet of us, and it briefly looked as if he was contemplating whether he should have Paula and me for lunch! Seeing the lion is an absolute must while in Africa.

After concluding our morning game drive which was nothing short of breathtaking, we were taken by boat to a location called The Raft Floating Restaurant located on the river. This was quite the experience, as it was again just Paula and I at this venue. Here we were, sitting right in the middle of the river of Chobe National Park looking out over the beautiful scenery as hippos and crocodiles were roaming nearby. The restaurant is actually located right across the border in Namibia so if you want to say that you stepped foot in this country as well then here is your chance. I would highly recommend this experience.

After our delicious lunch on the raft, we departed for an afternoon river cruise. Aboard a small vessel that was manned by our guide for the day, we roamed the river looking for more close-up shots of some of the animals. We took pictures in front of several crocodiles, some of which were more than ten feet long. It is important to be careful with the crocodile, as they have been known to be dangerous to humans. I was surprised to hear that the African crocodiles live an average of 70 years. There were hippos spotted along the shallow water and grass inlets. Surprising to most, the hippo accounts for the most human deaths of any large land animal in Africa, killing an estimated 500 people per year in the continent alone. It made me slightly nervous cruising around the river on our small pontoon boat with all these predators in the area, but certainly added to the experience. We were fortunate enough to encounter a rare elephant water crossing while we were out on the river. Our wonderful guide roared ahead when he saw the development taking place in the distance. Now within 50 feet of a herd of 30 elephants crossing the Chobe River, we sat there in the boat debating whether we were watching *Planet Earth* or whether we were really witnessing this firsthand. One after another, the elephants crossed single file with the older members of the herd assisting the youth. I could have sat there for hours watching these incredible animals.

That evening was our last in Camp Kuzuma. We had a barbeque dinner sitting by the fire pit overlooking the elephant watering hole. The staff got Paula and me to join in on a local dance around the fire as they were all singing. To top off the whole experience, as we were taking turns telling stories by the fire after our meal, a herd of about 20 elephants came to the watering hole right in front of us. I am not sure how seeing this ever gets old, as it is so relaxing. I thought to myself, "This is Botswana."

At about 1:00 a.m., I awoke to a vehicle thundering toward our camp. I jumped up, as Camp Kuzuma lies about 50 miles from any other form of civilization. My immediate thought was that we were surely about to be robbed, as I could not think of any other reason that a vehicle would be in the area at this hour. As I told Paula that I was going to rush over to the main part of the lodge, she started yelling at me and suffered a panic attack. Trying to calm the situation but failing spectacularly to do so, I insisted that I seek out members of the staff to figure out what was going on. At this point Paula could sense the worry in my voice and stopped breathing for a short period of time. Given her situation, I had to remain in our tent, as I could not risk what would happen to Paula if I scrambled back to the main lobby area. I stayed up until 5:30 a.m. that morning, holding a blow horn in my hand in the event that strangers raided our tent which I believed was imminent, or that an animal came crashing through the barrier. Only to add to the terror, I could hear two lions roaring nearby. As far as I was concerned, this was the least of my worries. Hours came and went, and nobody came rushing to our tent. I was convinced that there were men on foot in the bushes, as I could hear what I believed to be humans walking nearby but I am sure that this was exacerbated by the sound of the vehicle very close by. I asked the staff why a vehicle had approached our area the next morning and equally as alarming they said that they had somehow not even heard the vehicle! Ever nonchalant about a potential threat that would alarm most sensible individuals, they guessed that it was just the Botswana Defence Force searching for poachers.

Additional Activities and Recommendations

Despite the scare that we had on our last night at Camp Kuzuma, we made it out of Botswana safely and loved the country. If you are looking for a place to experience animals in their truly wild natural habitat, then Botswana is just the place for you. We did not have time along our journey, but adventure seekers may want to visit the Okavango Delta. Located 196 miles from Kasane, this large inland delta is known for the fantastic wildlife experience and scenery that it provides. Designated as one of the Seven Natural Wonders of Africa, this UNESCO World Heritage Site which includes the Moremi Game Reserve is nothing short of breathtaking. A quick Google search of the delta will have anyone with an appreciation for nature eager to make the journey to this destination. I would recommend planning to spend at least a couple days here if you decide to make the trip, as it is a little out of the way, but many have said that the expedition is well worth the time.

I would advise taking the time to research and inquire as to when the animals are most active at the specific location that you are looking into visiting. While wildlife was at or near the peak in Chobe National Park while Paula and I were in Botswana that may not have been the case at Camp Kuzuma. The experience was incredible nonetheless, but the grass around our lodge was high at this time of the year and could have prevented us from seeing more of the animals in the area. It is worth sending a quick email to the local lodge and asking.

If you are not planning to stay in Zambia or Zimbabwe, then I would recommend doing a day trip to Victoria Falls from Botswana. A couple hours drive from Kasane, Victoria Falls lies on the border of Zambia and Zimbabwe. Victoria Falls is one of the seven natural wonders of the world and is nothing short of breathtaking.

Fishing is another activity option in the country. Have an opportunity to try catching the rare Tiger Fish in the Chobe River. These fish can be caught using traditional methods in addition to fly fishing.

As you can see, there aren't nearly as many tourist options as some of the other countries discussed. Most of the options revolve around various safari activities which is where tourists will focus pretty much all of their time in Botswana. You likely won't have too many other opportunities to experience the natural wildlife that you can find in Botswana so take advantage.

Business Outlook

I do not find Botswana to be overly attractive from an investment perspective at this time because of the heavy reliance on two major industries, diamonds and tourism, with the former having a highly uncertain future. With that said, they do have a lot of potential in a few areas discussed below.

As discussed above, the government of Botswana has done a remarkable job over the years especially considering their resources. It is vital that the country continues to diversify the economy over the coming years which will dictate Botswana's future. Given the relative instability of most of the surrounding countries in the region, Botswana has been given a golden opportunity to continue to attract foreign investment despite the declining diamond business that they have relied on for so many years. According to recent reports produced by the World Bank, Botswana has made doing business easier for local entrepreneurs and they ranked third in the region for ease of doing business behind Mauritius and Rwanda. This is certainly a big positive, as they could ultimately become a technology or start-up hub or play a more prominent role in manufacturing with exports such as automobile components if they continue down this path of providing a business-friendly environment. To fully bear the fruit of any technological renaissance in Botswana, the government has a long way to go in terms of investment in infrastructure such as cellular towers, road systems, and other things that we simply take for granted in the United States. During much of our stay in the country, we had little access to cellular data via Wi-Fi as Botswana is still largely operating on a 2G network. Again, I see a large opportunity in the future for cellular data-related investment in Africa.

I think tourism is still in the early innings in Botswana. Investors and entrepreneurs looking to start a new tourism company or invest in one will have to navigate a heavily regulated industry but could well be rewarded with some of the best wildlife in the world. There is a long growth runway for lower and middle-tier accommodations.

Botswana could benefit from the help of an operations and logistics firm. Anywhere there is a place where truck drivers sit there and do nothing for up to a month while they wait for their turn on a river is ripe for disruption in terms of logistics and operational assistance. There simply has to be a better way to go about this business which would only be expedited by additional spending on infrastructure developments by the local government.

Given the business-friendly environment in the country, Botswana could take advantage of the high demand for medical products in the country in addition to the surrounding countries. Investors looking at this space should explore opportunities in pharmacy distribution, the manufacturing of medical products and supplies, and services pertaining to the medical field. Again, the government would likely have to be involved to some degree to further capitalize on this opportunity by placing a greater focus on education pertaining to the medical field in addition to encouraging foreign direct investment in areas such as medical manufacturing facilities and pharmacy distribution.

Updates Since Visit

Not much has changed in regard to the Botswana economy. The local economy is expected to grow 3.8% in 2019 with minerals being the largest contributor to revenue at 35.62% of output. The government has continued to focus on opening the economy up to tourism, but they will have to further encourage growth in other areas to ensure sustainable long-term success.

A potentially cautionary tale pertaining to the environment comes in the form of the government weighing lifting a hunting ban with what they say is an eye on reducing the elephant population. This is a stunning development for a country that has gone to such extreme lengths to preserve the local wildlife. It sounds to me like the Botswana government is trying to make some quick, easy money on big game hunting, like what we have seen in Zimbabwe and other African countries. I think they have to be overly cautious when navigating these waters, as the abundance of exotic wildlife is one of the few natural competitive advantages that Botswana possesses. "Some people are worried that elephants have recovered in greater numbers than the environment can sustain, and there is significant concern over increasing human-elephant conflict," says Elephants Without Borders, a conservation nonprofit. "During the past 20 years the elephant range in Botswana has expanded by 53%, causing increasing concern about the impact of elephants on biodiversity, the viability of other species and the livelihoods and safety of people living within the elephant range." These statements may be well grounded, but I think they should thoughtfully weigh the long-term positives and negatives of such a drastic turnaround in conservation policy. Unfortunately, as my writing was coming off the press Botswana did ultimately lift the ban on elephant hunting. This is a short-sighted measure to please the farmers that have claimed that elephants have hindered their crops. Given the reliance on tourism, this could be a costly decision over time.

Some have called on Botswana to diversify the economy by taking advantage of the 200 billion tons of coal reserves that the country has. Unfortunately, Botswana does not have the physical infrastructure in place to transport this natural resource to prospective buyers. Government investment in infrastructure could provide at least a short-term economic boost while building the foundation for industries such as coal.

The main focus for Botswana has to be on expanding the number of qualified skilled workers along with making improvements in the education sector. Botswana has regularly ranked in the bottom five countries in the world in terms of income inequality and improvements in labor and education would not only go a long way in helping diversify the economy, but also would help reduce the extreme income gap. Botswana's education expenditure is among the highest in the world at 9% of GDP and includes the provision of nearly universal free primary education but has not created a skilled workforce. So, the issue here is not the amount of financial resources being allocated to education, but rather how they are being used. Botswana's government should spend time studying how top performing global education systems such as Singapore, Finland, and South Korea have allocated their resources.

As I sounded the alarm about in regard to the lack of diversification of the local economy, Botswana will face a reckoning after the COVID-19 pandemic. As previously discussed, the economy is heavily reliant on tourism and diamonds. Tourism has come to a standstill globally and it looks likely that the diamond industry will enter a recession. The diamond business accounts for more than 80% of Botswana's export earnings so this is a serious challenge for the country. Many of the world's top gem dealers can't even enter Botswana to see the diamonds as of the time of this writing due to travel bans enacted by the country. Botswana should take my previous advice and look to diversify the local economy by educating, incentivizing, and training the local workforce to participate in other industries. As discussed in the South Africa chapter, it would be advised for Botswana to place additional focus on areas that are true utilities. It is a major problem when virtually a country's entire economy is dependent on two industries that I believe are heavily tied to discretionary spending. People can and will put off spending on areas such as diamonds and tourism under challenging economic circumstances and this has only been exacerbated by the extreme conditions enacted by the COVID-19 crisis.

Elephant crossing at Chobe National Park

When the lion stared us down from feet away!

Beautiful Botswana sunsets

The rolling Botswana grasslands

Luxury "camping"

Doing the safari experience right; complete with food and drinks

Zimbabwe

Introduction

After briefly settling into our hotel, we were off on our next adventure. We would be heading into Zambezi National Park, which was nearby, in search of the endangered black rhinoceros. Despite the name, the color of the black rhino varies from brown to grey, and the animal has a hook-lipped shape compared to that of a white rhino, which is described as being square-lipped. According to a 2016 report published by the IUCN, it is estimated that there are a little over 5,000 black rhinos remaining, which is slowly recovering given the recent emphasis on protection efforts for the species.

Zambezi National Park was a stark contrast to Chobe National Park, as I would describe it as being dry and somewhat desolate compared to the lush vegetation that comes to mind with Chobe. Despite the initially more visually appealing components of Chobe, Zambezi has a lot to offer in its own right. Paula and I were thrilled when our guide provided us with the opportunity to get out of the safari vehicle and take pictures standing a few feet from zebra. Our guides at Chobe National Park and Camp Kuzuma never allowed us to get out of the vehicle possibly rightfully so, so this was a plus in our mind. We were cruising the park in the afternoon hours, which we were informed was a pretty slow time of day for animals in this specific area with the exception of the black rhino, which was relatively active at this time. I found this to be another big positive for Zambezi National Park. We had the entire park to ourselves, as we did not come across a single other vehicle during our drive. While I would not classify Chobe National Park as being overcrowded, there were a fair amount of other safari vehicles in the area at most locations we were visiting.

After searching the park for roughly an hour and a half, something very special happened. Sitting right there in the middle of the path in front of us was a female black rhino along with her calf. I was happy with the view of this otherworldly sight from where we were, but our fearless guide literally drove us within feet of the pair. If you do not know anything about the black rhino, it has a reputation for having a short temper and they have been known to be dangerous to humans. A quick YouTube search reveals a highlight reel of clips showing angry black rhinos ramming safari vehicles at up to 30 miles per hour! Part of this is attributable to their extremely poor vision, which is said to be so bad that they can't distinguish a human and a tree at less than a hundred feet away, making it likely the animal with the worst vision on earth. None of this is reassuring information for the series of events that developed over the next few minutes. Sitting a matter of feet from the ill-tempered animals, Paula and I snapped pictures and simply could not believe what we were seeing. The feeling of exuberance and admiration turned to fear and hesitation as I could sense that the mother was beginning to get uncomfortable with our presence, which she was able to smell. The mother started to make grunting noises and walked over toward our vehicle. I signaled for Paula to get on my side of the vehicle, but she was simply frozen with shock as the adult female rhino was now sticking its head inside the vehicle in the row directly behind where we were seated! At this point, we realized that our guide was indeed crazy, as he was telling us to keep taking pictures and videos as the rhino was rocking our vehicle! Fortunately, Paula and I lived to see another day after this incredible series of events. As we pulled away, our guide was hysterical with laughter. We stopped a short distance ahead at a clearing, and he was high-fiving us and ecstatic with joy, which made me think more than ever that what he had just done was a large gamble that had fortunately paid off. The three of us rejoiced with a round of beers right there in the middle of Zambezi National Park all by ourselves. I will likely not have too many events as wild as this for the rest of my life, as this was undoubtedly the highlight of the trip in terms of thrill factor.

The Republic of Zimbabwe is bordered by South Africa to the south, Botswana to the west, Zambia to the northwest, and Mozambique to the east. As of 2017, Zimbabwe had a population of 14.2 million people. The eastern portion of the country is mountainous and 20% of Zimbabwe is made up of what is described as low altitude areas. Zimbabwe is also home to Victoria Falls, which lies on the border with Zambia in the northeastern part of the country where the Zambezi River lies. Zimbabwe's climate is defined as tropical, although this varies throughout the country. The rainy season runs from November to March.

Zimbabwe is still a relatively new country only gaining independence in 1980, making it the last of the United Kingdom's African colonies to do so. Despite the ceasefire that Britain helped negotiate in 1979, the country has suffered from violence and unrest ever since the peace agreement was reached.

Economy

The government of Zimbabwe is classified as a republic with a presidential system. Regardless of how the government is technically defined, it doesn't require much research to come to the conclusion that Zimbabwe is ruled by a dictator who has, unfortunately, run the country into the ground. Walk into any hotel or restaurant establishment in the country and you will be reminded of this with what must amount to be a mandatory picture of President Robert Mugabe. Elections in recent years have been widely criticized for vote-rigging, intimidation, and fraud. A period of currency instability began in the late 1990s after the government began confiscating private farmers from landowners. Once known by locals as being the "breadbasket" of Africa that provided food for the continent, farmers have fled to Zambia (and even Botswana), which has taken advantage of the dismal economic state of Zimbabwe. Zimbabwe has suffered from hyperinflation that peaked in 2008 at an estimated 79.6 billion percent! The country stopped printing its own currency in 2009 and in mid-2015 declared that they were to completely switch to the United States dollar. The Zimbabwean dollar remains largely worthless today and more recently issued bank notes have proved insufficient.

The largest industries in Zimbabwe are mining, agriculture, and services. While mining conditions remain extremely dangerous, the sector is important to the local economy. Zimbabwe has one of the world's largest platinum reserves along with relatively recent diamond field findings that could help the economy if governed properly. Unfortunately, much like the rest of Zimbabwe, large swaths of profits from the diamond fields have gone to corrupt politicians (see the 2012 reports regarding an alleged $2 billion government theft from Zimbabwe's eastern diamond fields) and army officers responsible for the area. Additionally, the indigenization law was passed in 2007 which states that foreign firms operating in Zimbabwe must sell a 51% stake of their business to local partners, which discourages outside investment in the mining sector.

While agriculture is still an important part of the local economy, the dismal economic policies instilled by the government have turned Zimbabwe into a net importer for food products. An example of how far this sector has fallen is illustrated by the annual wheat output which plunged from 250,000 tons in 2000 to 60,000 tons in 2016. If the country has any hope of turning the fortunes of this fallen industry around, it must incentivize farmers to return to the country with generous tax policies and guarantees that they will keep their hard-earned profits without any government intervention. Until this happens, expect more of the same for Zimbabwean agriculture.

Much like the state of the agriculture industry, local tourism has been plagued in recent years by economic instability. Tourist arrivals reached an all-time high in 2007 with over 2.5 million arrivals which fell to below 1.8 million by 2012. The industry has rebounded since 2012 and appears to be back on the right track. Despite all of the issues that Zimbabwe faces, they are fortunate to have some incredible natural wonders that no government policies can ruin. Victoria Falls has been designated as one of the Seven Natural Wonders of the World and is often debated along with Iguazu Falls in Argentina as the most beautiful waterfall on earth. Victoria Falls is the waterfall with the most water flowing over it in the world with an estimated 550 million liters of water plunging into the depths of the Zambezi River every minute! Adventure tourists can experience an array of activities at Victoria Falls ranging from a helicopter tour over the beautiful area to whitewater rafting and bungy jumping just to name a few. I will go into more detail regarding the whitewater rafting on the Zambezi River later, but it is regularly heralded as the "wildest one-day whitewater run in the world" attracting thrill seekers from all over. There are various wildlife and game reserves in Zimbabwe as well with Hwange National Park being the largest in the country.

While data is pretty limited in regard to the Zimbabwean workforce, some estimate that the 2017 unemployment rate is as high as 95%! Estimates have the country pegged at $600 to $700 a year per capita GDP. To get a sense of how poor this is, England would have been in a better economic state at the start of the Industrial Revolution in the late 1700s. In addition to the previously described issues regarding the agricultural, mining, and tourism sectors, the dangerous state of the country's roadways continue to kill citizens at a high rate along with a catastrophic state of the hospitals which plagues many other countries in Africa. Companies have continued to flee the country in search of a more business friendly environment. As far as I am concerned, every business class should study the spectacular downfall of Zimbabwe to know what not to do when running a country.

According to the 2017 World Bank report regarding ease of doing business, Zimbabwe ranked 161 out of 190 countries which isn't particularly surprising given the dramatic downfall the country has experienced. It costs men and women an estimated 119% of income per capita to start a business in the country compared to the Sub-Saharan African average of 54%. It takes men and women an average of 91 days to open a business (as of 2016) compared to an average of 27 days for the region. If the Zimbabwean government wants to bring companies back to the country, they can start with making it easier to set up a company. Again, the government must also instill confidence that they will not confiscate the productive assets from people who are producing real output for the country much like they did with the agricultural sector. Until this happens, I do not see why any rational individual would be investing in Zimbabwe.

The Zimbabwean government has admitted in recent years that the education system is in crisis. Despite these statements, Zimbabwe has actually maintained one of the highest literacy rates in Africa which some believe to be at least partially attributable to the education policy dating back to the 1980s that guarantees free primary school education to all citizens. Locals are concerned that new sweeping changes to the education system threaten a small bright spot in the country that hasn't had much to cheer about in the last decade.

Zimbabwe has faced worldwide scrutiny over their hunting policies since Cecil the lion was legally killed in 2015 (and, more recently, Cecil's son was killed by a hunter in 2017) by an American recreational big-game hunter. To partake in a legal hunting expedition in Zimbabwe with a guide, the price runs around $1,500 per day in addition to 2017 trophy fees such as $12,000 for an elephant and a whopping $35,000 for a lion! Illegal and frowned upon in countries such as Botswana, Zimbabwe can't seem to resist the high fees charged for this "sport." While there has been a renewed emphasis on cracking down on poachers within the country, this has been a major issue for Zimbabwe in recent years. The problem has been so bad that wildlife authorities began to dehorn rhinos in 2016 to curb the rampant poaching.

Adventure

We left Camp Kuzuma and started our expedition to Zimbabwe by road which was only about 45 minutes to the border and an additional 45 minutes once inside the country. In conducting research prior to the trip as to how I could acquire a joint Zimbabwe and Zambia visa online, I found that this was not possible which made me uneasy. I had read various horror stories online about individuals reaching the Zimbabwe border and being forced to pay excessive bribes to enter the country with no alternative. The simple fact that there is no option for online visa purchase makes the opportunity for corruption all the more probable. Additionally, I found it interesting that there were different prices for citizens from various countries to enter. For example, a U.S. citizen wishing to purchase a joint visa was quoted at $45 compared to a Chinese citizen, who would have to pay $90. I would highly recommend using a tour guide to get across the border, as our guide knew the immigration officer and likely saved us from any potential absurd bribes and expedited the process. Despite the fact that the paper clearly stated that the 2017 rates for a joint visa were $45, I was happy to pay $50 each and be on our way.

Once across the border, we had to stop on a couple occasions to wait as elephants crossed the road. I am not sure how anyone ever gets used to seeing this on a regular basis. We continued on our way until we arrived at Batonka Guest Lodge. Unlike our previous locations, Batonka had what appeared to be an electric fence sitting atop the gated wall enclosing the hotel in addition to a security guard who was present 24 hours a day. This was likely necessary given the extreme financial difficulties that the country is facing.

That evening we enjoyed a dinner at the famed Lookout Café, which provides spectacular views of the Zambezi River. We had scheduled in advance to eat here for dinner, as it was the night of a full moon and this restaurant is only open evenings when a full moon is present. I would recommend making arrangements in advance if this is of interest. Paula and I, ever so exhausted from our relentless pace of exploration, toasted as we glanced over the railing at the beautiful river that lie below with the bright moon shining down on us.

The following day we again arose early, as we were scheduled to visit Victoria Falls with our guide. If you are considering pairing a Victoria Falls adventure along with a visit to Botswana, I would recommend going in the June to August timeframe as we did. This allows for prime game viewing in

Botswana paired with plenty of water running over the falls. If you are solely interested in visiting Victoria Falls, then it is advised that a visit take place between February and June, which is when the water is flowing at its greatest volume. I would still personally recommend the June to August timeframe for Victoria Falls, as this is winter in Zimbabwe and provided for what I would consider to be excellent weather conditions with daily temperatures mostly in the 70s and sunny every day. Additionally, the low water season from the end of July or August to December is more optimal for most considering the whitewater rafting.

Paula and I grabbed our ponchos and headed to Victoria Falls. This location is nothing short of spectacular, and I would strongly recommend a visit even if you do tend to avoid areas with higher tourist volumes. We walked around the area for what amounted to be a couple hours taking in the views. Visiting several marked lookout points along the way, we put our ponchos on for about the last five areas, as water came raining down upon us at times. We were fortunate to get some magnificent pictures on this beautiful day.

We then transitioned via bus to a small local village in Zimbabwe. This was probably the only unpleasant part of the entire trip excluding our night-time scare in Botswana. As we were introduced to an older man who looked worn down and tired, he started to speak to Paula and me regarding life in the rural villages of Zimbabwe. Interestingly enough, he started preaching about how great life was here and how we were "slaves" to our political system in the United States. The man went as far as personally insulting my profession when I told him that I was an investment advisor. Not having any of this, particularly considering that I paid for the experience, I informed him of my issues with his statements and basically why I did not agree and reasons for why he was ill-informed on many of the topics he was addressing. Despite the fact that he largely had no clue as to what he was talking about, he did provide me with some valuable insight into the Zimbabwe culture during our conversation that turned increasingly heated at times. He told us that the rural villages in the country do not pay tax to the government and are completely self-sufficient, which I found interesting. Even more intriguing to me was the fact that these rural villages obtain the equivalent of small business loans that are lent to a group of individuals located in villages such as this. I was in disbelief, as I could not fathom any bank lending money to such an operation especially considering that I could not see what possible collateral could be repossessed in the event that payments were not made on the loan. He said that the bank takes livestock as a form of collateral in the event of a default. Could you imagine Bank of America being in the business of repossessing cows and going on to find a market for these animals?! I didn't think this could possibly be true but sure enough after some online research I did come across articles citing banks such as TN Bank that discussed accepting cattle as collateral for loans.

We walked around the village for a short period of time which was an eye-opening experience. The houses that we were looking at cost a total of $19 to build. They were made of clay and ran on solar power. While our conversation with the man at this village was not pleasant at times, I would still recommend visiting a local village in Zimbabwe or Zambia if nothing else but to provide some context on the state of the world in certain areas.

Our guide proceeded to drive Paula and me to a local Zimbabwean woman's house for lunch. Here we were provided with a full spread of local food which even included more adventurous options such as fried caterpillar. A little hesitant at first, we bit into the crunchy caterpillar that we found to have little taste. The rest of the meal was delicious, as we spoke with the overly kind host. Again, this was a truly grounding experience, as this lady by relative Zimbabwean standards was probably well off but by most American standards was extremely poor. She told us that most families that she knew of had seven to nine children so that they can take various roles within the family. This is in direct contrast to most developed countries, where families have been shrinking over the years due to increasing costs in areas such as higher education.

The last stop on our extremely busy day was to a local reserve that allowed us the opportunity to ride elephants. Paula was very eager to climb onto one of these precious animals and ride out into the sunset. We climbed aboard our new large friends and took a tour of the gated park for the next 45 minutes. What I found to be most incredible about the entire experience was the sheer volume of food that the elephants consumed while we were on the trek. My elephant constantly roped in branches with its trunk along the way. It is estimated that adult elephants consume between 200 and 600 pounds of food a day and feed for an astounding 12 to 18 hours per day! We came across animals such as buffalo and a crocodile along the trek. Everywhere you turn in Botswana and Zimbabwe, you are bound to come across some form of animal. The ethics of elephant-back safaris have been widely debated in recent years. Some animal rights activists argue that the animals should be free to roam in their natural environments, but I do not see how this is any different than being contained in a national park. I do hope that these companies treat the elephants well. I can say that I did not see any visible distress among any of the beautiful creatures that accommodated us on our short journey.

The following day, I arose to what may have amounted to my most anticipated part of our entire trip: whitewater rafting on the feared Zambezi River. Google searches in regard to this activity will reveal various recounts of near-death experiences and a lot of caution in addition to what I would consider to be tall tales about hippos and massive crocodiles roaming the rapids. Let me briefly dissect what I would consider to be fact from fiction. Rafting on the Zambezi is undoubtedly a dangerous activity in which individuals have lost their lives in attempting to navigate some of the treacherous Grade V rapids present at this location. However, the river is deep in most parts where the rafting takes place, which lessens the chance of an individual crashing into a rock during the excursion. Additionally, adult crocodiles die as they fall over the waterfalls, so there will not be any large crocodiles where the rafting takes place (it is possible that there could be some smaller crocodiles). Hippos really can't swim, so there is virtually zero chance that they will be roaming around anywhere near the rapids. We did not encounter any crocodiles or hippos along our journey. This is in stark contrast with the Upper

Zambezi where the canoeing takes place which is infested with crocodiles and hippos. I will take my chances on the Grade V rapids!

Any nervousness that Paula and I shared going into the day was immediately washed away upon hitting the first rapid. With my adrenaline pumping ever so hard, we proceeded to launch into and over the surrounding rapids over the course of the next couple hours. The highlight of the day came when we approached two consecutive rapids called The Terminator 1 and The Terminator 2. I briefly looked ahead, as the two boats in front of us who were also bravely charging ahead into what appeared to be oblivion had already flipped over. Increasing my focus and being responsible for the pace given my position at the front, I paddled aggressively as we were barreling headlong into what seemed like the wave from the movie *The Perfect Storm* crashing down on all sides. Unbelievably, we somehow remained upright despite the fact that the water had thoroughly obliterated us from every angle. I attribute this to our very experienced guide who was the best I have had in my various whitewater adventures over the years. Toward the end of the rafting, our guide did inform us that he had been on trips where individuals had lost their lives rafting the Zambezi. This is a cautionary tale for anyone considering this adventure activity. While my prior experience rafting over the highest available commercial waterfall in the world on the Kaituna River in New Zealand was memorable, nothing tops the Zambezi River. It lived up to the hype of being the greatest rafting experience on earth and was likely our favorite overall experience of the trip. If you are an experienced rafter, I would strongly recommend conducting extensive research prior to the trip, as some of the river is not open at certain times of the year due to varying water levels. We were unable to raft the full set of rapids because of the low water levels.

Just as you would expect the adventure to be ending, it is just beginning in the minds of some as the rafting part of the excursion is completed. I was well versed on this, as I had done considerable research prior to the trip on the rafting as well as the notorious hike out of the gorge after the rafting was complete. Be warned that the hike is difficult and there is no way around this. Over the course of the next 45 minutes, we climbed up the steep hill that was very uneven along the way. At certain points, Paula and I had to crawl and also had to climb up unstable "ladders" that actually consisted of a couple tree branches strung together by a piece of rope. I would consider this to be the most dangerous part of the day, as we were already exhausted from being barreled into by waves for the preceding two hours. For this leg of the adventure, I was grateful that we were there during the winter. I would have not wanted to do this during the summer months when temperatures are much warmer. While we were tired and out of breath upon reaching the top of the gorge, there was a sense of accomplishment in the air as we looked down over the Zambezi River. This excursion is not for the lighthearted but for those who dare to test the boundaries of what you may believe is possible, great potential rewards lie ahead.

That afternoon we took a helicopter tour over Victoria Falls. I believe the view from the helicopter provides the most stunning images of the falls. If you are interested in this activity be prepared to pay up, as a 12-minute helicopter ride runs around $150. There are longer and more expensive helicopter options, but I believe that this short option was perfectly sufficient, as we were able to capture prime views of one of the Seven Natural Wonders of the World from overhead with pictures that would make anyone salivate.

Additional Activities and Recommendations

Unsurprisingly, Victoria Falls is by far the most popular tourist attraction in Zimbabwe. I went into great detail regarding the whitewater rafting at the falls, but there is an array of other adventure sports available. Have the urge to try bungy? Victoria Falls Bridge offers bungy jumping allowing for individuals to plunge 365 feet over the Zambezi River. Surely this option is reserved for only the most adventurous. Along with the bungy, there are an array of high-altitude activities over the Zambezi River. This includes the gorge swing and zip-line. The gorge swing is the more extreme of the two, being at a higher elevation and the fact that you plummet 230 feet in the form of a free fall before arching back up toward the gorge. This is another activity reserved for only the most adventurous and those who are not bothered by heights. There are also intriguing prospects such as Devil's Pool, where thrill seekers can swim to the edge of the falls from the Zambian side. When water levels drop, the natural rock walls of the Devil's Pool form a barrier that allegedly prevents swimmers from being carried over the waterfall. The online pictures and videos of this activity appear surreal, as it looks like the people should be swept over the waterfall any second. Keep in mind that this is a high-risk activity and is expensive for the relatively short duration. If doing the Devil's Pool excursion is a high priority, make sure to time the visit when the pool is open, as water levels need to be appropriate.

Hwange National Park is located about 124 miles south of Victoria Falls and day and overnight trips are offered to the largest natural reserve in Zimbabwe. Located close to the Kalahari Desert, Hwange is home to more than both 100 mammal species and 400 types of birds. Other popular destinations include Mana Pools National Park, The Great Zimbabwe Ruins, and Chimanimani Mountains.

There are various canoeing options in Zimbabwe. You will have the opportunity to get up close and personal with animals such as hippos, crocodiles, elephants, etc. It is highly recommended to take great caution if you are considering this activity. Many areas of the Zambezi River (outside of those with rapids) are infested with crocodiles and hippos, which can make this activity dangerous. Conduct research regarding the best time of year for the various multiday options. I prefer the winter months due to the high-quality rafting conditions, best time of year to see most of the animals for the safari options, along with prime viewing of Victoria Falls.

Business Outlook

If Zimbabwe could ever get its act together, I again think there is potential opportunity for a well-respected low-cost global carrier such as Ryanair. Air Zimbabwe was recently barred from Europe in March 2017 after failing to address safety deficiencies detected by the European Safety Agency operator audits. Victoria Falls will always be a tourist attraction, and the industry would be significantly boosted if the government could instill any form of economic confidence or stability.

Given the currency issues that Zimbabwe has faced in recent years, there is a massive opportunity in dollar alternatives. Companies such as EcoCash have tried to take advantage of this environment by "providing an alternative medium of exchange from physical dollars." There is such a high demand for dollar alternatives in Zimbabwe that Bitcoin was trading at nearly double the price in Zimbabwe as the United States in 2017! Digital currencies likely will be a hot topic in the country over the coming years as locals look for additional ways to resolve the ongoing currency crisis.

The rise in hunger in the country has set the stage for an interesting ongoing battle. One would think that there is substantial opportunity for entrepreneurs looking to capitalize on products that increase food efficiency such as fertilizer and certain GMO products that have not been proven to cause any harm to health. Zimbabwe continues to place bans on many GMO products despite the fact that many citizens are starting to die. As with the 2016 *Wall Street Journal* op–ed titled "We May Starve, but At Least We'll Be GMO-Free," I do not see how the government can continue to enact such policies. Regardless of the governmental ineptitude in this area, there is still opportunity for creative farm efficiency products that can assist with the rising hunger issue in Zimbabwe.

Zimbabwe will remain uninvestable until the authoritarian regime decides that it wants to reverse policies instituted in recent years and run the country for the good of the citizens. The road to recovery must start with protecting individual's rights and productive assets by allowing them to keep their hard-earned profits in the mining and agricultural sectors. Substantial investments must be made in infrastructure and healthcare as well.

Updates Since Visit

Despite the geopolitical issues, the Zimbabwean economy is projected to expand 4.2% in 2019 and 4.4% in 2020. I will again touch on some of the long-term issues that the country faces but wanted to highlight a few economic tailwinds. The agricultural and mining sectors are expected to be the main drivers of economic growth at least in the short-term. While most of the youthful population remains unemployed, Zimbabwe does have one of the youngest populations on the planet, with ages 15-34 accounting for more than 36% of the total. Disastrous government policies have helped keep many of these individuals out of work, but if these economic policies can ever be addressed, the young, cheap labor pool provides for potentially robust macroeconomic upside. The potential regarding the youthful population is only compounded by the fact that Zimbabwe has maintained one of the best education rankings in Africa despite the ongoing political turmoil. The challenge is just creating a constructive environment for these young, relatively skilled individuals to maintain a career.

Former Zimbabwean president and strongman Robert Mugabe ruled the country for nearly 40 years until he was ousted by a coup in 2017. Many in Zimbabwe hailed the development, as Emmerson Mnangagwa at least brought hope to a country that was in desperate need of a change. Unfortunately, Mnangagwa's skeptics have had many of their fears come to fruition. In 2018, inflation in Zimbabwe hit its highest rate since 2008, and inflation has continued to be a major problem. This prompted another new currency called the RTGS dollar, which has a "fixed exchange rate 1:1 parity policy on the surrogate bond note currency" (the other failed local currency) and the U.S. dollar. Only time will tell whether this latest currency is successful, but this move will likely follow the path of the other unsuccessful currencies if the government does not provide adequate foreign currency reserves to maintain the value of the RTGS dollar along with having a sustainable pipeline of foreign direct investment and line of credit. I think we are a long way off from most sensible foreign countries allocating huge dollar sums to Zimbabwean investment.

Riots in Zimbabwe erupted in early 2019 when Mnangagwa announced that the government would more than double gasoline prices. After the protests turned violent, police and soldiers beat civilians, shot and killed 12 people, and detained at least 600 individuals. The government called the protests and unrest "terrorism," and social media avenues were temporarily blocked. These are dark signs for a country hoping that democracy would be restored or at least improved after the dramatic fall of Mugabe.

Following the global outbreak of COVID-19, a local Zimbabwean economist had this to say: "I can say with certainty that Zimbabwe will fail to come out of this Covid-effected recession with a functional economy. It was already dead before this pandemic. Many companies will certainly fail to come back. We had our own fair share of troubles before this. What guarantee do we have that we will come out of this and recover?"

As I had written before, Zimbabwe was a disaster heading into this crisis and it will be extremely challenging for the country to recover. It is reported that food shortages are impacting over half the population of Zimbabwe. This is attributable to the catastrophic policies related to farm ownership that I previously discussed that have only been compounded by issues such as the disallowance of GMO-related products which was also talked about earlier in the chapter. The government has taken notice and belatedly enacted some welcome reforms that I screamed for. In a bid to avoid a nationwide famine, Zimbabwe lifted a ban on genetically modified corn imports in early 2020. This policy does not go nearly far enough, but it is a step in the right direction. Additionally, the government is allegedly reversing the devastating farming land reforms that I documented in what is surely a bid to incentivize locals to grow more food to help mitigate this ongoing crisis. It is infuriating to me that measures such as this are only being enacted after a crisis of this scale. Countless lives in Zimbabwe will be lost that could have otherwise been avoided if sensible policies were put in place earlier.

Benefit of Zimbabwe safaris: close proximity to the animals

Picture taken right before the rhino rocked our vehicle!

Time to ride the elephants

Rafting the notorious Zambezi River

Victoria Falls

Chile

Introduction

I awoke to a pleasant surprise: The rain had finally ceased, and visibility was good after the mostly atrocious conditions we endured the previous two days. I started taking pictures of the EcoCamp grounds in case the clouds rolled in and the early morning conditions were just a teaser. Fortunately for us, the conditions for the most difficult and rewarding trek of the trip were much more favorable than the other days. The 16-mile hike up to the Torres (or "the towers" as which they are commonly referred) was grueling by even the most advanced trekker's standards. A woman in our group had completed 87 marathons and was open to admit that this hike was a challenge.

On the way up to the top, we stopped at various points to take pictures as the scenery was possibly the most impressive I have ever seen. One could see two enormous snow-covered mountains separated by a river running through the middle. What makes the pictures here so amazing is the sheer vastness of everything that surrounds you. A person looks like a tiny blip, as they are engulfed by a sea of beautiful snowy mountains and green trees.

The real challenge of the hike comes near the top, where hikers literally have to get on their knees to crawl at times due to the perilous conditions. By the time we had reached the final ascent, snow had begun to rain down on us, as we had gained quite a bit of altitude since our initial starting point. The hiking path was but only a few feet wide at this point, and it became crowded as anxious trekkers were now pushing to get to the top in anticipation of one of the best views in the entire world. I would be lying if I said I was not

219

scared at this point, as I looked six inches to my right and there was a drop of several thousand feet without a railing, and I unfortunately did not have the luxury of having a hiking pole. These factors combined with the sudden pushing that occurred along with the snow that had made the terrain incredibly slippery set up what could have been a nightmare scenario. Fortunately for us, the group came together led by our amazing guide and we willed our way to the top of the mountain.

There it was. The image that is as synonymous with Patagonia as the Lakers are to Los Angeles. My breath was taken away by the cold beauty, as the fresh snow from the day and the previous evening made the sight all the more spectacular. The entire set of mountains was visible which had been extremely rare in recent days after talking to others along the way. We took several pictures in front of the lake with snow covered "towers" looming in the background. Little did my Instagram followers know that I had climbed 7.5 miles uphill through the snow and at times was crawling on the edge of a several thousand-foot cliff to get here. The challenges that we endured over the course of the three days to get to this point made the experience all the more memorable.

I had injured my knee at some point along the way during the hike the previous day, but it did not become overly taxing until our descent from "the towers," which is even more challenging at times than the way up, especially near the top. For the latter half of the trip down, it felt as though someone was repeatedly stabbing me in the knee with a razor-sharp knife. I was doing everything I could to not draw attention to myself since I have been known to be stubborn about things such as this, but the pain simply became too great to hide. I let out a howl of pain, and the group stopped for a few moments. Fortunately for me, there was a doctor in my group and she wrapped my leg with a brace that helped ease the pain. I borrowed a hiking pole from another group member, and we were again on our way. Finishing the 16 miles that day under those conditions was a life achievement and didn't come easy, but I had told my group along the way that I would have to suffer two broken legs in order for me not to finish the total 30 miles that were covered over the course of the three days. I kept my word and we had a nice celebration that evening back at EcoCamp.

I departed for Chile on March 9, 2018. Websites such as Lonely Planet highlighted Chile as their top travel destination for 2018 because of the diversity of the activities available within the country ranging from the Atacama Desert, the driest location on earth with an average of less than one inch of rain per year, in the north to the Patagonia region in the southern part of the country. Despite the attention on sites such as Lonely Planet, I think Chile's tourism is still significantly underpenetrated relative to the offerings in the country. I opted to visit Chile in March because this was off-peak season for Patagonia, which provided lower pricing as well as more manageable crowds along the trails along with what is usually relatively decent weather. I was also enthralled by the idea of seeing snow on the mountaintops, which is not often possible during the peak summer travel months of December to February. In March the average temperatures in Torres del Paine National Park are usually in the 40s (Fahrenheit) and 50s with Santiago seeing daytime temperatures reach the 80s (although the temperature here has a wide daily range). I haven't visited the country during their summer months, but if I were to do it over again, I would still visit in March despite a challenging two days we faced while in Patagonia. The opportunity to see all but several hundred fellow trekkers out on the Patagonia hiking trails over the course of some days is too much to pass up.

Chile is a long and narrow nation geographically which stretches over 2,670 miles north to south, making it the longest country in the world, but only 217 miles at its widest point east to west with a coastline spanning over 4,000 miles. The strange shape of the country provides for a variety of climates and landscapes for the country, which is bordered by Peru, Bolivia, and Argentina. About 80% of Chile is covered in mountains, which is one of the big reasons that 2.17% of Chile's land is considered arable. As of 2018, Chile had a population of 18.7 million, which ranks the country 65th in the world. A whopping 90% of people in the country live in urban areas, with capital city Santiago's metropolitan area housing over seven million people which comes out to roughly 40% of the country population.

Chile is one of the most earthquake prone countries on earth and lays claim to the largest earthquake ever recorded, which measured 9.5 on the Richter scale in 1960. One of my tour guides informed me that they get a magnitude 4 earthquake every few months and they are accustomed to the natural disasters. The country has strict building requirements, which are aimed at limiting earthquake damage because of the extreme risk present.

Chile's government is a representative democratic republic where the president is both head of state and head of government. 2005 was a historic year for the Chilean democracy, as President Ricardo Lagos signed into law several constitutional amendments passed by Congress. These amendments included eliminating the positions of appointed senators and senators for life, granting the president authority to remove the commanders-in-chief of the armed forces, and reducing the presidential term from six to four years while removing the option for immediate re-election. I found the last point interesting, as I could not imagine a United States president going from office to being a regular citizen and then deciding that they want to lead the country again after experiencing the significantly less stress involved with not being depended on to make a nation's most critical decisions.

Research suggests that Native Americans inhabited what is modern-day Chile 10,000 years ago. Ferdinand Magellan discovered the southern passage, which is now called the Strait of Magellan and which made him the first European to set foot on what is now Chile. The Incas briefly conquered northern Chile in the 1400s, but they were then overtaken by the Spanish in 1533. The Napoleonic Wars raged during the early 1800s and ultimately led to the formal independence of Chile in 1818. Despite formal independence from Spain, the next 70 years saw authoritarian regimes, wars, and recessions. Toward the turn of the 19th century, the Chilean presidential powers were reduced, but there was a constant power struggle in the country until 2005 when the executive powers were substantially reduced.

An interesting oddball fact about Chile is that it was the last country in the Western Hemisphere to recognize divorce when it did so in 2004. Chile still has one of the lowest divorce rates globally.

Economy

Chile has been one of the fastest growing Latin American economies in recent decades, which has enabled the country to significantly reduce poverty. The World Bank provides an example that supports this claim, noting that "between 2000 and 2015 the population living in poverty, defined as $4 per day, declined from 26% to 7.9%." Despite this dramatic improvement and what one would have to consider to be the best-performing and most stable economy in South America as reflected by the strongest sovereign bond rating in South America and highest GDP per capita in the region, GDP growth plummeted in 2016 to 1.6% which was largely attributable to declining copper prices. Copper accounts for roughly 50% of the country's exports, making it the largest copper exporter globally and 20% of the government's revenue. So, despite the focus on economic diversification, the country's economic success will still fluctuate with the price of the precious metal. The rebound in copper prices since the 2016 lows has seen a recovery in private investment within the country, which should continue if the price remains on its current trajectory.

Despite the 2018 trend against free trade and towards protectionism, Chile has been a strong champion of free trade. In May 2010, Chile signed the OECD Convention, becoming the first South American country to join the OECD. In October 2015, Chile signed the Trans-Pacific Partnership trade agreement. Chile is an export-driven economy in which roughly one-third of GDP comes from the export of goods and services, so it is in their best interest to support free trade. Other top Chilean exports include fish, fruit, and wine. Some may find it surprising that Chile's wine industry is still very much in its infancy, as the first wave of the country's boutique wineries only began to spring up toward the end of the 1990s as Chile started to embrace positive developments pertaining to government democracy. Chile is considered to be one of the new wine countries, like Australia and South Africa, that are now competing with old wine countries such as France, Spain, and Italy. Expect growth in this industry to continue, especially as more international travelers come to realize all of the potential that Chile has to offer in terms of a vacation destination.

Chile's economy is dominated by the industrial and service sectors, which account for almost 96% of GDP. Chile's main sectors are "mining (copper, coal and nitrate), manufactured products (food processing, chemicals, and wood) and agriculture (fishing, viticulture and fruit)."

The agricultural sector contributes 4.3% of the country's GDP, and the industrial sector accounts for 32.4% of overall GDP. The service sector has increased in importance and now contributes 64.4% of GDP. Roughly 10% of the population works in the agricultural sector, 22.7% in the industry sector and 68% in the service sector. Tourism in Chile is growing at a robust pace, and I think that they are just in the early innings of a tourism boom. In 2017, a record-setting 6.4 million people visited the country which represented a 14.3% increase over 2016. Like many other countries, Chile has been investing in renewable energy, which they aim to account for 20% of the country's total energy by 2020.

According to the 2018 Index of Economic Freedom, Chile had the 20th freest economy in the world and the highest regional ranking behind Canada and the United States. Chile remains among South America's least corrupt countries, and citizens have generally seen property rights and contracts protected by the government. The Chilean tax policies are pretty much on par with what you will find in the United States. What many admire about Chile has been their responsibility and management pertaining to public debt which was just 23.6% of GDP in 2017 compared to 106.23% in the United States. Despite the plunge in copper prices in 2016, they did not resort to excess federal borrowing to fill the void.

Despite the successes that Chile has had in reducing overall poverty levels, the country still had a huge inequality issue that the OECD says is the highest among member countries. Much of this inequality is attributable to the difference in education quality. Statistics have shown that the private schools that charge high enrollment fees have had higher test results than their public peers. After years of protests and complaints, the Chilean Congress passed landmark legislation in January 2018 to provide free higher education, which had been the case until 1981, aimed at reducing the income inequality.

While I was visiting Chile, in March 2018, there was a change in president of the country, as Sebastián Piñera, a billionaire entrepreneur, again took the reins. Piñera oversaw growth of 5.3% during his term from 2010–2014, which was aided by rising copper prices, pro-business policies, and a drastic rebuilding effort following a February 2010 magnitude 8.8 earthquake prior to taking office. Goals for this presidency have included lowering the corporate tax rate to stimulate economic growth, injection of money into the healthcare sector, a more restrictive immigration policy, and pension reform due to the increasing number of individuals over 65.

Expect to see Chile remain one of the star economies of the region over the coming years. Despite the issues that they have seen in regard to income inequality, the reality is that they have had a pro-business government for the most part since the change of government in 1990 and have not fallen victim to the level of corruption that other South American countries such as Brazil has seen. Having said that, Chile was overtaken by a military dictatorship in 1973, which remained in power for almost 17 years. This is a cautionary tale for any long-standing democracy.

Adventure

From the moment I stepped into Chile, it was immediately apparent that this country was on the right track in terms of tourism and overall business philosophy. I always think a quality initial indicator of the business climate of a country can be found at the airport. At the Santiago airport, I was impressed with how they moved people through the customs lines without sacrificing the integrity of the process. Another positive sign was that there was a drug-sniffing dog, which tells me that the country is serious about keeping narcotics out and thinking about the long-term health of the country as opposed to trying to make a quick dollar on illicit substances and corruption. I spent only a few minutes in Santiago on the way down, as I had to catch a connecting flight to the southern part of the country. The nonstop flight from New York to Santiago was 10.5 hours and then a little over three hours from Santiago to Punta Arenas.

Upon arrival in Punta Arenas, one does truly feel like they are at the end of the world. This town of around 125,800 individuals, according to 2012 Census data, looks like it could be found in Antarctica. It may surprise some to find out that a flight to Antarctica from this area is only about four hours, so calling it the "end of the world" as some have been known to do is not too far from the truth.

Punta Arenas is the capital city of Chile's southernmost region, Magallanes and Antarctica Chilena. Magallanes is Spanish for Magellan which is of course named after Ferdinand Magellan who sailed close to the current location of Punta Arenas in the year 1520. It is best known for being one of the entry points to the Patagonia national parks, which are about a five-hour drive from the city. Given that there is not a large airport in Puerto Natales, which is located about two hours outside of Torres del Paine National Park, the famous national park that attracts many visitors in the region, many fly to Punta Arenas and continue on from here. The other popular option is to enter via El Calafate in Argentina, which is also four to five hours from Torres del Paine.

There is not a whole lot to do in Punta Arenas, and most tourists, particularly those with a limited amount of time, land and drive straight to either Puerto Natales or Torres del Paine. Given my adventure interests, I opted to stay in the area for a half day to check out Magdalena Island, which is a small island in the Strait of Magellan and about a 45-minute boat ride from Punta Arenas and is home to thousands of Magellanic penguins until the end of March, when the penguins head north to seek food. In 1982, Magdalena Island and nearby Marta Island were declared a national monument: Los Pingüinos Natural Monument.

On the day we went to Magdalena Island, the water was not too rough, but we were informed that this is not always the case. After our 45-minute adventure via boat, we stepped out onto the small island. Everyone else on the boat immediately began taking pictures of the adorable little penguins, but my newfound friend, Rob, and I headed toward the lighthouse on the opposite end of the island. I would recommend this approach, as we avoided the crowds and were able to capture pictures without any other humans in the background. We took countless pictures of the penguins, some of which were just a few feet from us. There are ropes on the island that are supposed to separate the tourists from the penguins but that does little, as the penguins are perfectly capable of going under the ropes and people are able to reach under or over the ropes if they please. I thoroughly enjoyed watching the penguins walking around with their famously peculiar waddle and seeing some burrowed underground in the self-made holes they call home for a portion of the year. We spent about an hour on the island just walking around and enjoying the company of the penguins.

Given that the water was relatively calm on that particular day, we were able to proceed another ten minutes on our boat ride to find a colony of sea lions. While we couldn't get off the boat at this location like we did for the penguins, it was worthwhile to see the hundreds of female sea lions along with their children. We were informed that the males were out fishing and would return in the coming weeks with food for their families. It was entertaining to watch these creatures, some of whom were just playing around with each other and others who were clearly in a fierce battle over territory, food, or whatever else it may be that sea lions in the Strait of Magellan get angry about. I was fixated on a trio of sea lions that were battling it out, hitting each other violently with their upper bodies. Ultimately, the largest of the group prevailed and could take temporary pride in knowing that she was the queen of the area. The four-hour trip out to Magdalena Island is worth the $130 and recommended for individuals who have the time to spend a half day in the Punta Arenas area.

The five-hour drive from Punta Arenas to Torres del Paine starts along the coast, as you will initially see water on one side and mostly uninhabited flat plains on the other side with mountains in the distance. As you pass some farms along the way, the environment starts to transform into more of a hilly setting. As we started to near Puerto Natales, dark clouds were located over the mountaintops in the distance, giving the land somewhat of a mythical feeling. We saw more wildlife along the drive to Torres del Paine than we did during our hikes through the national park. Along the drive, I spotted flamingo, horses, cows, llamas, guanaco, sheep, various birds, foxes, and nandu. The Puerto Natalas area is much more scenic than Punta Arenas and the reason that many decide to proceed directly here following their arrival. Green hills can be found in the surrounding Puerto Natales area with large mountains looming in the distance complete with a lake at the front of the town and rock walls that are often used by the locals for climbing.

Most of the jobs in Puerto Natalas are related to tourism given its proximity to one of the most beautiful locations on the planet. To a lesser extent, there are fishing jobs in this area as well.

Anticipation starts to build as you are closing in on Torres del Paine. I thought that the scenery in the surrounding areas were somewhat similar to the South Island of New Zealand in that there were a lot of rolling green hills with majestic mountains that could be seen in the distance. By this point, it should already be clear to a visitor that some of the roads need to be repaired. There are areas where a driver must nearly come to a complete halt because the roadway had completely eroded to rock. The country will have to further invest in infrastructure pertaining to the southern part of the country in the coming years if it wants to continue to attract tourists. I think this requires a delicate balance with not commercializing the area too much, which would turn off a segment of hardcore hikers and adventurers. For example, if Chile decided to build a larger airport in Puerto Natales, it would attract more visitors to Torres del Paine because it would require only a two-hour drive from this area to reach the national park. The other side of this is that it could potentially lose some of its luster if the trails become too overcrowded, like what you have seen in places like Peru around the Machu Picchu area. Regardless of further potential commercial development pertaining to a new airport or increased lodging capacity within the national park (we were informed that they are currently working on developing a second EcoCamp), Chile will need to further invest in the roadways in the area.

Along our drive, something happened that brought out a stark cultural difference between Chile and the United States. An individual along the side of the road flagged us down, and my driver stopped to speak with him. They were lost and friendly, and my driver informed them of which direction they needed to go, and then we were again on our way. First and foremost, it is not often that someone in the United States would pull over to speak with a stranger out of fear in regard to personal safety. Secondly, why did this person not have navigation? Who in the United States that owns a car wouldn't have access to some form of navigation on their cellphone? I think this part of the equation pertains to the dismal cellular service that is found in the southern part of Chile. As I have discussed in other chapters and have identified as one of my mega trends in the upcoming years, Chile will have to aggressively invest in cellular infrastructure in locations outside of Santiago such as the Patagonia region if they want to take the country to the next level. Chile's 2017 smartphone penetration rate of 52% isn't strikingly low, but it also isn't excessively high for a relatively advanced economy, either. I would expect to see this number converge with the United States' 2017 rate of close to 70% in the coming years if the country invests further in areas outside of the major cities.

Upon arrival at Torres del Paine, it was a relief given the vast distance that I had covered to get here. Since I arrived in the evening, I could not yet appreciate the unbelievable location where I was. EcoCamp lies at the base of "the towers," which are the famous set of mountains that you will often find on Instagram with the Torres del Paine tag. EcoCamp was founded in 2001 by Cascada Expediciones and accommodates up to 80 guests and has 100 staff members on hand. Despite the remote location of the lodging, I never felt unsafe in the slightest bit as security appeared to be above average for a setting such as this. It didn't take long for me to experience what Chileans refer to as there being four seasons in one day in the Patagonia region. It was pouring, and this aggressive pace of rainfall would continue on and off for the ensuing two days.

Now it was time to meet the group of complete strangers I would be trekking with during the next three days. Having booked this trip with Adventure Life, as I had done with other trips such as Southern Africa and Belize and later to Southeast Asia, I was able to share accommodation at EcoCamp with another traveler to split the cost and was also provided a high-quality networking opportunity with like-minded individuals that I wouldn't have met otherwise. Our group of eight, along with our two guides, hailed from various locations across the United States and Canada. I struck an accord with my new friends and discussed traveling adventures, investing, and philanthropic opportunities over a delicious three-course meal that consisted of soup, conger (Chilean eel, which was tasty), and fruit assortment. Each meal at EcoCamp was a three-course meal, of which we had a few options—and none of them disappointed.

Regarding the philanthropy, I later joined the Board of Directors for CanEducate, which is a Canadian-based charity that supports schools in developing countries founded by two members of my Patagonia hiking group. In the chapter on India, you will read about my experience visiting a local school supported by CanEducate. In addition to learning about various cultures and economies firsthand, the global connections that I have made through my years of traveling has been the next largest benefit. It is amazing to think that I would go from hiking with a couple strangers in Patagonia to planning a school-funding project in Haiti with those same individuals in less than a year. I also went on to join the Board of ZERV Inc., an innovative

Canadian technology start-up, in partnership with Rishi and Dave whom I met in Patagonia.

I had arranged for a "standard dome" at EcoCamp, which meant that I did not have electricity or heat. There are more luxurious rooms to be found here, complete with electricity and heat, but travelers must be willing to pay a large premium which I think can be better spent on tours and activities. Despite wrapping myself in no less than six blankets at all times in the evening, I still found myself to be cold and had difficulty getting to sleep due to the incredibly high winds and rain that continued to slam at a relentless pace into the roof of the tent. Some in the group had no trouble at all sleeping at EcoCamp, but others slept very little while we were there.

The following day, I arose at 5:30 a.m. to prepare for our day-long trekking adventure to the French Valley. We had arranged to complete a short version of the world-renowned W Circuit, which is ranked in the top ten treks around the world on almost every list and some consider it to be the most beautiful trek bar none. The full W Circuit is a four to six-day trek, but I opted for the short version, as travelers often do, so that I would have time to do other activities and explore Santiago. The morning began with a two-hour car ride up a switchback mountain with steep cliffs with fog covering most of the area. Fortunately, the sun started to burn the fog off, and we were able to capture a couple pictures of the legendary mountain scenery in the park. We passed an area that had been ravaged by a fire, which, our guide informed us, happened in 2011, lasted for about a month, and resulted in more than 43,000 acres of land being destroyed. The Chilean government responded to this incident by banning all outdoor fires within Torres del Paine. This was just one of many measures that I learned about along my journey that the Chilean government does to protect the beautiful local national parks.

The wind was howling, and we encountered torrential rains as we took a 30-minute boat ride across the emerald looking water. The Patagonia weather of legend was living up to its word. Throughout the day, the weather would go from a downpour with heavy winds to sunny and calm within a matter of minutes.

Our determined group did not let what was at times the most appalling weather I have seen in my entire life ruin our trek through the French Valley that day. Winds gusted as high as 62 miles per hour at times and nearly blew some individuals over as sleet and freezing rain continued to pelt us head-on as we navigated the foothills. On the bright side, what my guide referred to as the worst weather she had ever seen in the month of March in Patagonia made for a better story later on. I accepted the weather for what it was and took in the surrounding beautiful lakes, rainbows hanging over them at various points because of the rapidly changing weather. The hike went up and down for several miles mostly through wet mud, which provided another unexpected challenge. We passed along various bridges along the way that were only made to handle one to two individuals at a time.

After trudging through the mud, sleet, and rain for several hours, we stopped to have our lunch in a clearing where other groups found to be suitable as well. As you will find throughout Torres del Paine, there are no trash cans anywhere in the park aside from at sporadic rest stations. The thinking is that this will hold visitors more accountable for the waste that they produce and make them bring the garbage back with them. Our guide informed us that heavy fines are instilled upon individuals who are found to violate the garbage laws, which was another sign of the Chilean government going to great lengths to protect that natural beauty in the Patagonia region and is why I am bullish on the tourism prospects for the region in the future.

Due to the mostly dismal weather conditions that day, we were unable to capture the best views of the surrounding mountains on our hike through the French Valley. That being said, on our return hike we did get lucky. As we were making our way back to our accommodation, the sun came out and lit up the lakes in the area that could now be seen with a miraculously beautiful light blue hue that was compared to that of Moraine Lake in Banff National Park in Alberta (which I could later confirm after visiting Moraine Lake myself). I took this as a gift from nature for enduring high winds, precipitation, and low visibility for the majority of our seven to eight-mile hike that day. This was the highlight of the day, and I made sure to take several pictures at what I thought could very well be the best weather conditions that we would experience for the duration of our stay in Torres del Paine.

That night, we stayed at Paine Grande Mountain Lodge, which housed roughly 100 trekkers who had come from all over the world to see the natural beauty that resided in Torres del Paine. Our group headed straight for the bar after our arduous but rewarding day in the French Valley, and we sat around for drinks and stories as we further bonded and met others at the camp. Our sleeping conditions that evening was pretty comical for a group of well-to-do adult travelers, as I slept in a room with six bunk beds that were shared with two couples and a 73 year-old man in my group. Surprisingly, I slept much better at Paine Grande than I did back at EcoCamp because we were actually indoors, and the temperature was much warmer. The rest of the group laughed, but I was sad to say goodbye the following morning.

The next day, we arose early again to set out for our hike to the Grey Glacier. I did not think that the weather from the previous day could possibly get any worse, but the second day took the cake. As we slogged through the mud on a trail that lies parallel to a lake that was home to several glaciers, sleet relentlessly pelted our group in the face with continuous high winds. Despite the array of challenges that nature had provided us along the way, I remained overly positive and took in the scenery, which was nothing short of otherworldly. We stopped at various points along the way to take pictures that could find the snowy mountaintops as a beautiful backdrop to the scenic lake area. Smaller light blue glaciers could be found in the lake, which provided additional appeal for photographic opportunities.

Despite the mostly abysmal weather conditions, I thought we once again got very lucky in that the rain came to a complete halt as we boarded the boat for our hour-long ride to get an up-close view of the three large glaciers in the area. This experience was nothing short of incredible, and the visibility was good enough with the clouds hanging over the mountains making the setting look mysterious in a way. This boat ride reminded me of Milford Sound in New Zealand, but I think that the glaciers here in Patagonia made the scenery all the more spectacular. I spent the next hour outside on the boat taking pictures of the various glaciers and miraculous snowcapped mountains in the background. Many opt to visit Patagonia in the summer, but I could not imagine this scenery without the snow, which I think adds to the appeal.

I touched down in Santiago around midnight. Much to my surprise, there was a ridiculous traffic jam getting out of the parking lot at the airport at this hour, which lasted about 30 minutes. As I would see over the coming days, traffic in Santiago would be a consistent theme and should be a central focus for the government in the coming years. It was a huge relief being able to get an actual quality night's sleep in an indoor hotel room that evening despite having to rise early the next morning.

The next morning, I again got an early start, this time for a wine tour of the famous Concha y Toro. I was gathered from my hotel by my tour guide, and we picked up a few others along the way. One pair of individuals that we picked up noted that they had booked all of their local activities through Viator, a TripAdvisor company that serves as an intermediary for tours and excursions, as they had done in various cities all over the world. They noted that their experience in Santiago in regard to tours was disappointing in that the local tour companies had not contacted them in advance of the tour to confirm details such as time of pick-up or even that the tour was to go on as scheduled. I had the exact same experience leading up to my tours in Santiago and the guide explained that the Santiago tourism industry really just started to develop in the past 15 years and is still in its infancy. I found this interesting given the plethora of available activities in the area such as top-notch wineries, skiing, hiking, rafting, and even beaches within a few hours distance. I took note, as this is an issue for Viator because they are ultimately responsible for facilitating a successful transaction since the match between the customer and tour company occurred on their platform (as is discussed in the excellent book *Modern Monopolies: What It Takes to Dominate the 21st Century Economy*).

We arrived at Concha y Toro, which is located about 45 minutes outside of Santiago. The winery was founded in 1883 and is the largest producer of wines in Latin America. Wineries such as Concha y Toro are located in the Maipo Valley region, which are home to some of the oldest Chilean wineries and are famous for their red wines as opposed to the thriving white wine industry in the Casablanca Valley area.

The morning weather was nothing short of perfect, as it was similar to what you would expect to find in San Diego. Our group proceeded to wander around the enormous winery grounds, which could fit a small city inside its acreage. Plants can be seen sprawling into the distance with mountains completing the scenic backdrop. We were lucky enough to be able to pick as many grapes from the vineyard as we wanted, which was a pleasant surprise. This wine tour was not your usual wine tour, as we took a look inside the indoor wine cellar, where we were briefly locked in to witness a short description of the legend of the devil located in the cellar, which was broadcast via projector in the dark. Our tour guide informed us that most of the wineries in the area tried to do something to differentiate themselves from the others, so one is to expect a different unique element at each Chilean winery. Everyone in the group left Concha y Toro thoroughly satisfied with the experience and the wine. I found the tour to be a bargain at $59, which included hotel pickup and wine during the tour.

Without more than a few minutes to spare after arriving back to my hotel, I set out for an afternoon tour of Santiago with another local tour guide. I was picked up by a driver who did not speak English, so he had a translator talk with me and show me around the city. For $27 for what turned out to be over a three-hour experience, I am still trying to figure out how this was a viable business model for the two individuals involved, given that the local tour company had to take a cut as well as Viator for arranging the booking.

Traffic that afternoon was about the worst I have ever seen, so we spent much of the time walking around on foot.

Despite the gridlock traffic and fairly consistent graffiti, I was pleasantly surprised by Santiago. It has a good amount of green spread throughout the city, unlike many others. The views atop some of the taller buildings provide a treat with the mountainous backdrop on the city outskirts providing for a picturesque view. One building stands out from the rest on the city skyline and that is the Gran Torre Santiago which sits at 984 feet, making it the tallest building in Latin America and the second tallest in the Southern hemisphere. My tour guide informed me that this physically imposing office building sits mostly unoccupied, as there have been constant battles over the years in regard to building permits. Upon conducting further research, it is not uncommon for developers to argue with government officials over the impact of real estate buildings and projects on areas of concern such as pollution and traffic. This is a huge red flag in terms of business competitiveness because what you will find is that nobody will develop real estate in the future if they know that it will just be a constant bureaucratic struggle in doing so.

The fine afternoon tour that highlighted various locations such as the business district as well as La Moneda, the presidential palace, also took a pit stop at a coffee shop called Café con Piernas. It didn't take long to realize that this was not an ordinary coffee shop, as the women were dressed in unusually revealing outfits that you would expect to find at a strip club instead of a coffee shop. Ironically, the majority of the individuals in attendance that day seemed to be higher-class businessman who were completely oblivious to the fact that they were being served by ladies that were wearing dresses so tight that they might rip if a false sudden movement occurred (I was later informed by my surfing tour guide that there are various locations that this coffee shop chain operates. Some of them are classier business locations, which I seem to have gone to, and others are actually brothels with a coffee shop as a front). After we consumed our espressos, we were on our way again.

I enjoyed speaking with my tour guide about a wide range of topics, the most interesting of which pertained to immigration. Chile, like many countries in Europe in recent years, has seen an influx of immigrants because the country comparatively has done much better economically than its neighbors. The country has left its borders open, but it will be interesting to see how this plays out across the world over the coming years. It is a serious problem with no good solution.

I had made a reservation several weeks in advance at a restaurant called 99 Restaurante, which was ranked as the #14 restaurant in Latin America in 2017 according to eater.com and surprisingly came at a value price (my six-course meal along with a local beer and tip came out to $75). I like to try at least one high-quality restaurant on each trip I go on and thought this was a good choice given the superior food, array of local food choices included in the six courses, and value given the stature of the restaurant.

The ambiance at 99 is soothing, as it has a relaxing outdoor garden-type setting and is intimate in that it probably seats only about 30 individual's total. Each dish here is brought out separately and thoughtfully decorated, just like you would expect at any high-end restaurant. The highlight for me were the razor clams and the raspberry cake, which were simply delicious. The stuffed red pepper dessert was an interesting choice and just showed the versatility of the menu at 99. I would strongly recommend this restaurant for anyone visiting Santiago who would like to experience the high-quality local seafood and desserts at a price that is not overly demanding. Not sure you can do any better for the combination than here.

The following morning, I was picked up by my tour company to head to the Maipo Valley to do some rafting. The drive to Maipo was around an hour and a half and was interesting because my driver spoke but only a few words of English. I found this to be consistent theme throughout Chile as well as other Spanish speaking countries that I have visited such as Spain. This is intriguing because in most other cultures it is much closer to being universal that English is a well-versed second or third language. I cobbled together the relatively limited Spanish sentences that I am comfortable with to hold some basic conversations along the way.

Going through the safety procedures and doing the actual rafting was a bit of a challenge, as I was the only member of the entire 30-person group that was English speaking. Fortunately for me, one of the guides did speak English and was kind enough to teach me the Spanish commands so that I could fit in with the group.

The rafting down the Maipo River that day was far from exhilarating (they list the rapids at a Class III at that time of year, but it is questionable if they are even at that level), but our group enjoyed the ride, and our guide did an excellent job keeping us engaged and making it even more fun along the way by having us jump in the water and stunts such as getting up and running around the raft as we were plowing through some of the rapids. Additionally, the hour-long ride through the valley provided for some high-quality views of a gorgeous area. The river is surrounded by the Andes Mountains on both sides.

I had told my driver that I wanted to be taken back to Santiago at 4:30 p.m. so I had some time to kill after the rafting excursion and thought it would be a good idea to try what they referred to as the canopy and zip-line tour. Not thinking too much of it, I was provided with a bit more adrenaline than anticipated. The first two lines went back and forth across the Maipo River and were probably at an altitude of somewhere in the 100-foot range over the water. The lengthy ride across the river was good fun, as I glided along the wire and spun around in midair, taking in the beautiful Andean scenery. The intensity picked up further on the final three ropes. To even get to the next set of lines, one has to climb up a steep ladder. Once the summit has been reached, the real excitement begins. I don't think I am exaggerating when I say that I think one of the lines reached 30 miles per hour along the way. Adventurers whip through the high trees in the area and then again across the Maipo River at around 82 feet in the air. As you are passing across the line at such as rapid pace, the eventual stop is sudden and does provide for some temporary pain but likely worth it in the end. This activity was far more exhilarating than the zip-line excursion that I did in Belize and is suitable for a quick activity for adventurers looking to get some high-wire exposure. Both the zip-line and rafting cost about $30, but the real trick is actually getting to the Maipo area. Reputable companies such as Cascada de Las Animas will charge about $150 for roundtrip transport from Santiago. I had initially negotiated a better deal with another company only to eventually decline given their inability to provide me with transportation and hesitancy as to the legitimacy of the company, not wanting a repeat of my Peruvian adventure where I went sandboarding with what I later discovered was an illegal company.

The following day, I arose and prepared for my day trip to surf along the coast. Our destination was Maitencillo, which is a small beach town located about two hours and 15 minutes outside of Santiago. The drive along the way is an experience in and of itself, as you pass through various wine vineyards along the way, often surrounded by beautiful mountains with the sun shining ever so brightly.

I was picked up by my tour guide from a local company called Ride de Vuelta, again arranged via Viator, in the morning. The overly kind man would later inform me that his tourism start-up just consisted of himself at the moment, but I would come to be thoroughly impressed with him, as he made me feel at home being able to fluently speak English and he acted more as a friend than a guide. Interestingly enough, he brought along his friend, who went to the same college as I did: James Madison University (JMU). What are the odds of this happening? Here I am in Chile, and the one individual my tour guide decides to bring along is from the Virginia area and went to JMU. I bonded with the pair throughout the day and felt like I was back in the United States given the level of comfort.

This was my first attempt at surfing, and I must say that it is not easy. We practiced for a short time on the sand and then proceeded into the water. Despite it being a relatively low season for tourism in the area, there was a surf school going on at the beach while we were there, which made me feel even more comfortable. Over the course of the next several hours, I was mostly pummeled by what came to be pretty large waves but did get up on my board three or four times and ride the waves in despite the fact that it was far from graceful. If you are interested in surfing in the area, note that the water temperatures here in the Pacific Ocean are cold with the average water temperature in Maitencillo for the month of March being 55 degrees Fahrenheit. I found this to be a high-quality use of time, as I was able to see an entirely different area of Chile along the drive that I wouldn't have seen otherwise, tried a new sport, which I enjoyed doing despite not being overly successful at it, and seeing a beautiful little beach town. The $140 price tag for the full day activity included roundtrip transportation, full surfing equipment, and lunch. I would consider this to be a high-value purchase especially considering the fact that companies such as Cascada de Las Animas charge $150 just for the transportation to a location that is not nearly as far. More experienced surfers flock to Punta de Lobos, which is often considered the best surfing destination in the country and plays host to international surf championships because of the high-quality waves that can be found here that can reach up to 50 feet. Punta de Lobos is a three hour and forty-five minute drive southwest of Santiago.

Additional Activities and Recommendations

The biggest regret from my outstanding trip to Chile was not doing a puma tracking adventure while in Patagonia. This can be done as a single or multi-day excursion through various local travel companies. The top predator in the area is known to be elusive, but from the reviews that I read in regard to those who went with a puma tracker, the odds of successfully spotting the animal are high. One of my roommates while I was staying at EcoCamp came all the way from Moscow to the Patagonia region, and one of the items on his short bucket list was to track the local pumas.

Kayaking amongst the glaciers while in Patagonia is another popular adventure activity that I would have liked to do. This is commonly done as a half-day activity. If you would like to take your glacier experience to the next level, it is popular to do glacier hiking, where you will have the opportunity to walk on the glacier equipped with crampons.

Fly fishing is an enticing option while in Patagonia. Trout can be found in remote waters in the various parks located in the Patagonia region. A man whom I met along my travels did this activity and enjoyed it, saying that he did not see a single other person along the way. Those who enjoy fishing and like to do so in extremely remote areas may find this activity of interest.

The most popular activity to do while in Patagonia is, obviously, hiking. While we did all of our hiking in Torres del Paine, there are various other beautiful locations where this can be done. The other most popular hiking location lies on the Argentina side where individuals go to see the spectacular Fitz Roy in which adventurers can start the trek from El Chalten.

High-quality rafting can be found in various locations throughout the country, but the pinnacle of Chilean rafting can be found on the Futaleufú River, which is regularly rated as a top 10 whitewater destination on the planet. The river is located in the Patagonian highlands and surrounded by the Andes Mountains, which provides for a scenic backdrop while you are working your way through some of the class V rapids.

Located more than 2,000 miles west of South America, Easter Island is still one of the more popular tourism draws in the country despite the extreme level of seclusion and difficulty to get to. The oversized, mysterious, monolithic carvings scattered around the island are the main attraction here, but other activities consist of star gazing, visiting the local museum, and viewing the horses roaming the nearby hills.

Probably the most widespread summer activity in the Santiago area is wine tasting. As previously discussed, the Maipo Valley (red wine) and Casablanca Valley (white wine) are extremely popular given their high-quality wines and scenic areas. There are various half-day and full-day tours to these regions where individuals can visit one or several vineyards if they so choose.

It is common to visit the coastal city Valparaiso while in Chile. This can be done as a day trip from Santiago, but travelers often opt to spend a few days at this attractive beach town. The street graffiti art is popular to view here as well as your standard water activities such as going out on a boat. A day trip to this town could be paired with other excursions such as a wine tour or even surfing at a nearby beach.

Skiing in the Santiago area is a big attraction even though the season is relatively short and is the reason that the high season for tourism in the area is during the winter months. Locations such as Valle Nevado near Santiago are considered good slopes for beginners whereas Portillo near Valparaiso is known to attract more experienced skiers.

Mountaineering in the Santiago area, as well as Patagonia, is another attractive option for adventure seekers. Those looking for a real challenge will opt to climb Mount Aconcagua, which is located across the border in Argentina and, at nearly 23,000 feet, is the tallest mountain in the Southern Hemisphere. Despite the enormous size of the mountain, the climb is not overly technical and is considered doable for an individual who is determined enough. This is just one of the seemingly limitless options for mountaineering in the region.

The northern portion of Chile is home to the Atacama Desert, which lies in stark contrast to the southern Patagonia region. Interesting adventure activities in this region including riding a hot air balloon over the desert, seeing the stars at night, and sandboarding in Death Valley, with dunes reaching over 300 feet!

Business Outlook

I am bullish on the long-term outlook for Chile. As I stated earlier, I expect the Chilean tourism industry to see continued robust growth in the coming years as outsiders come to fully appreciate all that the Santiago region has to offer and Patagonia sees continued expansion. Another wildcard is the arctic tourism industry, which I believe is a compelling offering for adventure seekers. Chile offers cruises to Antarctica out of Punta Arenas. Keep in mind that any potential economic optimism will always come with some form of contingency, as Chile remains heavily at risk for major earthquakes.

Even though the Chilean wine industry has seen enormous growth in recent years, I would expect to see big growth on the domestic front. As recently as "2010, Chile was exporting over 70% of their wines," which was the highest ratio in the world. I would expect to continue to see robust growth in the wine export market and even more explosive growth domestically due to further increases in local wine tourism. The global wine tourism business has been booming and shows no sign of slowing down; as I noted before, the Santiago tourism market remains heavily underpenetrated relative to the offerings as evidenced by local tour companies that are still unorganized due to their lack of experience. Chile saw 6.4 million foreign visitors in 2017, which may seem like a lot, but roughly half of this total was from Argentina. The geographic location of the country remains a challenge for many potential visitors, but Chile simply has too much to offer to turn down.

After leaving Chile, I connected with my Patagonia tour guide on Facebook and posted on her wall, letting her know that I notified my tour company that she was the best tour guide I had ever had. Within a day's time, 45 individuals who I had never met before around the world "liked" and responded to this message on her wall. This made me think deeper about what a truly powerful tool Facebook is. Facebook and Instagram have enabled me to keep in touch with people that I have met all over the world through my travels. It just so happens that this trip coincided with a rare period of Facebook stock market futility, as the stock had plunged over 20% over a period of weeks due to privacy concerns after the Cambridge Analytica fallout. I reexamined the company and concluded that much of the current concerns were likely overblown, as Facebook's product offerings are so ingrained in users' lives that it would have minimal impact on user engagement and the overall business model. Take the original Facebook tool for instance. I have virtually all of my photos uploaded to Facebook, and it serves as my personal photo album. What would it take for me to consider switching to an alternate service of which no viable alternative currently exists? The answer is a whole lot. Plus, from an advertiser's perspective, where else can they find a platform that can reach over two billion monthly users that can tailor their advertisements more effectively than a traditional television advertisement? There is simply no alternative at this point in time. The runway for growth at Facebook and Instagram is still long, with studies showing that 70% of smartphone users use Facebook and data points such as U.S. consumers using their mobile devices for over five hours per day. As I have previously discussed, the worldwide rise in smartphone penetration in the coming years will be one of the big trends to watch and Facebook will be one of the prime beneficiaries from this development. Chile's 2017 smartphone penetration rate was an underwhelming 45% but countries such as India only had 25%, and this market opportunity is well over a billion people. Facebook is not even in the first inning of monetizing WhatsApp and Messenger, which each have well over one billion monthly active users. The India market specifically remains a huge opportunity for Facebook with WhatsApp if they can come close to replicating the success that Chinese-based Tencent has seen with WeChat pertaining to services such as payments. The India market is more similar to China than the United States in that they are more likely to adopt a payment system through an application such as WhatsApp because credit cards are not ingrained in their culture like here in the United States. I haven't even spoken about Facebook's virtual reality opportunity, which Mark Zuckerberg believes will reach one billion users and why would you doubt him when he has grown four different services to at least 800 million monthly active users (Facebook, Instagram, Messenger, and WhatsApp)?

There are various opportunities for investors looking for exposure to the infrastructure segment within Chile. The president has proposed a $20 billion infrastructure program which would emphasize highways, airports, and the metro system. As I noted in my observations, Santiago has a lot of room for improvement in regard to their transportation system. Additionally, given that such a large proportion of individuals currently reside in Santiago, I would expect people to move to other locations within the country over time which would present an even greater need for infrastructure investment. Recent accurate statistics for cities outside of Santiago are hard to come by, but 2017 data shows Puente Alto as being the second largest city in Chile at 568,000 residents, which is far below the more than seven million people who reside in Santiago.

Updates Since Visit

"According to the Chilean Central Bank, GDP is expected to grow 3.4% in 2019 and 3.2% in 2020." The Doing Business 2019 report produced by the World Bank highlighted recent reforms such as the faster introduction of an electronic system which made starting a new business easier and significantly improved contract enforcement made possible by plaintiffs now being able to file an initial complaint electronically. The World Bank ranked Chile 56th globally in terms of doing business in the same report, which is a solid score.

In regard to the infrastructure investment previously discussed, according to export.gov new infrastructure investment in the country is projected to be $174.5 billion between 2018 and 2027. This investment is expected to be in three main areas: base infrastructure (water resources, energy, and telecommunications), logistics infrastructure (inter-urban roads, urban roads and bridges, airports, and railway roads), and social use infrastructure (public spaces, hospitals, jails, and education). Fortunately, this report covers the areas of need that I talked about in regard to rural cellular communications and urban and rural roads.

As for Facebook, the outlook has not changed. The company has continued to be in the news regarding privacy-related issues, but underlying business fundamentals remain as strong as ever. Facebook has yet to monetize WhatsApp and Messenger, which could wind up being the company's most valuable assets, and Instagram still has a huge ramp ahead. I previously noted a comparison of the messaging platforms to WeChat in China, and it will be interesting to see if the company proceeds with back-end integration for Messenger, WhatsApp, and Instagram. This would overwhelmingly create the largest messaging platform in the world, on top of which basically the entire Internet can be built. The ultimate vision for the messaging services is that chats, calls, e-commerce, gaming, and everything else will be done within the messaging platform, which would essentially replace app stores operated by Apple and Google.

Of all of the countries that I have documented in this book, the most stunning series of events took place in Chile after visiting the country. In October 2019, what began as protests over a hike in metro fares quickly turned into violent riots that turned deadly and spread throughout the country with social unrest lasting months. Seemingly out of nowhere, there was social unrest not seen since the transition to democracy in 1990. I had previously highlighted the ongoing inequality problem in Chile, and it seems as though the increase in metro fares was the breaking point for an issue that had been building for years in the country. I think the timing of these riots is important because we are in a period during which capitalism is under global assault. It is stunning to see U.S. presidential candidates peg their entire campaigns on tearing down the rich with the idea that this will make conditions better for the less fortunate. As anyone who has ever studied economic history would know, this is not how economies work. I hope that Chile can recover from this tough period, which has crippled economic activity in the near-term.

Already reeling from months of protests, Chile's economy will be battered by the spread of COVID-19. As previously discussed, Chile is the world's largest copper producer and the COVID-19 pandemic has negatively impacted copper prices due to lower industrial demand. Copper accounts for nearly half of Chile's export earnings and the country needs to further diversify the overall economy. I think these recent developments have shined the light on some of the same issues that Chile's economy has in comparison to Australia. Both of these countries are too reliant on exports and demand-side factors that are out of their control. In a recent report by ING, Chile and Australia both ranked in the top ten in terms of being, "Value-added dependent on Chinese final demand as % of total value-added." Some of this is to be expected given the relatively small populations that both countries have, but Chile and Australia must do more to diversify their economies. According to the 2019 Global Entrepreneurship Index, Chile clocked in at 19, which was well ahead of more established countries such as China. Chile should double down on their local innovation where they are seeing success.

French Valley

The hike up to "the towers"

Grey Glacier

EcoCamp

Penguins at Magdalena Island!

Concha y Toro

Rafting

Zip-line adventure

Santiago

Maitencillo

Canada

Introduction

My girlfriend Paula and I drove 50 minutes south from the Lake Louise area back toward Banff to Mt. Norquay, where we would be having our first Via Ferrata experience. If you are not familiar with a Via Ferrata, it is traditional rock climbing in conjunction with an array of man-made ladders and suspension bridges that provide for a unique experience that can be performed by climbers at any experience level. I wouldn't describe this activity as being for the faint of heart, as there are points along the way where the drop-off is several thousand feet. Having said that, during the majority of the activity, you are attached to a harness that is being pulled along a metal bar used for support. Even though the harness should catch you in the event of a misstep or fall, I did not want to rely on this technology for safety. Fortunately, nobody in our group had to resort to this safety measure.

We opted for The Explorer Route, which lasted 2.5 hours at a cost of $122 a person, which I thought was a good deal given the activity. To get to the point where you will begin the climb, a chairlift is taken to the base. Even from the point where you will begin the climb, the views are stunning, overlooking the town of Banff with surrounding mountains and a body of water running through the town. The clouds on that particular day separated, which provided for beams of sunlight shining down which made it seem like it was the work of an angel given our vantage point situated high above Banff.

For the next 2.5 hours, our group worked our way along the mountain. We proceeded at a careful pace, as the group of beginner climbers stayed focused on the path ahead and couldn't fully appreciate the scenery until we stopped for breaks along the way. Our harnesses had two connectors, which were disconnected and reattached to the next cable as we moved along. This took a little getting used to but seemed almost natural after about 30 minutes.

The group moved across a suspension bridge that lay high above the rock floor below. The bridge shook as we were crossing, and the movement only became more pronounced as the next climber started to cross the bridge. The bridge portion was a highlight, but the peak excitement came when we opted for a segment of the trail that included a full-scale rock climbing effort. I found myself utilizing my long limbs as I reached for solid rock and at times even held onto the rope itself to pull myself upward toward the next flat landing. I would be lying if I said that this part of the excursion was not exhausting and a bit frightening at times. I did manage to take a few moments to appreciate where I was along the way, as I turned around to gaze out over the town of Banff in the distance thousands of feet below us. Again, I would say that this activity is not for those that are terrified of heights to the point that the fear can't be overcome. If this is not the case, it is good fun and provides for some exhilaration. I was thoroughly impressed with how Paula handled the climb.

I had booked us a reservation at Eden, which was located at the Rimrock Resort Hotel a few miles outside the town of Banff. According to TripAdvisor, Eden was ranked as the third best restaurant in the area and was ranked as being number one, two, or three according to most other websites. While expensive, we paid around $230 for our meal which included drinks and tip, this type of fine dining would likely set you back two or three times that amount in the Washington, DC area.

We opted for the three-course meal option and tried new food items such as squab (pigeon) and sturgeon, which came with caviar. Both of these items were delicious, as they were impeccably paired with side sauces and seasonings. We had ostrich, which we had tried along our journey to Africa. I did not find the ostrich to be as tasty, as it was sourced from Australia, and

I could tell that it just wasn't as fresh as the other options. We had a palate cleanser in between courses that came with an impressive smoke show that we captured on camera. Overall, it was a fantastic meal that I highly recommend for visitors looking for an upscale dining experience that won't cost you nearly as much as some cities in the United States.

Paula and I departed for Calgary, Alberta, in August 2018 to spend a long weekend primarily in Banff National Park. Paula was drawn to the images of the lakes and mountains in the area that she had seen on Instagram, which was the driving force behind our travel decision. A host of factors, such as the Instagram publicity along with National Geographic Traveler Magazine naming Banff National Park as one of the top destinations in the world to visit in 2017, has led to a surge in tourism for the area in recent years. The numbers have only been helped by the weak Canadian dollar, which has made the destination much more affordable than in years past. Banff National Park has seen a surge of Chinese visitors, with the number increasing by 25–30% every year between 2010 and 2016.

We opted to venture to Banff National Park during the summer months because we wanted to see the lakes when they were unfrozen. Additionally, we were more excited about the idea of hiking and doing activities such as mountain climbing as opposed to skiing and snowboarding. Those who are skiers would want to consider Banff National Park or Whistler, British Columbia during the winter. During June, July, and August, Banff National Park sees highs in the upper 60s to low 70s, Fahrenheit, with lows in the 40s, which makes for ideal hiking and camping conditions. The weather was cool in the mornings and evenings, but we found it to be perfect for active adventures other than rafting which sees water temperatures that are frigid.

Canada is the world's second largest country in terms of total area, after Russia, and constitutes 41% of the area for North America. Despite the large area controlled by Canada, the population of the whole country was only 37 million as of June 2018, with the most densely populated area being along the border in the east. To get a sense of how few people this is, the Tokyo metropolitan area alone is home to over 37 million people. When we flew from Toronto to Calgary, I did not see a single city or anything that came close to resembling one along the way. The vast, mostly empty expanse is divided into ten provinces and three territories.

Canada lays claim to more lakes than the rest of the world combined, with the country boasting around two million lakes. Another interesting fact is that Canada has the most doughnut shops per capita of any country in the world. I found it fascinating that Canada has a strategic maple syrup reserve to ensure global supply in the event of an emergency.

The Government of Canada was established through the Constitution Act, 1867 as a federal constitutional monarchy where the Canadian Crown acts as the building block. It is an interesting structure in which the monarch, Queen Elizabeth II at the time of this writing, is represented by the Governor General of Canada. It may be surprising to many that Canada's royal family is the same as Great Britain's. The Cabinet is led by the Prime Minister, Justin Trudeau, who is the head of Parliament. While the government is established as a constitutional monarchy, it is also a parliamentary democracy where citizens elect representatives that are responsible for legislation and decisions of Canada. Canada's government is similar to that of the United States in that it has three levels that each have different roles and responsibilities.

The official languages of Canada are English and French. If you are wondering why French is included as an official language, one must look at the history of the country. Beginning in the late 15th century, French and British expeditions explored what is modern-day Canada and New France was established in 1534. This area was later lost to the United Kingdom in 1763 after the French were defeated in the Seven Years' War. Britain continued to set the foreign policies for the territory all the way up until the end of the First World War. The last remaining clauses of legal dependence on the British Parliament were not removed until 1982.

Economy

The Canadian economy is highly developed, with the 10th largest nominal GDP globally for the second largest country by land area. Canada has a wealth of natural resources, as it is estimated to have the fourth highest estimated value as of 2016. Despite having the world's third largest petroleum reserves, being the fourth largest exporter of natural gas and being ranked third in the world in proven oil reserves behind Venezuela and Saudi Arabia, the Canadian economy is dominated by the services sector, which employs three-quarters of the nation's workforce.

Other industries of importance to note are logging, oil, automobiles, aircraft, seafood, and commercial fishing. Given that Canada has the 9th longest coastline in the world, this leaves room for opportunity in the fishing and seafood industries.

As of 2018, Canada was ranked as the 9th freest country in the world by economic freedom score, according to the Index of Economic Freedom. This high score, which has led to sustained economic prosperity, has been driven by strong rule of law and the support of an open market system, which recently has come under fire from the United States. The average applied tariff rate of 1.6%, to go along with longstanding free trade agreements such as NAFTA, have been pillars of stability for the Canadian economy, which has encouraged foreign investment. Only time will tell how recent trade negotiations will shake out and how they will impact the local economy. The fact that three-quarters of Canada's exports go to the United States makes the country overly reliant on one country and gives the United States outsized bargaining power in any negotiations.

In addition to the favorable marks regarding economic freedom, Canada ranks highly on ease of doing business as studied by The World Bank. According to 2018 rankings, Canada ranked second on the ease of starting a business. To me this seems like common sense, as more individuals will go to countries where they can easily open new businesses and will do so at higher rates if it is not difficult, but many countries continue to enact additional regulations to open new businesses. The World Bank ranks Canada in the top 10 regarding protection of minority investors, which supports the high marks given by the Index of Economic Freedom.

At least some of the sustained economic success exhibited by Canada over the years is attributable to the education system, which is ranked among the best in the world and has outpaced the U.S. in recent years. Canada's education system has excelled despite the lack of centralization that delegates schooling authority to each province. The Canadian education system has no federal level education ministry and instead has three territorial and ten provincial governments responsible for developing education curriculum which is supported by the Council of Ministers of Education, Canada.

One of the concerns regarding the Canadian economy in recent years, much like that of Australia and New Zealand, which I have covered, has been the scorching housing market, which has made home ownership unrealistic for many in several top markets. Recent market data has hinted that the Canadian housing boom may have come to an end, as a period of rising interest rates may finally be denting demand. The majority of home loans in Canada carry a five year balloon payment and a 25 year amortization, which makes the borrowers especially susceptible to interest rate increases. To put it simply, in past years, Canadian homeowners had always seen their adjustable home payments go lower since interest rates were declining. Now that interest rates have been rising, the adjustable mortgage rate payments have been going up. This is particularly worrisome given that Canadian households are more indebted than their U.S. counterparts and coming from higher base home values in many markets after seeing years of torrid price appreciation. I won't go into extensive detail here given my commentary on the Australian housing market, but I wanted to at least note the risk present in this sector, which could have a dramatic impact on the Canadian public banking sector, as it could see soaring default rates on residential loans.

Adventure

Upon landing in Calgary, Alberta, we picked up our rental car and proceeded with our two-hour drive to Lake Louise. If you are considering visiting the Alberta and British Columbia area, I would recommend renting a vehicle, as scenic highlights can be spread out and ridesharing options are limited and inconvenient relative to what one would expect in other countries. Driving out of Calgary, one of the first points of observation is how close the houses are together. This may not be all that surprising given the rapid rise of housing costs across Canada in recent years which has left Calgary with an average cost of a home of $479,266 as of August 2018. This amount outpaced the median income of a one-person household by 9.1 times, which is high considering that real estate agents generally say that you can afford a home if the price is equivalent to 2.6 years of household income.

We arrived at our accommodation, Paradise Lodge & Bungalows, which was about a 30-minute walk from the town of Lake Louise and a 15-minute walk to Lake Louise itself. I thought that the lodge was well positioned for an adventurer to take advantage of the various outdoor activities that are present in the area. Paradise Bungalows offers individual cabins that sit in the midst of trees that make you feel like you are at a mountain escape. Sitting on the back patio of your cabin looking out over the beautiful tree lined landscape with that potent pine tree smell that reminded me of Christmas time provided for an enjoyable experience.

The following morning, we arose at 5:00 a.m. to visit Moraine Lake. Moraine has limited parking and often fills up around 6:00 a.m. depending on the time of year, so make sure to plan in advance if you are looking to visit this beautiful area. Our lodge was located just up the street from the road that led to Moraine, so we were better positioned to take advantage of this natural beauty than anyone. We were lucky enough to get one of the last parking spaces available even though we arrived just prior to 6:00 a.m.

It was still dark out at this hour but that did not stop us from admiring the gorgeous bright blue lake supported by the snow-covered mountains in the background with green trees seemingly everywhere in the area. The distinctive blue color of the glacial lake is due to refraction of light deposited in the lake. The lakes in the area do not thaw until late May to early June, so if you are planning to see the unique colors that the lakes have to offer, you must keep this in mind.

We walked around the lake via the hiking trails for the next hour or so as the sun was rising. If you are walking alone, you must be cognizant of bears in the area, as the narrow trails are lined by the forest and the park recommends that visitors make noises while walking to trails to scare away potential predators. As we were walking around the lake, it seemed like every picture was better than the next. I will note that I thought the best views were those taken facing away from the entry to Moraine Lake because I thought it more fully captured the majestic mountain landscape that lined the lake.

The trail at Moraine that is most commonly taken by tourists is The Rockpile Trail, which is only a 10 to 20-minute walk from the parking lot. Here on top of the rocks you will find the most spectacular views of the area that you have most likely seen on Instagram that have made Moraine Lake famous around the world. I could have sat there for hours admiring the unique blue water below. We found that the color of the water of lakes in the area is best appreciated from higher elevations, as this brings out the full color that can't be seen as well when sitting just above the water. While some may view the parking situation at Moraine as a hindrance, we found it to be an overwhelming positive because it keeps the crowds here low, especially when compared to other locations such as Lake Louise. We found Moraine to be more scenic than Louise and far more enjoyable because of the lack of "touristy" feel that comes with Louise because of the ease of access.

We then proceeded onto Lake Louise. As previously noted, this area was far more crowded than Moraine Lake, which took away from the experience. Having said that, the lake still provides for beautiful scenery, but isn't as impressive as Moraine. Both Louise and Moraine offer canoeing options, which can be an interesting way to take in the views. I should note that this activity is expensive at over $90 an hour at each location (we were told that canoeing at Emerald Lake was less than $60 an hour), but we opted to try it at Louise because the temperature had warmed since it was now later in the day and we did not know if we would ever be back to this area. I think this is an interesting point to recognize. I would be considered by many to be overly frugal on a daily basis, but when it comes to spending on tours and attractions, there are many options that are close to inelastic in nature. I have been bullish on the travel and leisure sector in general for many years now and have come to appreciate the tours and attractions sub-segment because many people are not nearly as price sensitive on spending for this area as they are with other expenses.

We set out for our hour-long canoe ride around Lake Louise. We were lucky enough to capture some frame-worthy pictures, as the sun came out along the way and made the color of the water all the more beautiful. The almost total lack of current in the lake did make the canoe experience a bit challenging for a novice like me. We found ourselves having to stay out of the way of other canoes in the area a few times, but the lake is still large relative to the amount of people exploring it via canoe, but Moraine does again see far less traffic on the water.

The following morning, we set out on a day-long journey to explore more of Banff National Park in addition to Yoho National Park. The first stop on the trip was Takakkaw Falls, which is located in Yoho National Park and is the second tallest waterfall in Canada. It is worth visiting and makes for some fine pictures, but I think the surrounding area is even more picturesque. We couldn't help but take some pictures in front of the beautiful streams that would seem to inspire a Coors Light Rocky Mountain advertisement.

We then proceeded to Kicking Horse Mountain, where we took a 20-minute gondola ride to the top of the 7,700-foot-high mountain, which is home to Canada's highest restaurant. I will be honest and say that this part of the trip could be skipped unless you are a mountain biker. The trails at the top of the mountain looked enticing for bikers, and those who were flying down the mountainside seemed to be having a blast. Other than that, the views from atop the mountain were not very impressive and the food at the restaurant was underwhelming.

The next activity on the agenda was visiting The Kicking Horse Grizzly Bear Refuge that was home to a 700-pound grizzly bear named Boo. Boo's mother was shot and killed by a poacher in 2002, which left him defenseless at just five months old. Boo has lived here since that tragic event occurred. The refuge is used for grizzly bear research and observations.

To reach the refuge, one must take a chairlift back up Kicking Horse Mountain to a point that is about halfway to where the restaurant on top of the mountain lies. We took our trip up and were delighted to see Boo awake and moving around upon arrival. I should note that his caretaker had brought food out, so this awakening could be viewed as induced by human activity. We sat there in awe as this enormously beautiful and fluffy animal walked around. I do believe that Boo seemed happy to be living in this area. He played with his caretaker, who led him on several sprints up and back, which Boo was excited to play along with despite his age and size. We were informed that Boo had escaped twice during his tenure at Kicking Horse Grizzly Bear Refuge and both times came back to his home on his own accord. If this is in fact true, then it goes further to show that he does call this place home and enjoys living here.

We learned a few interesting facts about bears in the Banff area and in general. There are black bears (which we would see the following day) and grizzlies in the Banff area with the grizzly bear being the larger of the two. The bears in this area are 80–90% vegetarian, which may surprise some folks. Some of these bears can consume an astounding 200,000 berries in a single day! I thought I was being aggressive when I wolf down a half package of Costco raspberries in a single sitting. Perhaps most interesting is how the mother bears grow their cubs. The mothers will grow the amount of cubs that their body deems they can sustain based on the size of their body which is fascinating.

The final stop of the day was at Emerald Lake, which is located in Yoho National Park and is the largest of Yoho's 61 lakes and ponds. Perhaps unsurprisingly given its name, this lake has more of a green hue than either Moraine or Louise. We did not spend too much time here, but we were fortunate enough to capture some beautiful pictures of the shiny green lake which was again outlined by countless fresh green trees and mountains. Unlike Moraine Lake, the mountains here were not heavily covered in snow and were not nearly as high, which I think left a little to be desired, but it is still a stunning area. As I previously noted, the canoe activity can be done cheaper here than at Moraine or Louise.

This all-day tour across Banff National Park and Yoho National Park cost $174 per person, and I thought it was worth the expense given the ground that was covered and the difficulty that an individual unfamiliar with the area would have in reaching all of these destinations on their own in the allotted time. This activity pairs well with some of the more adventurous physical activities in that this provides for a much more relaxing day. It was a great balance given that we had done an abundance of walking and mountain climbing the day prior.

The following morning, we again arose early to go on a half-day rafting trip on the Kicking Horse River. Given that the temperature was in the 30s when we walked outside, I knew that we had to mentally prepare ourselves for what lie ahead. The 13.7-mile river that has class IV rapids is billed as the wildest ride in the Canadian Rockies.

Upon arrival, we suited up with several layers given the temperature of both the air and water. There was a woman in our group who I would estimate was in her 70s making the trip, so I knew that I couldn't look distressed about the cold temperatures. After the standard safety talk and the signing of liability waivers that basically says that the company is not liable in the event of a death, we set out for the 2 to 2.5-hour ride down the river.

Even though we were geared up with several layers, the ice-cold water did manage to seep into my boots as soon as I stepped into the river. The rafting ride was not that exhilarating, and I would rate the experience far behind that of the Zambezi River (Zimbabwe) or Kaituna River (New Zealand) but ahead of my international experiences in Chile and Peru. The water was a beautiful blue color, and the scenery, which again included trees everywhere, railroads running parallel to the river, and the mountainous landscape, was enjoyable to observe as we made our way down the Kicking Horse. There were moments of adrenaline along the river ride, but it was more subdued than I was hoping, most likely due to the water levels which were low at the time. Our guide informed our group that he spent six months of the year rafting in New Zealand and even served as a guide on the Kaituna River, which I had done while I was there. I found it hilarious when he said that the local New Zealand guides had lied to my mother and me when they told us that about one boat a month flips over the waterfall on that river. Our guide said that number can get to as high as one in five boats!

The $120 per person rafting trip, which included transportation was capped off with a barbeque lunch that was surprisingly delicious. If you are looking for a river ride that rivals the most extreme in the world, this trip is probably not for you. If you want to enjoy the scenery while having periods of excitement on the rapids along the way, then I would recommend doing the Kicking Horse River.

That afternoon, we decided to head north from Lake Louise on the Icefields Parkway which is a 144-mile stretch linking Lake Louise and Jasper. This road is rated as one of the top drives on earth by Conde Nast Traveler, and I can say with high conviction that our spontaneous decision to drive north to Columbia Icefield was a magnificent decision.

The entire drive up to Columbia Icefield was stunning, as it went from seemingly untouched blue lakes with a mountainous backdrop to snow-capped mountains in Jasper National Park. There were rightfully scenic stops frequently along the way. There were not nearly as many tourists along this road as you would find around Banff or Lake Louise, which would make this activity more suitable for those who seek places away from the crowds. Seeing the lakes and other sights along the way where Paula and I were by ourselves or with just a few others made the experience a lot more special than at Lake Louise, where the area was overrun with tourists.

We arrived at Columbia Icefield, which is located in Jasper National Park and is the largest icefield in the Rocky Mountains. If you are wondering what an icefield is, then you are not alone, as I had to look it up myself. It is defined as being a large area of connected glaciers that is usually found in a mountainous region. The temperature in this area is cooler than at Lake Louise, which makes sense given that it is over an hour and a half north by car. The icefield can be seen from the road, but there is an array of activities available in this area pertaining to the icefield. If we had more time, I would have liked to take advantage of the Ice Explorer activity, which is an all-terrain vehicle that takes you out onto the Athabasca Glacier.

On the journey back to Lake Louise, we came across something unexpected as we were cruising down the highway. Up ahead we saw a few cars parked along the side of the road with their cameras out. It didn't take long before I noticed a black figure on the side of the road that I quickly identified as a black bear! Paula and I were thrilled, as we were desperately hoping to have a bear encounter that did not occur in close proximity to us walking along a hiking trail. We watched in awe, as the bear ate some plants right there on the side of the road and eventually crossed the street, managing to hold up traffic in the process! We were ecstatic to have this spectacular encounter, and it was the perfect ending to an unbelievable trip.

Additional Activities and Recommendations

After having traveled up the stunning Icefields Parkway to Jasper National Park, my biggest regret of the trip was not being able to spend any time in Jasper, which is three hours from Lake Louise. Jasper is less crowded than Banff National Park and provides for beautiful scenery in addition to activities that are not offered in Lake Louise and Banff. For example, canyon tours are popular in the Jasper area. For around $150, you can spend a day hiking and rappelling waterfalls in Jasper National Park. Like most of the tours that have been discussed, this is only offered during the summer months since the water freezes as the temperature cools. The formal wildlife tours seem to be more popular in Jasper, as there are numerous tours that head out in search of bears, elk, moose, wolves, and other animals.

Camping is one of the most popular summer activities in Banff National Park. While visiting, I had a friend who camped out in the wilderness and went on hikes each day. This is an appealing option for those looking to get away from the crowds at Lake Louise and enjoy the beauty of nature. Prime backcountry camping season runs from May until October. Hot springs can be enjoyed during both the summer and winter months. Fishing is popular in Banff National Park, but make sure that you acquire a permit if you are looking to do this activity. Lake Minnewanka and Bow River are popular for fishing. While I did not enjoy my lone horseback riding adventure in Peru, horseback rides are a summer attraction in Banff National Park.

An array of winter sports and activities is available in Banff National Park. The most obvious activities to note are snowboarding and skiing. The most adventurous individuals may consider the heli-skiing option. The Canadian heli-skiing industry is considered to be highly regulated and relatively safe, but this is considered to be among the most dangerous adventure sports on earth. Keep in mind that this activity is expensive, as it runs over $800 per person for only a five-run excursion. A unique winter activity is offered by KingMik Dog Sled Tours. The Great Divide Tour costs $150 for the two-hour excursion that travels ten miles from Banff National Park to Yoho National Park. Other winter adventure sports such as snowmobiling and ice climbing are offered. As I described in the chapter on Iceland, ice climbing is by far the most difficult sport I have ever personally attempted and should be reserved for only the most adventurous individuals. A much less hardcore winter activity that is popular is to ice skate on Lake Louise, which is free.

Looking at Canada more broadly, I would be remiss if I didn't mention a visit to Niagara Falls. Most would consider Niagara to be among the top three waterfalls to visit on earth. It is usually ranked behind Victoria Falls (Zimbabwe/Zambia) and Iguazu Falls (Brazil/Argentina). While Paula and I found our visit to Niagara to be nothing short of amazing, I would definitely say that Victoria Falls is more impressive and is visited by far less people given its geographic location. If planning a visit to Niagara Falls, I would recommend staying on the Canadian side, as the sights are superior from this vantage point. While it will set you back $235 per person, I would recommend the all-inclusive day and night tour, which includes both a day and night boat ride and is capped off with a fireworks show in the evening.

Located in the far north of the country, some consider the tiny town of Churchill to be the best place in the world to see polar bears. Prime viewing season is between October and December, when the bears are moving to seal-hunting territory. Do note that it is difficult to get to Churchill, as most individuals catch a flight to Winnipeg only to proceed on a smaller plane for another two-hour ride to reach Churchill. You can imagine that is an expensive endeavor, as multi-day guided tours run into the thousands of dollars.

Whistler, British Columbia, is a famous skiing destination popular among Canadians and Americans alike. Whistler boasts over 200 trails that appeal to skiers and snowboarders at all skill levels.

Likely the most famous urban adventure activity in Canada is EdgeWalk at the CN Tower located in Toronto. Individuals take a roughly 30-minute walk around the outside edge of the tower which stands at close to 1,200 feet! $175 is a steep price to pay for this short adrenaline rush, but some looking to add this item to their bucket list may not want to pass up this opportunity. I have been to the top of the CN Tower and recommend the experience for anyone visiting Toronto. The views from the top of the tower are impressive and shouldn't be passed up. Having said that, those afraid of heights will want to be cautious. High structures don't usually bother me in the least, but even I felt myself getting a bit imbalanced at the top of the CN Tower.

Business Outlook

If the Canadian government continues to promote a strong rule of law and free trade to pair with an environment that is favorable to maintaining a business, the long-term business outlook remains positive. Having said that, Canada should work to diversify the economy so that it isn't so reliant on the United States. Downturns in the U.S. economy or bargaining tactics employed by the United States, which holds all the cards given the Canadian reliance, can have profound negative impacts and create uncertainty in the Canadian economy, which could lead to decreased investment in the country.

One Canadian industry that has received a lot of publicity recently is the cannabis business. If this industry wasn't already firmly on the radar of investors and multinational corporations, the $4 billion bet by Constellation Brands on Canadian cannabis producer Canopy Growth put the business further into the spotlight. Constellation Brands has publicly stated that they believe marijuana will soon be legalized across the United States, which is similar to the thoughts held by many others as reflected by the recent roll-back of regulations. Some estimates have the U.S. legal marijuana opportunity being pegged at $75 billion by 2030 with a belief that the business could even surpass that of soda one day. With slowing sales seen in soda and beer in recent years, it is not a secret why other companies such as Diageo PLC are conducting their due diligence on the industry.

Canada could further take advantage of the increasingly strict immigration policies posed by the United States when thinking about the education sector. Prospective college students have been shunning United States colleges and universities in favor of their Canadian counterparts at an increasing rate due to more relaxed visa policies and lower cost. Opportunistic investors could take advantage of this trend by pursuing education programs and training boot camps located in Canada. The CFA Institute has held one of their most in-depth review programs just across the border in Windsor, Canada, likely because of the easier access to the country relative to the U.S. I would expect more programs looking to attract a global audience pursue similar opportunities north of the border.

A Canadian industry that is poised for explosive growth is esports. It is believed that esports viewership will soon surpass that of both Major League Baseball and the National Hockey League. Goldman Sachs is projecting that esports will reach a global monthly audience of 167 million in 2018 and will see 300 million viewers by 2022, which would put it on par with today's NFL viewership. Didn't believe that esports has arrived in the mainstream? That would be hard to dispute after ESPN's recent TV deal to broadcast the play-offs for the esports Overwatch League. In the past year, I spoke to a member of the Washington Wizards' ownership group, who told me that he believes that the value of esports franchises will dwarf those of traditional sports. Whether this is an accurate forecast or not is to be determined but what is undeniable is that esports are a serious force to be reckoned with. Canada has quickly become a leader in hosting some of the most prestigious tournaments and events that the industry has to offer. Events such as Get On My Level held in Mississauga, Ontario have shown that Canada's strength as a growing global esports player. Expect to see continued robust growth in this business, as we are in the early innings of a prolonged growth story in the Canadian esports industry.

Canada is poised to take advantage of the exploding adventure tourism market, which is projected to register a 17.4% annual CAGR from 2017 to 2023 according to a 2018 report published by Allied Market Research. Whether it be British Columbia cruises offered in conjunction with Alaska, outdoor adventure packages done in Alberta or British Columbia, polar bear experiences in Churchill, or exploring the high arctic to see unique polar scenery and wildlife, Canada is well positioned to capitalize on this trend.

Updates Since Visit

It was only a matter of time given the valuations and lack of profitability in the cannabis industry, but the cannabis bubble ended up popping in 2019. The long-term outlook for the cannabis industry remains bright, but the market fundamentals had gotten far ahead of reality. There have been a lot of growing pains on the way to realizing the potential growth that many foresee in the U.S. cannabis industry. For example, while legal at the state level in U.S. states such as Colorado, marijuana use is still illegal at the federal level. This means that business in Colorado still needs to be done on an all cash basis. Even employees have to be paid in cash. The cannabis industry may well realize most of the market potential at some point in the future, but it will be a bumpy ride getting there.

As I had previously cautioned, the COVID-19 outbreak looks like it will have a significant impact on the Canadian housing market. Some estimates show a 30% decline in home sales, as buyers are staying at home and not attending open housing or making home purchases. I had no idea that a global pandemic would be the trigger, but it was only a matter of time before the Canadian real estate market came back down to earth. Only time will tell whether this will lead to broader issues in the Canadian financial system.

One of the few businesses in the world that has actually done better since the COVID-19 pandemic began is related to video games and esports which was previously discussed. It was reported in mid-March 2020 that consumers spent 65% more on video games compared to the year prior. With consumers across the globe cooped up indoors with little in the way of entertainment options, video game demand has skyrocketed. This is a welcome development for the video game and esports businesses which should see well-above average growth relative to GDP for many years to come.

Rafting on the Kicking Horse River

The black bear that crossed the road!

The Columbia Icefield

Stunning views along Icefields Parkway

Emerald Lake

Boo: The friendly gigantic grizzly bear

The beginning of the Via Ferrata adventure

Lake Louise

Moraine Lake

Our house at Paradise Bungalows

Colombia

Introduction

The final part of our day-long Medellín city tour, which took us to various different locations, was by far the most moving experience: a visit to Comuna 13. This neighborhood was once called "the most dangerous community in Medellín" back in the 1990s when Medellín was declared "the murder capital of the world". I would be lying if I said I was not nervous, as I had read in the local news that four individuals were murdered in Comuna 13 just in the previous 24 hours. I gave the benefit of the doubt to our tour guides, having grown to know and respect their judgment over the previous four days. Just like what you would find in American cities such as Baltimore, New Orleans, and Chicago, the level of safety can change dramatically from one street to the next, so to classify an entire neighborhood as "safe" or "unsafe" can be misleading.

To witness the transformation taking hold in this neighborhood was one of the most special experiences I have had in my lifetime; in fact, I am shaking at this very moment just thinking about our three-hour stay. The entire history of Comuna 13 is spelled out through murals painted on the walls. One of our tour guides, who knows an incredible amount about the neighborhood and is active within the community, told us the whole story of Comuna 13 that he has learned in talking to the locals over the course of several years. Comuna 13 was a stronghold for guerrilla groups up until 2002. Even though the guerrilla groups controlled the area, our tour guide informed us that most of the locals he had spoken to were relatively happy

281

with how things were despite the high levels of violence. On October 16, 2002, the Colombian military carried out the controversial Operation Orión, a strike to overthrow rebel groups in Comuna 13. Our tour guide told us that this was a bloodbath, as they brought in tanks and helicopters and unloaded on the neighborhood in a siege that would take the lives of hundreds of individuals. The murals in the neighborhood recounted this traumatic experience, even detailing the innocent children that lost their lives during this operation.

It may seem like a given that an operation such as this would still mostly be viewed as a positive given that guerrilla groups had controlled Comuna 13 and violence was rampant. In talking with many of the locals, our tour guide said that many believed that the invasion by the Colombian military and paramilitary groups was all a lie in that it was just another way for the government to profit. To this day, Comuna 13 is still controlled by paramilitary groups that local residents have to pay taxes to.

Despite the controversy within the neighborhood, the Colombian government realized the potential of this neighborhood as a tourism destination and has been investing in Comuna 13. For example, the government opened escalators in the impoverished district in 2011 (that assist in navigating the steep streets), and it since has become a model for urban planning around the world. We walked by learning centers that had been set up to benefit the locals in the neighborhood. Another basic business lesson can be learned from this: thoughtful investments in infrastructure and education will bring positive results. In my studies of various economies around the world, this has been a common theme.

As we walked through the neighborhood, we noticed a special development taking hold. Many children here who previously aspired to be drug dealers could now look up to the local artists that had risen to fame within Comuna 13. For example, a local artist and role model named Chota had documented a lot of the history of Comuna 13 in his mural drawings and now runs a successful restaurant in the neighborhood. We sat and enjoyed a hip-hop concert that was happening while we were passing by. I couldn't understand almost anything the artists were saying since all of it was in Spanish, but the message to me was more powerful than if it were being spoken in perfect English: there is hope for Comuna 13 and for Colombia more broadly. Don't let this depiction distort the reality that this full neighborhood transformation will take decades to fully take hold, if ever. We briefly walked through part of the very poor part of the neighborhood, and I did feel uneasy. As we were doing so, fireworks went off; this was an ongoing phenomenon at all hours of the day leading up to Christmas, and my girlfriend Paula and I immediately jumped, surely having registered the explosion as gunshots in this neighborhood. Two local boys got their amusement for the day from witnessing our reactions. Paula would later inform me that she was a bit startled when she noticed a gun tucked into a local's pants when we were walking by. As I said, this area is far from perfect but rewarding for those that make the trip. Our tour guide told us of the saying about Pablo Escobar that some would repeat: he was poor since all he had was money. Nowhere does this ring more true than in Comuna 13, as we found some incredibly "poor" children that were running around singing Christmas carols and were as happy as can be.

We made our trip to Colombia during the peak travel season in Medellín, which is around Christmas time (although people have differing views on when peak travel season is for Colombia). We were told that the rainy season had just wrapped up a few weeks prior and it had rained every day for an extended period of time. Travelers looking at Colombia for their next destination should weigh what would likely be a discounted rate during the rainy season with how much this would hamper the travel experience. Our weather in Medellín was beautiful every day, with consistently sunny weather in the 70s (Fahrenheit).

Colombia is located in northwest South America and is home to 49.8 million people as of December 2018. The country shares a border to the northwest with Panama, to the east with Venezuela and Brazil, and to the south with Ecuador and Peru. Colombia is characterized as having a tropical climate but is diverse geographically, with five main natural regions that present their own unique characteristics. Colombia is home to the Andes Mountains, Amazon rainforest, and a Caribbean coastline. Like we saw first-hand on our visit, Colombia has relatively low deforestation compared to peer countries in the area. Colombia is part of the "Ring of Fire," a group of countries in the Pacific Ocean vulnerable to earthquakes and volcanic eruptions. I was shocked at just how mountainous the Medellín area was, as I was not expecting this. If traveling to the Bogotá area, do consider the 8,660-foot elevation above sea level since this can be an issue for some travelers.

Bird lovers will love Colombia, as it ranks first in bird species globally. Colombia is home to 10–20% of the plant species on earth and is the second most biodiverse country in the world.

Colombia lays claim to the oldest democracy in South America. Similar to that of the United States, the president is elected by popular vote to serve a four-year term. In 2015, Colombia's Congress approved the repeal of a 2004 constitutional amendment that eliminated the one-term limit for presidents. We were told that President Iván Duque Márquez had already become unpopular amongst the locals despite having been installed in power only a matter of months prior to our arrival. One of his first initiatives as President was to raise taxes on middle and upper-class earners and reduce the corporate income tax rate. Even if this initiative was well grounded in helping balance the budget, it will never be popular amongst the people if the first thing you do as President is say that you are raising taxes, especially while reducing taxes for corporations.

Colombia was inhabited by hunters around 12,000 years ago. In 1500, the Spanish explored the area and began to colonize Colombia; Santa Marta was founded in 1525. Spanish rule extended from about 1525 until 1808. Various unsuccessful rebel movements marked the Spanish period, but, in 1811, Antonio Narino's rival movement resulted in Cartagena's independence. In 1821, the Republic of Colombia was created with a constitution. A two-year civil war eventually led to the creation of the United States of Colombia, which endured from 1863 to 1886, when the Republic of Colombia was established. A century later, the 1970s proved to be a period during which powerful drug cartels, fueled by the likes of Pablo Escobar, influenced all of society. Instability, violence, and corruption have plagued Colombia really up until the past few years. Hopefully, the recent progress we witnessed on our visit is a sign of what is to come for Colombia as opposed to a brief blip in history during which the country seemed to be finally finding its footing.

Here are some interesting facts about Colombia: the Amazon rainforest makes up one-third of total land area of the country, the law requires the Colombia National Anthem to play on TV and the radio each day at 6 a.m. and 6 p.m., Colombia is the world's leading source of emeralds, and the government has periodically imposed a "Dry Law" prohibiting alcohol consumption during major events such as World Cup matches and elections in order to stem public violence.

Economy

As of 2018, Colombia's economy was South America's third largest behind Brazil and Argentina. The economy is still heavily dependent on energy and mining exports despite the efforts to expand in service-related areas such as information technology. As of 2018, Colombia was, "Latin America's fourth largest oil producer and the world's fourth largest coal producer, third largest coffee exporter, and second largest cut flowers exporter," according to the CIA's *World Fact Book*. Colombia's economic growth in a given year will swing based on commodity market prices, and that has hampered economic growth in recent years with lower oil prices. Having said that, economic growth in the country has been surprisingly stable over the past several years, rising by an average of 3.8% annually from 2010–2017 and having nearly doubled GDP per capita in the past 15 years. This relative economic success story has come despite challenges related to infrastructure (I would rate the public road system as being very poor in aggregate), narco-trafficking, and poverty.

Other important industries for the Colombian economy include manufacturing, information technology (as of 2017 Colombia was the fastest growing country for IT in the Latin American region), and shipbuilding. Another rising star within the Colombian economy is the tourism sector, which set a new record in 2018. I have seen estimates that have pegged the tourism of Colombia at 3.8% of GDP as of 2018 and this compares to 10% of GDP for the average country. As you can see, Colombia has a lot of runway in the tourism space since it has so much to offer potential tourists as long as they feel safe visiting the country.

Despite having corruption that is still rampant throughout the country, the 2018 Index of Economic Freedom produced by the World Bank has Colombia ranked as the 42nd freest country in the world and the 6th most favorable score in the Americas region, which may surprise some readers given the history of Colombia. The World Bank notes that issues such as intimidation of judges are still common which threatens the rule of law. In speaking with our tour guides, bribes paid to the local police are still common even though most would say that the situation has improved since the Pablo Escobar days.

The World Bank ranks Colombia 65th (as of 2018) in terms of ease of doing business. The country ranks favorably in categories such as ability to receive credit and protecting minority investors but falls flat when it comes to starting a business, enforcing contracts, and paying taxes. The message from this brief summary is simple: If Colombia wants to take the next step in its quest to diversify the economy further into the services area, it needs to loosen regulations and make it easier to start and maintain a business. Colombia benefits from a geographic location that makes it an enticing trade partner for the United States. You should start to see more American companies shifting manufacturing and service-related operations to the country given the location, cheaper cost of labor, and now relative economic and political stability. These economic benefits would only be further accelerated by lighter regulations that would make operating a business within the country easier. Despite the additional opportunities that can be presented when it comes to trade-related opportunities with the United States, the reliance on the country for exports presents a potentially large risk to the Colombian economy. As of 2017, the United States accounted for 28% of total exports. As we have seen in recent history with countries such as Mexico, an economy that is overly reliant on a single trade partner could wreak havoc should trade negotiations start to collapse.

Another thing that the Colombian economy has going for them is the relatively efficient tax structure compared to neighbors such as the United States. The overall tax burden came out to 19.9% compared to 26.4% in the United States.

Colombia has produced solid scores when it comes to the education system, as the 2018 QS Higher Education System Strength Rankings place Colombia 34th, which is just ahead of Portugal and a few spots behind Chile. Colombia has stated that their goal is to become the "most educated" country in Latin America by 2025. There are statistics that support the fact that Colombia is taking education seriously. For example, in 2017 Colombia had an education budget larger than that of Brazil despite the fact that Brazil has more than four times the population of Colombia. It has been written that possibly the most visible outcome pertaining to improvement in the education sector is the expansion of access to education at all levels which Colombia has made a priority. These initiatives should bode well for the long-term health of the Colombian economy if they remain on this upward trajectory.

Adventure

Paula and I landed in Medellín, Colombia on December 20, 2018. On the airplane approach into the city, we could not help but be amazed by the lush green mountainous landscapes that our pilot was navigating. Most of the world is still unaware of the natural beauty that Colombia has to offer because of the violence that has plagued the majority of the previous generation. We were picked up at the airport by our two tour guides from the local tour company, which partnered with Adventure Life, called PathRider Experiences, that I have traveled with on a number of occasions. The entire cost of our private tour trip was $1,500 per person which included hotel for five nights, all breakfast and lunches (we ate at nice restaurants for lunch most days), and all tours, attractions, and transportation. Given all of the ground that we covered over this five-day period, this may have been the best travel deal I have encountered up to this point.

Along our roughly 45-minute ride down from the airport we stopped at a restaurant overlooking Medellín. We scarfed down some local food items, including empanadas, which were paired with Colombian juices such as lulo, a small, orange-colored fruit with a tangy and citrusy taste, which are largely unheard of outside the country. We gazed out over the beautiful city that is home to 2.5 million people to go along with four million individuals in the total Medellín metropolitan area as of 2018. The city is sprawling, as it winds around the valley in which it resides and has homes scaling the mountainsides that look down on the rest of the city.

We proceeded to check into our hotel, Hotel Poblado Alejandria, where we would reside for the next five nights. I would rate this hotel as nothing more than solid, as it was perfectly clean and has everything that a traveler would need in a hotel, but I would not classify it as luxurious by any means. Highlights of the stay included a quality breakfast each morning (which included omelettes, an array of fruits, various breads, and local items such as rice with beans, and soup), a beautiful rooftop view overlooking the city, good location in the El Poblado district, and an overly helpful staff on hand. I do feel obligated to note that we found the hotel to be noisy on some nights, as there were hotel room parties going on well into the night on some occasions and some would say that the rooms are a bit loud because of the location.

I had made a dinner reservation in advance for that evening at a restaurant named Carmen. This restaurant was recommended by our local tour company and was written up on various local blogs documenting fine dining in the area to go along with its 4.5-star rating on TripAdvisor. Just a short cab ride from our hotel, which cost less than $2, our taxi navigated one of the more vibrant nightlife scenes in Medellín. At the time of our stay, Uber was still illegal in Medellín even though the company was operating in the city. Adventure Life had advised us to use local taxis, as there was ongoing hostility between taxi and Uber drivers. I think this brings up an important point, which can be observed in other cities around the world. Policies and unions meant to preserve legacy businesses such as taxi companies are unquestionably not a good development for overall society. The rise of ride-sharing in the United States has improved the overall quality of life despite the adjustments that some in the taxi business have had to make to adapt to this shift. It is rarely beneficial to fight technological change, as this can often hold a society back.

Nearly all of the bars and restaurants were partially outdoors given the climate and there were locals seemingly everywhere sitting outside eating, drinking, and listening to music. I was a bit surprised by the amount of people out on the town given that it was a Thursday evening. One of my first observations in driving around the city was that it has not been Americanized yet. Our tour guides informed Paula and me that the entire city had but only a handful of chains such as Starbucks and McDonalds. To me, this is a major plus because it keeps the local heritage intact.

Upon our arrival at Carmen, we took in the elegant atmosphere that included a jungle-like feeling similar to many restaurants in Medellín. This was our best meal in Medellín (we tried Oci.Mde, which many have rated higher than Carmen, but we gave the edge to Carmen), as we found each food item to be of the highest quality to go along with exquisite presentation. We started with pulpo (octopus) and ceviche for appetizers. The pulpo was likely the best octopus I have ever had, as it was perfectly paired with a delicious dipping sauce and vegetables and was great for taking pictures. The ceviche also may have been the best of its kind that I have indulged in up to this point, as it was explosively flavorful and even included caviar in the dish. The main entrees lived up to the billing of the appetizers. Paula and I shared near impeccable dishes that consisted of dry-aged pig and seared beef tenderloin. Both were cooked to perfection and the beef was about as tender as it gets. I tried the 20 Mission IPA at Carmen, which I found to be my favorite beer while I was in the country. Our tour guides laughed when

I shared with them my theory of gauging economic development within a given country. My theory is that economic development can be observed by looking at how many local craft beers a country has. I have found that a broad craft beer selection correlates with high levels of economic development and sparse assortments correlate with lower levels of economic development. As Colombia is still early on in its path to becoming a more developed country, the fact that it has a small but growing selection of craft beers like what I found in my ventures across Southern Africa makes perfect sense. The cost of the whole meal came out to $93, which included four drinks, two appetizers, and two entrees of the highest quality. This meal would set you back several hundred dollars back in the United States. Carmen is a must-visit for anyone looking for fine dining in the Medellín area.

The following day, we arose in anticipation of our mountain bike ride in the area outside of Medellín on the way to Santa Fe de Antioquia. This scenic area is filled with green pastures and dotted by beautiful haciendas. The ride takes individuals through a lush cloud forest with open views of the Cauca River valley. The Cauca, Colombia's second most important river, flows from the mountains all the way to the Atlantic Ocean. The environment substantially changes along the ride, as we found it to be a little chilly near the peak, but this atmosphere transcends into tropical lowlands by the end of the ride, and the landscapes overflow with bananas, mangos, coffee, cacao, and yucca plantations. Advanced mountain bikers can opt for more technical single trails. The ride ended in a small village called Cordova, where we proceeded on to Santa Fe de Antioquia.

I would compare the stunning mountain bike experience to something you would expect to find in the Ireland countryside, only with a more favorable climate and an added jungle component which I think makes the area even more beautiful. The bike adventure felt like we were temporarily transported back into the 1800s for a matter of hours, as we saw children carrying pigs on their backs up hills, witnessed mules transporting wood and other products, and saw countless individuals selling coffee beans along the road (which I found hard to comprehend given the dearth of traffic that passed along this road). Much like the rest of Colombia, we found the local people along the way to be overly kind. Locals wanted to tell us more about their farms and heritage, which would be unheard of in many parts of the United States unless this was ultimately to be used as a sales tactic.

While I would strongly recommend this experience to individuals of all biking skill levels, I caution that the road quality along the way is poor to put it mildly. I have a torn labrum in my left shoulder which became increasingly sore along the way as we continuously pounded our way across large holes in the road. We even came to a point where a bridge collapsed altogether which was the result of heavy rain that had occurred for several days prior to our arrival. If you have any body ailments, this should be a consideration prior to booking your mountain bike excursion.

Our journey then continued onward to Santa Fe de Antioquia. This small town of 23,000 inhabitants that was founded in 1541 is located 36 miles north of Medellín. I noticed that there were few tourists in this town, which might have been because of the travel advisory put in place by the U.S. Department of State that had recommended against travel to the Antioquia department north of Medellín. I consulted various individuals prior to our travels to get a feel for the safety of this area and determined that it was indeed fine to visit. Having said that, the heavy presence of the National Army of Colombia in the town of Santa Fe was easily noticeable. Individuals can either take this as a peace of mind in knowing that they are there to protect individuals or that it has been or can be a dangerous place to be.

We sat and enjoyed a beer at a restaurant outside in the main town square. The atmosphere was festive, as Christmas was just a few days away and the town was dotted with decorations with Christmas music playing everywhere. An interesting development occurred as we were people-watching in the town square. A young man approached our table with a large stack of dollar bills and offered to sell them to our group. The man was not offering Colombian pesos but was making a proposal for Venezuelan bolivars, which were basically worthless because of the well documented hyperinflation being experienced in the country. In May 2018, it was reported that the value of Venezuela's currency had become worth less than the fake gold found in the video game World of Warcraft! This was a sign of the times for the country. Many people would have thought it to be unfathomable that Venezuelans were pouring into Colombia in large numbers, as it has historically been the exact opposite scenario. The immigration has become a hot-button issue for Colombia, as more than one million Venezuelans have recently arrived in the country. Colombia needs to act quickly to ensure that the migrants are successfully assimilated into society, which is not an easy task.

After we finished our beers, we walked around the array of shops that Santa Fe has to offer and ate lunch in the town. We then proceeded to walk a nearby bridge called Puente de Occidente, which is a suspension bridge that connects Santa Fe and Olaya. If in the area, you may want to consider this activity, as it is a peaceful exercise to walk across the bridge.

The following morning, we arose early to make a stop at one of Pablo Escobar's former homes, Edificio Monaco, which is located in the El Poblado district. Ironically the government was set to implode this home only about a month after our visit, so we were going to be one of the last people to see the home. There were signs all over the home reminding visitors of the lives lost because of Pablo Escobar. It may be hard to believe, but even though Escobar was killed in 1993 and was responsible for taking the lives of an estimated 4,000 people, he is still often perceived as an idol in many of the more impoverished neighborhoods. If you have watched the *Narcos* series on Netflix, this may be easier to understand, as Pablo handed out money to the poor, built soccer fields in some of the toughest neighborhoods, and often campaigned in these areas when he was aspiring to be a politician. The Colombian government has ongoing efforts trying to educate the public about all of the atrocities that Escobar committed. I won't go into extensive detail in regard to facts about arguably the most notorious drug lord the world has ever seen, but here are a few: at the height of his drug empire he was smuggling an estimated 15 tons of cocaine per day, Escobar was pulling in an estimated $22 billion per year at the peak of his "business" in the mid-1980s and made the

Forbes list of international billionaires for seven straight years from 1987 to 1993, and by the end of the 1980s Escobar was believed to be supplying 80% of the world's cocaine. While Escobar dominated the global cocaine trade for years, Colombia continues to break records for cocaine production in 2018. This remains an ever-present challenge for the Colombian government.

After our short period of reflection at Edificio Monaco, we continued to drive just outside of Medellín into the hills where we would be visiting a local coffee farm branded Café Cereza. I surveyed the stunning parcel of land located in the hills looking out over Medellín that had trees and bushes of all kinds and was growing various types of fruits such as bananas (coffee trees are often surrounded by banana plants which provide shade) and mangos in addition to the coffee beans. We were informed that this piece of land was optimal for coffee growing because it is located between 1,000 and 2,000 meters above sea level. Colombia is known to have the perfect soil and right amount of rainfall for coffee harvesting, as coffee thrives in locations where there are at least 80 inches of rainfall per year, has tropical climates with the optimal amount of sunlight, and the temperature does not drop below freezing.

We would be introduced to our new friend, Fabian, who was by far the most passionate man I have ever come into contact with when it comes to coffee. Fabian walked us through the seven-step process of making coffee and showed us various birds located on the property along the way. Paula and I were able to participate in the process by hand-picking coffee beans from the trees, cracking them open using one of Fabian's manual machines, and then washing the coffee beans using a well-designed water cleansing process. The locals emphasize that Colombian coffee is set apart from the rest because they hand-pick each and every bean unlike processes in locations like Brazil that are done with machines. I found it interesting that almost all of the Colombian coffee is exported. This is done to preserve the global reputation of Colombian as serving some of the highest quality coffee beans in the world.

The final step in the process was to taste the local coffee. I found it entertaining when Fabian criticized those who put additives such as sugar and cream in their coffee, as he asked if those same people would consider putting sugar and cream in a fine wine. I completely agree and believe that sugar and other additives taint the taste of a high-quality cup of coffee. Paula and I were not disappointed with the locally grown product and supported Fabian in purchasing five pounds of his higher-quality branded coffee.

Prior to my arrival in Colombia, I had already taken note of the rise of global coffee consumption and investment opportunity in this space, which led to my interest in Starbucks Corporation. I don't think it is difficult to see the appeal here, as coffee is in the early innings of a prolonged growth cycle in many countries around the world. For example, at Starbucks' recent 2018 Investor Day, they conveyed that, in the United States, we consume 300 cups of coffee per capita per year. Compare this to China, where they consume one cup of coffee per capita per year. This extreme dispersion would not matter if it weren't for the fact that coffee consumption in China is growing at a robust pace and expected to increase 50% over the next four years. Starbucks as well as local coffee harvesters such as Fabian have some strong macroeconomic tailwinds at their back operating in this business that I believe will continue for years to come.

After our enjoyable experience at the coffee farm, we continued up the mountain on our way to La Catedral. Likely the most infamous prison in the history of the world, La Catedral was a prison overlooking Medellín that was built to the specifications of Pablo Escobar under a 1991 agreement with the Colombian government. Pablo cut this deal with the government in exchange for a promise that they would not extradite him to the United States. If you watched the *Narcos* series, you know that La Catedral was far from a normal prison. While it looked run-down on the outside, it included lavish amenities such as a football pitch, jacuzzi, and waterfall. Even though Escobar was technically "imprisoned" here for one year and a month before going on the run again, he continued to operate his vast drug operation from the confines of the prison and brought the entertainment to him, often playing host to soccer matches in addition to basically any form of entertainment that he wanted which included prostitutes. It isn't hard to see the strategic appeal of the location of La Catedral, as it sat up in the hills where the guards had advanced notice of approaching intruders that could allow for an escape plan if necessary.

Ironically, in 2007 the Colombian government granted control of La Catedral and the surrounding land to a group of Benedictine Monks who transformed the former prison into a monastery. Pablo Escobar's helipad at this location remains intact, and Paula and I captured some stunning images here that encapsulate the entire Medellín valley. Despite being in "prison" here, Pablo must have felt like he owned Medellín given the generous vantage point.

We then continued on to do a 1.5-hour hike from La Catedral to Salto del Angel and Campanas Waterfalls to Arenales Viewpoint. I would describe this enjoyable hike as fairly challenging considering that you wade through the pine forest through a series of inclines and declines that require individuals to use ropes and frequently climb rocks along the way. The end point of the hike reveals a waterfall view that shows water cascading down the rocks surrounded by an array of lush green vegetation. Paula and I did not brave the water that resides at the bottom of the waterfall, but others were wading into what was described by our tour guide as the coldest water he had ever felt in his life. I would strongly recommend this beautiful hike to those who can withstand the rock climbing component that comes with this experience.

The following morning, we set out for Guatapé, which is close to a two-hour drive from Medellín despite only being about 50 miles from the city. We found this to be a consistent theme throughout the country given the combination of poor road quality and lack of major highways that would allow for faster speeds. The Colombian government has properly designated transportation as one of their three core current focus areas, and they have a lot of work to do here.

Guatapé is the name of an intriguing town that is also located in the Antioquia Department of Colombia. One of the main tourist attractions in this area is La Piedra, also known as El Peñol, which is a 656-foot high rock formation that came to be 70 million years ago. Tourists can climb the over-sized rock via the 649 steps built on the side of the rock (some have written that this is overly difficult, but as long as you are in reasonable shape, it should be fine). When we arrived at the top of La Piedra, we took in the tremendous views looking out over an area that I would compare to the Everglades in Florida. There was water surrounding the rock dotted with small green islands with trees, which makes it one of the top attractions in this region. Perhaps surprisingly to most given the appearance of a natural formation, the lake area is actually a man-made reservoir created by the Colombian government for a hydro-electric dam that was started in 1979. One of our tour guides was deeply disappointed with the area because the Colombian government took land from locals in the area and demolished a town in order to build this present-day reservoir. He went as far as to describe the top of the rock as a "massacre" given that restaurants and the like had been constructed upon this natural formation.

Here is where I often tend to kindly disagree with many tour guides. Most tour guides believe that the government should preserve the natural environment 100% of the time no matter the circumstances. I firmly believe that this requires a delicate balance between natural environment preservation and revenue-generating initiatives. In this instance Guatapé, La Piedra, and the surrounding reservoir have become a prime tourist attraction and are at the very least partially responsible for the employment of various tour guides despite their dismay with the area. What you can also find in areas like this is that tourists will come and then find their way to other areas that tour guides would describe as having more natural beauty and heritage. I too share a higher personal appreciation for old heritage locations such areas within the old town of Guatapé, but the reality is that La Piedra was jam packed with tourists and some of the most beautiful and oldest streets within Guatapé sometimes were completely vacant.

After La Piedra, we went on to the town of Guatapé, which is a beautiful place with a lot of history and small shops and restaurants. I have seen Guatapé labeled as "the most colorful town in Colombia" and rightly so, as the streets and lined with brightly colored paintings and decorations on the outside of homes with the illustrations often meant to describe the inside. If you have seen pictures of colorful streets in Colombia, they likely were taken in Guatapé. Unlike in the United States where most homes have locked windows and doors, you will find most of the homes in Guatapé being open and more welcoming.

Our next activity was a boat ride in the reservoir where we would be making three stops along the way. The first stop was the actual dam named Punchiná Dam, which is the reason this reservoir on the Guatapé River was built. The hydroelectric dam provides 30% of the electricity supply of Colombia and provided a whopping 70% of the country's power supply when it was completed in 1983. The dam was dry when we were visiting, but the man driving our boat showed us recent videos during the rainy season in which the area was completely flooded.

We continued to cruise around this beautiful reservoir area and arrived at a secluded place where adventurers can choose to cliff jump from rocks perched above the reservoir if they so choose. Paula and I opted to jump from the much smaller assortment that I estimate probably stood 15 feet above the reservoir. One of our tour guides got a running start and launched himself off of a 60-foot cliff and plunged into the depths of the water. I had done a similar stunt years ago in the islands of Greece and did not have the appetite to repeat the activity here, as one slip at the edge of the rocks could have been catastrophic.

The final stop along our enjoyable boat cruise was the ruins of La Manuela, which was one of Pablo Escobar's mansions. This stunning 20-acre property located on the water was complete with an array of exotic trees imported from around the world and was surrounded by a pool, tennis courts, a soccer field, stables, a guest house, a seaplane dock and provided views looking across the reservoir to a green hilly landscape. Our guides informed us that some of the wealthiest individuals in the country own homes in this area.

La Manuela was torn apart by a bomb in 1993 by Los Pepes (also known as "People Persecuted by Pablo Escobar"). Pablo had been tipped off about the assassination attempt and had evacuated the compound, only to be shot dead later that year in Medellín. The entire area is eerie but definitely worth a visit. In the guesthouse are several areas where the walls have been ripped open by individuals in search of money stashed away (to this day there are still people digging all over the country in search of Pablo Escobar's hidden money). The guesthouse is now home to one of the more interesting paint-ball venues the world has ever seen.

As we were standing on the top floor of the guesthouse and discussing the history of the area, Pablo Escobar, and the state of the Colombian drug business, we got to talking about the legalization of drugs. Our tour guides were under the impression that all drugs should be legalized, which would remove most of the incentive and profits to harvest narcotics such as cocaine and, in turn, dramatically reduce overall violence. Their argument was that the government could take a small fraction of what they would have spent on supporting jailed drug-related criminals and policing the illicit drug trade and use the tax proceeds from legal drug sales for programs to educate the public about topics such as drug addiction. I think this is essentially what you have seen many governments conclude in regard to marijuana as countries such as the United States and Canada are in the process of legalization. This topic is far more complex than our tour guides would have liked their clients to believe. While their opinions in regard to removing the incentive to produce illegal narcotics are well grounded, there are many other factors to consider. For example, even though we are in the process of legalization of marijuana how are we going to test for impaired driving when using the substance? I would imagine a solution is on the way, but this is a major road-block for widespread adoption and could be responsible for thousands of lost lives. According to a 2018 *Wall Street Journal* op–ed piece, in Colorado, the number testing positive for marijuana in fatal crashes has risen each year from 2013 (47) to 2016 (115), more than doubling (145%) in those four years. Of the 547 traffic fatalities in 2015, 99 were due to marijuana, 187 to alcohol and 35 to both. The most common drug in all fatal crashes is marijuana.

Another paramount issue that experts have studied in Colorado in regard to marijuana legalization is the fear that legal marijuana use will trickle down to children and young adults when they are at a vulnerable stage. We can't discount the fact that the majority of illegal drugs are addictive substances and often have debilitating long-term health effects, and even risk of immediate death in some instances. At this stage it is unclear as to what eventual impact marijuana legalization will have in this area, but it is something to consider.

I am not saying that drug legalization across the board should not happen, but to make a blanket statement such as that all drugs should be legalized without considering the potential downside implications to such a radical decision is simply not intelligent. There are many benefits that would come with widespread drug legalization, which include tax benefits, legal job creation, freeing up law enforcement to tackle other crimes, and most importantly removing the incentive to harvest illegal drugs on the black market. I can say with a high level of certainty that we will not be seeing the legalization of cocaine anytime soon, but I would not say never, as there are various ongoing studies in this field that may prove prior beliefs wrong. Having said that, to get the public support of a bill supporting the legalization of cocaine would take many years to develop.

The following day was, sadly, our last in this stunningly beautiful country that both Paula and I had fallen in love with during our brief stay. We would be taking a city tour of Medellín on December 24th, which was the day that they celebrated Christmas in Colombia so it was not as crowded as usual. The main religion in Colombia is Catholicism, with roughly 75% of the population falling under this designation and often being considered the most Roman Catholic of the South American countries. Our tour guides informed us that many people left Medellín during this time to spend time with their families in the countryside.

We hopped aboard the local metro which was clean and had a flat rate for a single trip of less than $1. This was a good value for those taking longer trips across the city but actually expensive for those in need of just going a few stops. We would then be taking a cable car onto our final destination. I have to admit that I was a bit nervous for this portion of the trip, as our guides had informed us just days prior of one of the local cable cars outside the city having collapsed! Of course, this story was followed up with reassurance that the cable car to Arvi Park, our final destination, was using more robust technology. The cable car ride rises above some of the poorer neighborhoods in the city and provides some unique vantage points of Medellín. The experience provided for some nice photos and videos on the descent back into the city.

Arvi Park is an open park developed on land for public use and is located 20 miles from the center of Medellín in the surrounding hills. We first stopped to enjoy some delicious fruits and empanadas from a local market located nearby. We then hiked a brief portion of the 33 miles of walkable trails available within the park. As far as fauna goes, the park is filled with an array of rare birds even though we didn't encounter many on our time along the trails. On the information pamphlet, there were also listed to be animals such as armadillos and porcupines within the park confines, but we did not come across any of these more exotic creatures. Arvi Park is a nice experience but if you are pressed for time and are not an avid bird watcher, this activity could be skipped if necessary.

The next stop along the tour was the city center area where we would learn more about the history of Medellín. This part of the city used to be where the majority of the expensive homes resided until the mass transit drove many to areas such as El Poblado (where our hotel was). There is a lot to learn about how modern-day Medellín came to be around here, so almost any tour will at least stop by here. Despite other parts of the city being relatively quiet on this Christmas Day, there were people everywhere here.

We then stopped to each lunch at a delicious Peruvian restaurant called Mistura, which is located in Laureles and is one of the nicer neighborhoods in Medellín. Unlike the El Poblado neighborhood, you will find that the streets here are flat, so it is much easier to navigate by foot. I would recommend a visit to this area, as there are various high-quality restaurants and the scenery is enjoyable.

Additional Activities and Recommendations

While we opted to visit a local coffee farm just outside of Medellín, some travel to the Coffee Triangle region, which is also located in Antioquia and has now officially been named a UNSECO World Heritage Site. This area has been popular amongst tourists because of the attractive mountainous scenery and the fact it has avoided most of the violence that is still present elsewhere in the country. This area is a six-hour trip from Medellín.

There is a plethora of attractive trekking opportunities within the country, but none is perhaps more intriguing than the four-day trek to the Lost City. These hidden ruins located in the jungle of the Sierra Mountains were built in 800 CE. Online reviews describe an "epic" adventure that takes trekkers through mud and across rivers. Since this area is along the coast in the same region as Cartagena, this adventure activity could be paired with a stay here.

Colombia offers a variety of adventure activities. Paragliding can be done in near San Gil, Cali, Medellín, and Bogotá. We were offered to do one of the many rafting excursions available in Colombia. Popular rafting destinations include Magdalena River near San Agustin, Rio Negro River in Cundinamarca, Barragán River in Quindio, Suarex, Fonce, and Chicamocha Rivers in Santander. Another adventure activity that can be found in the San Gil area is rappelling. Here thrill seekers can try their hands at the intimidating 230-foot Juan Curi falls. A unique activity can be found near Cartagena is mud bathing at the Totumo Volcano, which is 8,202 feet deep. Why not splurge for a $1.50 mud massage while you are here? Given that Colombia is home to close to 1,900 miles of coastline on both the Pacific and Caribbean side, there is an array of available water activities such as scuba diving and kite surfing. In the area around Providencia and San Andres there is the third largest coral reef barrier on earth classified as a UNESCO world heritage.

As far as cities go, Bogotá is another obvious choice. Bogotá lays claim to the best food options in the country, so food lovers make this city a priority. Tourists will want to consider a visit to the Gold Museum. There are various graffiti and historical tours available in addition to hikes and biking opportunities that can be done around the city. In conducting my research, I did not find as many adventure-activity options in Bogotá as Medellín. Additionally, the weather in Bogotá is not as favorable as in Medellín during the dry season since Bogotá is located on a high plateau in the Northern Andes Mountains and is often cloudy and rainy.

Cartagena is the most popular beach destination in Colombia, but the popularity comes with a price, as it is substantially more expensive than what you will get in Medellín. I have consistently seen Playa Blanca being rated as one of the top beaches in Colombia. This small jungle-covered island is located about 45 minutes from Cartagena. Given that it is so consistently rated as a top beach destination, it will likely drop off the list with time unless the country goes to extreme measures to preserve the natural beauty that can be found here.

In talking to our guides and others, the city of Jardín is a recommended visit for those looking to experience the small-town local heritage of the country. This city is located about 3.5 to four hours from Medellín and looks beautiful from the pictures that I have seen.

I won't go into depth here in regard to the Amazon rainforest since it is so well documented on various media outlets, but Colombia does offer cheaper Amazon experiences than neighbors such as Peru.

Business Outlook

I know this will sound crazy to those that have never been to Colombia and still think of a country being ruled by Pablo Escobar and the drug kingpins, but the Colombian peso is an intriguing investment option. While I was visiting the exchange-rate was roughly $1 USD for every 3,200 Colombian pesos. To give you an idea of how far the dollar goes in Colombia see the following: $2 will get you a taxi around the El Poblado district in Medellín, $20 will get you the best dinner entrees in Medellín, and if you booked a truly budget five-night all-inclusive travel package in Medellín and the surrounding areas I am sure you could find a deal for well under $1,000.

Deutsche Bank had the Colombian peso listed as one of their three most undervalued currencies of 2018. Not even taking into account current over or undervaluation, the currency could converge closer to the U.S. dollar over time, as the country leverages their prime geographic location, favorable climate, and a more friendly business environment, which should continue the upward trajectory in tourism, service-related businesses, and manufacturing. Why favor an investment in the local currency over purchasing a Colombian equity ETF such as iShares MSCI Colombia ETF? The ETFs available for Colombia are heavily skewed toward energy and financials, which may not be as attractive of an asset mix compared to some other less developed countries. The problem is that normal retail investors aren't even offered the option to buy emerging currencies such as the Colombian peso through a standard ETF. The only option for most investors would be to purchase the physical currency and pay around an 8% commission on each end of the transaction. Because of this, there is a lack of liquidity in many emerging currencies which could see future appreciation if there was just an easier and more efficient investment vehicle.

I am bullish on almost any and all businesses related to tourism in Colombia. I don't think it is difficult to see why, as the country is stunningly beautiful, has a tropical climate, has an expansive coastline, is culturally rich with one of the more interesting histories to learn about and study, and is well positioned geographically to take advantage of an influx of tourists from the United States, Western Europe, and Northwest Africa. Colombia may no longer be the travel sector's best-kept secret when it comes to tourism, but there is a huge growth ramp ahead for the country in this business. It is up to the Colombian government to ensure that tourists continue to have a positive and safe experience and can freely travel popular areas such as Medellín, Bogotá, and Cartagena. If it seems like I have been optimistic about the travel industries in many countries, that is because the travel and leisure-related markets are a play on the shift to spending more on "experiences" as opposed to "things." In 2017, one in five jobs created globally was due to travel and tourism and the global business grew 4.6% that year (making it the fastest-growing broad economic sector), outpacing overall economic growth for the seventh consecutive year. I would expect the worldwide travel and leisure industry to grow much faster than overall GDP for years to come.

For those who have visited Medellín, it isn't hard to see how the city could be an enticing value proposition for a real estate investment. I saw a real estate investor post online about how the present-day Medellín real estate market is the equivalent of getting in on markets such as Costa Rica and Belize 10–20 years ago before they experienced their prolonged bull markets. This may be the case, as the market has become an attractive destination for American retirees due to the tropical climate, low cost of living, and a healthcare system that has been known to be low in cost and high in quality. I would not expect the real estate prices and cost of living in Medellín and Colombia more broadly to remain this low for too long, as the secret is getting out that the safety in the country has improved dramatically in many areas and has a plethora of attractive attributes.

Updates Since Visit

As of the time of this writing following the outbreak of COVID-19, S&P Global was still projecting economic growth for Colombia in 2020 which was in contrast to GDP contraction projections for Latin American counterparts such as Argentina, Brazil, Chile, and Mexico. Even more impressive is the fact that Colombia's 2019 economic growth trounced all of these Latin American countries in 2019 with 3.3% growth. This strong relative performance does not surprise me, as I had written positively about the future of Colombia. Relative to many other countries, Colombia produces more goods and services that I would consider to be utilities that are needed in any economic environment. For example, I had previously mentioned that Colombia was the world's third largest coffee exporter. I would say that the majority of people that drink coffee on a daily basis will continue to do so even during deep recessions. It has helped that the commodity price of coffee has actually increased since the COVID-19 outbreak while the price of many other commodities has plunged. This data point lends some support for my claim that demand for coffee will remain strong in any economic environment.

There is commentary in this chapter as well as other chapters about the global growth of travel and tourism. This growth has been at least temporarily put on hold following the COVID-19 pandemic. I have confidence that we will continue to see growth in this segment in the future but it will likely be a long, arduous road to recovery.

Our beautiful bike ride

Local coffee farm experience

Hike with a view

Pablo Escobar's helipad overlooking Medellín

The top of La Piedra

Beautiful Guatapé

La Manuela

Comuna 13

India

Introduction

I was picked up early in the morning and taken to the local train station, from where I would be taking a six-hour journey down to Ranthambore National Park from New Delhi. On the way to the train station, it became immediately apparent to me that nobody in the country paid any attention to the traffic lights. We had a red light, and four cars went full speed through the intersection as if it were green. I was informed that the traffic enforcement officers would not be coming on duty until 11:00 a.m. and many people are aware of this and do not abide by the laws. I was told that, unlike many areas in the United States, there are no traffic cameras for enforcement. It is no wonder that over 400 people a day in India fall victim to traffic-related fatalities (as of 2018). Perhaps the most stunning development of the entire trip was the fact that we did not witness a single car collision along our tour of five Indian cities.

The train ride to Ranthambore was in and of itself one of the most memorable experiences of the entire trip. Seeing as I was booked in first class, I would have assumed that I would have a nice, private compartment complete with comfortable seats and amenities such as Wi-Fi. I should have known better than to assume that this train experience would come anywhere close to resembling a first-class experience back in the United States. I navigated the narrow corridor of the train to find a small unmarked compartment that was filled with four beds that I would have expected to see in a homeless shelter rather than a first class train compartment. I don't know what I would have done without the assistance of my travel guide. This entire process would have been nearly impossible without any of the local knowledge.

The whole train experience was a circus. Locals would walk by, trying to sell everything under the sun. One of the individuals in my compartment purchased a soda and immediately smelled the bottle to see if it was, in fact, a brand new, unopened bottle. The bathroom in the first-class train consisted of a hole in the ground that reeked of a horrible odor. If it weren't for the fact that two of the others in my compartment were also getting off at Rantham-bore, I have no idea how I would have known where to depart. It is not like in the United States where they make an announcement at each stop. The stations are poorly marked and difficult for a foreigner to recognize the train stop. I was so happy to finally arrive in Ranthambore, as I had been secretly praying the entire ride that I would arrive safely. Despite having the best rail-way safety record in 57 years in 2018, there were still 73 accidents reported across the railway network.

There was not a whole lot between Delhi and Ranthambore other than a slew of farms. All I kept thinking about over the course of the train ride was that this was the "rural India" where Amazon has been spending billions of dollars per year to build its distribution network within the country. I do not see how these investments are ever going to pay off, as there were few people in these areas and the math just doesn't seem to work. I have much favored the capital light approach that Facebook has taken in building out their dominant software ecosystem in emerging markets such as India with their family of products which includes Facebook, Instagram, WhatsApp, and Facebook Messenger.

The reason I traveled all this way to Ranthambore National Park was that there are only believed to be 3,900 tigers left in the wild with India laying claim to over 50% of this number. To give you an idea of how few this is, it is estimated that there were 100,000 tigers living in the wild in 1900. The global tiger population has been slowly recovering in recent years due to increased conservation efforts, but the population has been decimated by human encroachment and poachers over the years. Ranthambore is home to 70 tigers, and many would consider the park to be the best tiger viewing location in the world because of the large clearings present in the park that make it more optimal than some other national parks where visitors may find it more difficult to actually spot the tigers. I had done my own extensive research on this prior to arriving in India and had informed my guides that my sole purpose for traveling six hours alone by train to the middle of nowhere in this foreign country was to see a tiger.

Upon my arrival at Hotel Vivanta by Taj, I quickly set down my things and went out for an afternoon safari that turned out to be one of the most special experiences of my lifetime. I hopped aboard a small safari jeep and we went on to pick up five other strangers staying at various hotels in the area. For most, the drive from the hotel just to get into the park would be a memorable experience. I witnessed some things that you don't get to see every day in the United States, including men on the road herding groups of 20-30 goats, wild cows crossing the road in every direction, and monkeys pestering people for food, among many other interesting developments.

Within minutes of entering the park, I knew it was going to be a special day. We saw a black sloth bear roaming an open clearing (many would be unaware that there are bears in this part of India) to be followed up by spotting several large crocodiles set up around a beautiful lake area. Spotting these animals was great, but I did not travel all the way to Ranthambore to see a crocodile. In our pursuit of a tiger visual, we parked next to a handful of safari vehicles that were patiently waiting in front of a clearing. How could this group be so sure that a tiger was in the area without having actually spotted it yet? As was reinforced by National Geographic on television later that evening, the deer give out a warning call to their friends to inform them of a tiger in the area. If you witness an entire group of deer issuing the warning call at the same time, it is likely that there is in fact a tiger nearby. We sat and waited for what could have been close to an hour, as the nearby deer continued to vocally warn their peers despite our lack of visual evidence.

Then, it happened. I was the first one in the group to spot the full-grown female tiger that had just stood up in the distance. If you have ever seen a tiger in person, you will be able to recall that distinctive walk the majestic animal has. Even though the tiger was still at a distance and difficult to peg for certain, I immediately knew it was in fact a tiger because of the swagger with which it walked in comparison to all of the other animals in the ecosystem. It was essentially saying it was the top predator and there was nothing anyone else could do about it with its body language. I will never forget the ensuing 30 minutes for as long as I live, as the tiger walked within ten feet of our safari vehicle and proceeded to attempt to hunt deer in the area. While ultimately unsuccessful in her efforts, it was otherworldly to witness the game of cat and mouse that the animals played with the deer. I know that we were lucky in having this rare experience, as even one of the safari guides requested that I send a video from my phone to him of the tiger walking by our vehicle and hunting the deer. Even though I had only been in Ranthambore a matter of hours, the long journey to this national park was already worth the effort.

Over the course of four game drives in Ranthambore National Park, I saw three tigers, a leopard (which is rarer to see than a tiger), multiple sloth bears, several crocodiles, wild boar, mongooses, a honey badger, and countless deer and various birds. The park is split up into zones that are chosen at random for the visitor. I visited zones 2, 3, 4, and 5 and had the best luck in zones 3 and 4. While our up close and personal tiger experience came in zone 3, I do feel as though the highest percentage chance of spotting a tiger would be in zone 4 given the large size and layout of this area. We did not have as much luck in zones 2 and 5 but that isn't to say that others haven't had the best experiences in these parts of the park. Zones 3 and 4 are around a lake area while zones 2 and 5 are more similar to what you would expect to see in *The Jungle Book*.

Not even taking into account the array of wildlife present in Ranthambore, the park itself is beautiful and for some would be enticing enough to visit just for the scenery. While I was overly fortunate in my four game drives within the park, some others who stayed at my hotel did not have a single tiger sighting over the course of several game drives. Even though Ranthambore is world renowned for the ease of seeing tigers, it is far from guaranteed that a visitor will actually see even one. We were told that the time of year with the highest percentage chance of seeing a tiger is in the summer months prior to monsoon season (although some online research contradicts this statement) when the park closes July through September due to heavy rainfall. Having said that, the most popular time of year to visit Ranthambore is still around when I went in January because of the overall favorable weather in India at this time of year. If you do travel to Ranthambore during the summer months, you may have a higher percentage chance of seeing a tiger, but you will also find that the temperature is sweltering hot.

How India handles their tiger conservation efforts over the coming years will play a role in overall tourism arrivals. It says something that a good portion of the individuals I met in Ranthambore National Park had come from Southern Africa. Even though many of these people had lions, giraffes, zebras, rhinos, and elephants in their backyard, they still found it enticing enough to come to Ranthambore to attempt to spot a tiger. I should note that most individuals had traveled to Ranthambore from Jaipur, as one can drive just a few hours from that city to arrive in Ranthambore. Unfortunately given my insanely busy schedule, I did not have this luxury.

In talking with various other travelers staying in the Ranthambore area doing the safaris, I was the only one who visited the Ranthambore Fort. This makes sense, as I saw but one other tourist along my trip to the top.

This UNESCO World Heritage Site was likely built in the 10th century (depending on who you ask) and sits high up in the hills overlooking the beautiful Ranthambore National Park. It is utterly incredible that this project was possible at the time, as the building materials came from 50 miles away and had to be transported to the area via transportation such as elephants only to be completed with bare hands.

In my experience, walking to the top of Ranthambore Fort, it felt as though I was temporarily transported back to the 10th century. The locals go to the top of the fort to pray, and it makes for a much more authentic Indian experience than what you will find on a safari in Ranthambore. Along the way, you will get to see the various gates and other inclusions that you would expect to see in a well-planned fort, such as lookout holes that likely doubled as a path to shoot arrows if necessary.

At the top of the fort, you will find the temple where the locals pray. Here I rang a loud gong before being blessed by a local man. It was a very different experience than anything you will find back in the United States.

Along the way you will find monkeys all over the place. We even witnessed one of the monkeys snatch a box of food from a visitor only to sprint up a cliff before the man realized what had happened! Visitors can feed the monkeys if they so choose, as I did, by opening their palm and the monkeys will simply come and happily retrieve the food from the palm area and scarf it down.

Overall, this is a worthwhile experience for visitors looking to learn more about the history of the area and in search of a more authentic local Indian experience. I didn't have much time so I completed the entire activity in less than two hours, but visitors could spend a lot more time at the top depending on their schedule while in Ranthambore.

I traveled to India in mid-January, which is a popular time to visit many parts of the country due to relatively favorable weather. Weather in areas such as Delhi, Jaipur, and Ranthambore was cool in the mornings and evenings and often in the 60s (Fahrenheit) or low 70s during the daytime. Because Bengaluru and Mumbai are further south, these areas did not require any form of jacket at this time of the year and the weather was nice.

My trip to India was arranged through Fairfax Financial Holdings Limited, which is a Canadian-based insurance company that owns Fairfax India Holdings Corporation, which owns and operates several businesses throughout India. I traveled with a group of over 40 investors who came from all over the world to get a better sense of the businesses that Fairfax owns as well as to gauge the overall business climate in India and the Far East in general. The reality is that more and more of the global growth is going to be coming from this part of the world, so every investor needs to be well versed on developments in countries such as India, China, and Indonesia whether or not they have any direct investments in these countries. During our stay in India, we met with countless Fairfax executives and board members, listened to presentations on Fairfax businesses in India and on the country more broadly, and went on various tours to see some of the sights the country has to offer.

India is the 7th largest country in the world by land size and the second most populous country on earth, as it now boasts over 1.3 billion people. India is the most populous democracy in the world and the second largest English-speaking country.

India is a constitutional federal republic made of 29 states, each of which has significant control over their own dealings. The country is bounded by the Indian Ocean to the south, the Arabian Sea to the southwest, and the Bay of Bengal to the southeast. India has land borders with Pakistan, China, Nepal, Bhutan, Bangladesh, and Myanmar. The island country of Sri Lanka is only about 40 miles removed from the southeast coast of India. The coastline of the country measures approximately 4,671 miles and the Himalayas form the northern limit of India. The geography of India is diverse, with the landscape ranging from snow-capped mountain ranges to deserts, plains, and hills.

The government of India is created by the constitution of India as the legislative, executive, and judicial authority of the union of 29 states and six union territories. India has a parliamentary democracy which operates under the Constitution of 1950. Like the United States, India has a federal structure of government in which the constitution divides power between the central government and the state governments. The government has three branches: the executive, the legislative, and the judiciary. The Indian President is the head of the state and exercises his or her power directly or through subordinate officers.

The history of India is still somewhat of a mystery, as not much was left behind from the cities that existed in the Indus River valley thousands of years ago. The history is divided into three periods: Ancient India, Medieval India, and Modern India.

The Indus Valley Civilization is believed to have flourished around 2,500 BCE in what is today Pakistan and Western India. Until the 1920s, little was known about this civilization. Then, the Archaeological Department of India made discoveries that unearthed history and insights into the society that would be described as an urban civilization where people lived in well-planned towns which were the centers for trade.

The Europeans came to India in the 17th century, and by the latter part of the 18th century, the English had established themselves as the dominant power in India. This helps explain the widespread English-speaking culture present in India today. The British controlled India for a period of about two centuries before the anti-British movement became a mass struggle with the arrival of Mahatma Gandhi leading up to the 1900s. The British were eventually driven out of India in 1947 when the British Parliament passed the Indian Independence Act of 1947. This also declared Pakistan a free nation, and India has had a contentious relationship with Pakistan ever since. We were told at a dinner that an individual from Pakistan would not be welcome to join our table given the relations between the two countries.

There is no one state religion in India; 80% of the population classifies as Hindu and 14.2% as Muslim. India has more Muslims than any country other than Indonesia. India has had a history of religious violence that remains an issue to this day. Since independence, hundreds of religious riots have been recorded in which thousands have been killed. While you may notice that some women have opened up to clothing that would more resemble that of western culture, you will still find a portion of the female population that heavily covers the face, and overall Indian culture would still be classified as conservative. India remains a male dominated society despite improvements in regard to women's rights. Men don't have to wear wedding bands while the expectation is that females do. Roughly 90% of marriages in India are still arranged. Our tour guide informed the group that families take out local newspaper advertisements to look for a potential spouse for their children that would be from a family of a similar background.

Here are some additional interesting facts about India: India is the largest producer of movies in the world, the legal drinking age varies by state, but is as high as 25 years old in cities such as Delhi, and India is the world's largest milk producer.

Economy

India is the world's 6th largest economy by nominal GDP and third largest by purchasing power parity. India had the fastest growing major economy in 2014, 2015, 2016, and 2018. India is expected to be one of the top three economic powers in the world over the coming years, along with China and the United States.

The foundation of the Indian economy lies in its 1.3 billion people that are hardworking for the most part. The current average age in the country is 29 years old, and the country is very early in the consumption cycle relative to the United States and China. This is illustrated by the fact that India ranked 122nd globally in per capita GDP in 2018 despite having the 6th largest global economy in terms of nominal GDP. The flow-through impact can be seen in the growth projections for the ecommerce industry, which is expected to grow from $39 billion in sales in 2017 to a whopping $200 billion in 2026. As I will discuss later, this does not necessarily mean that the profits will follow this massive growth trajectory. Despite challenges that I will highlight, the economic potential is enormous if properly harnessed. India will continue to face challenges when it comes to physical infrastructure, poor secondary education, and bureaucracy that I would classify as extreme on any scale.

The IT industry continues to be the largest private-sector employer in India. We saw firsthand the skyrocketing growth that was taking hold in this sector in Bengaluru. Another important point to note about the Indian economy is how far ahead they are in terms of transition to a mobile-first economy when compared to the United States. How did a developing country like India leapfrog the U.S. in this space? India skipped the entire desktop and laptop revolution that we had in the West. Many Indian consumers went straight to mobile and do everything on their phones, such as buying all products on mobile. I personally still use a desktop or laptop to make purchases on websites such as Amazon because this is a habit that I spent years building prior to ever having a cellphone.

Despite my commentary on the bureaucracy in India, the World Bank boosted the country by 23 places over the past several years to 77th in terms of global ease of doing business. This tells you how low the baseline is and how deeply rooted bureaucracy is in the Indian culture. The World Bank has specifically highlighted improved business climate for small and medium enterprises. An example would be how Mumbai recently abolished the practice of inspections for registering companies under the Shops and Establishments Act, which cut the time to start a business from 30 days to 16 days. This makes sense to me because most of the regulation that I have followed in India has been targeted at large multinational corporations which is ultimately bad for future foreign investment.

Any discussion about the Indian economy would not be complete without looking at the controversial 2016 Indian banknote demonetization that is estimated to have wiped out at least 1% from India's GDP and cost the country 1.5 million jobs. To make matters worse, it is estimated that over 99% of the currency that the government said was going to be destroyed had subsequently made its way back into the financial system and diminished government credibility in the process. The government was introducing new currency bills and said that everyone would have to exchange their old bills for the new currency. The logic behind this was that in doing so the Indian government would be able to register individuals and account for their money for income tax purposes. At the time of demonetization, it is believed that fewer than 2% of Indians paid taxes! From my understanding, the demonetization process was a failed attempt to significantly move the needle when it comes to getting more citizens to pay taxes. Unless something changes on this front, I don't see how the country is going to fund all of these infrastructure projects (such as the current underground subway being built in Mumbai) that they are building and proposing. India is in desperate need of physical infrastructure to catch up with the exploding population, but it is a mystery to me as to how these projects are going to be paid for given present conditions and lack of clarity as to how things are going to change.

Adventure

Arriving in India for the first time from an overnight flight coming from the United States can be an overwhelming experience. It feels as though you have been transported to a whole different world altogether, as sleep deprivation takes hold and the stark contrasts from society in the Western world become readily apparent. For one, the plane you arrived on was likely full of nearly all Indian passengers. I was one of but maybe five Caucasian individuals on an airplane that likely held up to 500 people. I held my breath as the customs agent checked my E-visa, as I always play out the worst-case travel scenarios in my head prior to arrival in a foreign country to try and anticipate nearly everything that can go wrong. After a long wait to collect my bags, I was met by an agent from Thomas Cook India and transported to my hotel.

I was fortunate enough to be staying at the Leela Palace in New Delhi, which is considered by many to be the finest hotel in the Delhi area. While I may be a bit biased considering the fact that I was only staying in the top-of-the-line hotels around India, I think I can say that the country has by far the best customer service I have ever witnessed, even when compared to luxury hotel chains in United States and other more expensive countries, which is a bullish signal for the tourism sector.

Visitors are greeted with a cotton thread necklace upon arrival. I was personally shown to my room and walked through all of the amenities the hotel has to offer. The concierge was incredible, as they even opened the gym just for me at 4:00 a.m. when I couldn't sleep and helped me with things such as exchanging currency for smaller bills. Even though many others in our investor group preferred hotels such as Rambagh Palace (in Jaipur), my favorite was Leela because of the state-of-the-art technology and my personal preference for modern hotels. The history and natural beauty of Rambagh Palace and The Taj Mahal Palace (Mumbai) were more impressive, but I found the practicality of Leela gives it the edge over the other luxury hotels. I will admit that I was at least a little nervous to stay at The Taj Mahal Palace given the 2008 terrorist attack that claimed the lives of 31 individuals at this hotel. I would have expected more security at all of these hotels and would have felt more comfort in seeing the guards holding weapons given the history of the hotels such as the Taj in Mumbai.

After arriving at the hotel late at night and having completed my 4:00 a.m. gym session, I proceeded to read the local newspapers, which I did most days while in the country. What stood out most was how much it talked about implementing new regulations. I have been well versed on the Indian regulatory environment since I have many investments that operate in the country. Perhaps the pinnacle of the Indian regulatory insanity came in 2016 when the Supreme Court passed an order banning the sale of alcohol along national and state highways, ordering the cancellation of liquor licenses issued to shops by April 1, 2017. The order stated that no liquor stores should be visible from highways or located within a distance of 500 meters of the highways or be directly accessible from a national or state highway. The government has since retraced its footsteps on this ban, but if you are a multinational corporation such as Diageo PLC, how can you with full confidence continue to invest substantial sums of money in the Indian market if you know that the government is fully capable and willing to ban your main product at any point in time? It is government actions such as these that are terrible for foreign investment. Similar to the newspapers, the news on television said that social media fake news is one of the country's largest problems. Shouldn't most of the responsibility be on the consumer to not be so gullible and fact check sources before immediately assuming that everything they read is true? How is this remotely close to being as high of a priority when compared to improving education or physical infrastructure? I wouldn't be surprised if foreign companies started to become more skeptical in regard to investing huge dollars in the country.

After arriving back in the capital city of New Delhi later in the evening following my visit to Ranthambore National Park, I rested up for the slate of activities scheduled the next day. The following morning, I was introduced to the investor group that was a mix of people from all over the world. The majority of individuals were from Canada and to a lesser extent the United States but there were representatives from Europe, South Africa, and Australia. Many in the group ran their own investment firms, and some worked as executives at larger investment outfits.

We set out by bus for Old Delhi. Most visitors' first observation regarding Delhi would be how sprawling and crowded the city is. The 2019 population of Delhi is believed to be around 29 million people (if the statistics are to be trusted). The populations of the mid-tier and major Indian cities is difficult to comprehend if you live in the United States, where the largest city is New York City which is home to 8.6 million people. Old Delhi is 380 years old and is much more what you would think of in terms of a foreigner picturing India. Many areas of New Delhi could be mistaken for anywhere else in the world given the various newer and more modern projects.

Our group went on a brief rickshaw ride through the markets in Old Delhi. This area was overly congested, chaotic, loud, and smelly. It is everything that you likely have read about in regard to the real India experience. We then visited the local spice markets, where we couldn't help but take pictures and videos and digest this foreign experience that was being provided to many of us westerners. The sheer crowds and hustle and bustle of this area can be overwhelming for many but for those looking to get a peek into the local marketplaces in a country of 1.3 billion people, this is one of the places to do it.

We had lunch at The Spice Route located in the beautiful Imperial Hotel in New Delhi. Each day for lunch, we indulged in some form of high-end Indian cuisine (often meeting with executives from Fairfax Financial) that was always located in a decadent atmosphere. I am sad to say that I was disappointed with the food overall and became extremely tired of what I would consider to be similar meals by about the sixth day in India. I think it was likely partially attributable to lack of sleep along the journey, but I should note that most in the group did get sick at least once along the way. Discerning whether this was directly related to the food, water, exhaustion, or other factors is difficult to pinpoint, but many did not feel well after our dinner at City Palace in Jaipur. Despite eating various upscale dinners in Delhi, Jaipur, Bengaluru, and Mumbai, my favorite meal in India was our lunch at Peshawri in Agra. Every food item that I tasted at this restaurant which included chicken, lamb, prawns was delicious, and the sauces were equally as good. This restaurant provides for a unique atmosphere in that diners eat with their hands and wear an apron while eating their meal. If I could choose only one meal to have again in India it would be at Peshawri.

In the afternoon we visited Qutub Minar, a 240-foot tower that was established in 1192 and is a UNESCO World Heritage Site. The tower is surrounded by several historical monuments that are part of the Qutab complex. At the foot of the tower, you will find a mosque called Quwwat-ul-Islam, which was the first mosque built in India. The design of Qutub Minar has been compared to other minarets such as the Minaret of Jam, which is a UNESCO World Heritage Site in western Afghanistan.

Continuing my relentless schedule, I had arranged to be picked up to visit a local school called Pragati Wheel, which I support through my efforts with CanEducate, a Canadian-based charitable organization that provides ongoing support to schools in developing countries, as a Board Member for the entity. The school called in about 70 students on a Sunday just to greet me. Could you imagine the reaction if a school in the United States requested that their student population come in to school on a Sunday to greet a supporter? Over the past 11 years with the support of CanEducate,

Pragati has grown from 30 students to 300 students. The students attending this school are mostly from a nearby neighborhood where they live in houses that are essentially makeshift huts, which I passed by in reaching the school. These children are the poorest of the poor, and if it were not for Pragati Wheel they would be out on the streets, so just getting them into school is a major victory. Every now and then, you have a real life-changing experience, and this was one of them for me. Seeing the smiles on these children's faces, even though they had nothing other than this school, was special to say the least.

India has made great strides in recent years when it comes to education. For example, the 2018 Annual Status of Education Report (ASER) reported that the enrollment of children in the age group 6-14 has reached 95%. However, for India to take the next step, it will have to dramatically improve the college level education system. In 2016, only one Indian university made it to the top 200 in the world. This has been a consistent theme for India over the years and a major reason that the country loses a lot of the top talent to the United States and other countries.

That evening, we were lucky enough to have dinner at the residence of the Canadian High Commissioner to India. Given the location in New Delhi and size of the estate, I have little doubt that this complex would be valued north of $50 million. For all of our other dinners while in India, we met with Fairfax Financial executives. Given that we woke up most mornings around 5:00 a.m. and often didn't get home from our dinners and meetings until 11:00 p.m., I was exhausted by the end of the trip. I don't know how the more senior members of the group survived.

The following morning our group took an approximately two-hour train ride to Agra. This city of roughly two million people was founded in the early 16th century and is best known for being home to one of the New 7 Wonders of the World: the Taj Mahal.

The Taj Mahal is a modern marvel that rests on the right bank of the Yamuna River and is considered the greatest architectural achievement in all of Indo-Islamic architecture. There have been arguments over the years as to the purpose of the Taj Mahal. Claims that the UNESCO World Heritage Site was originally a Hindu temple have been refuted by archaeologists who say the Taj is a Muslim mausoleum built by a Mughal emperor to honor his dead wife. The Taj is significant to India in terms of tourism, as it attracts 6.5 million visitors per year. Perhaps most surprising to me was how few people there were when I was visiting. I would have expected four to five times the amount of visitors given how impressive the area is. It is highly unlikely that another Taj will ever be built, as it is made of marble and would likely cost hundreds of billions of dollars to construct today. We were told that the Treasury nearly went bankrupt when constructing the Taj all those years ago in the early 1600s. The project was believed to have taken 11 years to build, employing 20,000 artisans and 1,000 elephants!

I was overly impressed with the lengths to which the Indian government has gone to preserve the Taj Mahal, which is a positive sign for the future of Indian tourism. Only electric vehicles were allowed in the area surrounding the Taj to avoid further pollution and the building was immaculately clean, looking as though it was built in January 2019 instead of having been completed in 1653 (although this date is disputed). The structure looks bigger and even more impressive in person than in pictures. We snapped photographs and walked around the complex of structures for an hour or so. It was the absolute perfect day to visit the Taj, as there was not a single cloud in the sky and the temperature was around 70 degrees Fahrenheit. I think that everyone with the means to do so needs to visit the Taj Mahal at least once in their lifetime. Some historical monuments and structures tend to disappoint when a visitor finally sees them in person, but it is rare for someone to come back from the Taj without being blown away by the architectural mastery.

That afternoon we took a charter flight from Agra to Jaipur, which was less than an hour in terms of flying time. This was an experience in and of itself, as we took a private Jet Airways plane out of a military base located outside of Agra. Prior to traveling to India, I had done extensive research regarding the safety of the regional airlines that we were taking while in the country because I knew that India did not have the best reputation when it comes to aviation safety. According to airlineratings.com, Jet Airways and IndiGo Airlines (the two we would be taking along our journey) were scored a 6/7 in terms of safety, which is on par with the likes of South African Airways. This rating, combined with other research that I did, confirmed that Jet and IndiGo were the best available when it comes to safety and product offering. The caveat is that this may not carry substantial weight, as there have been numerous reports the past few years of the Indian skies becoming more dangerous due to factors such as relaxed regulation, pilot fatigue, and air traffic controls that are struggling to keep up with the surging demand for air travel in the country. As of July 2018, there were four near mid-air collisions in the past year that were narrowly avoided by IndiGo planes, and it is believed that there is at least one such event happening every day in Indian skies with many going unreported. India is in the top of the first inning in regard to growth in airplane travel and this will be an enormous 20 to 30-year growth story like what was experienced in China over the past 20 years. As of May 2018, India recorded double-digit air passenger growth for the 45th consecutive month. How the government handles this robust growth market going forward in terms of regulation and infrastructure will play a role in determining the ultimate success of this market. They have a lot of work to do in terms of getting the infrastructure to a place that would comfortably fit current demand and they will be playing catch-up.

The following day we were set to take a tour of Jaipur. Jaipur is the largest city in the Indian state of Rajasthan, which makes up 10% of the country by size. This city of close to four million people is often referred to as the "Pink City" because walls in the historic city center are painted with a terracotta pink color. Visitors to Jaipur who have arrived from Delhi will immediately notice that Jaipur is, on aggregate, a much cleaner, less congested, and, in my opinion, a more visually appealing city. Many in our group agreed that their favorite city that we visited along the journey was Jaipur.

Our first stop was Amer Fort, which is a UNSECO World Heritage Site that has intriguing architecture that combines Mughal and Hindu styles. This top Jaipur tourist attraction dates back to the 16th century and sits atop a hill named Cheel ka Teela, which allows for generous views of the Jaipur area. This impressive fort comprises an extensive palace complex built from pale yellow and pink sandstone along with white marble and is divided into four main sections, each with its own courtyard. While I would disagree, some members of our group found Amer Fort to be even more impressive than the Taj Mahal. Regardless, Amer is a must-see for all visitors that come to Jaipur.

In the afternoon, some of us in the group went to visit some of the local textile businesses in Jaipur. The textile industry has been growing exponentially in recent years and, according to the Union Minister, Foreign Direct Investment for the industry tripled in the three years ending 2017. The textile industry employs the second largest number of individuals in the industrial sector.

It was an enjoyable experience watching local hardworking Indians produce works of art such as carpets. Some found the Indians in general to be aggressive and persistent in their sales tactics, but I would have to disagree. I would consider the Moroccans to be by far the most persistent in this area and found the Indian people to be relatively relaxed when it came to trying to push the sale of their products. I did find some similarities between the Indian textile sales approach when compared to the Peruvian sales tactics in that the people wanted to provide a presentation of a given product in order to increase the likelihood that a potential consumer will make a purchase, which I think is a good sales strategy.

We also visited one of the finer local jewelry stores in Jaipur. We were told that Indians have always had a fascination with jewelry with a particular interest in gold. Be it Hinduism, Sikhism, or Jainism, India's religions have a deep connection with gold. Not only does bullion make up an integral part of major ceremonies, it is used to shower newlyweds, newborns, and individuals celebrating their birthdays. Gold is a major form of gifting in the Indian culture and is a status symbol in the country. The diamond district in Antwerp, Belgium, (I visited this area in 2011) long held the crown as the diamond cutting capital of the world but has ceded this designation to India in recent years where some estimates say that 80% of the world's diamonds are now polished in India. Some estimates claim that Surat, India (now known as the "Diamond City") handles 90% of the world's rough diamond cutting and polishing.

After visiting Jaipur and Delhi, one of the conversations that I had with another investor on the trip was that for a supposedly booming economy, where were all of the cranes? We saw but maybe two cranes in total in Jaipur and Delhi. We would later see a different picture in Bengaluru and Mumbai where construction was widespread, but it is at least something to consider. My new friend Bill said he had been traveling to developing countries for well over 30 years and had never seen such a lack of construction for an economy that was being pitched as having robust economic growth. It did make us at least pause to ask ourselves if the GDP metrics being reported by the Indian government were in fact true.

The next stop on our journey around India was in Bengaluru (formerly called Bangalore until the name change in 2014). Like Mumbai, which was renamed from Bombay, we were told that a nationalist wave riding through India has been a driving force behind these name changes in the capital of India's southern Karnataka state. Bengaluru's population is estimated to be around 12 million, but this number is set to explode to over 20 million by 2031. This makes sense from our observations, as there was a lot of building going on in this city, especially when compared to Delhi and Jaipur. Bengaluru is considered the IT hub of India and has at times been referred to as "India's Silicon Valley".

We didn't get to spend much time in Bengaluru, but in our brief stay here, it was clear to me that this was the most visually appealing city that we visited. While we were told that Bengaluru had somewhat been losing its reputation as being the "Garden City" because of all of the construction, it was still far greener than any city we saw while in India. The city resides in the southern part of the country and unlike its northern counterparts, it has a tropical savanna climate and is known for its pleasant weather throughout the year.

The main reason for our stop in Bengaluru was to visit and tour the airport, Bangalore International Airport Limited, which is now 54% owned by Fairfax India Holdings Corporation after the additional 6% interest they purchased from Siemens in May 2018. We were fortunate enough to have the opportunity to tour the facilities and even get to see the air traffic control room and walk around the outside of the tower overlooking the entire complex. The amount of construction going on at this airport was astounding and perhaps a sign of what is to come for the Indian aviation sector. During the investor presentation that we saw, air traffic at the airport had been tripling every eight years with no signs of slowing down. Given the geographic location of the airport, the Indian government has been positioning it as another gateway to Asia to compete with Dubai International Airport, which had the third most annual passengers as of 2017.

The last stop on our trip was Mumbai, which is still known as Bombay to the older generation that grew up using the name. During our stay here, we took a city tour and had a slew of meetings like at our other stops. I had three experiences that were of particular note while in Mumbai: the dabbawala experience, visiting the local marketplaces at dawn, and my first attempt at sailing.

The Mumbai dabbawalas are world famous (they have been visited by the likes of Richard Branson), but I had never heard of them prior to my arrival. They run a lunchbox delivery and return system to people at work that has been around since 1890. Many rational individuals would ask why on earth this business is even necessary, as workers in the United States who don't eat out for lunch simply just carry their lunch to work. Understanding this makes more sense if you watch a YouTube video of the Mumbai metro, as there is zero excess space for accessories such as a lunch bag on the morning and evening commutes. The dabbawala business has 5,000 employees that deliver 200,000 dabbas, lunches, every day. One of the most interesting parts about the business is the complete lack of technology used, as they use a special "coding" system that consists of writing brief letters and numbers on the top of the box to denote the route and drop off point along the way. Many of the employees are partially or completely illiterate so this simple coding system is the best way to communicate to fellow coworkers. The cost of the service is only $20 per month and a customer can get up to six deliveries per week for the fee! Many in our group were wondering how the rise of Uber Eats and Swiggy will impact the dabbawala business. While I disagree with their response, they argued that these businesses were not direct competitors with the dabbawala business. What I will say is that the price point is completely different between their business and the established food delivery players. Additionally, the dabbawalas claimed that because their business utilizes metro delivery on their routes, they could get the food to their customers far faster than Uber Eats or Swiggy could by car due to traffic congestion. I can see how the dabbawala business will continue to carve out a niche given the differentiated price point and at least for now the only offering that delivers lunches by train. But to say that Uber Eats is not a competitor is misguided, as there will be a segment of the target market that does prefer the advanced technology and other parts of the business that the dabbawalas do not offer. For example, I have always found it helpful that Uber responds almost immediately to any customer service requests. However you break it down, the dabbawala business is a modern marvel when it comes to logistics and operations. They claim a near 100% success rate in their deliveries despite the complete lack of technology. It was evident that the employees took a great sense of pride in their work despite the extremely low pay.

I had separately arranged for a tour named Mumbai by Dawn with about ten members of our larger group. We arose before 5:00 a.m. to visit the location where the fish comes in, newspaper distribution hub, fruit and vegetable market, flower market, and location where they do laundry outdoors. Despite having taken various tours in several cities in India, I was craving to see more of "the real India," which I think we only really witnessed in Old Delhi and during our brief meet with the dabbawalas (and I thought I had a real India experience visiting the local school in Delhi).

I am so glad that I opted to take the tour of the local marketplaces in Mumbai, as I was able to get a peek inside the hardworking culture present in the country. What I witnessed was an average work ethic that arguably surpasses that of the United States. Most people work six days a week with many individuals working three or four jobs to make ends meet. The average person here worked tirelessly and did so with a smile on their face. I believe that if countries such as India and China can ever make large advancements in secondary education, physical infrastructure, and regulatory reform to encourage a more business friendly operating environment they will be able to gain ground on the United States. This is a major caveat, and I don't know if it will ever happen, but the declining work ethic and determination of the average U.S. citizen does worry me. India and China have much larger and hungrier populations that, if properly harnessed, could make a leap past the United States.

Most from the West would have envisioned something a little different in hearing that the plan was to visit markets such as a newspaper distribution center and a flower market. The Mumbai reality of these business centers was that the newspaper center consisted of a bunch of locals sitting outside on a sidewalk organizing and getting individuals set up with their personal pile for which they would be distributing that day. The flower market wasn't much different in this sense. To arrive here, we had to walk through a crowded street to arrive at a sidewalk area that was overflowing with locals passing by and perusing the flower offerings. A few interesting sights we saw along the way that you don't get to see every day: a man slitting the throat of a live chicken on the side of the road, seeing thousands of articles of clothing being dried out in the open as part of the local laundry business, and live auctions conducted at the fish market where women would sell a bag of the recently caught fish.

Some interesting points to note about the newspaper business are that India now has the most paid newspapers in the world. Unlike the United States where physical newspaper sales plummeted for years, newspaper sales are still rising at a solid pace for the Indian market due to the demand for newspapers that cater to the various local languages. My prediction is that online resources such as Facebook will take note of this trend and take market share from physical newspapers, especially considering the rising smartphone penetration in India, but only time will tell. What will help keep the physical newspaper business afloat is the extremely low cost of them, as they were only $.10 at time of visit. The rest of the money made from the issues was in the advertisements.

One of the points that our tour guide noted along the way was the ongoing belief that automation is bad for society. This is ever present in how they handle many businesses that we saw along our tour such as the newspaper distribution where many of their current roles would be filled by robots in other markets such as the United States. While there are always individuals in the United States and other more developed markets that voice these worries, it scares me as to how deeply-rooted this philosophy is in the Indian culture. If the United States never embraced automation as a society, we would have never advanced past making individually hand-crafted automobiles in the late 1800s and early 1900s. Make no mistake about it, there will be a segment of the population left behind in this latest industrial revolution where we are becoming a data centric society. I would be worried for any job that is pure manual labor and does not include any human analytical component. As a whole, we will have to adapt to this new reality that robots can help us become more efficient in many manual labor categories as demonstrated by companies such as Amazon that have utilized them in their warehouse distribution facilities. We should be focused on creating new jobs and roles that entail monitoring the tasks and efficiency of these robots, explaining the output, and thinking about what we can do to make the process better. More than ever, a premium will be placed on education in this evolving data centric society which in addition to productivity advancements will likely only widen the inequality gap, which we will have to be mindful of in charting these waters. Despite the forthcoming societal challenges faced by automation, to restrain innovation on these grounds would be the peak of regulatory irresponsibility and lead to an overall society worse off over the long-term.

In touring Mumbai, one can't help but notice the extreme inequality present in the city that is a widespread issue in India as a whole. Mumbai is home to 28 billionaires and also lays claim to miles of slums that were made famous by the movie *Slumdog Millionaire*. India's 1% owns 58% of wealth compared to 42% in the United States. This will be one of the major challenges the country will look to tackle in the upcoming years.

The final activity on this jam-packed itinerary was a sailing lesson that I did on the Arabian Sea that departed next to the Gateway of India, which was just outside of our hotel (The Taj Mahal Palace). I was surprised at how easy one can pick up this leisure activity, as I was fully capable of guiding our boat in my desired direction after about an hour of practice. From the water view it made the pollution in Mumbai all the more apparent. I did have a bit of trouble breathing in Mumbai, and others noted that it was somewhat of a challenge in Delhi. This will be a challenge area for India going forward.

Additional Activities and Recommendations

Given the vast size of India, there are near limitless opportunities when it comes to exploring the country, but I will keep this list to a handful of items. Before making travel arrangements, do make sure to carefully research the weather in the portion of the country under consideration for the time period of interest. Keep in mind that monsoon seasons in India vary throughout the country and certain areas get hot and uncomfortable during the summer months.

If I had more time in India, I would have gone straight to Uttarakhand. This area located in the far north of the country is bordered by Nepal and Tibet, which has a backdrop of the Himalayan peaks. There is a lot of relatively undiscovered natural beauty here and an array of adventure options that include trekking, rock climbing, whitewater rafting at locations such as Rishikesh, and visiting parks such as the famous Jim Corbett National Park (home to Bengal tigers, leopards, and elephants). There seems to be near infinite possibilities for an adventure seeker such as myself to explore.

Another wildlife related destination that caught my eye was The Hemis National Park in Ladakh, Jammu, and Kashmir, which has the highest density of snow leopards in any protected area on the planet. Visitors can hire a local expert to track these elusive animals. In addition to Ranthambore National Park and Jim Corbett National Park, which I have covered pertaining to tiger wildlife, Bandhavgarh National Park, Pench National Park, and Kanha National Park are some of the other popular tiger destinations in India. Around two-thirds of the estimated 3,500 one-horned rhinos remaining in Asia reside in Kaziranga National Park, so those looking to spot this animal will make this destination in Assam a priority. Many would be surprised to find out that Gir Forest National Park is home to Asiatic lions, which is also an enticing option.

Goa has gained international recognition as a popular beach destination in India. Adventure seekers looking for nightclubs and other nightlife offerings that keep the parties going until the morning hours may find something to like here. Given the reputation that has made Goa a tourist hotspot for the beaches and nightlife, this does not appeal to me, but it remains as popular as ever. Having said that, there is a wealth of adventure options here, which includes scuba diving, surfing, parasailing, hiking, water sports, and fishing. Some of the investor group that I was traveling with was stopping in Goa after our tour was over. Those with a keen eye on scuba diving will want to head to Andaman Islands, which is the top-rated scuba destination in India.

Kashmir is a significant draw for skiing and other winter activities. This Himalayan area is often considered a hub for adventure sports. It should be noted that the U.S. Department of State recommends not traveling to Kashmir due to terrorism and civil unrest.

For a unique experience, adventurers may want to attend one of the world's largest camel fairs at Pushkar, which takes place in the Thar Desert in Rajasthan. This event attracts more than 200,000 visitors and is a cultural phenomenon. 30,000 camels come to this fair, where they are sold to families. Activities and performances such as temple dancing, folk music concerts, and spiritual walks take place during the festival. This is an event that I would like to witness for myself one day.

For those looking for a nature experience that does not involve viewing exotic and rare animals, you may want to consider visiting the Tea Gardens of Darjeeling. If you aren't convinced by this writing, then do a Google image search of this stunning area located in eastern India of the West Bengal state. I was informed that the southern portion of India is dominated by coffee drinking while the majority of the rest of the country still sticks with tea.

Veranasi is often considered a high priority for visitors to India. This is one of the oldest inhabited areas in the world that is still populated. There are various temples and forts such as Ramnagar Fort that travelers will want to observe and learn more about along the way.

Udaipur is another city that often comes up in conversation because of its beautiful lakes, forts, temples, and palaces. This city located in Rajasthan has been the setting for many movies such as the 1983 James Bond film *Octopussy*.

Business Outlook

While in India, I was told that, when comparing India to China, a famous investor said, "With China, the opportunity is apparent and the risk is hidden and with India the risk is apparent and the opportunity is hidden." I am not sure I could summarize my thoughts on India in a more succinct manner. India operates the largest democracy in the world with 1.3 billion people, and growing quickly, that I would classify as hardworking for the most part. Additionally, the average age of the population is 29, and the consumer is early in the consumption cycle. The million-dollar question is whether these robust demographic tailwinds will be offset and to what extent by poor physical infrastructure, a dismal secondary education system, and extreme bureaucracy.

While the cost of everyday items can be had for a bargain, upscale and luxury services and products are expensive relative to other developing markets. For example, fine dining in a city such as Jaipur, Delhi, or Mumbai would set you back several multiples of what you would expect to pay in Medellín, Colombia. Having said that, one could purchase a pair of sandwiches at McDonalds for $1. I still get the feeling that the Indian rupee and the overall Indian equity market may have gotten ahead of itself relative to business reality in 2019. The 20 to 30-year projections for the Indian rupee and stock market could look completely different, but that is just my gut feeling about the country right this second.

In speaking with an array of local business executives and investors along my trip, I concluded that the largest Indian businesses opportunities were in physical infrastructure, aviation, and mobile technologies. As discussed previously, the physical infrastructure opportunity will play out in full only if the Indian government figures out a rational plan for paying for all of the infrastructure projects the country needs to keep up with the population growth. I talked about the opportunity related to the Indian aviation sector and this applies to the travel and tourism business, which is projected to establish itself as the third largest in the world by 2028 in terms of total GDP, up from 7th in the world today. One of the major focuses of India on the infrastructure side has been building secondary airports to support this robust growth in travel and tourism. I have talked about the developments in India when it comes to mobile habits and widespread phone adoption, but I haven't touched on the rising smartphone penetration rate in India. The 2019 smartphone penetration rate is 46% compared to just 29.8% in 2016 (and a projected 71.4% in the U.S. in 2019). Given that India has the lowest cost of data in the world, a cellular network that I found to be even better than that of the United States, and consumers that have been trained to use their mobile devices for almost everything, it is easy to see a perfect storm of opportunity in this space.

One of the other large opportunities I discussed was vehicle adoption. By 2040, the number of vehicles per 1,000 inhabitants is projected to increase nine times! This projection could be altered dramatically by widespread adoption of autonomous vehicles and ridesharing, but current predictions are calling for an enormous increase in vehicles in India.

Another area of focus is healthcare pertaining to some of the lesser diseases. I was told that for the majority of India's existence, they have focused almost solely on tackling major diseases. As the country gets more developed, some of the focus and budget is going to shift to second and third-tier priorities like what we have seen with the evolution of other developed countries.

One of the things I struggle with when it comes to emerging markets in general is the correlation between GDP growth and the ability to actually profit from this growth. There is an enormous misconception that just because a country is growing fast and has demographic tailwinds for years to come, every investor will make a lot of money in that country. I think this is a trap that Amazon and Walmart could be falling into in India when it comes to the e-commerce industry. While the growth projections for the industry are staggering, I do not believe there is a clear route to substantial profits in the Indian market. Even though Indian GDP has been growing at a rate that has been several multiples of the United States in a given year, iShares MSCI India ETF returned 7.25% in the five years ending 2018 compared to 8.44% for iShares Core S&P 500 ETF, which may surprise some individuals. The correlation between country GDP growth and earnings per share growth is far below what most believe and causes this disconnect between GDP growth and stock market returns. Additionally, price always matters, and the stock index or individual companies could reflect this optimism.

In my view, the jury is still very much out on India. I am not as convinced as many others that investors will be able to come away with outsized returns from investments in the country. I would have to see severe changes to government policy related to business for me to get excited.

Updates Since Visit

Since my visit to India, chaos erupted in Kashmir after India's only Muslim-majority state had its statehood removed. Protests ensued, and the digital rights group Access Now claimed that the Internet was shut down for the longest period of time on record for any democracy. The ongoing religious tension between the Hindu and Muslim populations remains a considerable risk for the long-term health of the Indian economy and the well-being of the country as a whole.

According to a report by the World Bank, "The Covid-19 outbreak came at a time when India's economy was already slowing, due to persistent financial sector weaknesses."

I have followed the developments in India closely and believe that some of the economic weakness even before the outbreak of COVID-19 was attributable to ineffective economic policies implemented by the government. On an almost daily basis I read about additional protectionist measures being enacted by the Indian government that will ultimately harm foreign investment. In what is perhaps a more ominous signal for the future of the Indian economy, almost every well-funded business in the country that you read about loses money. A 2019 report cited eight Indian start-ups with billion dollar valuations that were all losing money. Amazon's India business continues to report losses along with nearly every other company I cover that operates in India. Disney recently release their Disney Plus streaming service in India for a cost of $20 per year compared to $70 per year in the United States. I do not believe that Disney turns a profit at a rate of $70 per year per consumer so I would estimate that the loss per year in India will be massive. In short, the economics of operating almost any business at this moment in time have not made sense outside of possibly Facebook and Google's advertising juggernauts. The long-term potential for the Indian economy is still present but I am not as optimistic as most others that this potential will ever be fully realized.

Ranthambore National Park

Ranthambore Fort

Meeting with the students at Pragati Wheel

Perfect day at the Taj Mahal

Amer Fort

Air traffic controls at Bangalore International Airport Limited

The world famous Mumbai Dabbawala business

The Mumbai laundry business

Cuba

Introduction

We had a tobacco tour in the Viñales area, which is located about 2.5 hours from Havana. This tour costs $60 per person and the total transportation cost from Havana starts at $150. This full day tour included a hike, lunch, and a visit to a local tobacco farm. There is an option to pair horseback riding with this tour, and hiking options vary depending on the group's preference. This activity was my most anticipated part of our trip to Cuba.

On the ride from Havana to Viñales, it doesn't take long to realize that there is not much other than farms and open land along the way. It is a scenic drive, as most of the landscape is green. The most striking observation on the drive is that all of the farmers and workers in this area were using machetes to cut the grass. There was no sign of any lawnmowers. Could you imagine cutting several acres of land in the 100 degree (Fahrenheit) Cuban heat by hand with a machete?! Ironically, Mr. Bellini informed me that the Cuban Revolution under Castro started in the countryside and the farmers were supplied with state-of-the-art technology such as lawnmowers. Fast forward 60 years, and the Cuban countryside has gone back hundreds of years in time. The misguided and unethical communist government policies have made it so that farmers in 2019 can't afford to purchase a lawnmower.

While most of the land between Havana and Viñales is flat, the Viñales area brings hills and mountains. Our hike in this area was done in a relatively flat open area, but there is the option for more challenging hikes up in the mountains. In just looking at the potential mountain hiking paths from the lower altitude, I would recommend this option for more adventurous individuals who have the means to conquer hikes that pose a bit of a challenge. We hiked around the wide-open area for a couple hours and took in the views. As we navigated the open terrain on this hot, sunny day, we intermittently stopped for pictures to capture the rolling, green farmlands that were dotted with tropical trees and had green mountaintops in the background. Again, it felt like we were transported back hundreds of years in time as we were passed by men that were transporting goods via wooden carriages being pulled along by oxen.

After our 2.5-hour drive from Havana and a couple hours hiking around the open countryside, we finally arrived at the location where we would be learning about the local tobacco process. Our group entered what I would describe as a tent that was being used to hang thousands of tobacco leaves. As soon as we stepped into the tent, the cigar aroma hit us like a ton of bricks. I thought it was a fine smell, but I am sure there are plenty of people that would disagree.

We were informed that tobacco grows best during the winter months. Tobacco seeds typically are planted in late October and harvested in March and April. The harvesters don't like rain because the mosquitos swarm after periods of heavy rainfall and eat the tobacco plants. If you do any independent research on tobacco harvesting, you will find that in order to process tobacco for smoking you will need to ferment the product which requires quantities at least in the hundreds of pounds if done through a natural process. This explains the massive inventory that this older man had built up inside this tent. After the tobacco leaves are picked, they are hung up in a tent or barn to dry for 45 to 60 days, which is what we were witnessing. After the drying process, the tobacco leaves are dampened, aired, and flattened at which time the fermentation process is completed. To naturally ferment tobacco, the product is placed into a pile where the humidity starts to build, and the temperature rises. This process is repeated after the desired temperature is reached. This recurring fermentation process can take up to three months. Only then is the tobacco rolled into a cigar.

As far as I could tell, the man here in charge of this tobacco process had likely been harvesting and rolling cigars for 60 years and had probably never left the small town of Viñales. If you closed your eyes and envisioned a Cuban cigar roller, this guy was what you would picture. He went through the process of rolling several cigars right in front of us. We all placed natural honey on our lips because we were informed that this would mitigate any burning feeling on the lips from the cigar. We sat there and enjoyed our authentic Cuban cigars in the tent. This was an informative and worthwhile experience for anyone visiting the country. This was my favorite part of the trip.

Unfortunately for this local man who knew far more about cigars and tobacco than any human I have ever encountered, he had to sell 90% of his harvest to the Cuban government at whatever price the government determined to be fair. He could only keep 10% of the harvest to smoke or sell to tourists. The cigars were sold to tourists at a fixed price of $3 each, which is far below what they would fetch in the United States or other capitalist markets. Additionally, the harvesters aren't allowed to put labels on the cigars or brand them in any way. This talented individual could make a fortune building a real cigar brand in the United States given his knowledge and expertise, yet here he is in Cuba selling nearly all of his product to the government for pennies on the dollar and is not even allowed to build a brand. This man seemed to be at peace with this reality, but it is not right or fair. My blood is boiling inside my body as I write these words.

I traveled to Cuba toward the end of May 2019 along with my girlfriend Paula's family. It was hot during out visit, with temperatures during the day in the 80s and 90s (which was above the normal temperatures for this time of the year) with little in the way of cloud protection. We were told that the high tourism season occurs in November and December.

This was a special trip for the Bellini family because Mr. Bellini had grown up in Havana and fled the country just as Fidel Castro was consolidating power. Up until a few years ago, Mr. Bellini had not returned to Cuba for

351

over 50 years. Unlike many Cubans who now reside in the United States, Mr. Bellini has generally fond memories of the country because he experienced the better times before the Cuban Revolution and got out before conditions really started to deteriorate.

Cuba is the largest island in the Caribbean and has a population of 11.5 million people as of 2019. The recorded history of Cuba began with the arrival of Christopher Columbus in 1492. Spain colonized the island in the 16th and 17th centuries and the Spanish influence in the country is ever present to this day. The rise of Cuba really occurred in the 19th century with the increase in sugar production which benefitted from the success of the United States and the downfall of Haiti as a sugar producer. Cuba remained loyal to Spain until the end of the 19th century. The Ten Years' War against Spain occurred between 1868 and 1878, but ultimately failed in establishing Cuba as an independent nation. The Cuban War of Independence, which occurred between 1895 and 1898, was the last of three wars between Cuba and Spain. The United States entered this war in 1898 and tipped the balance of power in favor of the Cubans. On December 10, 1898, the United States and Spain signed the Treaty of Paris, which demanded the formal recognition of Cuban independence from Spain.

I wish I could say that after Cuba achieved independence from Spain, the country had a long and prosperous democratic history. As anyone with the most cursory knowledge of Cuba after Fidel Castro took power knows, that is not the case. The seeds of the Cuban Revolution were planted in the 1920s when Gerardo Machado y Morales was president of the country. Machado became Cuba's first clear dictator and crushed the prosperity that came as a result of the successful sugar business in the early 1900s. Machado suspended freedom of speech, press, and assembly as a result of the proclamation of martial law. Cuba was thrown into economic crisis and Machado's attempts to stabilize the price of sugar were unsuccessful. Fortunately for the local Cubans, the army forced Machado to flee the country in 1933. Fulgencio Batista disrupted the Cuban democratic process with a military coup in 1952.

By this action, he provoked a popular discontent that Fidel Castro exploited with an idealistic democratic rhetoric which he later cynically betrayed.

Fidel Castro is by far the most famous individual in Cuba's history and, unfortunately, not because of the prosperity that he brought to the country. Castro served as Prime Minister of Cuba from 1959 to 1976 and then as President from 1976 until 2008. Castro successfully overthrew the Cuban government led by Fulgencio Batista in 1959. This was the start of the Cuban Revolution where Castro assumed political and military power as Cuba's Prime Minister. For nearly the next 50 years, Fidel Castro consolidated power into a one-party communist system that was the first in the Western Hemisphere. Under the Castro rule, all private businesses were nationalized, free press became nonexistent, political opposition was squashed, and free elections became a fairy tale. Cuba aligned itself with the Soviet Union under the Castro regime while the United States placed embargoes on the country and attempted to overthrow the Cuban government. The U.S. broke off diplomatic relations with Cuba in 1961 and unsuccessfully attempted to take out Castro with the Bay of Pigs invasion where a group of 1,400 American-trained Cubans stormed the island only to be captured or killed by Castro's forces. Castro would go on to run the country into the ground over the next 47 years and attempt to spread the revolution in countries such as Chile and Nicaragua.

Woefully misinformed individuals have praised Fidel Castro for bringing free education and healthcare to Cuba, but these benefits were far outweighed by the negatives. I really doubt that anyone depicting Castro as a hero has ever personally visited Cuba, because even years after the Fidel Castro autocracy, it is clear that Cuba is still one of the least desirable places to live on earth. Why do you think that so many Cubans over the years have lost their lives trying to make it to the United States on low quality rafts? Fidel Castro held an entire country hostage for five decades for his own benefit and was arguably one of the most evil humans to ever live. Despite what would seem like overwhelming evidence of this line of thinking, this is far from a universally held opinion. For example, Castro is popular in many African nations because of the active assistance from Castro's Cuba that shaped the political reality of vast parts of Southern Africa. Castro will likely continue to be a controversial historical figure for many years to come.

What Machado failed to understand was that in order to maintain authoritarian power, you must have the military in your pocket. Unfortunately for Cubans, Fidel Castro understood this from early on. Cuba has maintained a law that establishes compulsory military service for those aged 17–28 in making a two-year military service stint necessary for both sexes. Known as the Cuban Revolutionary Armed Forces, the military has maintained great power since the Cuban Revolution. In fact, the Soviet Union provided the Cuban military with subsidies from 1966 until the early 1990s. The Cuban military has 50,000 active military personnel, but the capable firepower is greatly in excess of this number in the event of an emergency because of the obligatory military service requirement. Each year Global Firepower puts out a list of most powerful militaries in the world and the 2019 rankings put Cuba at 71st globally.

An important part of Cuba's history when thinking about the relationship with the United States is the Cuban Missile Crisis, which was a tense 13-day nuclear standoff in October 1962. Nuclear missiles were installed in Cuba by the Soviet Union and had been discovered by an American spy plane that photographed the nuclear missile sites being built by the Soviets. President John F. Kennedy met with advisors for several days to discuss the pressing issue. While some advocated for the immediate invasion of Cuba, which could have prompted a nuclear war, Kennedy opted to place a naval blockade around Cuba to cut off further supplies from the Soviets. It was an incredibly scary period given that the armed nuclear weapons were located a mere 90 miles from the American mainland. After a series of negotiations, the United States agreed to a deal whereby the Soviets would dismantle the nuclear weapon sites in exchange for a U.S. pledge not to invade Cuba and separately agreed to remove nuclear missiles from Turkey. A nuclear miscalculation was narrowly averted, and this series of events went a long way in helping shape American foreign policy in the coming years. In subsequent years, the U.S. would have a much lower tolerance for communism and potentially dangerous authoritarian governments in the Western Hemisphere. For example, it was later confirmed that the U.S. government played a role in the 1973 Chilean Coup which was reportedly at least partly attributable to the fear of rising communist influence in South America.

Here are some interesting facts about Cuba: Cuba is one of only a few countries that employs a dual currency system, Cubans were not allowed to own cell phones until 2008, until 2013 there was an import ban on cars in Cuba, and Cuba is one of only two countries in the world where Coca-Cola can't be bought or sold.

Economy

The Cuban economy and country more broadly are dominated by state-run enterprises with the majority of the labor force being employed by the state. The communist economy provides most Cubans with free education and healthcare along with food subsidies. Sugarcane production has always been important to the local economy and a crash in sugar prices in the early 1990s had a devastating impact. Tobacco, coffee, rice, beans, and various types of fruit are some of the other products grown locally. As of 2015, Cuba imported 70–80% of the country's food, which makes it overly reliant on other countries for basic needs.

Tourism surpassed sugar in the mid-1990s as the primary source of foreign exchange for Cuba. 2018 saw a record number of international visitors, with close to five million people visiting the country. These numbers and the broader Cuban economy will likely be significantly impacted if the United States places further restrictions on travel to the country, especially since the U.S. and Canada are the two leading markets for visitors.

Cuba's primary import partner is Venezuela with Canada being the second largest trade partner. Prospective foreign investors must form joint ventures with the local government in order to do business (the only exception to this rule is for Venezuela).

The World Bank does not even report on Cuba in reports such as their Ease of Doing Business rankings, which tells you pretty much everything you need to know about the economy right there. If Cuba was ranked alongside other countries, they would be ranked near the bottom in terms of virtually every metric. The 2019 Index of Economic Freedom ranks Cuba 178th out of 180 global countries with only Venezuela and North Korea lagging behind. The report goes on to say that the economy is run by the nearly bankrupt Cuban government and is economically one of the least efficient in the world. There were some pro-market reforms adopted a decade ago with the goal of raising productivity, but there wasn't much follow-through on this plan. The report cites issues such as property seizures by police without justification being common. Corruption is widespread, and there is no separation of powers in the legal system. Prices are controlled by the state, and the country is dependent on subsidized oil from Venezuela and Russia. Low, state-dictated wages punish workers and keep most locals below the poverty line.

Recent U.S. embargoes against Cuba have impacted the local Cuban economy. Having said that, I have seen many misguided and likely politically motivated news articles almost solely blaming current U.S. policies for the economic crisis on Cuba. The food rationing that has been reported on in Cuba has been in place since the Cuban Revolution in 1959. While the food rationing has likely become more dire in recent months partly due to the U.S. policies, to infer that this is a new development is simply untrue. The Cuban economy has also suffered a great deal from the collapse of the Venezuelan economy. Part of the reason Cuba's economy grew in the late 1990s and early 2000s was due to the high amount of oil being imported from Venezuela.

Venezuela, the country that has the largest proven oil reserves in the world, has plunged into crisis since the 2014 drop in oil prices. The country has been hit harder than any other oil producers because according to OPEC, oil accounts for 98% of the country's export earnings. Venezuelan oil production has dwindled in the last two decades, from more than three million barrels per day at the beginning of the century to between 1.2 million and 1.4 million barrels per day by late 2018. This drop has had an outsized impact on the Cuban economy given the importance of Venezuela as a trade partner.

This conversation brings us back to an important development for Cuba regarding relations with the U.S. On December 17, 2014, President Barack Obama announced the beginning of a process normalizing relations between Cuba and the U.S. and in March 2016 Obama became the first U.S. President to visit Cuba since 1928. In talking to the Cuban locals, Obama is widely hailed as a hero in the country. We now know that President Trump has gone to great lengths to reverse many of these Obama-era policies, but I think this warrants discussion. Was President Obama really helping the Cuban people with the easing of relations with the U.S? This provided a short-term boost to the Cuban economy, especially in the tourism sector, but the Cuban citizens are not participating in this upside because the government essentially takes all of the benefit. While the intention may have been good, I would argue that these policies were disastrous when thinking about the long-term picture for Cuban citizens. In my view, the open policies toward Cuba were an endorsement of the oppressive communist dictatorship being employed in the country and only further entrenched the government. The Cuban people will never get what they deserve until there are significant changes made to the government and endorsements for the Cuban government by powerful nations such as the United States will only make this dream ever more distant.

Adventure

I arrived at our Airbnb in Havana that was located in a tall building with nice views overlooking the water. In 2016, President Obama relaxed U.S. travel restrictions to Cuba and the laws have been changing since. At the time of our visit, one of 12 categorical exemptions as a U.S. citizen was to obtain a Cuban visa under the provision that you were supporting the local people, which meant that you had to stay in an Airbnb. After putting my items down in my room, we were off for a tour of the city.

The 1950s cars in Cuba are famous, so it was only natural that we opted to take an old, light blue convertible taxi to our destination for the start of our walking city tour. My taxi driver from the airport told us a fascinating story about cars in Cuba. He informed Paula, Paula's father, and me that Cuban cars are first rented to tourists and then passed along to a government-run taxi company. The cars are run for over 300,000 miles and sold only to local citizens at that time for between $70,000 and $80,000 for the average vehicle! Could you imagine going to CarMax and being offered a 1950s car with over 300,000 miles for these prices with no alternatives?! This was just one of the many ways in which the Cuban Communist system was broken. Cuba must be home to some of the best mechanics in the world with all of these old cars still on the streets.

My first observation of Havana was that the city was even more run down than I was expecting. Having said this, there have been ongoing restorations in Old and Central Havana for at least a decade. The four major plazas, main churches, connecting streets, as well as the Great Theatre of Havana and the National Capitol, have been undergoing restoration as part of the plans for the 500th anniversary of the city. Outside of these developments, there hadn't been much updated or restored since the 1960s era and most buildings and structures were essentially crumbling to the ground. There were many hotels that were upscale Las Vegas-style hotels at one point in time but had been largely neglected for decades. This is what happens when you take away free market economics. The condition of the buildings was so bad that I mistakenly thought I was looking at a prison when in reality I had my eyes set on a college campus.

Over the course of the next several hours, we walked around Old Havana. We toured various courtyards and learned about the architecture of the buildings. I found this part of the city to be depressing overall. We passed the building that at one time housed the local stock exchange. The stock exchange was shut down during the Castro-led Cuban Revolution at about the same time other buildings such as the Supreme Court and Federal Reserve likely closed. This is tyranny at its core.

Along our tour we stopped for mojitos at La Bodeguita del Medio, which Mr. Bellini informed us was an iconic tourist destination. A quick Google search will tell you that this is Cuba's most popular bar. This place was packed with people dancing to Cuban music being performed by a live band. I didn't order a mojito for myself since I was not feeling well from the lack of sleep from the night before but found Paula's drink to be tasty. Most visitors to Havana will want to put La Bodeguita on their list of locations to visit.

That evening we visited the famous Hotel Nacional de Cuba to have a drink. This hotel that opened in 1930 has been visited by an array of celebrities over the years, as shown in the form of pictures in a room located within the hotel, and is one of a handful of buildings in Havana that the government has made a priority to keep in good condition. Most visitors staying in Havana will want to stop at this iconic location. We enjoyed a drink and some dinner outside in the large and impressive grounds area. I found that the local beer selection in Cuba managed to surpass even Iceland for worst in the world among countries that I have visited. I would compare the popular beer Cristal to a local Natural Light and there wasn't much in the way of competition. As far as I am concerned, my theory as to the number of local craft beers a country has being an indicator of overall economic development has more merit than ever. While eating dinner, we found out that the real version of a Cuban sandwich is not like the American version. The Cuban version is essentially just a bunch of meats put on a piece of bread, and my girlfriend, Paula, did not find the authentic edition to be appetizing (Mr. Bellini informed us that the original local Cuban sandwich was delicious but not possible to be found in Cuba today). While there were exceptions such as the delicious broad selection of local fruits, I found the food in Cuba to be highly disappointing. I did not find the shredded pork to be very good.

The following day we did a tour of the National Capitol Building along with the Great Theater of Havana and explored other parts of Havana. The National Capitol Building, which opened in 1929, was under restoration for eight years and only re-opened in 2018, so we were lucky to be able to see the inside of this impressive building. I should note that it does cost money to see the inside of buildings such as the Capitol and the theater. The price probably fluctuates, but expect to pay around $10 per visit. The Great Theater of Havana was under construction while we were visiting, so we were unable to see a show, but we could still tour the building. Many visitors will opt to see a show at this well-preserved building. Unless a building is so different than that of western culture such as the Taj Mahal, I do not find building architecture all that interesting, but architects and those intrigued by architecture have said that Cuba is fascinating in this regard. The outdoor space outside of the Great Theater of Havana, Parque Central, is much nicer than the Old Havana area over by La Bodeguita del Medio that we toured the day prior. There is a nearby street, Paseo del Prado, which is similar to Las Ramblas in Barcelona where artists and vendors line the streets with local products.

We saw the building that used to be home to Bacardi production. The Bacardi family business began in Cuba in 1862. It remained a Cuban company up until Fidel Castro came to power in 1959. Initially the company closely aligned itself with the Castro revolution but only a year and a half after Fidel took power Castro confiscated all of the Bacardi properties and most of the Bacardi family was exiled from Cuba. Fortunately for the family and the Bacardi brand, they had created independent companies outside of Cuba, which enabled the business to flourish to this day. This is yet another example of the perils of communism and dictatorship. Who in their right mind would put in the effort to create an innovative business knowing that the government will strip it away if there is any success? Unfortunately, under the current model it is not even possible to create a capitalist business of any kind without government involvement even if the unwarranted motivation was there.

While back at our Airbnb, Paula's father told us some fascinating stories about his family's experience in Cuba. Mr. Bellini was still in Cuba when Fidel Castro came to power, and, fortunately for him, his mother could see that conditions were rapidly deteriorating and fled the country before it was too late. The Castro regime had already nationalized the news and was consolidating power under his rule. Mr. Bellini said that there were individuals who were in charge of essentially making sure that everyone was cooperating in a given neighborhood. His mom had to lie and say that the family was going on a two-week vacation out of the country and had to leave valuable possessions such as their car so that the neighborhood watchman wasn't suspicious of their "vacation" plans. The neighborhood watchman went as far as to ask Mr. Bellini, who was still a child at this time, about their upcoming trip. Fortunately for the Bellini family, they were able to get out of Cuba just before the Bay of Pigs invasion and full travel restrictions kicked in. Their lives would have been dramatically different if they remained in Cuba under the Castro regime.

Mr. Bellini told Paula and me a story about his uncle's attempts to escape Cuba. His uncle had arranged with two separate groups to construct a boat to leave the island. On these first two occasions, both groups ended up leaving without his uncle. Frustrated and willing to again risk his life to escape the oppressive conditions brought on by the Castro regime, he arranged for a third boat attempt to leave Cuba. This time, one of the members of the group was working with the Cuban government, so policemen were waiting for everyone at the boat when they tried to leave! The government was sentencing those involved to 20 and 25 years in Cuban prison but something strange happened when it came time to punish Mr. Bellini's uncle. The police had found $50,000 in the boat that belonged to Mr. Bellini's uncle, of which there was no mention at the sentencing. He was sentenced to one year of house arrest and then deported out of the country. It was inferred that the policemen involved took the money and split it amongst themselves and saw Mr. Bellini's uncle as a liability and wanted him as far away from Cuba as possible! I am sure this type of corruption is rampant in the country.

That evening we went to the famous Tropicana show. Tropicana has been a mainstay as a part of Cuban entertainment dating all the way back to 1939. Most people associate feather headdresses and revealing sequin showgirl outfits with Las Vegas, but these elements of popular culture began at Havana's Tropicana Club.

Prices for a show at Tropicana vary depending on seat location, but a ticket and dinner starts at $85, which includes a welcome drink, a cigar, and a portion of a bottle of Havana Club rum. Expect to pay well upwards of $85 for good seats. If you are expecting the food here to be tasty, you will be wildly disappointed. Everyone agreed that the food was well below average, and one of our friends who ate at Tropicana the month prior had a similar opinion.

As far as the quality of the show, if you like Las Vegas style entertainment, then this attraction is for you. I think a lot of people come away surprised at the level of glitz and glamour present at this venue, considering the overall quality of infrastructure in the Havana area. I would have to say it is rather unsuspecting that you would find entertainment that is arguably on par with Las Vegas here in Havana. The Tropicana venue is outdoors and is pleasant if the weather cooperates.

The show lasts a couple hours and includes around 50 performers who dance, sing, and perform acrobatic acts with no real breaks to be had. A few of the notable highlights of the show were when a group of women balanced chandeliers on their heads and when two performers did an impressive balancing act using ropes and ladders. There was a plethora of talented individuals involved with this production. While the entire production and venue was impressive and beautiful, I had a difficult time enjoying the experience because I couldn't help but to think about the deal that the entertainers were getting. They were at worst being forced to put on a lavish spectacle for wealthy tourists and at best getting a raw deal because the government would end up reaping the lion's share of profits from this endeavor. Perhaps those involved were better off than most in Cuba, but this is not much of a statement. I would prefer to see a show in Las Vegas, New York, or any other capitalist market where I know that those involved are willingly participating and not because they may not really have any other choice.

Mr. Bellini talked to all of our local guides and taxi drivers about the local government and what their thoughts were. The more educated individuals were aware that they were getting a raw deal from the government, so this knowledge base is at least a step in the right direction. Perhaps this is partly attributable to the rise of Internet access in the country, which has only gone mainstream in the past few years. It is hard to believe that Internet access was rare to have in private homes prior to 2016 and only in December of 2018 did the government start to allow mobile phone customers to use the Internet via its 3G network. Make no mistake, the Cuban Internet is still censored but the information flow to the local people has improved substantially and the more educated citizens know that the government is taking advantage of them.

The following evening, we ate dinner at San Cristobal Paladar in Havana. This restaurant has been visited by many famous individuals, such as Barack and Michelle Obama and Beyoncé and Jay-Z, which is documented in pictures inside the restaurant. It is believed that Michelle Obama recommended the restaurant to Beyoncé given that they are friends. The venue has a lot of character and feels as though you are eating in a home dining room rather than a restaurant. Each room has a story that goes along with it, and tours of the restaurant are offered. This was my favorite meal while in Cuba. I had one of the local fish which was good. Our waiter went out of his way to ensure that we enjoyed our experience by offering our table 12-year aged rum. Along with Michelle Obama, I endorse this restaurant.

My favorite part of the trip to Cuba was that I came back home feeling much more appreciative of the government we have in the United States. Regardless of what you think about Donald Trump, Barack Obama, or any other United States president or how the U.S. government runs more broadly, it is indisputable that what we have is orders of magnitude better than in Cuba. While it was an incredible learning experience hearing the stories from Mr.

Bellini, talking to the locals, and seeing parts of Cuba for myself, I couldn't help but feel a tremendous amount of anger in visiting Cuba. The citizens of Cuba did nothing to deserve this cruel punishment and unfortunately many of them do not have enough money to ever leave. So, while our itinerary was meticulously planned by the Bellini family and included a high-quality mix of activities, I can say that I will not be returning to Cuba unless there is a change to the local government. In my opinion, visiting is an endorsement of the brutal dictatorship and I want more for the local Cuban people.

Additional Activities and Recommendations

If I had more time in the country, I would have gone scuba diving. Cuba is known to have quality diving options with the highest rated being Jardínes de la Reina. This government-protected area (there is a commercial ban on fishing) is considered to be among the most beautiful dive destinations in the Caribbean. Here you will find various types of fish, sea turtles, and, of course, sharks including hammerheads, black tips, leopards, and reefs. Nearly 100 of the world's 500 shark species can be found around Cuba.

For the hikers reading this, you may want to consider climbing Pico Turquino. This mountain is the tallest peak in Cuba at nearly 6,500 feet. There are two different routes hikers can take to the top, both of which take two to three days to complete. It is considered the best to climb during the dry season which extends from October to May.

While I didn't make a visit while I was in Cuba, almost all travelers at least make a stop to one of more of the famous beaches. In doing my research, Varadero was most often ranked the top beach in Cuba. Located a couple hours north of Havana, this 15 mile-long white sandy beach offers scuba diving, sailing, snorkeling, fishing, and boating. There are beaches all over Cuba, and my personal preference would be to opt for a less crowded beach, but many will flock to locations such as Varadero due to the natural beauty and available infrastructure.

Rock climbing is a popular sport that is done in Viñales. Interestingly enough, in 2012 climbing was banned in Viñales National Park and the entire western province of Pinar del Rio, but it was reported that the climbing continued in the wake of the ban. It is unclear if the climbing ban still stands, but research shows that climbing in the Viñales area continues with over 250 routes being found in the area.

The town of Trinidad, a UNESCO World Heritage Site, is popular to visit. It is a 200-mile drive and takes close to four hours to complete from Havana. Much of the architecture found here dates back to the time between the 17th and 19th centuries when Trinidad was flourishing from the sugar and slave trades. Travelers can opt to do a multi-day tour of Trinidad and explore the local beaches and Topes de Collantes National Park, which has waterfalls and quality hiking options.

I regret not going to the Museum of the Revolution in Havana. I think it would have been interesting to compare what the government depicts as the history of the country to reality. I am sure this dispersion is colossal.

Business Outlook

Cuba will be almost completely uninvestable unless dramatic changes are made to the government structure. The Communist dictatorship that Cuba employs reaps nearly all of the benefits of the local economy, removes any incentive to work hard or do anything innovative, and has an ownership interest or sole ownership of any business that would otherwise be valuable in the private sector. Unfortunately, I don't see how this is going to change outside of an invasion by a more powerful foreign government. I was told that the Cuban military is treated well by the government, has a vested interest in the success of the current government structure, and is advanced because they frequently go on ambitious overseas training sessions. The government further maintains their stranglehold on the country by continuing to employ the neighborhood watch program that I discussed involving Mr. Bellini at the start of the Fidel Castro regime. Despite being diabolical in terms of morals, the government is smart in going about maintaining control of the country.

After experiencing a ruthlessly oppressive communist government first-hand, I think it warrants a revisit to the discussion about capitalism. While the socialist policies being proposed by presidential candidates in the United States are not as radical as what I experienced in Cuba, it is a disturbing trend. Supporters of communism and socialism are correct in the line of thinking that such policies reduce income inequality. However, these policies just result in everyone being miserable together as opposed to broad-based successful equality. This will be obvious for anyone who has spent time studying the successful global economies in history. Legendary investor Howard Marks put it best when he said, "When we look around the world, we see countries that have stressed equal sharing of the pie and others that have cared more about expanding the pie. The equal sharers include Cuba, North Korea, Venezuela and the USSR, while the expanders, in addition to the U.S., include South Korea, Hong Kong and Singapore. In which group of countries do people generally live better? In which group would you rather live?" Despite the rising belief that capitalism is evil and only benefits a few rich individuals, history says otherwise.

I know what you are thinking after reading the above paragraph: But what about China? Despite not being a democracy, China still employs several aspects of free-market economics. In short, ambitious individuals in China still have an incentive to innovate and get ahead which is not the case in Cuba. Let's just take a quick look at the Chinese powerhouse Tencent to understand what I am talking about. As of this writing, Tencent, best known for its popular messaging application WeChat, has a market capitalization of approximately $500 billion. Despite government restrictions and oversight on areas such as the publication of certain video game titles, the Chinese government has overall been supportive of innovation at Tencent and other local market leaders such as Alibaba. Private enterprise has built modern China and 2018 reports show that nearly two-thirds of the country's growth and nine-tenths of the new jobs come from the private sector. The Chinese success story could still be ruined or slowed if the government gets jealous and employs more state control in successful areas such as technology and e-commerce. It is widely known that the Chinese technology giants have close ties the government, with recent reports saying that Alibaba's Jack Ma has been a member of the Communist Party of China since the 1980s.

In discussing the current state of the Cuban government with Mr. Bellini, we concluded that China could be a viable government to model the local one after. While it seems extremely unlikely at this time, China has provided a blueprint for countries such as Cuba that wish to maintain a stranglehold on the country while seeing success by being supportive of areas of free markets. While far from perfect, this would be an enormous step in the right direction for Cuba. I want to be clear that I am not in any way endorsing the various aspects of ongoing human rights oppression in China. I couldn't disagree more with how China disallows basic freedoms such as freedom of press, but the reality is that a country like Cuba is not going to shift overnight from being a brutal communist regime to a capitalist society with human rights freedoms on par with the likes of the United States. A stepping-stone to this shift would be adopting elements of capitalism in the economy before making this leap.

It is sad to see what has been made of Cuba, especially considering the potential that the country has. After all, Cuba is an hour plane ride from Miami, has tropical weather, and has natural beauty in many ways. Foreign investors could get excited about the prospects for Cuba if there were ever a major government overhaul but after seeing the current state of Havana, I think it would take an entire generation to rebuild the infrastructure that the government has ruined.

I won't go into detail about the cruise industry since I have already discussed my optimistic outlook for the industry in the South Africa chapter, but this was the one investable industry that the country had since U.S.-owned cruise operators could offer for-profit Cuban services without the Cuban government taking control of the business. At the time of this writing, the United States government banned cruises to Cuba which had been a high yielding itinerary for Carnival, Royal Caribbean, and Norwegian Cruise Line. The beauty of the cruise business is that unlike the hotel business, if there are macroeconomic issues in a given country such as travel bans or political instability then cruise line operators can simply adjust their itineraries to go to different destinations.

I will not be providing updates since the visit due to the amount of time between the visit and publication and the lack of credible information released on the country.

Classic cars of Havana

Near the National Capitol Building and The Great Theater of Havana

Inside the National Capitol Building

Tropicana

Hike day at Viñales

That's a lot of tobacco!

The making of mojitos

San Cristobal Paladar

Singapore

Introduction

O ne evening while in Singapore, we continued our relentless schedule by getting a full taste of Gardens by the Bay. Gardens by the Bay is ranked the number one attraction in Singapore on TripAdvisor as of December 2019 and has reached more than 50 million visitors since opening in June 2012 according to the official Gardens by the Bay website. This ambitious $1 billion project was meant to further transform Singapore into what they refer to as the "Garden City" and is home to more than 1.5 million plants. At the time it was built, Prime Minister Lee Hsien Loong said the decision to construct Gardens by the Bay was not an easy one, but the project has clearly paid massive dividends by boosting tourism and pushing Singapore closer to its vision of a green future.

Our first attraction at Gardens by the Bay was the OCBC Skyway. Sitting 72 feet above the ground, this 420-foot long skywalk allows for a different perspective of the "Supertrees" that are the centerpiece of the Gardens by the Bay project. The skywalk allows for some interesting vantage points of the rest of the city. We did the OCBC Skyway experience at dusk; I think it could have been enjoyable to do this attraction during the light show but the lines would have been extreme at this hour, and we wouldn't have been able to fit in all of our other excursions. This could be a consideration for those that have the time.

Next up was the Cloud Forest which is a 115-foot mountain residing inside a progressive-looking dome structure. Inside you will find an abundance of lush vegetation and the world's tallest indoor waterfall. Tickets for the Cloud Forest are usually purchased in a bundle with Flower Dome and Floral Fantasy, which is $46 per adult ticket. We also went through the Flower Dome, which is the largest glass greenhouse in the world as listed in the 2015 Guinness World Records. The Flower Dome displays exotic plants from five continents, organized in nine different gardens. The Cloud Forest and Flower Dome will be worth a visit if you have enough time to spend at Gardens by the Bay. There are several other attractions at Gardens by the Bay that we did not go to that visitors may want to consider. Unless you are a plant expert, a 30-minute walk through is probably a sufficient allotment of time for each. The highlights from these locations for me were the waterfall at Cloud Forest and the wide array of massive cacti at Flower Dome along with the impressive Christmas decorations that were on display at the Flower Dome.

The main attraction at Gardens by the Bay is the free 15-minute light show named "Garden Rhapsody" that runs at 7:45 p.m. and 8:45 p.m. daily. For Paula and me, as well as many others, this was probably the highlight of our stay in Singapore. Thousands of people gathered for this spectacle. Paula and I had arrived around the Supertree Grove early, so we laid down and enjoyed the first couple minutes of the light show looking up from our backs as if we were stargazing. Even though thousands of locals and tourists were present, other than the serene music put on display you could have heard a pin drop. We watched in admiration as the 162,900 plants on the Supertrees lit up with orchestral music being played in the background. There are 68 hidden audio speakers around this area, eliciting the feeling of being front and center at an orchestra concert while you are following the lights and gazing out across the rest of the city, which also is illuminated. The Marina Bay Sands can be captured in pictures in the background of the Supertree Grove, which makes for some fine photography. I could have sat there for an hour absorbing the experience here, but I think the fact that the show only lasts 15 minutes makes the experience more special due the scarcity factor. Singapore did a marvelous job with the entire Gardens by the Bay area.

Paula and I had chosen to go to Southeast Asia in late November 2019 so that we could get some exposure to the Asia region. I had only been to India, and Paula had not been anywhere in Asia. Given the complexity of the itinerary, this was a very difficult trip to plan. But the combination of Singapore, Borneo, and Indonesia provided for a chance to see a global business powerhouse and beautiful Asian city with Singapore, arguably the best scuba diving site in the world and endangered species such as the Orangutan and Pygmy Elephant along with a natural rainforest in Borneo, and ancient Asian architecture along with an intriguing economic development story and Komodo dragons and beautiful scenery in Indonesia.

As I have done with many trips in the past, I booked the trip in the midst of the start of "rainy" season in all of the destinations. This allowed for better pricing and fewer tourists along the way. As expected, we encountered little rain since our travels began just at the start of the rainy season, but if a prospective traveler sees on Google that December is the start of rainy season, they will more than likely avoid this month. From my experience, even if December is the start of rainy season, it is rare that it will suddenly start pouring every day on December 1.

It may be confusing, but Singapore is both a country and sovereign city-state. There are references to Singapore dating back as far as the third century, but modern Singapore began with the arrival of the British colonists. Singapore was formerly a British colony with the British arriving in Singapore as early as 1819. It wasn't until 1826 when Singapore was declared a British Colony. Singapore was later merged with Malaysia to become a Crown British Colony in 1946. Singapore separated from Malaysia and formed the Republic of Singapore in 1965.

The Singapore government is self-defined as a democracy with separation of powers, but Singapore is a dictatorship in reality. Just because a country has been an economic success story does not change the fact that it is a dictatorship. I happen to agree with the study published in *Leadership Quarterly* that examined 133 countries between 1858 and 2010 and concluded that,

"Autocrats with positive effects are found at best as frequently as predicted by chance, while autocrats with negative effects are found in abundance." Prime Minister Lee Kuan Yew ruled Singapore from 1959 to 1990. By the 1980s, Singapore had per capita income second only to Japan in the East Asia region. But for every Lee Kuan Yew you have a Fidel Castro, a Kim Jong-un, a Vladimir Putin, and a Jacob Zuma. Winston Churchill said it best in 1947 with, "Indeed, it has been said that democracy is the worst form of Government except all those other forms that have been tried from time to time."

Today, Chinese, Malays, and Indians comprise three official ethnic groups in Singapore. As of 2019, approximately 76% of the country's population was Chinese. There are four official languages in Singapore: Malay, English, Mandarin and Tamil. Malay is the national language with English being the main working language. According to 2015 census statistics, 33.2% of the local population practices Buddhism, 18.7% Christianity, and 14% Islam.

Here are some interesting facts about Singapore: chewing gum is banned except with a medical prescription, it is a crime to not flush a public toilet after use, the country consists of 63 smaller islands, Singapore has changed its time zone six times since 1905, and Singapore is one of the only three surviving city-states in the world (the other two are Monaco and Vatican City).

Economy

According to the 2019 annual Global Economic Competitiveness Report by the World Economic Forum, Singapore overtook the United States to become the world's most competitive economy. This is an astonishing accomplishment for a country that has a surface area of 278 square miles and a 2019 population of 5.8 million people. In the first 25 years after Singapore became an independent republic in 1965, Singapore grew GDP as an average clip of 9.2%. GDP growth has been an average of 7.7% since independence as of 2019. According to 2018 statistics, Singapore outpaced the United States in terms of GDP per capita.

Why has Singapore succeeded where so many other Asia-Pacific countries have failed?

The first advantage Singapore has is its geographic location. A country wanting to trade between East Asia, India, Africa, Europe, or the Middle East needs to travel through the Strait of Malacca which runs right past Singapore. Singapore also has natural deep-water ports, which have benefitted the shipping industry and trade. Singapore has regularly ranked near the top of the world in terms of education, ease of doing business, healthcare, rule of law, and safety. This is a classic example of a country successfully employing free market economics while enforcing rule of law. This is capitalism! Singapore has employed few trade barriers, has had low taxes, and few capital restrictions. It is these factors which have made Singapore an economic miracle.

Singapore retained its number two position in the 2019 Ease of Doing Business rankings produced by the World Bank. Some highlights from the 2019 report included Singapore making the process of handling construction permits easier by streamlining the process, improving public access to soil information, and improving its approach to inspections. According to the report, Singapore companies spent the least number of hours in the world paying taxes at just 49 hours per year compared to 696 hours among the worst-performing countries. Singapore also spent the least number of hours enforcing contracts: 120 days per year compared to 1,340 days among the worst-performing countries.

The manufacturing industry is the most significant driver of Singapore's GDP at 20–25% of the total GDP contribution per year as of 2019. Singapore has placed extra emphasis on high-end manufacturing which includes semiconductors, consumer electronics, and transport equipment. Singapore should benefit further from their success in these areas because industries such as semiconductors will only continue to grow in importance.

The financial services industry is also very important for Singapore's economy. In the Global Financial Centers Index of 2017, Singapore ranked third in terms of competitiveness of their financial sector. Only New York

City and London were ranked above Singapore. The ongoing success in financial services has earned Singapore a reputation which has made the country a global financial center.

A couple other emerging areas for the Singapore economy are medical technology and aerospace engineering. Again, Singapore is thinking years if not decades ahead by aligning the countries future with major growth industries that happen to have attractive economics. Tourism in Singapore has surged in recent years, as 2018 set new records for international tourist arrivals with 18.5 million. That means there were over three times as many visitors in the year as there are Singapore citizens. Despite the increase in popularity, I never felt as though the city was so overcrowded that the tourism numbers were becoming a liability for the city in terms of quality of life.

Since I strongly believe that education is the foundation on which most success is built, I think that Singapore's education system has had a lot to do with the country's success. When Singapore became an independent country in 1965, it basically only had one natural resource: the local people. What did Singapore do? It invested heavily in this resource. Singapore now spends about 20% of the annual national budget on education and the adult literacy rate is 97%. As a result, Singapore has developed an education system that has consistently ranked among the top in the world. Unlike education systems in the West, the Singapore education system is highly centralized that is scripted and uniform across all levels and subjects. This type of strategy is more geared towards examination performance as compared to what you will see in the United States. The strict focus when it comes to a uniform curriculum has been paired with what has been called, "the best trained teachers in the world." Singapore goes above and beyond when it comes to teacher training by training all new teachers at the National Institute of Education. Singapore also focuses on retaining high-quality teachers by giving them continuous training and support. In addition to the support system provided to the teachers, teaching is also an attractive profession due to compensation. Starting teaching salaries in Singapore are on par with accountants and engineers in the civil service. In the United States, a typical starting salary for a teacher is nowhere near that of an accountant. There has long been a debate about the correlation between teacher salaries and the quality of a country's education system and a recent study sheds light on this topic. A 2019 study published in the journal *Education Next* found, "clear evidence that higher teacher pay is associated with an increase in teachers' cognitive skills—which, in turn, is associated with better student performance." At least to me, this is common sense, but there are still many that argue that there is zero correlation between average teacher salary and overall quality of education. The study also notes that teachers have stronger cognitive skills and their students perform better in math and reading in countries that pay teachers higher salaries like in Ireland, Canada, and Finland. Singapore teachers have achieved a perceived high social status among local peers which has been another component that has made teaching an attractive profession.

Despite all of the successes that Singapore has had since independence, they do have a few glaring long-term weaknesses. Singapore lacks arable land and natural resources which is hardly surprising given the geography. As a result, only 1.3% of the labor force is employed in agriculture as of 2019. This makes Singapore almost entirely reliant on imports for most agricultural products which is not an ideal situation to be in, especially during times of global turbulence. Another major weakness in the Singapore story is in the defense sector. According to globalfirepower.com, Singapore has 72,500 active military personnel as of 2019. To put this into perspective, the United States has nearly 1.3 million active troops. Put simply, if there were ever to be a military conflict Singapore could easily be overtaken. Given the size of the country and resources, they would not be able to put up a fight against other larger developed superpowers. Singapore could face backlash in the future in regard to the state of human rights in the country. The government has long controlled both the media and freedom of expression and Singapore ranked 151st out of 180 nations in Reporters Without Borders (RSF) world rankings on press freedom. Look no further than the recent "face news" law that made waves when the Singapore government demanded that Facebook correct an online post that the Singapore government deemed to be false information. The post in question happened to do with accusations of the arrest of a whistleblower and election rigging which the Singapore government claimed was "false" and "scurrilous." There has been a lot of debate about this topic recently, but government censorship is dangerous and the Singaporeans may ultimately demand more in terms of human rights. I see this as a potential game changer when thinking about the long-term picture of the country.

Adventure

From the moment you arrive at Singapore Changi Airport, you feel like you have come to a special place. The number one ranked airport globally for seven years running as of 2019, it has become a destination in itself, boasting a 130-foot indoor waterfall, its own IMAX movie theater, a $1.3 billion mall that is home to 280 shops and restaurants and is open to visitors without airplane tickets, among many other attractions. Upon arriving back home to O'Hare International Airport in Chicago, I was reminded how desperately the U.S. is in need of major infrastructure upgrades when it comes to our airports. Large international transit hubs such as O'Hare are the first experience that many will have in a given country and provide for an all-important first impression. Singapore passes this test with flying colors and the United States will have to find a way to finance these infrastructure upgrades to keep pace with other global superpowers. I would recommend that the U.S. government look into privatizing the local airports similar to what we have seen from Australia and New Zealand in recent years but countries such as Singapore have made airport upgrades a priority and backed the ambitious projects with federal dollars.

Upon quickly settling in to our local hotel, we set out for the Marina Bay Sands where I would have my first excursion in this city that I would grow to love over the next few days. Marina Bay Sands was a massive $5.7 billion project undertaken by Las Vegas Sands (LVS) that initially opened in 2010. LVS has recently reached out to lenders in 2019 in search of an additional $6 billion in financing for expansion plans, which include a fourth hotel tower and a 15,000-seat arena that could once again reshape the entire city. The Marina Bay Sands is a modern architecture symbol that has become as synonymous with the Singapore skyline as the Sydney Opera House has been for the Sydney Harbour. Everything about the Marina Bay Sands screams luxury, including The Shoppes at Marina Bay Sands where one can find a wide variety of luxury stores and restaurants, the upscale nightlife entertainment which includes the globally recognized Marquee nightclub brand, and an observation deck that sits 57 stories above the city providing marvelous panoramic views and famous Instagram shots from the Infinity Pool.

Prior to arriving in Singapore, I had arranged via Ultimate Drive located within Marina Bay Sands a reservation to test drive a Lamborghini in the streets of the city. Fortunately for me, I was provided a "free" upgrade to drive the Lamborghini Huracán, which has a 2019 retail price starting at $203,674. I will be perfectly honest, I was absolutely terrified about the potential liability that came with operating such an expensive vehicle and this was probably not the most intelligent decision I have ever made for that reason. I don't know what insurance plan came with this vehicle, but I can imagine that even a fender bender on a car like this could run into the tens of thousands of dollars in damages. To make matters worse, I would be operating this extravagant vehicle on the opposite side from which I was accustomed at home. It takes some time to get used to driving on the right side of the car, given that I have spent my entire life driving with the steering wheel on the left side of the car.

The Lamborghini Huracán claims the ability to accelerate from 0 to 62 miles per hour in a stunning 3.4 seconds (depending on the specific model). While still terrified about getting anywhere near other cars on the road, I thoroughly enjoyed blowing by other vehicles after a red light. Fortunately for me, this car had a fully automatic transmission or else I would not have been able to drive it given my lack of knowledge about manual systems. This was admittedly not one of my bargain purchases with a 15 to 20-minute drive around the city costing me $273, but I was sucked in by the extravagance of Singapore even before I stepped foot in the city. I was also intrigued by the opportunity to feel like a Formula One (F1) driver since the F1 race track also runs through the streets of Singapore. The Singapore F1 race takes place on the Marina Bay Street Circuit around the luxury resort around where I cruised the streets.

That evening we had a dinner reservation at KOMA, which is located in The Shoppes at Marina Bay Sands. One of the first observations that an individual from the United States would have is in regard to the transportation system in Singapore. Taxis are still widely used despite adoption of ridesharing companies such as Grab which is a prominent player in the Southeast Asia market. The taxi system is relatively efficient because there are taxi lines spread out throughout the city, but this process was still frustrating in comparison to hailing an Uber or Lyft back home. In 2018, Grab acquired Uber's Southeast Asia operations, pitting the company against Gojek, which is the other ridesharing powerhouse in the region. After Grab purchased Uber's operations there were increasing user complaints about steeper prices, delays, and customer service lapses but this brought newer market entrants such as Ryde and TADA along with an increasing focus on the market from Gojek.

A ride in your local taxi in Singapore will bring a U.S. businessperson to the quick conclusion that mobile payment adoption is far ahead of the U.S. like what I have witnessed in other markets such as India. There is fierce competition in this market that includes the likes of WeChat Pay, Alipay, GrabPay, Google Pay, among many other options. The reason that e-payment adoptions in countries outside the U.S. has risen so much more quickly is tied to the entrenched credit card system in the U.S. market. The Singapore government as part of its Smart Nation vision to become "a leading economy powered by digital innovation" has been active in promoting a number of initiatives to digitize the payments system which should be a boon for the local economy. Not only is the economy more efficient when the flow of money is digitized but it also allows for the government to better track money within the financial system and reduce the amount of money that is evading tax payments.

The reason that we had chosen KOMA for dinner that evening was a combination of the fact that it was a buzzy new Japanese restaurant with beautiful décor and desirable menu but also because I wanted to check in on my Madison Square Garden Company investment. Madison Square Garden owns TAO Group Hospitality which is a globally recognized premium nightlife company that operates well-known brands such as TAO, Marquee, and LAVO. TAO had recently opened KOMA in the months leading up to our stay in Singapore making it the newest addition to the TAO portfolio so I thought it would be prudent to stop by for a visit.

The atmosphere inside KOMA reminded me of the Asian scene in the movie *Inception*. Everything about the restaurant screams Asian fusion from the orange Japanese columns that line the entrance (which is a reference to Fushimi Inari Shrine in Japan) to the bridge over the waterway with a prominent Asian-style bell in the background. KOMA passed the test for me, as I was impressed with the layout, ambiance, and enjoyed a delicious assorted sashimi platter along with a thoughtfully prepared mushroom fried rice bowl. It was a good sign that the restaurant was full while we were there.

The following morning, we were picked up from our hotel by our driver that would be escorting us around Singapore over the next few days. First up on the agenda was the Singapore Zoo.

On our ride to the zoo, I conversed with our driver and learned a lot of valuable insights into the local economy. I was informed that an average car in Singapore costs about $100,000. The reason that cars here are so expensive is that half of the cost of a vehicle is for a Certificate of Entitlement (COE) that gives car owners the legal right to register the vehicle and use it in Singapore for a period of ten years. The cost of the COE varies depending on supply and demand and can even exceed the cost of the car itself. The craziest part about this vehicle registration system is that many citizens resort to scrapping their vehicles after ten years after paying these exorbitant fees just for the right to operate the car in the country. I don't understand how anyone in Singapore could justify purchasing a luxury vehicle knowing they will have to scrap the vehicle in ten years unless they just have so much excess money that it doesn't matter. Singapore does a lot of positive things that keep the economy humming but this is one of their most egregious policy decisions and it pushes up the cost of living for anyone that owns a vehicle.

One of my most interesting learnings from our conversation was that the Singapore government provides housing for all citizens. It was reported in 2018 that 80% of Singaporeans live in a government-built apartment and 90% of residents were reported to own a home. Many have praised Singapore as having the best public housing program in the world. I found this to be particularly confounding because this goes against what I have seen in many other countries in my travels around the globe. From what I have observed, there is usually a negative correlation between the amount of welfare-related programs provided by the federal government and the overall success of a given economy. This makes sense given that welfare programs in aggregate reduce the incentive to contribute to society. I don't think you can point to any one factor and definitively say why this system works for Singapore, but my hypothesis is that this government housing program is implemented in conjunction with a successful forced savings scheme. Singapore set up the Central Provident Fund in 1953 as a compulsory national social security savings plan. In simple terms, workers below the age of 56 are required to put 20% of each paycheck into their CPF account with employers contributing an additional 17%. The rate of required contribution has been as high as 50% in the past. The contribution money is then distributed into three buckets: housing, healthcare, and retirement. An added bonus for Singaporean workers in addition to the fact that they will have money put away for housing, healthcare, and retirement is that the government guarantees generous interest rates on this money. As of the last quarter of 2019, CPF members earned 3.5% on Ordinary Account dollars and up to 5% on Special and MediSave accounts. How does this compare to the system in the United States? The U.S. has a Social Security system for retirement where employees contribute 6.2% of earnings along with a 6.2% contribution from employers for a 12.4% total (as of 2019). As for healthcare, the 2019 Medicare rates are

1.45% for the employer and 1.45% for the employee for a 2.9% total. The U.S. does not have any "forced saving" for housing. Many will argue that forced saving programs violate individual freedoms with this group preferring to do as they please with their employment earnings. I think Singapore has proven that there is merit to the type of system that they have operated given the overall success of the economy and local housing numbers that most would consider to be a resounding success.

I was inquiring about the Singapore e-commerce landscape and our guide informed us that free e-commerce delivery takes about a month. He was raving about the speed of delivery, as not long ago packages for free delivery took two months to be delivered. Customers can opt for paid delivery through platforms such as AliExpress, which normally takes about three days. As I have seen in many other countries, the U.S. remains the unrivaled leader when it comes to efficiency in the e-commerce and logistics industries.

The Singapore Zoo has often been rated the number one zoo on earth, usually edging out other favorites such as San Diego Zoo (United States), Zoologischer Garten (Germany), and Taronga Zoo Sydney (Australia). After visiting Singapore Zoo, I would have to agree with this assessment. I have visited Taronga Zoo Sydney and San Diego Zoo and did not believe that these zoos came close to matching the Singapore Zoo. The Singapore Zoo is a vast green expanse that is famous for the "open concept" set in a rainforest environment. It boasts more than 2,400 specimens of over 300 species of which 34% are considered to be threatened.

The Singapore Zoo is home to animals that include orangutans, lions, elephants, giraffes, cheetahs, rhinos, zebras, and almost any animal you can think of but the highlight has to be the resident white tigers. According to the most recent 2017 data, there was only believed to be 200 white tigers left in the world and the Singapore Zoo is home to two of them. I watched in awe as these beautiful creatures took in the sunlight in front of us. We went to the zoo in the morning, and the majority of the animals seemed to be active at this time, as I have seen with most other zoos. The Singapore Zoo puts on various events throughout the day, such as feeding time for the elephants and an acrobatic show put on by the orangutans. I am not a huge fan of zoos since my preference would be to see animals in their natural habitat, but if you are looking to go to one high quality zoo in the world, this would be the one.

After departing the zoo, we headed back toward the city (Singapore Zoo is about a 30-minute drive from the city). We drove around Chinatown, which is regularly rated as one of the top attractions in Singapore and is the most prominent of the various ethnic neighborhoods located within the city (which makes sense given that 76% of Singapore's population is of Chinese descent). Chinatown includes various popular landmarks such as Sri Mariamman Temple and Buddha Tooth Relic Temple. We took some time to walk around the local market areas here and tried out some authentic Chinese cuisine at a local restaurant. I do not much care for the Chinese food at home in the United States but found the food at this Chinese restaurant to be delicious. The spices were much more pronounced, and it was readily apparent that not nearly as many genetically modified ingredients were used in the making of this meal. You wouldn't find those oversized fake pieces of General Tso's chicken here!

We then briefly stopped in Little India, which is another popular Singapore tourist attraction and often the second most popular neighborhood to visit after Chinatown. I would recommend a visit to both neighborhoods if you are visiting Singapore. These neighborhoods are loaded with character and are worthy of top-attraction status as rated by various online outlets.

Driving around Singapore, one of the most readily apparent observations that a visitor can have is the amount of plant life that has been infused into the city. I was informed that construction developers are required by law to incorporate greenery into the projects. This fits into Singapore's vision of becoming the world's greenest city, as Singapore calls itself the "Garden City." The Gardens by the Bay project went along with this theme. Singapore was the greenest major city I have ever seen by a wide margin.

The next stop on our busy schedule was the Singapore Botanic Gardens. The Gardens is the first UNESCO Heritage Site in Singapore, as it was labeled a UNESCO World Heritage Site in 2015. It happens to be the only tropical botanic garden on UNESCO's list. Entrance to the massive Singapore Botanic Gardens is free, and there are various attractions within this area, such as National Orchid Garden, Ethnobotany Garden, and Ginger Garden. We had purchased tickets to walk through the National Orchid Garden, which is believed to be the world's most extensive orchid garden. There are over 1,000 species and 2,000 hybrids on display at this impressive garden. I am not one to marvel at flower collections, but even those least knowledgeable about the flower field would be delighted to walk through this soothing environment. Everywhere you look there are plants and flowers along with thoughtfully placed fountains and a refreshing scent that is good for the soul.

I had made dinner reservations at an upscale French restaurant called Les Amis for that evening. Les Amis is one of the top-rated restaurants in Singapore and was ranked the 33rd best restaurant in Asia for 2019 by theworlds50best.com. Les Amis is located on Orchard Road, which is the Singapore equivalent to Rodeo Drive in Beverly Hills. Here you will find every luxury store one could imagine. Orchard Road in itself is a top-rated tourist attraction, and it is even more special to visit during Christmas season as we witnessed. The city goes to great lengths to decorate Orchard Road with Christmas lights. This may surprise many in the West who would not expect an Asian city to have such a large Christian following, but Christianity is the second most practiced religion in Singapore behind Buddhism.

At Les Amis, we indulged in meticulously prepared dishes that included venison and scallops. This was the type of over-the-top restaurant that included caviar with the dishes, palate cleansers between plates, a complementary bread cart, and a chocolate plate along with a take-home dessert as you are leaving. The best part about this experience was the people-watching. You could tell that the restaurant was a status symbol for many of the locals. Nearby a wealthy young Asian man, or perhaps one pretending to be so, was dressed in expensive sweats and trendy shoes on a date with a young woman dressed in revealing fashion who was clearly there to be wined and dined and to say that she ate at Les Amis. I am not sure she looked up once from her phone the entire meal. I don't see how this is enjoyable, but it made for some quality entertainment for Paula and myself. The food at Les Amis was good, but it did not measure up to some of the other fine dining experiences that we have had at locations such as La Colombe Restaurant in South Africa. That is a high bar to set, but my comparisons for all categories are usually to the best in the world and that isn't changing here.

The following morning, we set out for Universal Studios Singapore. This theme park is Southeast Asia's first and only Universal Studios theme park and is home to 24 rides, shows, and attractions. Universal is located on Sentosa Island and is just a piece of the broader tourism infrastructure that Resorts World has amassed on the island. The island is also home to manmade beaches, Adventure Cove Waterpark Singapore, S.E.A. Aquarium Singapore, Skyline Luge, among many other attractions. I was interested to see what an Asian theme park looked like, as I really didn't know what to expect.

I was surprised at how crowded the theme park was for a weekday. Perhaps unsurprisingly, the crowd at the theme park was full primarily of individuals of Asian ethnicity with few other Caucasians to be seen. I thought the theme park was impressive overall. Just as you would expect to find in American parks such as Disney World, Universal Studios Singapore is divided into seven zones or what I would call "worlds" that are modeled after icons from the movie world. At least temporarily, this allows for visitors to transport to an imaginary realm such as *Madagascar*. Any American visitor who has frequented theme parks back at home would notice that the average ride at Universal Studios Singapore is not as intense as you would expect to find at United States theme parks. The warning labels that you will find for the rides are comical and almost convince you not to go on any of the rides no matter how brave you are. Unfortunately, I couldn't find the exact wording online, but these cautionary messages were likely fueled by past liabilities or to prevent against future lawsuits.

The highlight of our time at Universal came on "TRANSFORMERS The Ride: The Ultimate 3D Battle." While we had to wait in line for an hour and a half to experience this attraction, I think it was worth the wait to experience one of the perennial park favorites. I know that Paula had never heard me scream so loudly, as we were momentarily fully immersed in a *Transformers* battle scene. I don't actually think the car we were in was physically moving all that much, but the visual effects made it feel as though we were falling from skyscrapers and getting launched all over a city. Despite being pretty fearless when it comes to most adrenaline activities, I have a weakness for theme park rides. The "stomach drop" feeling you get on a roller coaster or a 3D experience such as what this ride provided is much more difficult for me to handle than coming face to face with a shark or something of the sort.

The Universal experience reinforced my appreciation for the Walt Disney business model. The Universal Studios Singapore experience will be enjoyable for most visitors but the reality is that the majority of people do not have close to the extent of emotional connection with movies such as *Jurassic Park*, *Madagascar*, *Shrek*, *Transformers*, and *The Mummy* as they do with dominant Walt Disney franchises such as *Star Wars*, most of the Marvel Cinematic Universe including the global phenomenon that is *The Avengers*, all of the popular Pixar movies which includes the likes of *Toy Story* and *The Incredibles*, classic Disney animated franchises such as *The Lion King*, and even popular franchises that were spawned based on Disney theme parks and rides such as *Pirates of the Caribbean*. Disney has built and maintained unrivaled global franchises that span generations which has allowed them to continue to feed the overall Walt Disney flywheel that now includes by far the most successful movie box office, a profit machine in the theme park segment which has expanded with cruise lines, a media business that has recently gone all-in with a streaming strategy that has seen a lot of early success, and various other ways the company monetizes their franchises and overall brand such as the royalties they receive from Hasbro for selling action figures using the *Star Wars* brand. What an incredible company.

After concluding our time at Universal, we headed back over to Marina Bay Sands where we would be going to the Sands SkyPark Observation Deck. The observation deck sits 57 stories above the streets of Singapore and provides for panoramic views of this magnificent city. I walked around the top of the building and took pictures and videos and just marveled at the scenery. Some people like to go to the top at nighttime to see the city with lights, but I don't think this would have been the same experience. I think I was able to get a better appreciation for what may have been the most beautiful city skyline I have seen during the light of day. One of the most striking observations that could be noticed from atop the Marina Bay Sands was the amount of boat activity around the shipping ports. In all of my travels across the world, I have never seen a busier shipping port. This is yet another indicator that business conditions are strong in Singapore.

We capped off an amazing stay in Singapore by taking a river cruise, which was the perfect way to close out our time in the city. The hop-on-hop-off boat ride allowed for us to have one final vantage point, which only heightened my appreciation for the modern beauty present in the city. I think that some of the most beautiful cities in the world, such as Sydney and Paris, have waterways running through them and Singapore is no different. The choice to do the river cruise at night and as the last excursion was perfect, as it tied the whole experience together with the gorgeous lighting of the city ever present.

Additional Activities and Recommendations

The timing would have to align with a trip itinerary, but I think it would be worth the extra effort to arrange a visit to Singapore around a Formula One (F1) race. The Singapore Grand Prix takes place on the Marina Bay Street Circuit which was the first street circuit in Asia designed for F1 races. The F1 race weekend is a three-day event that draws 250,000 spectators at stands near the Marina Bay Street Circuit. I wish I could have fit this into our schedule.

If you are looking to splurge for a big life event, the restaurant Odette is rated as Asia's number one restaurant by theworlds50best.com for 2019. Odette is a French fine-dining establishment. I attempted without success on several occasions to get a reservation at Odette during the months leading up to our trip. If you are interested in booking a table at Odette, make sure to do so well in advance. Just like other restaurants in Singapore, the restaurant will only allow you to book a table within a given time frame, so an interested visitor would have to come back to the website at that exact time to increase the likelihood that a table is secured.

Paula and I had already gotten our Ferris wheel fix on the London Eye a few years prior so we opted not to take a ride on the Singapore Flyer which may interest others. The Singapore Flyer stands at 541 feet and was the world's tallest Ferris wheel until the High Roller opened in Las Vegas in 2014. I am sure the ride aboard this Ferris wheel provides for some fine views of the city.

For those who opt not to go to the Singapore Zoo, there are a couple other local wildlife options that may be of interest. The Night Safari is located next door to the zoo and is also one of the top-rated attractions in Singapore. The experience provides a 45-minute tram tour that allows visitors to see over 2,500 nocturnal animals in their "natural environments." By "natural environments," I think they mean that the exhibits are mocked up to resemble the natural environments of the resident animals staying here. Could be an interesting option for those looking for something a little different than a standard zoo experience. There is also the River Safari Singapore which is Asia's only river-themed wildlife park. This park is home to over 5,000 animals and is another animal option to be considered.

Business Outlook

Unless the country risk factors I highlighted related to defense, natural resources, and human rights bite the economy, the overall economic outlook for Singapore should continue to be bright. Singapore should continue to see large inflows of foreign investment as the country touts leadership in education, ease of doing business, healthcare, rule of law, and safety. Singapore has benefitted from the recent unrest in Hong Kong, which Singapore has long battled for the title as being the dominant financial center in the Asia-Pacific region.

Where there is current weakness, there is future opportunity. Singapore had a 2019 total defense budget of $11.4 billion, which may be significant by the regions standards, but this is still dwarfed by the $717 billion 2019 budget in the United States, $177 billion in China, and even more comparable regional countries such as South Korea at $42 billion. Singapore still dedicates a higher percentage of their annual budget to defense spending than the U.S even though absolute dollar figures for Singapore are much lower. There has been a military splurge in the Asia-Pacific region fueled by China, and I think Singapore will continue spending heavily on this sector to keep pace. Automation is at the center of Singapore's military strategy, and I would expect them to continue making major investments in autonomous military technologies.

After spending time in Singapore, Malaysia, and Indonesia, there was a striking observation regarding the wellness trends that we have seen developed in countries such as the United States. In recent years, there has been a wave of boutique gyms and a shift to more healthy food options in the United States. These developments have not taken place in places such as Singapore, Malaysia, and Indonesia. I would expect these markets to develop more quickly in Singapore just because this country is the furthest along in terms of economic development. Looking at the Asia-Pacific region as a whole, the entire fitness industry as of 2019 was only worth $16.8 billion. As a comparison, the U.S. health and wellness market alone is estimated to be worth $30 billion. The data has shown that these trends are gathering steam in the Asia-Pacific region from a low base. Health and fitness is projected to grow by 6.4% annually between 2018 and 2023. Given what I saw, I think we could be in for a multi-decade period of sustained high growth for the health and wellness markets in the Asia-Pacific region. You should start to see a lot more money flowing into fitness centers, protein bars, and food locations with healthy options.

As discussed above, Singapore has been investing in aerospace engineering which I think is a good bet given Singapore's geographic location and the regional trends. According to a 2019 report by Boeing, "Over the next 20 years, Boeing projects the demand for aviation services in Asia-Pacific will expand by 5.1%, or $3,480 billion." I have written extensively about the growth of the travel industry and the Asia-Pacific region will be at the forefront of this growth over the next few decades. Singapore is in prime position to take advantage of these trends in the context of a business such as aerospace engineering because they should be able to hire top industry talent in the Asia-Pacific due to all of factors that I highlighted that have made Singapore an economic miracle.

I won't provide economic updates for Singapore, Malaysia, and Indonesia since the time between our visit and the completion of this book was short in duration.

My ride in a Lamborghini Huracán at Marina Bay Sands

White tiger at the Singapore Zoo!

Singapore Botanic Gardens

Our visit to Universal Studios Singapore

Beautiful view from the Sands SkyPark Observation Deck overlooking Singapore

World's tallest indoor waterfall at Cloud Forest

Malaysia

Introduction

We were at Sukau Rainforest Lodge for less than a day and a half, but in that time, we went on three river cruises during the day and one evening river cruise, and we visited the nearby Gomantong Caves.

There were a couple of clear highlights during our marvelous stay here, the first being our sighting of the orangutans. We were fortunate enough to spend time alone with our guide watching a family of four orangutans climb around in a nearby tree along a waterway inlet. We sat there for around 20 minutes marveling at these beautiful creatures as they picked fruit from the tree and climbed along its limbs. Our guide told us that once all of the fruit was picked from the trees where they had been in recent days, they would move on to another area. I had informed our guide that our main goal during our brief stay at Sukau was to see the Orangutan, and this goal was accomplished by the morning after we arrived.

The other main highlight of our time at Sukau was the sighting of the Pygmy Elephant. We had paid extra for an add-on river cruise that was specifically tasked with finding the elephant. After taking a 40-minute boat ride to another area of the Kinabatangan River and aimlessly driving up and down in search of the endangered creature, things were looking grim. To put this situation in a little more perspective, many areas along the river are densely covered with trees and plants, which often makes visibility difficult from a boat on the river. Animals can easily hide from a tourist's line of vision if they so choose. Finding an animal like the Pygmy Elephant is not like finding a tiger. If you are on a search for a tiger, the best chance you have of finding one is to listen for nearby deer give an "alarm" signal in the form of a chirping sound. While in search of the Pygmy Elephant, we were literally just going up and down the river hoping that one would pop out of the rainforest.

Just as we were about to call it quits, our guide started violently waving and pointing to a large figure shaking the nearby trees. Despite what seemed to be improbable odds, we watched the elephant gracefully navigate the area along the river for the next few minutes. I attribute what seemed like sheer luck to our first-class guide, who knew all of the ins and outs of the area. He told us that it was rare to have accomplished everything we did in our brief stay at Sukau and was somewhat taken aback when I informed him of our proposed schedule given the amount of activities and excursions planned in such a short time frame. At least for us, a day and a half was the perfect amount of time to spend at Sukau because we would have found ourselves bored if we had spent another couple days and some of the novelty of the stunning lodge area would have worn off. We did it just right. This sentiment does come with the caveat of an alternate scenario where we did not see the Orangutan. I would have been devastated if we took two flights, drove 2.5 hours, then finished the journey on boat and to not have seen a single Orangutan. If we had not spotted an Orangutan in the first day and a half, then I would have wanted to stay longer.

I won't go into an in-depth analysis of our excursion to the Gomantong Caves, but I will advise skipping this activity if you are afraid of cockroaches and bats. These caves were crawling with roaches everywhere, which did make me uneasy. Having said that, it is a solid cave system and provides for some nice views looking up from the bottom. It is a decent way to spend a few hours when you include the time spent traveling from Sukau.

Malaysia consists of 13 states along with two primary regions: Peninsular Malaysia and East Malaysia (Malaysian Borneo). The two primary regions are separated by 400 miles of the South China Sea. Urban areas are largely concentrated on Peninsular Malaysia, while East Malaysia is dominated by rainforests. According to 2019 statistics, Malaysia has a population of approximately 32.6 million people, which ranks 44th in the world. Malaysia covers a total area of 127,355 square miles, making it slightly larger than Norway.

The Proto-Malays were believed to have migrated to modern-day Malaysia between 2,500 and 1,500 BCE. During World War II, Japan occupied Malaya, Sabah, Sarawak, and Singapore. The Federation of Malaya was created in 1948 under British protection. The independent state of Malaysia was created on September 16, 1963, as a federation of Malaysia, Singapore, Sabah, and Sarawak. As we read in the chapter on Singapore, Singapore withdrew from the federation in 1965 to become a separate nation.

The Malaysian government is technically a federal constitutional elective monarchy modeled after the British parliamentary system. In reality, Malaysia has long been dominated by corrupt dictators that have served in the prime minister role. For anyone who disputes this, I would recommend reading *Billion Dollar Whale: The Man Who Fooled Wall Street, Hollywood, and the World*. This highly entertaining book documents the stunning rise of Jho Low, a Malaysian "businessman" with virtually no prior credentials who stole billions of dollars from Malaysia's quasi sovereign wealth fund, 1Malaysia Development Berhad (1MDB). Former Malaysian Prime Minister Najib Razak is now on trial for his involvement in what could be the world's biggest financial scandal ever. This massive scandal has reverberated across the financial world and has led to companies such as Goldman Sachs admitting guilt for their involvement and agreeing to pay a $2 billion fine just to resolve the U.S. Department of Justice probe.

According to the Transparency International's (TI) Corruption Perception Index (CPI) 2018, Malaysia ranked 61st out of 180 countries. One of the big problems that Malaysia has faced in regard to corruption is that one ruling party has dominated the entire history of the country. When former Prime Minister Najib lost power, it was the first time in Malaysia's 61-year history that the United Malays National Organization (UMNO) lost control of the government. Without competition, there is always going to be less accountability, so it was a positive development when Mahathir Mohamad defeated Najib Razak in a stunning upset in the 2018 election.

Like Singapore, Malaysia has had a dismal record when it comes to freedom of expression. There is some reason for optimism, though. According to the 2019 World Press Freedom Index, Malaysia jumped 22 spots to 123rd out of 180 countries. This put Malaysia at the top of the rankings for countries in the Southeast Asia region. The report noted that the "general environment for journalists is much more relaxed, self-censorship has declined dramatically and the print media are now offering a fuller and more balanced range of viewpoints, including support for the new ruling coalition led by Prime Minister Tun Dr Mahathir Mohamad, and support for the old ruling coalition, now in opposition." Perhaps the current ruling political party is trying to gain some goodwill from the citizens, but I remain cautiously optimistic given the country history.

Malaysian students made significant strides in the latest Program for International Student Assessment (PISA), an international benchmarking study that tests how well students apply their knowledge and skills. Having said that, Malaysia's 6,111 students who participated in the exam scored lower than the OECD averages in categories related to reading, mathematics, and science. After conducting extensive research on the topic of the Malaysian education system, it seems as though overall quality has suffered from a lack of vision and stability. Political interference has caused several syllabus and instruction changes, which have led to setbacks for the education system as a whole. In contrast, Singapore has held a clear education vision that is highly centralized, scripted, and uniform across all levels and subjects. Malaysia has long been criticized for teaching in Malay as opposed to English. Many have argued that this has made access to information much more difficult, as acquiring information through a Google search in Malay is substantially harder than in English. The current government administration has laid out a roadmap for language education reform with the government declaring that English will be the main focus of Malaysian education. I think that these language education reforms could go a long way toward resolving some of

Malaysia's education issues if instituted properly. The next phase of Malaysian economic growth will have to be more knowledge-led as opposed to being tied to areas such as manufacturing so the effectiveness of ongoing education reform is critical.

The Expat Insider 2019 Survey, conducted by InterNations, which is the world's largest expat community with 3.6 million members, polled over 20,000 respondents and ranked 64 destinations. The survey found that Malaysia ranked 9th out of 64 nations. Why is this important? The survey ranks the best places to go based on experience, economics, and raising children overseas. Malaysia ranked 7th out of 64 countries in terms of the Cost of Living Index. According to the 2019 Global Retirement Index conducted by internationalliving.com, Malaysia ranked first out of 25 countries in the healthcare category. If Malaysia improves in areas such as education and working opportunities, I think you could see Malaysia rank even higher on the list related to most desirable countries for expats.

Why has the Malaysian healthcare system been consistently ranked as one of the world's top healthcare systems? Compared to countries such as the U.S. and Australia, the medical cost can be 40–80% lower for medical procedures. The healthcare infrastructure is up-to-date, there are private and public hospitals which visitors can choose from, a visitor doesn't need a referral from a general practitioner and can just register for a hospital visit, and the cost of a typical prescription is much lower than many developed countries. Having said this, the recent drug price controls to be instituted in Malaysia could have dangerous implications for the long-term future of the local healthcare industry. Lower drug prices may be a short-term win for politicians, but this reduces the incentive for pharmaceutical companies to innovate and in turn produce life-saving drugs. Pharmaceuticals account for only 14% of local medical expenses, outpatient services account for 46%, and inpatient services account for 24%. In my opinion, the government should first focus on efficiencies related to patient services where the majority of the healthcare costs currently are.

Here are some interesting facts about Malaysia: the Japanese invaded Malaysia on December 8, 1941, a day after they bombed Pearl Harbor, caning is a common punishment under Malaysian law with the maximum number of strokes that can be ordered being 24, Malaysia is home to one of the world's largest populations of king cobras, Malaysia has some of the strictest drug laws in the world with the death penalty available for those that sell drugs, and some Malaysian buildings don't have a fourth floor because the word four has a similar tone to the Chinese character for "death".

Economy

According to a 2019 report produced by The World Bank, "since gaining independence in 1957, Malaysia has successfully diversified its economy from one that was initially agriculture and commodity-based, to one that now plays host to robust manufacturing and services sectors that have propelled it to become a leading exporter of electrical appliances, electronic parts and components." The shift to a focus on exports has led Malaysia to be dependent on this part of the economy, as in 2015 "gross exports of goods and services were equivalent to 73% of GDP." This puts the country's own economy at the mercy of the health of economies in the countries to which Malaysia is exporting. Malaysia is one of the most open economies on earth as supported by the trade-to-GDP ratio, which has averaged over 130% since 2010.

Also according to The World Bank, Malaysia is expected to progress from an "upper middle-income economy to a high-income economy by 2024." Income inequality in Malaysia remains high relative to other economies in East Asia, but these numbers have been improving in recent years. Improvements in the education sector could well lead to a further reduction in income inequality in Malaysia.

Malaysia's productivity growth over the past 25 years has been below other comparable economies. According to the World Bank's Human Capital Index, as of 2018, Malaysia ranked 55th out of 157 countries. Productivity growth is going to be more important in the future for Malaysia with the transition to the more knowledge-led economies associated with more developed countries, which again reinforces the ongoing importance of education for the local economy.

According to the 2019 Index of Economic Freedom, Malaysia is ranked as the 22nd freest in the 2019 Index. Malaysia is ranked 6th among 43 countries in the Asia–Pacific region. According to the report, there is no minimum capital required to start a business and it takes fewer than ten procedures to start a business. Government policies such as these encourage entrepreneurs to start businesses, which in turn increases foreign investment in the country. Perhaps the most interesting note from the report is that there is no national minimum wage in Malaysia. Many have complained that Malaysia's minimum wage laws are confusing, as evidenced by the planned increase in minimum wages beginning January 1, 2020, which is for only 57 bigger cities and towns.

Roughly 31–40% of the Malaysian workforce, which numbers about 15.3 million people, is comprised of foreign workers. These foreign workers are primarily employed in dangerous and difficult jobs in the plantation, agriculture, construction, manufacturing, and service sectors. Local Malaysian media outlets have complained that wages have been driven down by an influx of foreign workers willing to take on low-skill work for little in the way of pay, which has kept many local Malaysians out of work. This is free market economics! Instead of complaining and instituting new laws such as the reduction of the number of overseas workers by more than 130,000 in five years, the Malaysian government should focus on educating and training the local Malaysian population to take advantage of the undesirable work these foreign workers are doing for low pay. For example, instead of the focus being on reducing the number of foreign workers planting crops in favor of local Malaysians, the focus should be on training the local Malaysian workforce to help make crop production more efficient. This would be a higher paying job than being the individual that does the actual planting of the crops and the overall economy would be able to support multiple parties and become more efficient in the process. We have recently seen the same nationalistic rhetoric coming out of the United States with anti-immigration policies. In the majority of cases (particularly for developed nations such as the United States that have low birthrates), immigration will be a net positive for a local economy if there is a plan for integration into the culture of a given country. Let free market economics run its course!

Looking at a list of the 30 largest companies on the KLCI index of Bursa Malaysia, the Malaysian stock market index, I realized that there was not a single company with a technology focus. In a world dominated by technology, this is an ominous sign. According to recent 2019 reports, top-funded local technology start-ups such as iFlix have opted to list their companies on the Singapore and Australia stock exchanges due to "poor responses and strict rules" in Malaysia. Grab is another example of a company that was started in Malaysia but ultimately moved to Singapore due to a larger pool of venture capital funding and a lower corporate tax rate. It is going to be difficult for Malaysia to stay competitive in the technology sector when Singapore has a developed start-up ecosystem and charges a 17% corporate tax rate compared to Malaysia's current 24% rate. Malaysia should consider a change to their corporate tax structure, as it will be difficult to be competitive when close neighbor Singapore is offering a lower rate paired with a stronger history of corporate successes and fundraising ecosystem. Look at what happened before the United States passed the Tax Cuts and Jobs Act of 2017. Countless major U.S. corporations, such as Burger King, Medtronic, and Seagate Technology, fled the United States (at least from a legal registration standpoint to avoid higher corporate taxes) under President Obama. What happened after the passing of the Tax Cuts and Jobs Act? Large American corporations stopped leaving for tax reasons. The U.S. likely also would have lost Pfizer were it not for the lowering of the corporate tax rate. This is basic free market economics.

Adventure

Our adventure to Borneo began at the Kuala Lumpur airport. The first observation a visitor coming from Singapore will have is that the national language of Malaysia is Malay, which is one of two official languages, the other being English. Fortunately for American travelers, airport employees relay information in both Malay and English. Visitors will also be quick to notice a population that is much more diverse than what you will find in Singapore. As of 2019, approximately, 50.1% of the population was Malay, 22.6% were Chinese Malaysians, 11.8% being non-Malay indigenous groups, and 6.7% being Indian Malaysians. Unlike in Singapore, you won't find many Westerners here. In fact, there was only one other Caucasian individual on our flight to Sandakan, Borneo.

I had seen some on my travels to India, but Paula received her first exposure to restrooms that literally consist of a hole in the ground here in Malaysia. Instead of finding a toilet seat in a stall like you would expect to find in most Western countries, a stall in many areas in Malaysia and Indonesia simply includes a hole along with toilet paper and a button to flush. This will likely be the first sign for many that they are navigating less developed countries while in Malaysia and Indonesia.

To say that it was an effort to get to Borneo may be a bit of an understatement. We had to fly from Singapore first to Kuala Lumpur and then on to Sandakan, Borneo, on the way to the island. Upon leaving, we had to fly from Tawau to Kuala Lumpur and then to Jakarta and finally Yogyakarta. These flight paths did not make any sense from a logistical standpoint, but there just aren't many flights offered in and out of Borneo each day. While this inefficiency makes for more difficult travel planning, it helps preserve the natural environment because there aren't many tourists going to Borneo.

On this trip, we had four flights on Malaysia Airlines, which may terrify individuals who have monitored the news in recent years. Arguably the highest profile airline incident of the last decade occurred on Malaysia Airlines Flight 370 on March 8, 2014, when the aircraft disappeared. While we likely will never know for sure what actually transpired, some reports found a similar flight path on one of the pilot's home simulators just six weeks prior to Flight 370's disappearance. I have read countless news reports and theories, and my personal opinion is that one of the pilots intentionally crashed the plane into the ocean, but this opinion likely will never be able to be fully validated. Given the data that have been released up until now, I just think that this was the most probable explanation.

Another high-profile Malaysia Airlines incident came just months later when Flight 17 was shot down by a missile over eastern Ukraine on July 17, 2014. Many will forever view Malaysia Airlines as unsafe because of the negative global press coverage, but the reality is that these incidents could have happened to any airline. I have always argued that airlines should be more careful about the airspaces that they fly over, but most airlines continue to navigate troubled countries due to time and cost savings. My Air Canada flights in and out of India, which went through locations such as Afghanistan, easily could have suffered the same fate. If the disappearance of Flight 370 was due to a rogue pilot, then I am not sure what the airline really could have done to prevent this other than screen the pilots more thoroughly in aggregate. Having said this, in the few weeks leading up to our trip the U.S. Federal Aviation Administration (FAA) downgraded Malaysia's International Aviation Safety Assessment (IASA) from a Category 1 country to a Category 2 country. This change puts Malaysia in company with Bangladesh, Thailand, Costa Rica, Curacao, and Ghana as the only Category 2 countries worldwide.

This report wasn't saying that Malaysia Airlines specifically was unsafe, but rather that the country was providing relatively weak oversight for the airlines operating within the country. This is not what I wanted to hear two weeks before my trip, but this was worth putting into perspective. The two incidents in 2014 for Malaysia Airlines were the first time since 1995 that a Malaysia Airlines flight had crashed. To go a step further, between 1977 and 2019, I could find only four plane crashes in the airline's history. It just so happened that two of these crashes came just months apart. Even though a flight on Malaysia Airlines remains statistically much more safe than driving a car, the mainstream media has convinced many that a flight with the airline is unsafe despite what the math says. I think that is why the exit row was empty on all of our flights with Malaysia Airlines!

Flying into Sandakan, Borneo I had similar feelings as to when we flew into a remote part of Botswana. Sandakan is a city located on the northeast coast of Borneo that had a 2017 population of 196,500. Peering out my airplane window I could see uninhabited rivers, streams, and marsh that stretched for miles. There was not much in the way of development until we got close to the immediate airport area.

Borneo is the third largest island in the world by area, and ownership of the island is split among Malaysia, Indonesia, and Brunei. Indonesia controls over 70% of the island. In August 2019, Indonesian President Joko Widodo announced a plan to move the capital of Indonesia from Jakarta to Borneo. At least for me, this only heightened my urgency to visit this remote island. According to the World Wildlife Fund, Borneo has lost half of its forests in the last century and a third have disappeared in the past three decades. If Indonesia does go through with its long-term project of shifting the capital to Borneo, there would be further potential for environmental destruction.

The main culprit of the environmental devastation in Borneo has been oil palm plantations. A 2019 research report cites that the palm oil industry was responsible for at least 39% of the forest loss in Borneo between 2000 and 2018. Having said that, analysis of recent trend data has shown that industry oil palm plantation-related deforestation has been steadily decreasing since 2012. Oil palm plantations produce 40% of the world's vegetable oil, and the use of palm oil in food products has doubled worldwide in the past 15 years, with about half of all items at the grocery store now containing it. Approximately 85% of the world's planted oil palm area is located in Indonesia and Malaysia with Borneo claiming 45% of the global planted area. One of the driving forces behind our decision to visit places like Borneo and Komodo National Park is that these destinations may not be the same in the future due to environmental impacts.

We had a 2.5-hour drive from Sandakan Airport to Sukau Rainforest Lodge, which is where we would be staying the next couple nights. Along the drive, there are trees as far as you can see and mountains in the distance. The scenery is exotic and screams "adventure," as there is little in the way of development here. As previously discussed, you will notice areas where some of the natural rainforest has been cleared for oil palm plantations. This 2.5-hour drive would have taken far less time if the roads were of decent quality. On several occasions the bumps were so bad that I found my head hitting the ceiling of the vehicle. There was also no drainage system, so the water just sits on the roads and creates massive potholes.

The final leg of the journey to Sukau Rainforest Lodge is to take a five-minute boat ride, as the lodge is not accessible at all by road. Upon cruising up to the lodge on our small motorboat, the overall excitement level was soaring. As I looked around, we were now fully immersed in the rainforest along the Kinabatangan River. Named by National Geographic as one of the "Unique Lodges of the World" the lodge consists of communal amenity areas and villas that are supported by wooden planks next to the river. There is not much else around in the way of development other than some locals living in the area and a couple other lodges dedicated to tourism.

Without a moment of down time to spare, we put our belongings in our room and set out for an afternoon river cruise along the famed Kinabatangan River. If you conduct an online search for the best wildlife destinations in the world, the Kinabatangan River and Sabah (the area in Borneo where Sukau resides) more broadly will make an appearance on many lists. The area is known for the Borneo Big Five, which consists of Orangutan, Proboscis Monkey, Pygmy Elephant, Rhinoceros Hornbill and Estuarine Crocodile. Sabah is often viewed as the best place in the world to see the critically endangered orangutans which the World Wildlife Fund estimates there to be around 119,000 remaining as of 2017. The Borneo Pygmy Elephant is listed as endangered by the World Wildlife Fund with only 1,500 believed to still be in existence according to the most recent estimates.

The scenery and overall sensation that you get riding down the Kinabatangan River is amazing. Everywhere you look there are proboscis monkeys climbing the tall trees along the river. These creatures are endemic to the jungles of Borneo and stand out because of their huge noses and pot belly stomachs. On a number of occasions, we just sat there and watched large families of proboscises play with each other. It is remarkable to see the animals swing from tree to tree and even leap large distances to another tree. Our guide said that in his years watching wildlife along the river he had only seen one monkey ever fall to the ground.

After concluding our outstanding action-packed brief stay at Sukau Rainforest Lodge, we set out for a four-hour drive southeast to the coast to Semporna. Semporna is a poor fishing town of 35,301 people (this is according to 2010 Census data, which is the latest searchable data) located on the east coast of Sabah, which is primarily known by tourists as the jumping-off point to beautiful islands and famed diving destinations such as Sipadan Island located in the Celebes Sea.

We had arranged to stay at the Mabul Water Bungalows which are 16 bungalow units built over water, similar to what many see in pictures in locations such as the Maldives. These floating units reside next to Mabul Island, which is a renowned scuba diving destination in its own regard but most well-known for its close proximity to what many in the scuba diving community consider to be the best diving destination in the world: Sipadan Island.

From the port of Semporna, we took a 45-minute boat ride out to Mabul Island, where we would be staying the next three nights. The boat ride is scenic, as you pass by other floating resorts and many beautiful islands along the way. The feeling you get when pulling up to the water bungalows at Mabul is similar to that of a 5:00 a.m. Christmas feeling as a child. The stunning overwater bungalows appear to pop up out of nowhere and provide for magnificent pictures sitting upon the clear blue waters below.

Paula and I walked around and took pictures of the resort area, which was likely the most stunning I have ever seen. Walking around, the first observation an individual from the U.S. would have is the lack of Western tourists here, which I fully expected from my prior research. We were one of only two American couples staying at Mabul Water Bungalows, and the other American couple said that they had been there for close to a month and hadn't seen any other Americans until we arrived. There were mostly Chinese tourists on the island, many of whom did not even scuba dive, which didn't make sense to me. While the bungalow area was beautiful and there were some small beaches on Mabul Island itself, there really is not a lot to do here other than scuba dive, and I would not recommend a visit to any non-divers. I would be remiss if I didn't at least include some commentary on the safety situation around the Mabul area and the greater region off the east coast of Sabah. I had done exhaustive research leading up to our trip because governments such as the UK, Australia, and Canada advise against "all but essential travel" to islands off the eastern coast of Sabah, which includes Mabul Island and Sipadan Island. Sabah has had a long running problem with kidnappings in the waters off the eastern coast which has been primarily attributable to kidnap-for-ransom terrorist groups operating out of the southern Philippines. There have been reported kidnappings of locals and fisherman the last few years but the last kidnapping I could find regarding an international tourist in the area was when a Chinese tourist was abducted in April 2014. The Malaysian government has made it a priority in recent years to significantly enhance security measures in the Sabah waters to promote tourism. For example, the Eastern Sabah Security Command (ESSCOM), a Malaysian security area covering the east cost of Sabah from Kudat to Tawau, was established in 2013 and restructured in 2014. The Malaysian government has invested substantial resources to upgrade the navy in recent years, including the launch of radar stations giving the navy the ability to track terrorists that continue to attempt to carry out cross-border crimes. While we were staying at Mabul, there was a large Malaysian navy vessel sitting alongside the water bungalows equipped with two large machine guns. There was also a police presence that worked in conjunction with individual resort security both at Mabul Water Bungalows and on Mabul Island. Sipadan Island, which is a 25-minute boat ride from Mabul, is a military base, and at night you can see the lights of Malaysian navy ships patrolling the region. Some will argue that these security measures are a reminder of some of the dark past of Sabah and some would say that the enhanced security makes them feel more secure. Unfortunately, past events such as the infamous 2000 mass kidnapping at Sipadan Island by Abu Sayyaf Group (ASG) still looms large over the region. Data has shown that enhanced security measures in recent years have dramatically reduced the number of incursions in Sabah waters, but many governments are still not convinced of the safety.

Now that I have covered all of the potential ways that we could have been kidnapped and taken to the notorious Philippine terrorist base in Jolo, let's discuss what was easily one of the greatest experiences of both of our lives. Over the next few days, we did a combined six dives around Mabul Island and Sipadan Island. While enjoyable, I did feel as though the overall scuba diving in the Mabul area was a little disappointing compared to the average reviews I had read online prior to the trip. It seems to me as though the area has been overfished and perhaps the aquatic life is not as abundant as it once was. Having said that, we still had an amazing time on our dives here and bonded with new friends living in Maine (U.S.) and Dubai. Our animal sighting highlights around Mabul included turtles, eels, large grouper, and various schools of fish.

Then came what I believe was the highlight of my entire life up to the time of this writing, which was our visit to and the diving around Sipadan Island. The reason that the aquatic life here is maintained so well are the strict regulations and limits on the diving permits allowed. At the time of our visit, only 120 permits were issued per day! For the lucky few who acquire a permit, the diving experience is unrivaled. The trade-off is that the Sipadan Island dive permits are extremely frustrating to secure. If considering a visit, make sure that the Sipadan Island dive permits are received many months in advance and to re-confirm the details several times leading up to the trip. Even though I had arranged for the acquisition of our Sipadan dive permits with my travel company about six months prior to our trip (and re-confirmed the details on several occasions), we still encountered issues upon arrival that were eventually resolved with me calling my travel company and explaining the situation. Those looking for Sipadan diving permits will have to work with the minimum room night requirements at the surrounding resorts, with Mabul Island being the most convenient location to access Sipadan. The diving around Sipadan is worth this extraordinary effort, trust me.

On our 25-minute boat ride out to Sipadan Island, the excitement levels were soaring as we knew we were about to experience something truly special. On our boat it was only Paula, myself, one other diver, and the dive masters which makes sense given my previous commentary about the intense regulations here.

Over the course of the day, we would complete three dives around Sipadan: Barracuda Point, Drop Off, and South Point. According to Scuba Travel, these dive sites are ranked numbers 1, 50, and 35 in the world. I had hired a private videographer in advance to capture all of our best moments of the day. The video turned out better than I could have ever imagined.

Sipadan became famous when diving legend and explorer Jacques Cousteau described it as one of the best diving destinations in the world. Visitors had the option to stay on Sipadan Island itself until 2004 when all diver operators and hotels on the island were shut down and the island was converted to a military base. These measures along with the extreme restrictions for allowing only 120 dive permits per day has allowed the local aquatic life to flourish.

Our first dive was South Point. Within minutes of submerging into the blue waters surrounding Sipadan Island, I was encountered with the very scenario that I had read about in detail for months leading up to the trip. Many scuba divers dream to encounter a "Jackfish tornado" in the magnitude that I found myself engulfed in at that moment. I had spotted thousands of swirling Jackfish and immersed myself in the middle of the spiraling vortex. I spun around taking pictures and videos in real time as our videographer captured Paula and I wrapped up in one of the marine-life wonders of the world. I spotted a couple reef sharks nearby gliding effortlessly through the Jackfish.

Over the course of the day of diving at Sipadan, we saw it all: massive schools of Barracuda, turtles everywhere you turned, reef sharks, beautiful coral, and everything in between. There is a reason that many divers have named Sipadan as the top diving destination in the world and I thought that it certainly didn't disappoint. My favorite dive overall was Barracuda Point, which is named by Scuba Travel as the number one dive site on earth. While all three were the pinnacle of spectacular, Barracuda Point was even one notch up. If you are making the adventure out to Sipadan, make sure to request this dive site. When I came out of the water after our dive at South Point, I said to Paula, "That was the coolest thing I have ever done in my life." That statement still applies, and I would extend it to our whole day diving at Sipadan.

After each exhausting day diving while staying at Mabul, we celebrated with a beer or two at the bars at Mabul Water Bungalows. I had read about it leading up to the trip, but Malaysia ties with Singapore as having the second highest excise duty on beer in the world after Norway. This was one of the few products in the country that wasn't an absolute bargain when thinking about it in the context of U.S. dollar purchasing power. Alcohol consumption in the country is generally frowned upon since more than 60% of Malaysians are Muslim. It is factors such as this along with things such as not having acceptable public bathrooms in several instances that will unfortunately keep a lot of Western tourists away. More adventurous tourists that can look past this and expand their horizons will be rewarded. Malaysia remains accessible, as Forbes named it one of the "16 best destinations for cheap flights in 2020". Much like most of the Southeast Asia region, you will find that the U.S. dollar goes far on most daily purchases.

Malaysia generally has a pretty good reputation when it comes to overall culinary reviews, but I think it would be delusional to say that we had a chance to experience the "real" Malaysian food since we were staying only at resorts that provided more westernized tourist food. Having said that, I enjoyed our food in Malaysia and found it to be much better than what we encountered in Indonesia. I don't think this is particularly surprising given that I can't recall ever seeing an Indonesian restaurant outside of Indonesia.

We had a breathtaking time on our adventures throughout Borneo, and it was the highlight of the trip for both Paula and me. Having said that, one of the downsides and trade-offs to our planned itinerary was that we never really had the opportunity to experience the daily life in Malaysia. Going to Borneo and saying that you experienced what life is like in Malaysia would be the U.S. equivalent of only traveling to Moab, Utah, and claiming that you have experienced life in the United States. We could have substituted both Kuala Lumpur and another area in Malaysia or just Sumatra (Indonesia) for Borneo, but I am glad we didn't. I think Borneo should be high on every adventure travelers' list and with a sense of urgency given the environmental and political challenges facing the island that may prevent this exotic gem from being the same in the future.

Additional Activities and Recommendations

Like many areas in Southeast Asia, Malaysia has monsoon seasons that vary depending on where you are within the country. This information should be researched prior to booking a trip. Obviously, prices will be much lower during monsoon season, so a prospective visitor will need to weigh the trade-offs of optimal time to visit and cost. As I have documented, my experience has been that the best time to visit is at the beginning of rainy season due to lower prices and weather that is usually not any different than a few weeks prior when it is technically not labeled as rainy season. As with all countries, make sure to check with a travel immunization specialist, particularly if you are planning a visit to locations such as rural Borneo. We had to get medication for Malaria and immunizations for Polio (yes, Polio still exists in certain parts of the world in 2019) and Japanese Encephalitis. Unfortunately, the Japanese Encephalitis vaccines are extremely expensive. This is a two-shot series with each vaccine costing around $300. While the risk may not have been great of contracting this brain swelling illness initiated by mosquitos, there is a 30% chance of death for those inflicted and the risk is higher during rainy season which is when we were visiting. If the choice is to spend $600 and virtually ensure survival or not spend $600 and have to worry about not putting on enough mosquito repellant and having my brain swell until death, I will spend the $600.

I had initially done everything I could to try and fit in climbing Mount Kinabalu with our itinerary. Mount Kinabalu, located at the West Coast Division of Sabah in Borneo, is the highest mountain in Southeast Asia at over 13,000 feet. Most tour companies run two-day climbs, but the logistics can prove challenging and time consuming if you are trying to pair this excursion with a visit to the east coast of Sabah given the distance. Similar to Sipadan Island, there is a strict limit on permits at Mount Kinabalu, with only 135 climbing permits granted per day. Make sure to get the arrangements done at least six months in advance. Mount Kinabalu doesn't require much in the way of technical expertise and can be done with a basic level of fitness. Do note that if the desire is to complete the climb in two days, training should be done prior to arriving in Borneo. I have read various blogs stating that while novice climbers can climb Mount Kinabalu, it can still be challenging from a fitness standpoint. The first day's trek will last between five and seven hours, with the second day lasting three to five hours followed by the descent. This mountain lays claim to the world's highest Via Ferrata, according to the 2011 Guinness Book of World Records. I won't go into detail explaining what a Via Ferrata is given my personal experience on one in the Canada chapter.

Some of the others staying at Sukau Rainforest Lodge were heading on to Danum Valley, which is also located in Sabah, Borneo. Danum Valley also has an excellent reputation for wildlife sightings, and some believe it is the best wildlife destination in Borneo and broader Malaysia. If you can't make it to Borneo, Taman Negara National Park, which is located in Peninsular Malaysia, is usually the top-rated wildlife destination outside of Borneo. Taman Negara is the largest national park in Peninsular Malaysia and is home to the longest rope walkway in the world. All the iconic animals of Peninsular Malaysia are believed to live in Taman Negara, but seeing larger animals here is pretty rare as confirmed by my research and speaking with guides while in Borneo. Elephants, sambar deer, tapir, barking deer, and wild boar sightings are possible but it would be highly unlikely that you would have a situation like we had at Sukau where we saw all of the big wildlife sightings in a day and a half.

The Cameron Highlands has been among the favorite places to visit in Malaysia since the end of the 19th century. The Cameron Highlands is a district in Pahang, Malaysia, that consists of beautiful emerald tea plantations. Visitors see the local tea plantations, take part in various guided walks and treks, and visit some of the local villages in the area. Regular buses make the 3.5-hour journey from Kuala Lumpur, so this destination is easily accessible as a day trip from Kuala Lumpur.

If we weren't visiting Borneo and wanted to see other parts of Malaysia, I would have gone to Kuala Lumpur, the capital of Malaysia. I had looked into first visiting Kuala Lumpur and taking an overnight train to Singapore which takes about seven hours. The Petronas Twin Towers, the tallest buildings in the world from 1998 to 2004 standing at 1,483 feet, continue to be a major tourist draw and modern architectural marvel. The Petronas Twin Towers are designed with a steel and glass façade resembling motifs from Islamic art. Like other famous towers such as the Eiffel Tower or CN Tower, visitors have the option to go inside the Petronas Twin Towers. Tourists are shown the Skybridge and the Observation Deck. The Skybridge is located on the 41st floor with the Observation Deck on the 86th floor.

There are many city tours and the like offered around Kuala Lumpur, but adventure seekers will want to head seven miles north of the city to Batu Caves. Here visitors will climb their way up 272 steps to a limestone hill, which is home to a series of caves that consist of Hindu shrines and temples. There is a 100-year-old temple that features statues erected inside the main caves. There are limestone formations believed to be 400 million years old and the temple is considered an important religious landmark by Hindus.

Visits to George Town are popular. George Town is the colorful, multi-cultural capital of the Malaysian island Penang. In 2008, George Town was declared a UNESCO World Heritage Site. Kuala Lumpur is known for its giant towers, and Kota Kinabalu is known for a massive mountain while George Town is famous for the art, heritage, and excellent food.

While the eastern coast of Sabah, Borneo offers many high-quality scuba diving opportunities and some fine beach destinations, there are also desirable opportunities for a beach vacation closer to mainland Malaysia. There are popular beaches such as those found on Langkawi, located off the north-western coast of Malaysia, but there are plenty of options for those looking for beach destinations that are less crowded.

Business Outlook

The biggest question mark going forward for Malaysian business is tied to whether Malaysia can have a sustained environment where rule of law is upheld. It was a positive development in 2018 when an opposition government party took control for the first time in 61 years, but it is yet to be seen if corruption can be rooted out of the system for a long period of time. As I have previously touched on, the development of the education system and in turn productivity growth will be the other critical piece of the puzzle going forward. How well will the Malaysian government help prepare Malaysians for this ongoing shift to a more knowledge-led economy?

Shaquille O'Neal once said, "I heard Jeff Bezos say one time [that] he makes his investments based on if it's going to change people's lives." This makes sense, as dollars usually ultimately flow to where the most value is being provided. Thinking along these lines related to what I saw in Borneo, anyone that comes up with an environmentally acceptable solution for the ongoing palm oil issue will make a fortune. As I previously stated, oil palm plantations produce 40% of the world's vegetable oil, and the use of palm oil in food products has doubled worldwide in the past 15 years with about half of all items at the grocery store now containing it. But as I saw firsthand in Borneo, oil palm plantations have come at a great cost to the environment, which is becoming a more important consideration in the world we live in today. The challenge is to create an environmentally friendly alternative that is healthy for humans to consume that comes at a cost that is competitive with current palm oil products. This would change the world and bring large profits in the process.

At least for now, one of Malaysia's biggest competitive advantages is the low cost of labor compared to other countries. Malaysian companies can offer a cost of living that is far below that of Singapore. According to a 2018 report by Loanstreet, the cost of living in Singapore was 58.55% higher than in Kuala Lumpur. This had me thinking about a couple different opportunities, the first being continued investment and growth in manufacturing along with segments of the service economy where the average salaries are relatively low. Additionally, there is an argument to be made that real estate prices in Malaysia will rise in the future given the current cost of living, geographic location of the country, solid infrastructure, and high-quality healthcare system. If Malaysia could continue to see improvements in terms of human rights, political corruption, and overall education along with more business-friendly policies related to sectors such as technology, Malaysian real estate could see more future upside than any other market that I have ever looked at.

Sukau Rainforest Lodge

Cruising down the Kinabatangan River

Orangutan!

Jackfish tornado at Sipadan!

One of the many turtle sightings

Sipadan Island

Indonesia

Introduction

Indonesia is a vast archipelago that lies in the Indian and Pacific oceans and spans the equivalent of one-eighth of the Earth's circumference. The estimated 17,508 islands that make up Indonesia are grouped into the major islands of Sumatra, Java, the southern portion of Borneo, and Celebes. Indonesia has an estimated 2019 population of 270.63 million, making it the fourth most populous country on Earth behind the United States. According to a 2017 population forecast done by Statista, the Indonesia population is projected to reach 321.55 million by 2050. Approximately 57% of Indonesia's population lives in Java, which is where we would be visiting Yogyakarta and some of the surrounding areas.

Human history in Indonesia is believed to date back to at least 1.5 to 1.8 million years ago. The ancestors of many modern Indonesians are believed to have arrived on the archipelago about 4,000 years ago. Hindu kingdoms were started in Sumatra and Java around 300 BCE under the influence of India. The Indian influence in Indonesia is still present to this day. The Portuguese took control of parts of Indonesia during the 16th century but they were overtaken by the Dutch in the 17th century. The Japanese eventually overpowered the Dutch in the 20th century, but they were viewed as being oppressive by the local people in Indonesia. There was a four-year independence war and Indonesia proclaimed full freedom in 1949.

The first two Indonesian presidents ruled from 1945 until 1998. Unfortunately, these two presidents ruled under autocracies and used the military to remain in power. While there have been flaws, since 2004 Indonesia's presidents have been elected through relatively fair election processes. Having said this, a growing number of observers believe that Indonesia has been sliding in the wrong direction and is now not a full democracy. Critics note that protections for minorities, freedom of speech, and freedom of organization have all eroded to the point that it does not constitute a full democracy.

According to worldpopulationreview.com, Indonesia has the largest Muslim population in the world in 2019 at about 229 million. According to the 2010 census, over 87% of Indonesian's were declared Muslim. About 10% of the population is Christian and less than 2% of the population is Hindu despite the early Hindu influence and Hindu majorities that still exist today in locations such as Bali.

In 2002, Indonesia declared that it would be a constitutional requirement that governments at all levels dedicate at least 20% of their budgets to education, which was a big step in the right direction considering that money spent on education was less than 1% of the budget in 1995. While the country literacy rate is now high at around 95% (according to UNESCO), there is still much to be desired when it comes to education in Indonesia. According to the Program for International Student Assessment (PISA) tests performed by OECD in 2015, Indonesian students were performing below average in mathematics, reading, and science. From my research, the poor education quality in Indonesia if often tied to corruption. For example, school management positions are said to often be sold to the highest bidder. Teachers have been reported to be promoted for supporting political candidates that have gained influence over schools. With these levels of corruption present, it really isn't going to matter if 100% of the government budget is reserved for education. For education in Indonesia to take the next step, there will need to be accountability for those taking part in these illegal and unethical practices.

The Indonesian government recently increased infrastructure investment needs to $430 billion for the period 2020–2024, which would account for about 50% of GDP by 2024. Indonesian Minister Bambang Brodjonegoro said that the "only way for Indonesia to have higher economic growth is connectivity." They are on the right path, but this is a massive challenge for a country that is dispersed across 17,000 islands. The plans call for constructing 25 airports along with other areas of need, such as power plants. Indonesia is trying to keep up with the ongoing flying boom taking hold in the country, as airline passengers skyrocketed more than 60% for the five years ended in 2018.

The World Health Organization ranked Indonesia as being the 92nd best healthcare system in the world out of 190 countries. This makes Indonesia one of the worst-rated healthcare systems in Southeast Asia. A poor quality of public health services can be attributed to factors such as doctors not being fit to treat patients and poor-quality health facilities. There is rampant corruption in the healthcare industry, which can be at least partially tied to low wages for doctors in the public sector.

Economy

The Indonesian economy differs starkly from many Asian neighbors such as Malaysia and Thailand in that the local Indonesian economy is driven by domestic activity rather than exports. In 2015, the industrial sector accounted for 40% of GDP, services at 43%, and agriculture at 14%. Large segments within the broad industrial sector include petroleum, natural gas, textiles, mining, apparel, footwear, and rubber. The industrial sector has been boosted by the large Indonesian workforce, which has made for a favorable country to locate industrial production. Due to a large land area and tropical climate, Indonesia is rich in natural resources such as minerals, oil, and timber.

According to a 2019 report by the OECD, "Two decades after the 1998 Asian Financial Crisis, and one decade after the Global Financial Crisis, Indonesians' living standards are far higher than before, and their economy is more resilient. GDP per capita has risen by 70% during the past two decades." Just since 2015 Indonesia has jumped 33 places in the World Bank's Ease of Doing Business ranking to 73rd globally. The World Bank highlights challenges related to urban infrastructure in Indonesia. According to the World Bank, since 1950 the share of the population living in urban areas has increased from 12% to 56% and this number is projected to be over 70% by 2045. Despite the heavy investments being made by the government related to infrastructure, the city infrastructure has not been able to keep pace with the ongoing population explosion that we have seen. The Indonesian government made a stunning declaration in August 2019 when it said that the country was going to move the capital city from Jakarta to a yet-to-be-built city in Borneo. The rationale behind this decision was reportedly related to heavy pollution in Jakarta, the fact that Jakarta is slowly sinking, and Jakarta infrastructure that is overburdened. From what I have gathered from my research, the main areas of focus for the Indonesian government should be infrastructure, education, and healthcare.

According to the 2019 Index of Economic Freedom, Indonesia ranked 56th in the world. Some highlights from this report include the implementation of measures to reduce the cost of launching a business, property rights that are generally respected, and positive reforms in recent years related to fuel subsidies. The report cites dramatic increases in overall business and investment freedom, but goes on to note ongoing corruption at least partially attributable to the fact that anticorruption efforts are registered from within the government as opposed to an outside independent body.

Indonesian President Joko Widodo declared in 2019 his vision to create "10 new Balis." Tourism has been a promising growth sector for the local economy, and about 40% of the 15.8 million visitors in 2018 visited Bali. This tourism development effort makes all the sense in the world since Indonesia is home to a vast expanse of beautiful islands, of which many have been undeveloped up to this point in time. While travel and tourism outpaced the Indonesian economy in 2018 at a 7.8% growth rate, I believe that there is a massive runway for the local tourism sector. 15.8 million visitors may seem like a lot, but when put in the context of the 270 million people for the local population and that Indonesia makes up one-eighth of the Earth's circumference with a tropical climate with only Bali being visited in large numbers, this vision is easy to see. As I previously discussed in regard to the condition of the bathrooms and cultural norms, it may be in the best interest of Indonesian tourism to westernize some of the development for the 10 New Bali initiative. I personally would not have any interest in this, but the success of tourism in Bali speaks for itself. The market has spoken, and mass tourism in Indonesia has been drawn to the area within the country that has the most developed infrastructure and is most closely tied to Western cultural norms.

In addition to the ambitious growth plans for the tourism sector, the government has stated that they will emphasize development in the manufacturing sector to support future economic growth. Unlike Singapore, which focuses on value-added areas of manufacturing such as semiconductors, Indonesia's manufacturing is largely dependent on simple manufactured goods and raw commodity-based exports. To be better set up for future success, Indonesia should align this sector with regional growth opportunities related to aerospace, semiconductors, and defense.

I received a lesson on the local Indonesian currency, the rupiah, when I was preparing for my trip to India. Instead of Bank of America supplying me with Indian rupees as requested, they mistakenly gave me Indonesian rupiahs. In the probably six-day period during which the currency was shipped and I realized the mishap that had taken place, the Indonesian rupiah had depreciated about 12%! I don't even have to do any in depth research to conclude that this is an unstable currency that is a problem for the Indonesian economy as a whole. There is also the fact that as of the time of this writing, $1 USD is the equivalent of 13,940 Indonesian rupiahs. If you want to take out $500 USD in the form of Indonesian currency you will be holding on to a stack of 6,970,090 Indonesian rupiahs! Currency reform and a long-term strategy is needed to prevent this from happening. As I discuss in the chapter on the ingredients for a successful economy, a stable currency is necessary.

Adventure

We arrived at Soekarno-Hatta International Airport in Jakarta and had to rush to our next flight to Yogyakarta. I had surmised this would be the case prior to arrival because this airport is the busiest in the Southeast Asia region. We had to hustle to make our next flight. Anyone who has ever been to this airport will know that the international terminal is nowhere near the domestic terminal. There were even pictures on the wall of individuals carrying their suitcases covered in sweat which was exactly the scenario that was playing out with Paula and me.

We would be traveling on Garuda Indonesia, which is a five-star airline as rated by Skytrax. The fact that any Indonesian airline has achieved a five-star rating is a stunning development considering the dismal history of the country's aviation safety record. In 2007, all Indonesian airline carriers were placed on the EU blacklist for safety reasons which was only lifted in 2018. In 2015, Indonesia airline carriers had more airlines with the lowest possible safety ranking than any other country on earth, according to surveys conducted by airlineratings.com. Just the fact that we were able to step onto an Indonesian airline with confidence at a reasonable price goes a long way to speaking about the improvements in quality of life in much of the developing world. The book *Factfulness*—one of the most useful books I have ever read—talks about all the ways the world is better than most think and the improvements in transportation safety in countries like Indonesia would be an example of this. Even just few years ago, the idea of me stepping onto an Indonesian airline would have been unfathomable.

One of the first observations that any visitors arriving from Malaysia will have is the difference in language practices. Unlike in airports in Malaysia, for example, where information is repeated in both Malay and English, English is often not used in Indonesia. The official language of Indonesia is Indonesian, which is a standardized form of Malay. Unlike in Singapore and Malaysia, where local newspapers written in English are accessible, I could not find local newspapers in Indonesia published in English. As further confirmed by my research, most printed books in Indonesia are written in Indonesian, and the language is incorporated into the education curriculum in Indonesia and used in the drafting of legal documents. Western travelers who aren't visiting tourist meccas such as Bali will have a more difficult time getting around Indonesia unless traveling with a guide.

We arrived in Yogyakarta late at night and then had to take an hour-long car ride to our hotel, which was conveniently located near the Borobudur Temple. That was where we would be going early the following morning. Our friends Chris and Jayne had joined us and would be traveling with Paula and me for the remainder of our journey. Having only slept a couple hours, we were picked up at our hotel at 4:15 a.m. to go to the famous Borobudur Temple for the sunrise.

This impressive UNESCO World Heritage Site is the largest Buddhist temple in the world and is regularly rated as a top three tourist attraction in Indonesia along with Bali and Komodo National Park and is Indonesia's single most visited attraction. The history behind this modern marvel is remarkable, as the temple was assembled entirely by human labor and took more than 75 years to complete (this estimate varies depending on whom you ask) in the 9th century.

Indonesia is believed to be the country where Buddhism first spread beyond India, and we are lucky enough to have some of these ancient Buddhist monuments still around today. The rulers of the Shailendra Dynasty were responsible for the construction of the temple, and the area was believed to be abandoned around the 14th century when the rulers relocated to another area in Java for reasons that are still unknown. The site was rediscovered in 1814 by Sir Thomas Stamford Raffles. Borobudur has been preserved through several restorations, with the largest projects completed between 1975 and 1982. Borobudur survived the massive 6.2 magnitude earthquake that struck in 2006 that caused great damage to many areas of Java. In 1985, nine bombs were detonated at the Borobudur Temple by terrorists, which destroyed major sections of the structure. Borobudur was also covered in volcanic ash following an eruption in 2010. Having survived all of this turmoil over the years, I only had a greater appreciation for the historic site that was kept in pristine condition.

Borobudur is a 95-foot-high step pyramid that has more than 500 Buddha statues situated around the temple. BBC has named this landmark one of the "Seven Wonders of the Buddhist World." We walked to the top of this impressive structure and waited until the sun rose. As the sun started to illuminate the surrounding area, we took pictures from all over the temple along with the other tourists visiting. I know that we were not visiting during the high season, but I am surprised that there weren't more tourists at the site. For being Indonesia's most-visited tourist site, I would have expected it to be more crowded. Borobudur is only open for religious ceremony one day a year so that tourists have the opportunity to visit on the other 364 days.

Clouds and some fog hung over the surrounding trees that day, which made the views looking out from atop Borobudur look mysterious. I marveled at the beautiful architecture that is just so different from anything you see in the Western world. I realize that some of the temple has since been restored, but it is still stunning to me that such an architectural achievement could have been accomplished thousands of years ago with the technology available at that time. How were the Buddha statues constructed with such precision? Like the pyramids in Egypt, this is a mystery we will likely never fully grasp. Borobudur is a must-visit for anyone traveling to Indonesia. It is a shame that most visitors often opt just to visit Bali and never have the opportunity to see the "real Indonesia."

Later that morning, we proceeded to explore Candirejo, which is a typical Javanese village not far from Borobudur. Our journey around the area was done via horse cart, which was my much-preferred method of horse-related travel after my horse riding experience in Peru. We rode through various small villages and areas where fruits and vegetables were being grown. There was papaya and cassava being grown, and we stopped to get a look at the process of soybeans being mixed with other products. The soybeans are imported, and then the locals mix the imported product with other ingredients.

Any conversation about fruit in this part of the world would be incomplete without the mention of durian. Durian is grown in countries such as Indonesia, Malaysia, and Thailand and is often labeled the "smelliest fruit in the world." In fact, when we were in Singapore, there were several signs in our hotel that we later realized said that visitors who brought durian into the hotel would be fined because the smell of the fruit is so bad! Naturally, I was intrigued. Many locals enjoy eating durian, and many tourists who try durian hate it. Could durian really be as bad as Greenland shark? I never came across anyone on the street selling durian after I had learned about the legend of the fruit, but I am 99.5% sure I accidently tasted durian soup when I was in the Hong Kong airport. It tasted as though I had bitten into a piece of soft egg-like garbage that had been baking outside in the sun for months. While I think that Greenland shark still has the edge for worst food I have ever consumed, I don't see how anyone could enjoy this food product. It was horrific.

Riding around these rural villages of Java, one will notice that almost all of the labor is being done in a completely manual fashion. There are no machines to be seen to help with any of the agricultural processes being done and even the construction of buildings seems to be done all by hand. Efficiency could be dramatically improved in developing countries such as Indonesia with increased automation. It is just a matter of getting affordable tools into the hands of the people doing the work. While this may be a current challenge, it paves the way for a lot of future opportunity.

The highlight of our adventures around the Java countryside came when we visited a local house where we had the opportunity to perform gamelan music using the instruments they had. Considering our group of four had almost zero combined musical experience, we really didn't sound all that bad. By the end of our performance, which lasted several songs, we were all laughing hysterically. I would recommend a visit to the more rural part of Indonesia for anyone contemplating a trip to the country. It provides a completely different perspective than what you will get from visiting the locations packed with tourists.

Traveling around that day, I had several observations and learnings from the conversations I had along the way. Anyone visiting from the United States will notice the prevalence of motorbikes as a method of transportation. According to the Indonesian Motorcycles Industry Association, domestic distribution of two-wheel vehicles in 2018 was 6.3 million units compared to 1.1 million vehicles for the auto market. The thought process that as income levels rise, transportation in Indonesia will shift from two wheels to four wheels has not played out as many have anticipated. There is reported to be only 87 cars owned per 1,000 people compared to "600 to 700" per 1,000 in many more developed countries as referenced by Prijono Sugiarto (president of a local conglomerate controlling the majority of Indonesia's car market). There are many theories as to why two-wheel transportation continues to thrive in Indonesia, but I believe that the main reason has to do with the rise of ride-hailing services and e-commerce development. It is readily apparent that motorbike transportation services booked through companies such as Gojek and Grab have become very popular in Indonesia. Everywhere you look there is a Grab or Gojek employee riding a motorbike with a customer on the back of the two-wheel vehicle. The other major disruption when it comes to motorbike use cases is in the e-commerce business. The last mile delivery services in Indonesia are dominated by motorbikes given the narrow streets and heavy traffic.

We were informed about the caste system which is still used in practice in Indonesia in the year 2019. The caste system present in Indonesia is a Hindu influence similar to the Indian caste system. We were told that the caste system is changing with the Muslim influence. Internet access has recently come to small villages such as around Candirejo, and there has been backlash against the idea of a caste system as citizens have gathered more information. The media often likes to document all of the negative impacts the Internet can have on society, such as disinformation, the spread of terrorism, and the lack of privacy, but the benefits of Internet access far outweigh the negatives. For the first time in their lives, locals in rural Indonesian villages can learn about the freedoms expected in countries such as the United States and why social mobility should be based on life accomplishments as opposed to the family that you are born into.

I have written extensively about the rise of transportation services such as Grab and Gojek in the Southeast Asia region, but I haven't touched on another development happening in the mobile technology space. These companies, along with others that provide different services on mobile applications, have been expanding into various new fields. For example, Grab offers a payments service with GrabPay, food delivery, videos, movie ticket purchases, hotel bookings, and many other services. On their website Grab states, "Say hello to your everyday everything app." This slogan is consistent with what I was told about the landscape of mobile technologies in Indonesia. The market is increasingly consolidating and being dominated by a select few companies that are offering a broader range of services.

That afternoon, we made a spur-of-the-moment decision to visit a waterfall located about an hour from our hotel in Borobudur. We were advised against this decision because the sky was ominous and afternoon storms appeared to be imminent. There are several local waterfalls around this region, and it is a popular activity to hike to these areas. The drive to the area where the waterfall was located passed through several small towns and villages full of various temples and churches. The hiking area provided views of Mount Merapi, which is an active volcano that we would have liked to have visited if we had more time in this area.

We hiked down into a valley that passed through rice fields and had to climb over flimsy bamboo bridges that crossed over several streams. The hike down into the valley to get to the waterfall was steep, and we are extremely lucky that heavy rains did not ensue prior to our hike back up. We had an enjoyable time taking pictures of the waterfall and the rolling rice field plains with Mount Merapi in the background.

The following day, we were picked up from our hotel at 8:30 a.m. for a full-day tour of Yogyakarta. The first stop on our tour was the Sultan's Palace (also known as Kraton Palace). Kraton Palace is usually listed as a top 10 attraction in Yogyakarta and with good reason. The sprawling compound could be confused for a small city, as it is home to over 25,000 people. This impressive palace was built between 1756 and 1790 and is an example of Javanese sultanate architecture. If you are wondering what a sultan is, you are not alone. The Sultan of Yogyakarta is similar to a governor in the United States. The difference is that once an individual is elected Sultan, they are ruler for life. At the time of our visit, there was a major ongoing power struggle regarding the Sultan title. The title traditionally has been passed down to the next son in line, but the current Sultan of Yogyakarta does not have a son. There has been widespread backlash because the current Sultan is believed to be in the process of transferring power to his eldest daughter. No official successor has been named, but this speculation has fueled anger amongst those that believe that a woman should never ascend to this position of power.

In the past, there was a large waiting area within the confines of the compound, where visitors remained until the Sultan was ready to see them. In this waiting area, they were provided entertainment, which is still the case today except the primary visitors are tourists. I was stunned at how few other tourists there were here, as there were likely only six other individuals touring this area. We watched the music performance in the waiting area and then walked around the massive compound and learned about all the history here. The palace still serves as the main seat for the Sultan of Yogyakarta and as a museum for past Sultan's artifacts.

Next up on our tour was Tamansari Water Castle, which is located adjacent to Kraton Palace. This area was an addition to the royal complex over 200 years ago by the first Sultan. Some of the original functions of this location were to meditate, work, hide, and defend the Sultan's family. Westerners will find the architecture of these palaces interesting, as it is far different than anything seen in the Western hemisphere.

In the afternoon we toured the UNSECO World Heritage Site Prambanan, which is located about ten miles outside of Yogyakarta. Those who have limited time in the Yogyakarta area will most likely make their top priorities Borobudur Temple and then Prambanan. Prambanan is Indonesia's largest Hindu site and one of Southeast Asia's major attractions. Built in the 9th century, this site consists of 240 temples and, I think, has architecture similar to the famous Angkor Wat in Cambodia. Unlike Borobudur, Prambanan suffered extensive damage in the 2006 earthquake.

On the morning we were set to leave Yogyakarta for Komodo National Park, we were abruptly awakened at 3:30 a.m. by prayers being blasted over the loudspeakers in the streets in what I believe was the local language. This went on for 45 minutes! I guess the earplugs at the hotel front desk could have been a warning sign! Unfortunately, it is stark cultural differences such as this that will continue to keep many Western tourists away. I personally see it as being more authentic and a learning experience when I find myself in these situations. This is similar to what I experienced in Morocco except that I was in Morocco during Ramadan, which made the prayers far more noticeable due to larger participation amongst the locals.

Over the course of our stay in Java, we saw hardly any Western tourists except at Borobudur Temple. This was inclusive of Prambanan, which had very few people visiting. If this site was dropped in the middle of Washington D.C. there would be thousands of tourists at any given time. When we were visiting Prambanan, there may have been 30 to 40 other tourists. There were only a couple other visitors staying at both of our hotels in Java.

Along the drive from Borobudur to Yogyakarta, I did not see any chain restaurants or stores. I think Indonesia is similar to India in many ways except that Indonesia is about ten years earlier when thinking about the country development curve. Other than prime tourism areas such as Bali, Indonesia hasn't gotten to the point where many Western brands have infiltrated the area, which I think is a positive from a tourist perspective for those looking to experience the authentic local culture.

If you spend time in Indonesia, you likely will notice brands and stores that are infringing on the patents of global brands. For example, I saw a "Popeye" fast food chain that was clearly ripping off the Popeyes name and brand. We were told of stories about various trademark pirates that have been responsible for stealing the Polo Ralph Lauren intellectual property and brand in Indonesia (this was confirmed by my independent research). Driving around the country and conducting even the most basic Internet searches, you will find that Indonesia has had long-running problems in regard to the regulation and enforcement of Copyright laws.

In 2016, the Global Intellectual Property Center conducted a global survey for an intellectual property protection index, ranking the level of intellectual property and trademark protection in the countries surveyed. From 30 surveyed countries, Indonesia was ranked 27th, only slightly better than Vietnam, Thailand, and India. Indonesia has placed a greater emphasis on Copyright regulations in recent years and ratified laws with sweeping changes in 2014 with the passing of Copyright Law No. 28, which was enacted to resolve more complex Copyright issues.

While Indonesia may have made relative progress compared to a decade ago on this area, my visit confirmed that there is still a long way to go in conforming to expectations that U.S. companies would have. This is a major issue because without strict enforcement and oversight of Copyright and IP protection, businesses and entrepreneurs do not have an incentive to innovate. Many intelligent individuals will just decide it is better off to wait for someone else to create a product or service and then steal the idea. In order for Indonesia to ever become a global business powerhouse, it will have to fix these problems.

Throughout our time in Java, everywhere we went we were told stories about local infrastructure being damaged by earthquakes. The powerful earthquake that struck the Java area in 2006 was responsible for most of the damage in recent years, but this leads to thought-provoking ideas regarding Indonesia as whole. Indonesia falls on the "Ring of Fire," which is a horseshoe-shaped area around the edges of the Pacific Ocean along which 90% of all earthquakes occur. Additionally, 75% of Earth's volcanoes are located along the Ring of Fire. The vast number of earthquakes along the Ring of Fire are caused by the amount of movement of tectonic plates in the area. The insurance risks in the country against natural disasters are so great that the Indonesian government recently agreed to assume a portion of the insurance risk for state-controlled assets. The devastating 2018 Sulawesi earthquake and tsunami that was responsible for the deaths of over 2,000 people again highlighted the risks and insurance gaps in Indonesia. The earthquake caused catastrophic damage in a region where building codes are not particularly robust and property insurance penetration rates are low. All of this had my wheels spinning. In a country that can't even protect against basic Copyright infringement, would I really trust a local insurance company to follow through on reimbursement for hundreds of thousands or millions of dollars in property damages in the event of an earthquake, volcano eruption, flooding, or any other prevalent natural disaster in Indonesia? At least for the time being, I don't see how a prospective homeowner would ever be able to get past this.

Driving around Java over the course of our stay, I noticed that I had not seen a single movie theater. How could this be? I did some research and, according to a 2019 Bloomberg report, Indonesia has entered a new "golden age" for the Indonesian movie theater industry. Indonesia sold 16 million movie theater tickets in 2015, a figure that soared to 43 million in 2017. To put this into perspective, 43 million was still just a quarter of the number sold in the UK, which has a fourth of the population of Indonesia.

It seems that luxuries afforded to more developed countries such as attending movie theaters are increasing in popularity in Indonesia but from a very low base. Having said that, from my travels across the globe to various developing countries, I have come to the conclusion that the advertising model is the best way to reach consumers in these areas. Global powerhouses such as Facebook and Google have achieved "platform lock-in" with

WhatsApp, Facebook, YouTube, and Google, which afford them the ability to make additional profits from the consumer in a variety of ways.

Luxury brands such as Apple have largely missed out on the next generation of consumers in developing markets like Indonesia because they have priced themselves out of the market. By looking at the data and talking to locals in Indonesia or India, you will conclude that only a select few can justify paying $1,000 for a new iPhone. Consumers in developed markets such as the United States were locked into the iOS platform many years ago, which has allowed Apple to achieve enormous margins on luxury product sales. This has not been and will not be the case in most developing markets because consumers have been locked into products and operating systems dominated by WhatsApp and Google, which have been fueled by the advertising model. Could this allow for large margins to be achieved by Facebook and Google on the next generation of hardware products such as virtual reality if they are fueled by software such as WhatsApp that has become indispensable to the daily lives of hundreds of millions of people in Indonesia and India? Apple has already proven this is possible. The great irony with Apple is that the biggest strength of the business model in developed markets has been the fact that most components of the iOS platform have been exclusive to Apple products which has driven Apple product sales for consumers that are locked into the iOS software. This will also be the biggest weakness for Apple in developing markets because most consumers in these markets have little exposure to most iOS software products and the data has shown that the big-ticket hardware purchases have not followed in these markets.

On our flight to Komodo National Park, we had the first big issue of the trip. Our friend Jayne left her passport on the airplane. By the time we figured out what had happened, the airplane was already on its way back to Jakarta. This potentially catastrophic situation was a learning experience for all involved: do everything possible to avoid losing your passport while overseas, and always carry copies of your passport since this information may be required to get an emergency passport. If in need of an emergency passport, find the nearest U.S. Embassy and apply for a replacement passport. There will be a passport replacement fee, but this will be the least of your worries if you find yourself in this situation. Consulates and embassies can't issue passports on weekends or holidays, so make sure to plan around this. Jayne may be one of the luckiest individuals to ever have walked this earth because Garuda Indonesia found her passport and brought it back to the remote Komodo National Park within a few days! If you are wondering how an Indonesian airline achieved five-star status, here you go.

All that said and done, flying into Komodo National Park is impressive in and of itself. Clear blue waters, scattered uninhabited islands with hills and mountains, and little in terms of human development. It has the feeling of flying into the Greek Islands except much more remote and with less development along with clearer waters.

Komodo National Park is a UNESCO World Heritage Site and has been named as one of the New 7 Wonders of Nature. This remote area can be reached by a short flight from Bali. This stunning national park is massive, as it covers roughly 847 square miles. As we would come to see during our stay, the popular sites located within the park are often at least a couple hours away from each other by boat. Komodo is most known for being the only place in the world where the remaining 6,000 wild Komodo dragons live. Komodo National Park is also home to several world-renowned scuba diving sites as well as quality hiking opportunities. At the time of our visit, the Indonesian government was mulling a $1,000 tax charged to tourists just to enter Komodo National Park. This would reduce the number of annual tourists to the area and make the destination only reserved for luxury tourism. I initially thought this proposition was outrageous, but a $1,000 fee really wouldn't be that out of line with industry norms when thinking about destinations tied to animal conservation. For example, Rwanda charges a $1,500 per person per day fee for gorilla tracking. The high fees contribute to conservation efforts with the unfortunate side effect of limiting the tourism opportunities to the wealthiest individuals.

We had two full days in Komodo National Park, and we would be doing five dives along with visiting Rinca Island, where we would hopefully be seeing the Komodo dragons. Most visitors stay around Labuan Bajo which is where the airport is located. Labuan Bajo is a small port town with a population of 221,430 according to the 2010 census. There was a plethora of boats at the harbor.

During our stay at Komodo National Park, we spent the majority of our time out on a boat with a group of other visitors who also were scuba diving. Even if you aren't interested in scuba diving or snorkeling, an extended boat ride in Komodo is a must. The scenery is nothing short of breathtaking as you pass by countless uninhabited islands and get a feeling of how remote this location is.

Perhaps it was because Paula and I had just come from Sipadan Island, but I found the diving in Komodo National Park to be a bit disappointing. This should come with the caveat that we did not go to famed dive sites within Komodo such as Castle Rock, which are notorious for strong currents and reserved for more advanced divers. The coral reefs were healthy, and the overall diving was solid, but the volume of large marine life in Sipadan dwarfed all of the dive sites in Komodo. I was hoping that we would see the manta rays since "manta season" within the park runs from December through February, but we did not see any. The highlights of our five dives were seeing a cuddle fish, several large turtles, reef sharks, and being able to do a drift dive (essentially going with the strong current on a dive). A popular option for diving enthusiasts is to do a liveaboard diving trip within Komodo National Park. This is where divers sleep on the boat, and I can see why it is popular given how spread out everything is within Komodo.

We had opted to see the dragons on Rinca Island as opposed to Komodo Island because Rinca has more dragons and is smaller, which allows for a greater chance of spotting these iconic beasts. Approaching Rinca Island feels like a scene from *Jurassic Park*. The barren island is sparsely populated by trees but mostly full of dusty hills and small mountains. The island is completely undeveloped with the exception of a couple houses where park rangers reside.

The remaining 6,000 Komodo dragons live on only five islands, all of which are located in southeastern Indonesia (four of which are within Komodo National Park). The Komodo Dragon is the largest living lizard in the world and can reach 10 feet in length. The dragons basically eat anything, including younger Komodo dragons! They are cannibals. In fact, 10% of an adult Komodo dragons' diet consists of newly hatched Komodo dragons! These ruthless animals can eat up to 80% of their body weight in one meal and usually only eat once a month. It may seem a bit frightening, but Komodo dragons are adept swimmers. Could you imagine seeing one of these massive lizards while scuba diving?!

Perhaps surprisingly, a tour at either Rinca or Komodo to see the Komodo dragons is a walking tour. The defense against the 200-pound carnivores are 150-pound park rangers holding a stick! According to Komodo National Park authorities, 30 people have been bitten by Komodo dragons since 1974 with five of the victims dying (as of 2017).

Having the opportunity to see the Komodo dragons on Rinca Island was a special experience. We probably saw 12 of them during our stay. I stood in awe as I watched several dragons crawling around with the infamous stalking movements that they use. Their long tongues were repeatedly put on full display while I was taking it all in. I am surprised at how close the rangers allow tourists to get to the animals given the potential looming danger. While not directly next to the dragons, we probably got within 15 to 20 feet of a couple of them which made for some excellent pictures. All of the Komodo activity at the time of our stay was around where the park rangers are living. If you would like to see the Komodo dragons wandering around other parts of the island, a morning visit is recommended because this is when they are more active. We visited during the afternoon hours when the dragons were mostly content sitting in the more shaded areas. Keep in mind that it is usually very hot on Komodo Island and Rinca Island. I could see how an extended hike here could become uncomfortable quickly.

We capped off our fabulous time in Komodo National Park with a short trip to nearby caves at Batu Cermin Cave, which is just 15 to 20 minutes outside of town by car. The more desirable local cave attraction is Rangko Cave, which offers a swimming hole, but we did not have the time to do this since it is over an hour outside Labuan Bajo. Batu is a fine place to go on the morning you are departing for the airport. Do note that you likely will have to bend down to enter the cave, as the height of the entrance is low. There were some bats and some cool scenery, but this is not a place where you can really spend more than 15 minutes exploring.

In hindsight, we should have stayed an extra day in Komodo National Park. I would really have liked to have done a boat ride, which would have taken us to Padar Island and Pink Beach, both of which are iconic destinations within Komodo National Park. Again, these destinations are a couple hours away from Labuan Bajo by boat, and this excursion is usually a full-day trip. Padar Island is the third largest island within Komodo National Park, and this is where you will often see Instagram pictures atop one of the mountains on the island. I am still bitter that we were not able to experience the panoramic views here. I did everything in my power to arrange for a private boat ride out to Padar, but I couldn't put our flight back to Bali in jeopardy.

On our long journey back home, we had a layover in Bali. While we were only here for a matter of hours, our stay was enough to convince me that one of the best travel decisions I have ever made was visiting Komodo National Park over Bali. I hated almost everything about Bali. It was like a combination of Las Vegas and Ocean City, Maryland, in the United States. The airport was full of Western tourists who thought they were the greatest thing on earth for being at this "exotic" destination. It has all of the chain beach shops that you would expect to see at an American beach destination. While I realize that I did not see top Bali locations such as Ubud, I don't see how you can tell what is authentic and what isn't in Bali. It all seemed fake to me. Additionally, Bali is predominantly Hindu, which is unlike the vast majority of Indonesia. That makes Bali a poor representation of the rest of the country. Visiting Bali would be the American equivalent to visiting a 100% Spanish town and saying that you experienced the authentic American culture. One of the main reasons that tourism has thrived in Bali is because the Hindus are less conservative than the Muslims in aggregate. If you are looking to party, go to Bali. If you want to experience local Indonesian culture, go anywhere else in the country. The only reason I could ever see anyone wanting to come here is to surf or scuba dive. Bali is renowned as a quality surfing destination and Liberty, a wreck dive, is regularly rated as a top 10 scuba diving destination in the world.

Additional Activities and Recommendations

Had we not chosen to go to Borneo, I would have opted to go to Sumatra, Indonesia, instead. Sumatra is much less frequented by tourists than destinations such as Java and Bali, but Sumatra is home to some high-quality wildlife experiences. Sumatra is home to 11 national parks, three of which are listed together as a UNESCO World Heritage Site. Sumatra is home to orangutans, rhinos, tigers, elephants, clouded leopards, and tapirs that all live in the same forest. Kerinci Seblat National Park, located in West Sumatra, is Sumatra's largest national park and one of the higher-rated parks in the area. Kerinci is recognized under the Global Tiger Initiative as one of the 12 most important protected areas in the world for tiger conservation. Travelers will usually take an eight-hour drive from the city of Sangai Penuh to the base of Kerinci Seblat National Park, which by itself is considered to be a very scenic experience. I personally would much rather explore relatively uncharted wildlife territory in Sumatra than go to a destination such as Bali, which is flooded with tourists and has lost all of the authentic local culture.

If you are into scuba diving, the Raja Ampat Islands located in West Papua is regularly rated as the top dive site in Indonesia and one of the best diving destinations in the world. Raja Ampat is an archipelago that consists of over 1,500 small islands and home to 530 species of coral, 700 species of mollusk, and 1,300 types of fish. Unlike many other formerly beautiful destinations spanning the globe, Raja Ampat has managed to stay this way due to its remote location. I am getting wanderlust just writing this passage, as I can envision myself swimming amongst the resident Whale Shark population that navigates these waters.

While the area will be crowded with tourists, Bromo Tengger Semeru National Park is one of the places that is worth dealing with all of the people around. Mount Bromo, located in East Java, is likely the most famous of the 147 registered volcanoes in Indonesia. An Instagram search of Mount Bromo and the surrounding areas will confirm why, as the scenery is absolutely stunning. There is plenty to do in this area to keep tourists occupied, with offerings such as hiking, jeep excursions, horse riding, and waterfall viewing, among many other activities. Lonely Planet notes that accommodation in the Bromo area is notoriously expensive so travelers should plan accordingly.

There are an estimated 17,508 islands in Indonesia, so I think it is safe to say that tourists can find one that suits their personal interests. Outside of Bali, Lombok and the Gili Islands have risen in popularity in recent years. It really depends on personal interests when thinking about which islands to visit. Interested in the widest array of nightlife offerings? Go to Bali. Looking for natural beauty that has tourist infrastructure but not as crowded as Bali? Go to Lombok. Looking for a more remote island to get away from the crowds? Consider a destination such as Seram Island which is much bigger than Bali but hardly sees any tourists.

I feel obligated to at least mention the current capital of the country and largest city in Indonesia: Jakarta. Bali has received the nightlife spotlight in recent years because of the tourist draw, but Jakarta remains the nightlife capital of Indonesia. Popular nightclubs such as Colosseum Club continue to be mainstays on the global nightlife scene, as Colosseum again ranked in the top 100 according to the 2019 djmag.com rankings. Conservatives are lobbying for club curfews and strict alcohol laws which could put an end to one of Southeast Asia's nightlife hotspots, but at least for now the party rolls on in Jakarta.

Business Outlook

As discussed in the section on the economy, tourism represents a major growth opportunity for Indonesia. We should see significant investments being made related to local tourism companies, tourism infrastructure, and global technology platforms related to tourism increasing partnerships and investments in Indonesia. Indonesia has become a focal point for Booking Holdings' Next Billion Internet user's initiative. Booking Holdings is the largest online platform in the world dedicated to travel, as measured by company market capitalization as of 2019. In addition to the tourism tailwinds previously discussed, the study by Booking highlights the high Internet penetration in Indonesia as an additional tailwind for online travel bookings in the country.

Another significant growth area is in the coffee market. As I discussed in the chapter on Colombia, the global coffee market offers a significant runway for long-term growth and Indonesia's retail coffee market is projected to grow at a compound annual rate of 11.4% between 2017 and 2021, which ranks it among the fastest growing coffee markets globally. According to 2018 reports, Indonesia was already ranked in the top five coffee markets in the world by volume, which is interesting because Indonesia has similar demographics to India and coffee has not caught on there nearly to the extent to what we have seen in Indonesia. This anomaly can at least be partially explained by the fact that Indonesia sources some of the highest quality coffee in the world locally, but I would still not expect to see the gap that we currently do. There has been high growth in the coffee market in the broader South and East Asia regions, with the share in coffee consumption increasing from 5% in the early 1990s to a 12% consumption rate in 2018 according to a report by the International Coffee Organization. The ongoing rapid growth in coffee consumption in Indonesia and Southeast Asia will benefit local coffee retailers and global powerhouses such as Starbucks that operate in the region along with the harvesters that are sourcing the coffee. Sumatra accounts for more than 60% of the coffee crop area in Indonesia. I thought the coffee and espresso was delicious and I enjoy drinking Sumatran coffee while back home.

While much of the international focus has been on the Indian growth story in recent years, I believe that much more attention will be paid to Indonesia in the years ahead. Indonesia is the fourth most populous nation in the world (and growing) with a median population age of 28. As I previously noted, Indonesia seems to be about ten years behind where India is in terms of overall development. I would expect Western consumer brands to invest much more heavily than in the past if they can work out the difficulties in navigating areas such as local Copyright laws. Global technology behemoths have taken note of the opportunity in Indonesia. A 2019 report on WhatsApp speculated that the company was in the process of launching a payments solution in Indonesia with the report citing the explosive growth in the e-commerce industry which is set to triple to $100 billion by 2025. In five years, I would expect the opportunity narrative on Indonesia to be similar to what we hear about India today: huge population growth on an already large base, young average age of consumer and workforce, and massive growth in many consumer areas such as e-commerce. I am surprised that Indonesia hasn't received more publicity at this point in time, especially considering the global starvation for yield with the ongoing backdrop of low interest rates. The lingering question will be if Indonesia can overcome corruption, insufficient infrastructure, poor education and healthcare systems, and a less favorable regulatory environment compared to more developed countries to fully take advantage of enormous consumer growth opportunities? Time will tell.

Sultan's Palace

Borobudur Temple

Prambanan

Komodo National Park is stunning

Scuba diving adventures at Komodo

Aboard our boat!

Travel Lessons Learned

Over my years of travel, I have accumulated a vast knowledge base in terms of travel tips that I would like to share with others. I hope that this list is helpful.

If you are looking to travel on a budget, look to countries that are less developed. For example, when I traveled to Colombia in 2018, this trip was a magnificent value purchase when compared to more developed destinations such as Western Europe, Australia, and New Zealand. In recent years, most of the budget travel indices and lists have rated Southeast Asia as the region that has provided travelers the best value for their money. I think there is a fine line when discussing this topic because countries with near completely undeveloped tourism industries can be over the top expensive. I recently did research on the potential cost of a safari in Gabon, located in Central Africa, and it would have set me back several multiples of a similar experience in South Africa. The best value destinations will be those that have moderately developed tourism industries in countries that are less developed than locations such as the United States and Western Europe.

Look at destinations where the currency is weak relative to where you are making your income. For example, South Africa entered recession in 2018 and the South African rand has been particularly weak against the U.S.

dollar the past few years, which has provided for a high-quality opportunity to visit this beautiful country. Temporarily weak economic performance in a country can provide an opportunity for travel value seekers.

I would recommend looking at destinations that may be temporarily misunderstood as to the safety of visiting. For example, when I visited Morocco back in Summer 2016, ISIS was more powerful, and there was a perception that every country and area in Western Africa was dangerous. As I saw during my visit, this perception was far from reality. The media coverage had temporarily prevented many tourists from visiting Morocco and provided even further value for a country that has historically been highly rated in this department relative to countries such as the United States. When checking travel advisories such as that from the U.S. Department of State, I would recommend comparing the advisories from several countries and doing independent research on top of this. What you will find is that there are often discrepancies and governments can take years to update a travel advisory in a given region or country that has improved in terms of safety and security. Putting in the effort in this area can save a prospective traveler a great deal of money over the years.

Everyone is different but to me a travel experience to a country that sharply contrasts with my life back home is much more valuable from a cultural perspective than an experience that is similar in nature. This is another reason why I haven't spent much time in Western Europe in recent years. I think that what you will see in Western Europe generally closely resembles that of the United States when thinking about this in comparison to countries such as India, Botswana, or Colombia. It took me years of traveling to realize this, but I now have a far greater appreciation for visiting countries that have a large cultural divergence from the United States because I find that I learn a lot more along the way.

In recent years, I have increasingly planned my travels around some of the "real" cultural experiences in various countries. There is a reason that I chose not to visit Bali on my trip to Indonesia. While I can't say from personal experience, it would appear from my research that visiting Bali and saying you have the slightest inkling as to what the culture of Indonesia is like would be comparable to going to Cancun and saying that you know how people live in Mexico (after visiting Bali during our brief layover, I couldn't agree more with this assessment). It has been challenging, but I have tried to balance this sentiment with opportunities for outdoor adventure activities, wildlife and other natural experiences, and "must-see" attractions such as the Taj Mahal.

Pick and choose countries and areas to travel without outside help compared to planning a trip with the assistance of a tour operator. I would increasingly recommend using a tour operator the more uncertain the safety situation is in a given country and if there is a large cultural divergence from the home country. For example, I would recommend using a tour operator for travelers planning to explore the rural areas of Colombia that have never visited the country. While there are many parts of Colombia that are completely safe, there are also areas that are rife with drug cartel operations and have a higher risk for terrorist acts. I will use my personal example from India when discussing my reasoning for considering a tour agency if there is a large cultural divergence from a traveler's home country. My train experience to Ranthambore National Park was nothing short of terrifying given that I could not figure out where I was and the stop that I was supposed to depart the train. It is times like these that I believe a tour operator could provide high value.

I always recommend looking for the unique features of a country when planning a visit. This could be in terms of wildlife, adventure activity offerings, physical structures, or natural wonders. If you approach travel from this mindset, I think you will find that it is much more rewarding than visiting a country and spending your time shopping or sitting on a beach that could be done just about anywhere else in the world.

I approach my travel budget planning with the logic that I am going to save some money in the accommodation and food areas so that I am able to allocate more financial resources to activities and experiences. 20 years from now, you are much more likely to remember the skydiving experience that you had in Queenstown, New Zealand, than the food you ate that day or where you slept. I don't ever like to miss out on a unique attraction that I want to do, but I will more than likely be willing to downgrade my hotel option or only splurge on one or two luxurious meals in a given country.

When thinking about the optimal time to visit a particular destination, I usually recommend visiting during "shoulder season" because there may not be too much of a sacrifice in terms of weather conditions and you can likely save a good amount of money and see less crowds during the visit. I have used this strategy in planning trips to locations such as South Africa and Chile and it worked out well.

I know that I would be viewed as an extreme planner by most, but I would advise making most of the excursion bookings prior to arrival. You don't want to spend half of your trip trying to figure out what you are going to do next. I find it to be much less stressful and a better use of time if the detailed itinerary is thoughtfully pieced together prior to arrival. I know that this philosophy has caused me to miss opportunities such as puma tracking in Patagonia, but the benefits have far outweighed the drawbacks.

If you are looking to save days off in terms of work, plan your travel around holidays. I almost always travel during holiday periods to lessen the amount of time I am out of the office. In 2018, I traveled to Chile, Canada, and Colombia and missed a total of 11.5 days of work by planning trips during holiday periods and running an efficient schedule.

I urge all responsible travelers to consider using travel-related credit cards to help cover travel expenses. If done properly, an individual should rarely have the need to pay for a single flight. It is largely a myth that opening new credit cards kills your credit score. This is a very small portion of the overall credit score, with most estimates placing this factor in the range of 10% of the overall credit score.

What Makes a Successful Economy?

I have learned more about the global business environment through my travels and the writing of this book than I probably have cumulatively through my extensive reading over the years. All of the research regarding various economies around the world made me interested in going back and studying the causes of America's rise to economic prominence along with some of the other most dominant empires in history. Many of the economic philosophies that made America great are getting lost in today's landscape, where we are witnessing an unprecedented backlash against capitalism that threatens the future success of the United States. It would be hugely beneficial if we all went back and studied what led to the economic rise of the U.S. and the other greatest empires in the history of the world and related these findings to the environment we see today. This chapter will discuss the common traits found in economies that are successful over the long-term by reviewing the past and providing comparisons that are found in the world today.

A sturdy infrastructure foundation is a common theme for economic success and played an important role in the rise of America as an international superpower. Prior to 1871, there was approximately 45,000 miles of railway track in the country. "Between 1871 and 1900, another 170,000 miles were added to the nation's growing railroad system," according to The Library of Congress. The railroad boom that America witnessed in the late 1800s and early 1900s laid the foundation for economic success for years to come because it provided for a relatively reliable and cost-effective way to transfer goods. The time period between 1870 and 1914 is often referred to as the Second Industrial Revolution because of the rapid territorial expansion that was fueled by the national railway system that had tied the country together for the first time. Successful economies in 2019 still invest in infrastructure similar to how the United States did in the late 1800s. For example, I witnessed Mumbai's ongoing construction of their first underground metro system, which should help alleviate some of the grueling traffic in the city that stifles economic progress because of all of the time that is wasted on the roadways. Sticking with India, it was abundantly clear that they have made airport infrastructure a priority and are investing substantially in this area. Improved airport infrastructure can boost economic performance in a variety of ways. For example, tourism is likely to see an uptick because there will be more flights available to India which will provide increased convenience and lower costs to visit. Much like how the railway system knit the United States together in the late 1800s, modern-day airports have a similar impact on a country. Strong airport infrastructure provides for a hub for goods to pass through and stimulates the urbanization of the surrounding area. To have sustained economic success, a country must maintain a solid infrastructure foundation.

The quality of the education system in a given country is vital for a variety of reasons. There is generally a direct correlation between level of education and personal income, which is why I became a Board Member at CanEducate to help tackle the issue of education in impoverished areas in developing countries. Income inequality results when you have a group of very educated people and then another group with little to no education at all. I firmly believe that the best way to close this gap is to focus on educating the less fortunate portion of the population. This focus on education across all segments within a country also benefits the local economy in that it provides for more skilled workers. As I have witnessed in countries such as Belize, a poor education system can result in consistently high unemployment and a shortage of skilled labor which is a drag on the economy. These themes can be traced all the way back to the ancient world.

The Roman Empire, often considered the greatest empire in the history of the world, ruled from 27 BCE through 476 CE and exhibited some of the same characteristics pertaining to education discussed above. I don't think it is surprising that the Ancient Romans placed a premium on education given the sustained success of the empire. The wealthier families received a quality education and were often taught by private tutors at home while the poor did not receive a formal education but still learned to read and write. This is one of the earlier examples of how inequality develops within an economy. I think that one of the main advantages that the United States maintains today is the unmatched quality of the secondary education system. For all of the advances that China has made in regard to education, they haven't come close to replicating the success that the U.S. has had in terms of college-level education. As I noted in the chapter on India, if they are to take the next step in terms of economic development, they are going to have to dramatically improve their university system.

Ease of doing business is another critical element to any successful economy. The World Bank produces a report each year that ranks countries regarding ease of doing business which evaluates factors such as corruption, property registration, time to start a business, ability to acquire credit, among various other factors. One of the four pillars of Ronald Reagan's strategy was to reduce regulations on businesses. While many will argue that Reagan did little to reduce regulations regarding health, safety, and the environment, he eliminated price controls on domestic oil and gas, deregulated cable TV, interstate bus service, long-distance telephone service, ocean shipping, and eased banking regulations. These pro-business policies helped lift the United States out of the 1980 recession by stimulating the economy. Fast forward to today and you see New Zealand sitting atop the global ease of doing business rankings. It takes just 0.5 days on average to start a business in New Zealand. Who wouldn't want to start a business in this country? When thinking about policies affecting businesses, governments should first think, "if I were running a business what would I want to see in terms of government policy?" and then weighing this thinking against potentially harmful long-term economic impacts such as reducing banking regulations to the point that we would be at risk of another global financial crisis similar to 2008–2009.

An important and often misunderstood element of sustained economic success is a sound currency. At times, President Trump has railed against the strength of the U.S. dollar especially when comparing it to the Chinese yuan because of the temporary disadvantages strength in a currency provides in terms of trade deficits. But let's think about this for just a minute. What great countries in the history of the world have had consistently weak currencies? Steve Forbes points out, "The floundering today makes it clear that the knowledge that enabled us to go from the late 18th century through the First World War, where we had the greatest increase in human wealth in history; in that one and a quarter centuries we created more wealth than all the previous centuries put together, and a key element was stable money, starting with the British pound." History does not lie, and I could not agree more with Mr. Forbes on this topic. It is for these reasons that policies related to the Icelandic króna have terrified me. The country is simply too small to have its own floating currency and the result has been a consistently erratic currency that has discouraged foreign investment over the years. I hope that President Trump, Iceland, and many other individuals and countries can learn from history on this topic and target a stable currency for the long haul.

Average citizens must have an incentive to work and innovate. The easiest way to discourage work participation and innovation is to offer generous entitlement programs. Depending on who you ask, Franklin Delano Roosevelt (FDR) is one of the most beloved or most hated presidents in the history of America. FDR famously passed a sweeping series of entitlement programs which included the Social Security Act in 1935. The problem with entitlement programs such as the Social Security Act is that citizens come to rely on this government funding for retirement and do little themselves to prepare. Additionally, once an entitlement is received it is extremely difficult to take this away given the government bureaucracy. Look no further than the Social Security Act for evidence to support this claim. The full retirement benefit age for Social Security is 66 years old (if you were born between 1943 and 1954), which is just one year older than when the act was signed into law in 1935. This is despite the fact that people live many years longer on average in 2019 than in 1935, which means that the U.S. government is paying more every year to cover these expenses and bankrupting the country in the process!

While visiting Peru, I witnessed the opposite end of the spectrum when it comes to prudent management of welfare and entitlement programs. Unlike the U.S., Peru does not have a welfare system. While this will lead to some negative consequences, there were people out on the streets in wheelchairs doing anything they could to make an impact on both their personal lives and society. In other words, their incentive to participate in the economy and society was high which is in direct contrast to the expansion of entitlement programs and welfare systems. Similar statements can be made regarding incentive structures pertaining to taxation. While an extreme case, do you think that UK residents had any incentive to innovate when the top income earners were being charged an astounding 98% tax on their income in 1974? Of course not! Why do you think The Beatles left the country? Incentive structures at the government, company, and individual level are critical to economic success.

I touched on this topic in the chapter on Singapore, but Singapore has been somewhat of an anomaly when it comes to case studies on entitlement programs. I won't recap my entire discussion, but it seems that Singapore has combined their housing program with a forced savings scheme in a country that has a world class education system. While I believe the history of successful economies would say that the expansion of entitlement programs is a negative for net economic growth, Singapore has proven that it is not impossible to subsidize a large percentage of the country's housing and achieve robust economic growth.

A strong healthcare system is an important component for prolonged economic success. A high-quality healthcare system encourages people to live in a given country. I don't think it is a coincidence that the World Health Organization's 2019 global healthcare rankings top marks go to mostly what I would consider to be highly developed countries. France, Italy, Singapore, and Spain are the larger countries that lead the list. The United States has a long and winding history in the healthcare area and has almost always outspent relative to GDP when compared to the results that the country has seen. This will be one of the biggest issues for the U.S. over the coming years and decades.

The healthcare landscape as we know it today really did not get formed until 1966 when Medicare was passed under the Social Security Administration. Medicare is a national health insurance program for the elderly. U.S. politicians dating all the way back to Teddy Roosevelt in 1912 had advocated for health insurance programs in some capacity. A country that I highlighted as having a strong healthcare system during my visit was Colombia. The WHO ranks the country as having the 22nd best healthcare system in the world in 2019. This is a boon for the Colombian economy because, when combined with the cheap cost of living compared to countries like the United States, it provides for a compelling retirement location. Foreign retirees will then buy up real estate in Colombia and invest their financial resources in the local economy. This is just one of the many reasons that a quality healthcare system is necessary for sustained economic success. The highest quality business leaders and even many average citizens will often not remain in a country with poor healthcare systems.

Having a strong foundation in terms of rule of law is a critical component to a country's economy. The rule of law category covers various items such as corruption at the government level, protection of property rights, and accountability for crimes. There will be corruption in any country you visit, but from what I have seen, the United States has a strong record in terms of rule of law compared to many other countries. I don't think it is a coincidence that elements of Roman law are still referred to today even though the Roman Empire collapsed in 476 CE. This tells me that they had a revered rule of law. I will use South Africa as a present-day example of a country that has been lacking in terms of rule of law under at least the past couple government administrations. Jacob Zuma's presidency was marred by a string of corruption scandals that staved off foreign investment in the country. Foreign investors will be more reluctant to invest if there is political uncertainty which will hurt the local economy. Additionally, there has been a lot of uncertainty surrounding property rights in South Africa. The African National Congress (ANC) passed an amendment to the South African Constitution allowing the seizure of white-owned farmland without compensation. Knowing this, why would anyone want to be a farmer in South Africa? How could prospective foreign investors have confidence that property rights are to be protected with legislation like this in place? The most successful countries over the long-term have a respected system in terms of rule of law.

The level of productivity is crucial to long-term sustainable economic growth. To put it simply, this is the ability to get more out of less when it comes to input resources. Labor productivity has been a widely debated topic in the United States in recent years. During the period 1995–2004, U.S. labor productivity clocked in at 3.2% compared to 0.5% for the years 2010–2016. U.S. labor productivity as measured by the Bureau of Labor Statistics has remained anemic in recent years, which has perplexed countless economists.

I won't go into great detail here regarding this topic, but it would seem to me that this is a measurement problem rather than a dramatic slowdown in real factor productivity. The productivity measured by the Bureau of Labor Statistics is only looking at output relative to labor and is not taking into account the productivity that we have seen on the consumer side. For example, consumers can now receive packages in the mail for almost any product in less than two days by ordering it online with the click of a button. In the past this would have required the consumer to go to a physical retail location and use their time searching for the product and waiting in line. How is this not increasing societal productivity if the consumer uses this time to work on their business instead?

Similar examples can be drawn from the likes of Google, YouTube, and other online platforms. A determined individual can figure out how to do almost anything in the world on these platforms given the astronomical amount of global data that has been aggregated. Time that was formerly spent by individual trial and error can more than likely be saved by referring to a YouTube video explaining how to perform a specific task. This leads to an increase in productivity especially if the individual uses the time saved to make a difference in other capacities. When looking at GDP per hours worked comparisons on a global scale is this really a fair comparison? I don't think it is a coincidence that many European countries often rank favorably according to these metrics. It is most often because they are working fewer hours! Is anyone really as productive after in their 13th hour of work as they are in their second? Of course not. Iceland has been one of the exceptions to this rule in that the statistics show that their strong labor productivity performance has not been the result of simply working fewer hours on average than countries such as the United States. Economic productivity is critical to the long-term success of a country, but this data can be read in a number of ways, so be careful in analyzing headline numbers in this area.

Safety and security are an important element of economic success. This can take a number of forms, but I will use the Incas as an example that I touched upon in the chapter on Peru. The Incas built a dominant empire that was short-lived and ended soon after the arrival of the Spaniards in 1532. The Incas were not able to defend themselves against the Spaniards, who intimidated the Incas with horses in battle.

While this example may not directly correlate with safety and security in the modern era, it is similar in nature. The lack of ability to successfully combat terrorism can have a profound impact on an economy. The Shining Path is a terrorist organization that ravaged Peru during the 1980s and

1990s. While still present today, it is not nearly the threat that once plagued Peru. At the height of the Shining Path's power, there were few schools in the countryside because of the threat of terrorism. We know that this increases income inequality because there will be a larger discrepancy in educational background between the highly educated and the least educated individuals. Terrorism threats also hurt the economy by limiting tourism potential and decreasing the ability to attract and retain citizens to live in a given country. All else equal, is a sensible individual going to choose to live in a country where they wake up every day fearing for their life or in a place where they feel comfortable going about living a normal life? In addition to being able to manage internal conflicts, a country must have the ability to protect itself against external threats in order to have success over the long haul.

Population growth is another element to be considered. It was much easier for the United States to record robust GDP growth metrics in the early days when the population was still growing at a high rate. According to U.S. census figures, the population of the United States in 1870 was 38.5 million, which exploded to 92.2 million by 1910. With the population growth rate at 6% a year, it is not really going to matter what happens on the input productivity front because 6% more individuals are going to have needs as consumers that must be met. Having said that, I have cautioned investors as to extrapolating this line of thinking to the local stock market because there is far from a direct correlation between GDP and population growth and overall equity returns. The U.S. population growth dropped to approximately 4% over the next 40 years following 1910 and increased at a rate of less than 1% in 2019. Productivity gains get more important as an economy becomes more developed, as the "easy growth" from robust population growth wears off. I would say that India is still very much in the stage of "easy growth." The population is expanding rapidly, and there is an increasing need for infrastructure to satisfy all of these new people. The Indian economy could grow at a rapid rate for many years to come just by continuing a building boom similar to what we have seen from China since 1979 when the country opened up to foreign trade investment and implemented some free-market reforms.

As an economy becomes more developed and domestic fertility rates decline, immigration becomes a more important factor for sustained economic growth. This logic is at odds with the recent rhetoric coming from President Trump having gone as far as saying that the U.S. is "full." Developed countries with low fertility rates that aren't open to taking immigrants will have to lean even more on productivity gains and will have a much more difficult time churning out economic gains. Look no further than Japan as to why a hardline immigration policy combined with nothing in the way of population growth can lead to economic stagnation.

This discussion about the various components of a successful economy over the long-term is by no means all-encompassing but should at least provide a solid foundation for understanding many of the most important elements.

ACKNOWLEDGEMENTS

I would first like to thank my wonderful girlfriend, Paula Bellini, for being so supportive of me throughout this challenging project in addition to sharing some of the best adventures and moments of my life. This book would not have been possible without her. I would like to thank my parents, Mark and Kelly, for providing encouragement even though they were skeptical at times when I informed them that I would be traveling to countries such as Colombia, which they knew more for cocaine distribution and violence than for beautiful landscapes and a wealth of adventure tourism options. Thank you to all of those with whom I shared my adventures along the way: my brother Connor and his fiancé, Meghan; my good friends Joe and Greg; and all of my new friends I met along the way, including Rishi and Dave, who I still work closely with on various projects. A final thank you to Kelli Christiansen who helped me fact-check this book. Kelli works with bibliobibuli and can be contacted at kelli@bibliobibuli.com.

LIST OF SOURCES[1]

(No Author Listed.) *"African Economies Adopt Record Number of Reforms, Says Latest Doing Business Report* (Press Release). October 25, 2016. Washington, DC: The World Bank. Accessed from https://www.worldbank.org/en/news/press-release/2016/10/25/african-economies-adopt-record-number-of-reforms-says-latest-doing-business-report

(No Author Listed.) "Agriculture Journals," *Open Access Journals* (Website). n.d. Accessed from https://www.omicsonline.org/agriculture-journals-south-africa/

(No Author Listed.) "All About Botswana," *Africa.com.* n.d. Accessed from https://africa.com/heres-what-you-need-to-know-about-botswana/

(No Author Listed.) "Are the Nazca Lines Flights Safe? What You Need to Know," *World Nomads.* n.d. Accessed from https://www.worldnomads.com/travel-safety/south-america/peru/nasca-lines-of-peru-safety-tips-for-choosing-your-flight

(No Author Listed.) "Chile: Democratic at Last—Cleaning Up the Constitution," *The Economist: The Americas.* September 15, 2005.

---

1   Arranged alphabetically by last name; unattributed websites, blogs, etc., not sourced; corporate websites not sourced

Accessed from https://www.economist.com/the-americas/2005/09/15/democratic-at-last

(No Author Listed.) "Chile's Congress Approves Free Higher Education," *TeleSur*. January 25, 2018. Accessed from https://www.telesurenglish.net/news/Chiles-Congress-Approves-Free-Higher-Education--20180125-0007.html

(No Author Listed.) "China Embraces Coffee Culture Craze, Thanks to Millennials," *CBS News*. June 6, 2018. Accessed from https://www.cbsnews.com/news/china-coffee-craze-millennials-embracing-culture/

(No Author Listed.) "Colombia Is the Fastest-Growing Country for IT and Digital Services in the Latin American Region," *CPA Practice Advisor*. June 13, 2017. Accessed from https://www.cpapracticeadvisor.com/small-business/news/12343542/colombia-is-the-fastest-growing-country-for-it-and-digital-services-in-the-latin-american-region

(No Author Listed.) "Conquest and Colony of Peru," *Discover Peru*. Boston: The Peru Cultural Society. n.d. Accessed from http://www.discover-peru.org/conquest-and-colony-of-peru/

(No Author Listed.) "Doing Business Report: Peru Enacts Reforms to Improve Business Climate," *Andina*. January 9, 2019. Accessed from https://andina.pe/ingles/noticia-world-bank-peru-economy-to-rise-38-in-2019-738546.aspx

(No Author Listed.) *The Economic Context of Botswana: Economic Indicators*. London: Export Entreprises SA/Lloyds Bank. Latest update March 2020. Accessed from https://www.lloydsbanktrade.com/en/market-potential/botswana/economical-context?vider_sticky=oui

(No Author Listed.) "The Economics of News Media and Why It's in Deep Crisis Because of Covid-19," *The Print*. April 24, 2020. Accessed from https://theprint.in/opinion/the-economics-of-news-media-and-why-its-in-deep-crisis-because-of-covid-19/407946/

(No Author Listed.) "Foreign Language Study in Compulsory and Upper Secondary Schools 2011–2012," *Statistics Ireland*. September 25, 2012. Accessed from https://statice.is/publications/news-archive/education/foreign-language-study-in-compulsory-and-upper-secondary-schools-2011-2012/

(No Author Listed.) "Historic Sanctuary of Machu Picchu," *World Heritage List*. n.d. Accessed from https://whc.unesco.org/en/list/274/

(No Author Listed.) "How Giant Outdoor Escalators Transformed a Colombian Neighborhood," *CNN*. December 14, 2015. Accessed from https://www.cnn.com/travel/article/colombia-medellin-neighborhood/index.html

(No Author Listed.) "How Napoleon's Conquest of Spain Led to Revolution in Chile," *History Hit* (Website). December 12, 2018. Accessed from https://www.historyhit.com/1818-declaration-chilean-independence/

(No Author Listed.) "Indonesia Proposes Grand $564 Billion Plan to Rebuild the Country," *The Straits Times*. May 16, 2019. Accessed from https://www.straitstimes.com/asia/se-asia/indonesia-has-a-grand-564-billion-plan-to-rebuild-the-country

(No Author Listed.) "Ireland's Residential Property Still in Deep Crisis," *Global Property Guide*. August 27, 2011. Accessed from https://www.globalpropertyguide.com/Europe/Ireland/Price-History-Archive/irelands-residential-property-still-in-deep-crisis-127018

(No Author Listed.) "Machu Picchu," *National Geographic*. November 15, 2010. Accessed from https://www.nationalgeographic.com/travel/world-heritage/machu-picchu/#close

(No Author Listed.) "Malaysia Ranks 1st In World's Best Healthcare Category," *The Star*. February 7, 2019. Accessed from https://www.thestar.com.my/news/nation/2019/02/07/malaysia-ranks-1st-in-worlds-best-healthcare-category/

(No Author Listed.) *The Modern Outback: Nature, People and the Future of Remote Australia*. Philadelphia: The Pew Charitable Trusts. October 14, 2014. Accessed from https://www.pewtrusts.org/en/research-and-analysis/reports/2014/10/the-modern-outback

(No Author Listed.) *Morocco Economic Outlook* (Website). n.d. Abidjan, Côte d'Ivoire: African Development Bank Group. Accessed from https://www.afdb.org/en/countries/north-africa/morocco/morocco-economic-outlook

(No Author Listed.) "Morocco Received Over 10 Million Tourists in 2014," *Morocco World News*. July 16, 2015. Accessed from https://www.moroccoworldnews.com/2015/07/163411/morocco-received-over-10-million-tourists-in-2014/

(No Author Listed.) *Zimbabwe Economic Outlook* (Website). n.d. Bidjan, Côte d'Ivoire: African Development Bank Group. Accessed from https://www.afdb.org/en/countries/southern-africa/zimbabwe/zimbabwe-economic-outlook

(No Author Listed.) "NZ Builds on Saudi Trade Ties," *Arab News*. December 16, 2012. Accessed from http://www.arabnews.com/nz-builds-saudi-trade-ties

(No Author Listed.) "Once Roaring, Canadian Home Sales Brace for 30% Drop on Coronavirus," *National Mortgage News*. April 2, 2020. Accessed from https://www.nationalmortgagenews.com/articles/once-roaring-canadian-home-sales-brace-for-30-drop-on-coronavirus

(No Author Listed.) "One of the New Seven Wonders of the World: Machu Picchu," *New 7 Wonders of the World* (Website). n.d. Accessed from https://world.new7wonders.com/wonders/machu-picchu-1460-1470-peru/

(No Author Listed.) "Orang-utans," *World Wildlife Fund* (Website). n.d. Accessed from https://wwf.panda.org/knowledge_hub/endangered_species/great_apes/orangutans/

(No Author Listed.) "Peru Economic Outlook," *Focus Economics*. February 18, 2020. Accessed from https://www.focus-economics.com/countries/peru

(No Author Listed.) "Peru: Growth Sinks to Two-Year Low in Q1," *Focus Economics*. May 24, 2019. Accessed from https://www.focus-economics.com/countries/peru/news/gdp/growth-sinks-to-two-year-low-in-q1

(No Author Listed.) "Peru: Infrastructure Investment to Benefit From Legislation," *Andina—Editora Peru*. November 2, 2018. Accessed from https://andina.pe/ingles/noticia-peru-infrastructure-investment-to-benefit-from-legislation-731496.aspx

(No Author Listed.) "School Uniforms and Learning How to Sew by Delsyia," *Varsity Tutors*. May 2019. Accessed from https://www.varsitytutors.com/scholarship_entries/delsyia-28248

(No Author Listed.) *Singapore Defense Report 2019: Market Attractiveness, Competitive Landscape and Forecasts to 2024* (Press Release). November 1, 2019. Accessed from https://www.globenewswire.com/news-release/2019/11/01/1939421/0/en/Singapore-Defense-Report-2019-Market-Attractiveness-Competitive-Landscape-and-Forecasts-to-2024.html

(No Author Listed.) "South Africa Has One of the World's Worst Education Systems," *The Economist*. January 7, 2017. Accessed from https://www.economist.com/middle-east-and-africa/2017/01/07/south-africa-has-one-of-the-worlds-worst-education-systems

(No Author Listed.) "Steering Chile Away From the Middle-Income Trap," *The Economist: The Americas*. September 29, 2018. Accessed from https://www.economist.com/the-americas/2018/09/29/steering-chile-away-from-the-middle-income-trap

(No Author Listed.) "Sustainable Agriculture: Palm Oil," *World Wildlife Fund* (Website). n.d. Accessed from https://www.worldwildlife.org/industries/palm-oil

(No Author Listed.) "Ten Signs We're Heading for 'Economic Armageddon,'" *New Zealand Herald*. February 11, 2018. Accessed from https://www.nzherald.co.nz/business/news/article.cfm?c_id=3&objectid=11992189

(No Author Listed.) "Thrilling Glacier Skywalk Opens in Canada," *Condé Nast Traveller*. May 2, 2014. Accessed from https://www.cntraveller.in/story/thrilling-glacier-skywalk-opens-canada/

(No Author Listed.) "VAT and Income Tax to Decrease?" *Iceland Review*. August 8, 3005. Accessed from https://www.icelandreview.com/news/vat-and-income-tax-decrease/

(No Author Listed.) "What Are the World's Deadliest Animals?" *BBC*. June 15, 2016. Accessed from https://www.bbc.com/news/world-36320744

(No Author Listed.) "What Can We Make of Ryanair's Holdings PLCs (ISE:RY4C) High Return on Capital?" *Simply Wall Street*. December 12, 2018. Accessed from https://simplywall.st/stocks/ie/

transportation/ise-ry4c/ryanair-holdings-shares/news/what-can-we-make-of-ryanair-holdings-plcs-isery4c-high-return-on-capital/

(No Author Listed.) "World Locations With Highest Attack Rates," *International Shark Attack File* (Website). Gainesville, FL: Florida Museum of Natural History. Accessed from https://www.floridamuseum.ufl.edu/shark-attacks/trends/location/world/

(No Author Listed.) "Zimbabwe Introduces RTGS Dollar to Solve Currency Problem," *BBC*. February 26, 2019. Accessed from https://www.bbc.com/news/world-africa-47361572

AAP. "House Prices Rise in Sydney and Melbourne for the First Time Since 2017," *9Finance*. July 1 2019. Accessed from https://finance.nine.com.au/personal-finance/australia-house-prices-june-corelogic-property-news/7fe42a30-e7f8-404d-b003-43c3c115e7a0

Béchir Abba-Goni and Marc Bidan. "Sending Selfies Just Got Easier: In Africa's 2G Mobile Economy, 4G Is Expanding Fast," *CNN*. Updated November 24, 2016. Accessed from https://www.cnn.com/2016/11/24/africa/the-conversation-africa-mobile-phone/index.html

Muntazir Abbas. "Jio-Led Data Price Reduction Fuels Smartphone Adoption in India: Cisco," *Economic Times*. June 28, 2018. Accessed from https://economictimes.indiatimes.com/industry/telecom/telecom-news/jio-led-data-price-reduction-fuels-smartphone-adoption-in-india-cisco/articleshow/64774860.cms

Abigail Abrams. "Rationing Begins, As Cuba Braces for Economic Impact From Venezuela Crisis," *Time Magazine*. May 16, 2019. Accessed from https://time.com/5590217/rations-in-cuba-venezuela-crisis/

Africa Check. "Does Gauteng Make Up a Third of South Africa's GDP? And Is It Africa's Seventh Biggest Economy?" *Africacheck.org*

(Website). November 19, 2018. Accessed from https://africacheck.org/reports/does-gauteng-make-up-a-third-of-south-africas-gdp-and-is-it-africas-seventh-biggest-economy/

Fumnanya Agbugah–Ezeana. "HIS Becomes Third African Telecoms Infrastructure Provider to Postpone IPO in 2018," *The Nerve.* June 28, 2018. Accessed from https://thenerveafrica.com/20038/ihs-postpone-ipo/

Agence France Presse. "Cuba Lifts 50-Year-Old Car Import Ban," *The Telegraph.* December 19, 2013. Accessed from https://www.telegraph.co.uk/news/worldnews/centralamericaandthecaribbean/cuba/10528233/Cuba-lifts-50-year-old-car-import-ban.html

Agence-France Presse. "Rough Ride for Uber As Morocco Cabbies Sabotage App," *The National.* January 8, 2017. Accessed from https://www.thenational.ae/world/rough-ride-for-uber-as-morocco-cabbies-sabotage-app-1.90023

Harriet Agerholm. "America Falls Short of Being a Full Democracy for Second Year Running, Report Finds," *The Independent.* February 5, 2018. Accessed from https://www.independent.co.uk/news/world/americas/america-democracy-rated-donald-trump-not-fully-democratic-us-president-report-the-economist-a8195121.html

Liz Alderman. "Iceland, Symbol of Financial Crisis, Finally Lifts Debt Controls," *The New York Times.* March 14, 2017. Accessed from https://www.nytimes.com/2017/03/14/business/iceland-economy-finance-capital-controls.html

Doug Alexander. "'This Is Freezing the Market': Once Roaring, Canadian Home Sales Brace for 30% Drop From Coronavirus," *Financial Post.* April 2, 2020. Accessed from https://business.financialpost.com/real-estate/mortgages/canadian-home-sales-30-percent-drop-coronavirus

Adriaan Alsema. "Medellin, 10 Years After 'Operation Orion,' Still Looking for Answers," *Colombia Reports*. October 16, 2012. Accessed from https://colombiareports.com/medellin-operation-orion/

Kimberly Amadeo. "Iceland's Economy, Its Bankruptcy, and the Financial Crisis," *The Balance*. May 30, 2019. Accessed from https://www.thebalance.com/iceland-financial-crisis-bankruptcy-and-economy-3306347

A. Ananthalakshmi. "Palm Oil to Blame for 39% of Forest Loss in Borneo Since 2000: Study," *Reuters*. September 19, 2019. Accessed from https://www.reuters.com/article/us-palmoil-deforestation-study/palm-oil-to-blame-for-39-of-forest-loss-in-borneo-since-2000-study-idUSKBN1W41HD

Jenny Anderson and Chad Bray. "Iceland to Lift Capital Controls Imposed After Financial Crisis," *The New York Times*. June 8, 2015. Accessed from https://www.nytimes.com/2015/06/09/business/dealbook/iceland-to-lift-capital-controls-imposed-after-financial-crisis.html

Jon Lee Anderson. "The Afterlife of Pablo Escobar," *The New Yorker*. February 26, 2018. Accessed from https://www.newyorker.com/magazine/2018/03/05/the-afterlife-of-pablo-escobar

APO Group and United Nations Economic Commission for Africa (ECA). "Coronavirus—Africa: The Economic Impact of COVID-19 on African Cities Likely to Be Acute Through a Sharp Decline in Productivity, Jobs and Revenues, Says ECA," *Africa News*. Last updated April 15, 2020. Accessed from https://www.africanews.com/2020/04/15/coronavirus-africa-the-economic-impact-of-covid-19-on-african-cities-likely-to-be-acute-through-a-sharp-decline-in-productivity-jobs-and-revenues-says-eca//

Marco Aquino. "Peru Readies $26 Billion Stimulus Plan to Mitigate Coronavirus Impact," *Reuters*. March 29, 2020. Accessed from https://www.reuters.com/article/us-health-coronavirus-peru/peru-readies-26-billion-stimulus-plan-to-mitigate-coronavirus-impact-idUSKBN21H08R

Mike Arnot. "How Does Ryanair Make Money? By Flying Bags Around Europe," *ThePointsGuy*. n.d. Accessed from https://thepointsguy.com/news/how-does-ryanair-make-money-by-flying-bags-around-europe/

ASER Centre. *Annual Status of Education Report (Rural) 2018 (Provisional)*. January 15, 2019. New Delhi, India: Author. ISBN: 978-93-85203-01-5. Accessed from http://img.asercentre.org/docs/ASER%202018/Release%20Material/aserreport2018.pdf

Adam Augustyn and the Editors of Encyclopædia Britannica. "Agra—India," *Encyclopædia Britannica*. n.d. Accessed from https://www.britannica.com/place/Agra

Adam Augustyn and the Editors of Encyclopædia Britannica. "Gerardo Machado y Morales—Cuban Dictator," *Encyclopædia Britannica*. n.d. Accessed from https://www.britannica.com/biography/Gerardo-Machado-y-Morales

Adam Augustyn and the Editors of Encyclopædia Britannica. "New France," *Encyclopædia Britannica*. n.d. Accessed from https://www.britannica.com/place/New-France

Adam Augustyn, Melissa Petruzzello, and the Editors of Encyclopædia Britannica. "Sydney Harbour Bridge," *Encyclopædia Britannica*. n.d. Accessed from https://www.britannica.com/topic/Sydney-Harbour-Bridge

Australian Bureau of Statistics. *Australian Demographic Statistics* (Website). June 2016 (3101.0). Canberra: Author. Last updated December 15, 2016. Accessed from

https://www.abs.gov.au/AUSSTATS/abs@.nsf/7d12b0f6763c78caca2
57061001cc588/2d2860dfa430d432ca2580eb001335bb!OpenDocum
ent

Australian Bureau of Statistics. *Year Book Australia, 2012* (1301.0).
Canberra: Author. May 24, 2012; last updated November 11, 2015.
Accessed from https://www.abs.gov.au/ausstats/abs@.nsf/Lookup/
by%20Subject/1301.0~2012~Main%20Features~Australia%27s%20
climate~143

F. Avvisati, A. Echazarra, P. Givord, and M. Schwabe. "Programme for
International Student Assessment (PISA) Results From PISA 2018,"
Country Note: Malaysia. 2019. Paris: OECD Publishing. Accessed
from http://www.oecd.org/pisa/publications/PISA2018_CN_MYS.
pdf

Devika Banerji and Rishi Shah. "India Overtakes Japan to Become Third
Largest Economy by Purchasing Power Parity," *Economic Times.* April
19, 2012. Accessed from https://economictimes.indiatimes.com/news/
economy/indicators/india-overtakes-japan-to-become-third-largest-
economy-in-purchasing-power-parity/articleshow/12722921.cms

Norma Barbacci. *Celebrating the 500th Anniversary of Havana, Cuba*
(Website). December 31, 2019. New York: World Monuments
Fund. Accessed from https://www.wmf.org/blog/celebrating-500th-
anniversary-havana-cuba

Susan B. Barnes. "Sleep in Glass Pods Suspended 1,200 Feet up the Side
of a Mountain in Peru's Sacred Valley," *CNBC.* October 25, 2017
(updated November 8, 2017). Accessed from https://www.cnbc.
com/2017/10/25/perus-skylodge-sleep-in-a-glass-pod-suspended-
off-a-mountainside.html

BBN Staff. "Belize Ranking Drops on Ease of Doing Business Index,"
Breaking Belize News. November 22, 2017. Accessed from https://www.

breakingbelizenews.com/2017/11/22/belize-ranking-drops-ease-business-index/

Alex Beggs. "Where Potatoes Pass From the Ice to the Sun," *Bon Appétit*. April 30, 2019. Accessed from https://www.bonappetit.com/story/mil-restaurant-peru

Matt Berrie and Craig Tyndale. "Australia's Economy Is a House of Cards," *Steve Keen's Debtwatch*. November 14, 2017. Accessed from https://www.debtdeflation.com/blogs/2017/11/14/australias-economy-is-a-house-of-cards/

Alma Romero Barrutieta. *Fiscal Sector in Belize* (Technical Note). May 2013. Washington, DC: Inter-American Development Bank, Fiscal and Municipal Management, p. 7.

Tarek Bazza. "Over 12 Million Tourists Visited Morocco in 2018, Up 8% from 2017," *Morocco World News*. January 23, 2019. Accessed from https://www.moroccoworldnews.com/2019/01/264155/tourists-morocco/

David Beirman. "Australia Needs to Invest If It Wants the Tourism Boom to Continue," *The Conversation*. January 19, 2017. Accessed from theconversation.com/Australia-needs-to-invest-if-it-wants-the-tourism-boom-to-continue-71407

Chris Bell. "Why Is Colombian Coffee So Good?" *Culture Trip*. March 9, 2018. Accessed from https://theculturetrip.com/south-america/colombia/articles/why-is-colombian-coffee-so-good/

Roland Benedikter and Miguel Zlosilo. "The Trans-Pacific Partnership: More Questions Than Answers for Chile?" *Georgetown Journal of International Affairs*. November 23, 2015. Accessed from https://www.georgetownjournalofinternationalaffairs.org/online-edition/

the-trans-pacific-partnership-more-questions-than-answers-for-chile

Beethika Biswas. "Iceland Imports About 1.65 Million Tonnes of Alumina to Feed Its Smelters, Australia Tops the Exporter List," *Alumina*. July 20, 2017 Accessed from https://www.alcircle.com/news/iceland-imports-about-165-million-tonnes-of-alumina-to-feed-its-smelters-australia-tops-the-exporter-list-28278#collapsePreferences

Bloomberg. "Malaysia Aims to Reduce Foreign Workers in Five Years," *The Hindu Business Line*. October 30, 2019. Accessed from https://www.thehindubusinessline.com/news/world/malaysia-aims-to-reduce-foreign-workers-in-five-years/article29829045.ece

Bloomberg. "The Pot Stock Bubble Has Burst. Here's Why," *The Los Angeles Times*. November 16, 2019. Accessed from https://www.latimes.com/business/story/2019-11-16/pot-stock-bubble-has-burst

BNAmericas. *Peru Mining Deaths Decline As Industry Improves Safety*. January 2, 2019. Santiago, Chile, and Newark, DE.: Author. Accessed from https://www.bnamericas.com/en/news/peru-mining-deaths-decline-as-industry-improves-safety

Alistair Boddy-Evans. "Chronological List of African Independence," *ThoughtCo*. Updated January 25, 2020. Accessed from https://www.thoughtco.com/chronological-list-of-african-independence-4070467

Boeing. *The Asia-Pacific Region: A Spotlight Destination for Aviation Services* (Press Release). October 15, 2019. Chicago: Author. Accessed from https://www.boeing.com/features/2019/10/asia-pacific-region-10-19.page

Jerry Bowyer. "Steve Forbes: 'Great Countries Don't Have Weak Currencies," *The New York Sun*. October 25, 2014. Accessed from https://www.nysun.com/national/steve-forbes-great-countries-dont-have-weak/88893/

Roger Boyes. *Meltdown Iceland: Lessons on the World Financial Crisis From a Small, Bankrupt Island* (©2010, getAbstract). New York: Bloomsbury USA, 2009. Accessed from https://www.economist.com/media/pdf/meltdown-iceland-boyes-e.pdf

David Bradbury and Michelle Harding. "Revenue Statistics—2018," *Better Policies for Better Lives.* n.d. OECD Centre for Tax Policy and Administration. Paris: Organisation for Economic Co-operation and Development. Accessed from *https://www.oecd.org/tax/revenue-statistics-australia.pdf*

Michael Brett. "Berber—People," *Encyclopædia Britannica.* n.d. Accessed from https://www.britannica.com/topic/Berber

James Brooke. "Shining Path Rebels Infiltrate Peru's Schools," *The New York Times.* August 30, 1992. Accessed from https://www.nytimes.com/1992/08/30/world/shining-path-rebels-infiltrate-peru-s-schools.html

Selene Brophy. "SA Sees +10m International Visitors As 2016 Tourism Growth Hits 13%," *Traveller24.* February 21, 2017. Accessed from https://www.traveller24.com/News/sa-sees-10-million-international-visitors-as-2016-growth-hits-13-20170221

Grace Browne. "What Is Palm Oil?" *Live Science.* April 2, 2020. Accessed from https://www.livescience.com/palm-oil.html

Michele Bullock. *The Evolution of Household Sector Risks.* September 10, 2018. Albury, Australia: Ai Group. Accessed from https://www.rba.gov.au/speeches/2018/sp-ag-2018-09-10.html

Colin J. Bundy, Alan S. Mabin, Andries Nel, Julian R.D. Cobbing et al. "Diamonds, Gold, and Imperialist Intervention (1870–1902)—South Africa," *Encyclopædia Britannica*. Last updated March 8, 2020. Accessed from https://www.britannica.com/place/South-Africa/Diamonds-gold-and-imperialist-intervention-1870-1902

Jason Burke. "Zimbabwe Warns Brutal Crackdown Is 'Foretaste of Things to Come'," *The Guardian*. January 20, 2019. Accessed from https://www.theguardian.com/world/2019/jan/20/zimbabwe-warns-brutal-crackdown-foretaste-of-things-to-come

Monica Burton. "Here Are Latin America's 50 Best Restaurant Winners for 2017," *Eater.com*. October 25, 2017. Accessed from https://www.eater.com/2017/10/25/16533894/latin-america-worlds-50-best-restaurants-2017

Business Research & Economic Advisers. *The Contribution of the International Cruise Industry to the Global Economy in 2016*. December 2017. Washington, DC: Cruise Lines Industry Association. Accessed from https://staging.cruising.org/-/media/files/industry/research/economic-impact-analysis/global_economic_contribution_2016.pdf. See also: https://cruising.org/-/media/research-updates/research/economic-impact-studies/2016-global-economic-impact-study.pdf

Jeff Campagna. "Pablo Escobar's Private Prison Is Now Run by Monks for Senior Citizens," *The Daily Beast*. July 7, 2014 (updated July 12, 2017). Accessed from https://www.thedailybeast.com/pablo-escobars-private-prison-is-now-run-by-monks-for-senior-citizens

Isaac Carey. "Why Iceland's Tourism Boom May Finally Be Over," *Skift*. January 16, 2019. Accessed from https://skift.com/2019/01/16/why-icelands-tourism-boom-may-finally-be-over/

Mark Cartwright. "Inca Civilization," *Ancient History Encyclopedia*. September 15, 2014. Accessed from https://www.ancient.eu/Inca_Civilization/

Damien Cave. "A Lucky Country Says Goodbye to the World's Longest Boom," *The New York Times*. March 27, 2020. Accessed from https://www.nytimes.com/2020/03/27/world/australia/australia-coronavirus-economy.html

Richard Cavendish. "The Australian Gold Rush Begins," *History Today*. Vol. 51. February 2, 2001. Accessed from https://www.historytoday.com/archive/months-past/australian-gold-rush-begins

Central Intelligence Agency. *The World Factbook: Australia–Oceania: New Zealand* (Website). Last updated February 8, 2020. Accessed from https://www.cia.gov/library/publications/the-world-factbook/geos/nz.html

Ronald W. Chan. "Investors Should Buy a Ticket to Indonesia," *Bloomberg*. April 5, 2019. Accessed from https://www.bloomberg.com/opinion/articles/2019-04-06/indonesia-s-movie-industry-should-attract-investors

David Chau. "Australia's Fortunes Are Linked to China's Economy—for Better or Worse," *ABC News*. January 14, 2019. Accessed from https://www.abc.net.au/news/2019-01-15/china-economy-slowdown-will-affect-australia/10716240

Joyce Chepkemoi. "The Top Export Products of Australia," *World Atlas*. Last updated April 25, 2017. Accessed from https://www.worldatlas.com/articles/the-top-20-export-products-of-australia.html

Max A. Cherney. "Facebook Stock Drops Roughly 20%, Loses $120 Billion in Value After Warning That Revenue Growth Will Take a Hit," *Market Watch*. July 26, 2018. Accessed from https://www.

marketwatch.com/story/facebook-stock-crushed-after-revenue-user-growth-miss-2018-07-25

Chester Chin. "Malaysia Ranked 9th Best Destination for Expats to Live and Work in," *The Star*. October 1, 2019. Accessed from https://www.thestar.com.my/lifestyle/travel/2019/10/01/expats-in-malaysia/

Julian T.S. Chow. *Tourism in Belize: Ensuring Sustained Growth* (WP/19/267). December 2019. Washington, DC: International Monetary Fund. Accessed from http://wits.worldbank.org/data/public/cp/en_USA_AllYears_WITS_Trade_Summary.csv

Lynsey Chutel. "Africa's Largest Phone Network Is Expanding Its Dominance With Its Own 'Smart Feature Phone'" *Quartz Africa*. November 20, 2018. Accessed from https://qz.com/africa/1464244/africas-largest-phone-network-is-expanding-its-dominance-with-its-own-smart-feature-phone/

James Clark. "Is This the World's Most Dangerous Sea Route?" *BBC Travel*. April 29, 2019. Accessed from http://www.bbc.com/travel/story/20190428-is-this-the-worlds-most-dangerous-sea-route

Laura Clark. "One-Tenth of Native Mammals in Australia Are Extinct: Blame Cats And Foxes," *Smithsonian Magazine*. February 11, 2015. Accessed from https://www.smithsonianmag.com/smart-news/why-one-tenth-australias-native-mammals-have-gone-extinct-over-last-200-years-180954216/

Nick Clark. "Education in Peru," *World Education News + Reviews*. April 6, 2015. Accessed from https://wenr.wes.org/2015/04/education-in-peru

Judith Clarke, Marsha Courchane, Cynthia Holmes, and Tsur Somerville. *The Subprime Crisis: Weathering the Storm in the U.S., Canada, and Australia* (Working Paper 2010–03). January 2010. Vancouver, Canada: Centre for Urban Economics and Real Estate. Accessed

from https://www.sauder.ubc.ca/sites/default/files/2019-06/The%20
Subprime%20Crisis%20Weathering%20the%20Storm%20in%20
the%20USA%20Canada%20and%20Australia.pdf

Harry Cockburn. "Taj Mahal Remains a Muslim Tomb, Not a Hindu
Temple, Archaeologists Tell Indian Court," *The Independent*. August
31, 2017. Accessed from https://www.independent.co.uk/news/world/
asia/taj-mahal-hindu-temple-muslim-tomb-india-shah-jahan-wife-
bhuvan-vikrama-a7922911.html

Helen Coffey. "Singapore Airport Named Best in World for Seventh Year
Running," *The Independent*. March 28, 2019. Accessed from https://
www.independent.co.uk/travel/news-and-advice/best-airports-2019-
world-changi-singapore-skytrax-awards-tokyo-seoul-a8843431.html

COHA. *The Rise and Fall of Shining Path* (Website). May 6, 2008.
Washington, DC: Council on Hemispheric Affairs. Accessed from
http://www.coha.org/the-rise-and-fall-of-shining-path/

Álex Colás, Josep Bada, and Joaquín Guerrero. "The Status of the 2G/3G
Network Sunset," *NAE*. July 31, 2019. Accessed from https://nae.
global/en/the-status-of-the-2g-3g-network-sunset/

Erin Conway-Smith. "Soaring Murder Rate Drives Cape Town up List of
Deadliest Cities," *The Times* (UK). July 1, 2019. Accessed from https://
www.thetimes.co.uk/article/soaring-murder-rate-drives-cape-town-
up-list-of-deadliest-cities-xhqw3k0ld

Adam Courtenay. "Aussie Banks the World's Most Profitable," *Finsia*.
March 29, 2016. Accessed from https://finsia.com/insights/news/
news-article/2016/03/29/aussie-banks-the-world-s-most-profitable

Cruise Lines International Association. *Cruise Industry Ocean Source
Market Report—Australia 2017*. 2017. Washington, DC: Author.

Accessed from https://www.cruising.org.au/Tenant/C0000003/Cruise%20Industry%20Source%20Market%20Report%20(1).pdf

Nick Dall. "The Salt That's Made From the Tears of the Incas," *OZY: Live Curiously*. November 12, 2017. Accessed from https://www.ozy.com/good-sht/the-salt-thats-made-from-the-tears-of-the-incas/81666/

Joe Parkin Daniels. "Colombia Continues to Break Records for Cocaine Production, Report Says," *The Guardian*. September 18, 2018. Accessed from https://www.theguardian.com/world/2018/sep/19/colombia-cocaine-production-breaks-record

Rob Davies. "CEOs Taking COVID-19 Pay Cuts 'Should Not Be Rewarded With Shares,'" *The Guardian*. April 11, 2020. Accessed from https://www.theguardian.com/business/2020/apr/11/ceos-taking-covid-19-pay-cuts-should-not-be-rewarded-with-shares

Khawaja Dawood. "Lonely Planet Names Chile World's Top Travel Destination for 2018," *The Santiago Times*. October 24, 2017. Accessed from https://santiagotimes.cl/2017/10/24/lonely-planet-names-chile-worlds-top-travel-destination-for-2018/

Gywn D'Melo. "Smartphone Penetration in India Is on the Rise, Set to Reach 37.3 Crore Users in 2019," *India Times*. January 15, 2019. Accessed from https://www.indiatimes.com/technology/news/smartphone-users-in-india-smartphone-penetration-is-set-to-reach-373-million-users-in-2019_-360475.html

Datablog Inequality. "Inequality Index: Where Are the World's Most Unequal Countries," *The Guardian*. 2019. Accessed from https://www.theguardian.com/inequality/datablog/2017/apr/26/inequality-index-where-are-the-worlds-most-unequal-countries

Thomas M. Davies, James S. Kus, John Preston Moore, Robert N. Burr, and Javier Pulgar-Vidal. "Achievement of Independence—Peru,"

Encyclopædia Britannica. Last updated September 23, 2019. Accessed from https://www.britannica.com/place/Peru/Achievement-of-independence

Glenn De'ath, Katharina Fabricius, Hugh Sweatman, Peter Doherty, et. al. *The Great Barrier Reef Has Lost Half of Its Coral in the Last 27 Years*. October 2, 2012. Townsville, Queensland: Australian Institute of Marine Science. Accessed from https://www.aims.gov.au/docs/media/latest-releases/-/asset_publisher/8Kfw/content/2-october-2012-the-great-barrier-reef-has-lost-half-of-its-coral-in-the-last-27-years

Cayla Dengate. "Australia Is Home to Heaps of the World's Most Dangerous Snakes," *HuffPost*. September 3, 2016. Accessed from https://www.huffingtonpost.com.au/2016/03/08/venomous-snakes-australia_n_9413542.html

Jeff Desjardins. "Here's How Copper Riches Helped Shape Chile's Economic Story," *Business Insider*. June 22, 2017. Accessed from https://www.businessinsider.com/how-copper-riches-helped-shape-chiles-economic-story-2017-6

Laura Dixon. "The Best Time to Visit Victoria Falls in Africa," *USA Today*. Updated May 1, 2018. Accessed from https://traveltips.usatoday.com/time-visit-victoria-falls-africa-17387.html

Taylor Dolvan and Rob Wile. "Cruise Industry Has Enough Cash for 10 Cruise-Less Months. But Will Passengers Come Back?" *Miami Herald*. April 17, 2020. Accessed from https://www.miamiherald.com/news/business/tourism-cruises/article242033816.html#storylink=cpy

Carl Duncan. "Seeking the Soul of India," *The Los Angeles Times*. November 21, 1999. Accessed from https://www.latimes.com/archives/la-xpm-1999-nov-21-tr-35844-story.html

Sarah Durant. "There Are Only 7,100 Wild Cheetah Left in the World," *Quartz Africa.* January 12, 2017. Accessed from https://qz.com/africa/883963/there-are-only-7100-cheetahs-left-in-the-world/

MacDonald Dzirutwe. "Zimbabwe's Inflation at Highest in a Decade As Dollar Shortage Bites," *Reuters.* November 13, 2018. Accessed from https://af.reuters.com/article/investingNews/idAFKCN1NI1H9-OZABS

The Economic Commission for Latin America (ECLA). *Economic Survey of Latin America and the Caribbean: Belize.* 2017. Santiago de Chile: United Nations ECLA. Accessed from https://repositorio.cepal.org/bitstream/handle/11362/42002/148/EEI2017_Belize_en.pdf

Alex Egerton, Paul Harding, and Daniel C Schechter. *Lonely Planet—Belize: Country Guide.* Melbourne, Australia: Lonely Planet. 2016. ISBN: 978-1-786-5711-06.

Holly Ellyatt. "Oil Markets Face Three Possible Scenarios in Venezuela," *CNBC.* May 2, 2019. Accessed from https://www.cnbc.com/2019/05/02/venezuela-crisis-and-how-it-could-affect-oil.html

Ron Emmons. *DK Eyewitness Travel Guide: Malaysia and Singapore.* New York: Dorling Kindersely, Ltd. 2008, 2010, 2013. p.238.

George E. Ericksen, Jamie Fernández Concha, and Enrique Silgado. "The Cusco, Peru, Earthquake of May 21, 1950," *Bulletin of the Seismological Society of America* (1954) 44(2A): 97–112. Accessed from https://pubs.geoscienceworld.org/ssa/bssa/article-abstract/44/2A/97/115702/the-cusco-peru-earthquake-of-may-21-1950?redirectedFrom=fulltext

ET Bureau. "Ease of Doing Business: India Among 20 Most Improved Countries," *Economic Times.* Updated September 29, 2019. Accessed from https://economictimes.indiatimes.com/news/economy/

indicators/ease-of-doing-business-india-among-20-most-improved-countries/articleshow/71357483.cms?from=mdr

ET Contributors. "For Thousands of Diamond Traders, a New Bourse in Surat Promises to Add to the Shine," *Economic Times.* March 29, 2019. Accessed from https://economictimes.indiatimes.com/small-biz/sme-sector/for-thousands-of-diamond-traders-a-new-bourse-in-surat-promises-to-add-to-the-shine/articleshow/68626309.cms?from=mdr

Evolita. *Smartphone Penetration Rate in India Between 2015 and 2020* (Website). n.d. Accessed from http://beta.evolita.com/explore/smartphone-penetration-rate-in-india-between-2015-and-2020/rngxa/

FactsMaps. *PISA 2015 Worldwide Ranking—Average Score of Math, Science and Reading* (Website). n.d. Accessed from factsmaps.com/pisa-worldwide-ranking-average-score-of-math-science-reading/

Bjorn Fehrm. "Ryanair: Cheapest and Most Profitable Airline in Europe," *Leeham News and Analysis.* February 22, 2017. Accessed from https://leehamnews.com/2017/02/22/ryanair-cheapest-profitable-airline-europe/

Deepa Fernandes. "Cuban Tobacco Farmers Involved in Cigar Production Face Tough Times," *Marketplace: Minnesota Public Radio.* June 2, 2017. Accessed from https://www.marketplace.org/2017/06/02/cuban-tobacco-farmers-involved-cigar-production-face-tough-times/

Charles Forelle. "As Banking Fairy Tale Ends, Iceland Looks Back to the Sea," *The Wall Street Journal.* October 10, 2008. Accessed from https://www.wsj.com/articles/SB122359763876821355

Ellie May Forrester. "Successful Translocation of Rhinos From Europe to Rwanda," *Discover Wildlife (BBC Wildlife Magazine).* June 25, 2019.

Accessed from https://www.discoverwildlife.com/news/successful-translocation-of-rhinos-from-europe-to-rwanda/

Fox News. "Venezuela Extends Expired Passports for Two Years Amid Paper and Ink Shortages," *Fox News Live*. October 13, 2017. Accessed from https://www.foxnews.com/world/venezuela-extends-expired-passports-for-two-years-amid-paper-and-ink-shortages

FP Analytics. *New Zealand: The 2018 Aging Readiness & Competitiveness Report: Small Innovative Economies*. 2018. Washington, DC: AARP International. Accessed from https://arc2018.aarpinternational.org/File%20Library/Countries/2018_New-Zealand.pdf

FPJ Web Desk. "India's Coastline! Some Amazing Facts and Figures," *The Free Press Journal*. October 18, 2018. Accessed from https://www.freepressjournal.in/cmcm/indias-coastline-some-amazing-facts-and-figures

Osbaldo France et al. *Mobile Chile 2016*. July 19, 2016. New York: eMarketer. Accessed from https://www.emarketer.com/Report/Mobile-Chile-2016-Updated-Forecasts-Key-Growth-Trends/2001820

Mark Frank. "Cuba Ends Restrictions on Cellular Phones," *Reuters*. March 28, 2008. Accessed from https://www.reuters.com/article/us-cuba-reform/cuba-ends-restriction-on-cellular-phones-idUSN2815132920080328

David French and David Goodman. "UPDATE 2—South Africa's MTN in Nigeria Mobile Tower Venture With HIS," *Reuters*. September 4, 2014. Accessed from https://www.reuters.com/article/mtn-group-nigeria/update-2-south-africas-mtn-in-nigeria-mobile-tower-venture-with-ihs-idUSL5N0R50KU20140904

Janice Friedman. "9 Interesting Facts About the Sahara Desert," *Conservation Institute.* June 12, 2013. Accessed from https://www.conservationinstitute.org/interesting-sahara-desert-facts/

FTN Editorial Team. "How a Free-Market Made Chile the Richest Latin American Country," *Freedom Today Network.* May 8, 2019. Accessed from https://ftn.media/how-free-market-made-chile-richest-latin-american-country

David Gaffen, Luc Cohen, Marianna Parraga, Jessica Resnick-Ault, Dmitry Zhdannikov, and Tom Hals. "Factbox: U.S. Sanctions on Venezuela's Oil Industry," *Reuters.* January 29, 2019. Accessed from https://www.reuters.com/article/us-venezuela-politics-usa-sanctions-fact/factbox-u-s-sanctions-on-venezuelas-oil-industry-idUSKCN1PN34I

Michael Gerrity. "Singapore's $5.7 Billion Marina Bay Sands Opens Doors," *World Property Journal.* May 17, 2010. Accessed from https://www.worldpropertyjournal.com/international-markets/vacation-leisure-real-estate/real-estate-news-singapore-marina-bay-sands-las-vegas-sands-corp-sheldon-g-adelson-skypark-sky-park-ceo-thomas-arasi-singapore-casinos-2547.php

Anne Gibson. "High Home Prices and Moderate Pay Make Auckland World's Fourth Least Affordable City," *New Zealand Herald.* January 23, 2017. Accessed from https://www.nzherald.co.nz/business/news/article.cfm?c_id=3&objectid=11785825

Kimutai Gilbert. "The Story of Hyperinflation in Zimbabwe," *World Atlas.* Last updated June 6, 2017. Accessed from https://www.worldatlas.com/articles/the-story-of-hyperinflation-in-zimbabwe.html

Indermit S. Gill, Ivailo Izvorski, Willen van Eeghen, and Donato De Rosa, et al. *Diversified Development: Making the Most of Natural Resources in Eurasia.* 2014. Washington, DC: International Bank for Reconstruction and Development/The World Bank.

GlobalPost. "Zimbabwe's Indigenization Law Provokes Controversy," *PRI*. May 30, 2010. Accessed from https://www.pri.org/stories/2010-03-28/ zimbabwes-indigenization-law-provokes-controversy

Piyush Goel. "OmniChannel Retail: What It Is, Value, Challenges, and Success Factors," *Brown Tape*. December 18, 2018. Accessed from https://browntape.com/omnichannel-commerce-what-it-is-real-value-challenges-and-critical-factors-for-success/

Vindu Goel and Jeffrey Gettleman. "Under Modi, India's Press Is Not So Free Anymore," *The New York Times*. April 2, 2020 (updated May 6, 2020). Accessed from https://www.nytimes.com/2020/04/02/world/ asia/modi-india-press-media.html

Christina Golubski and Anna Schaeffer. "Africa in the News: Impacts Of COVID-19 on African Economies and Elections Updates—Economic Challenges in South Africa, Tanzania, Angola, and Zambia," *Brookings*. April 4, 2020. Accessed from https://www.brookings.edu/blog/africa-in-focus/2020/04/04/africa-in-the-news-impacts-of-covid-19-on-african-economies-and-elections-updates/

Gustavo González. "Chile: Historic Reforms Complete Transition to Democracy," *Inter Press Service News Agency*. July 14, 2005. Accessed from http://www.ipsnews.net/2005/07/chile-historic-reforms-complete-transition-to-democracy/

Good Education Media. "Study Costs in Australia," *Studies in Australia* (Website). n.d. Accessed from https://www.studiesinaustralia.com/ studying-in-australia/how-to-study-in-australia/study-costs

Peter S. Goodman. "End of Apartheid in South Africa? Not in Economic Terms," *The New York Times*. October 24, 2017. Accessed from https:// www.nytimes.com/2017/10/24/business/south-africa-economy-apartheid.html

Gillian Gotora. "Zimbabwe Government Stealing Diamond Funds, Report Claims," *The Everett Daily Herald* (Associated Press). November 12, 2012. Accessed from https://www.heraldnet.com/news/zimbabwe-government-stealing-diamond-funds-report-claims/

Annie Gowen and Marnas Sharma. "Rising Hate in India," *The Washington Post*. October 31, 2018. Accessed from https://www.washingtonpost.com/graphics/2018/world/reports-of-hate-crime-cases-have-spiked-in-india/

Grand View Research. *Asia Pacific Nutritional Supplements Market Size, Share, and Trend Analysis* (Report Summary). November 2019. Report ID: GVR-4-68038-105-4. San Francisco: Author. Accessed from https://www.grandviewresearch.com/industry-analysis/asia-pacific-nutritional-supplements-market/request/rs2

Charlotte Greenfield and Greg Stutchbury. "'Utter Devastation' After Major Quake, Aftershocks Hit New Zealand," *Scientific American*. n.d. Accessed from https://www.scientificamerican.com/article/ldquo-utter-devastation-rdquo-after-major-quake-aftershocks-hit-new-zealand/

Xavier Greenwood. "South Africa Is the Most Unequal Country in the World and Its Poverty Is the 'Enduring Legacy of Apartheid,' Says World Bank," *Independent*. April 4, 2018. Accessed from https://www.independent.co.uk/news/world/africa/south-africa-unequal-country-poverty-legacy-apartheid-world-bank-a8288986.html

Garish Gupta. "Falling Oil Prices Turn Up the Heat on Venezuela's Maduro," *Time*. December 4, 2014. Accessed from https://time.com/3619052/oil-prices-maduro-venezuela/

Sharon Guynup. "Kaziranga: The Front Lines of India's Rhino Wars," *Mongabay*. April 4, 2017. Accessed from https://news.mongabay.com/2017/04/kaziranga-the-frontline-of-indias-rhino-wars/

Padraic Halpin. "Pilots at Ryanair's Largest Base Reject Pay Offer," *Reuters*. October 20, 2017. Accessed from https://www.reuters.com/article/uk-ryanair-pilots/pilots-at-ryanairs-largest-base-reject-pay-offer-idUKKBN1CP2CA

Catharine Hamm. "100 Facts for 100 Years of Machu Picchu," *The Los Angeles Times*. July 1, 2011. Accessed from https://www.latimes.com/travel/la-xpm-2011-jul-01-la-trb-machu-picchu-fact78-20110623-story.html

Kristen Han. "The Many Ways to Be Chinese Singaporean," *The Interpreter*. August 9, 2018. Accessed from https://www.lowyinstitute.org/the-interpreter/many-ways-to-be-chinese-singaporean

Virginia Harrison and Daniel Palumbo. "China Anniversary: How the Country Became the World's 'Economic Miracle'," *BBC News*. October 1, 2019. Accessed from https://www.bbc.com/news/business-49806247

Caroline Harsch. *Expat Insider 2019 Survey Reveals: The Best and Worst Destinations to Live and Work in 2019* (Press Release). September 5, 2019. Munich: Internations. Accessed from https://www.internations.org/press/press-release/expat-insider-2019-survey-reveals-the-best-and-worst-destinations-to-live-and-work-in-2019-39881

Hafsteinn Hauksson, Ed. *Tourism in Iceland: Investing in Iceland's Growth Engine*. 2018. London: GAMMA Advisory. Accessed from https://www.gamma.is/media/skjol/Gamma-Tourism.pdf

Michael Havis. "Mansion Where Pablo Escobar Stashed Cocaine and Cash in Secret Compartments Lies in Ruin," *Daily Mail*. July 2, 2018. Accessed from https://www.dailymail.co.uk/news/article-5908489/Mansion-Pablo-Escobar-stashed-cocaine-cash-secret-compartments-paintball-venue.html

Andrew Hecht. "3 Reasons to Position for a Rebound in Copper," *Seeking Alpha*. December 6, 2018. Accessed from https://seekingalpha.com/article/4226508-3-reasons-position-rebound-copper

Amy Held. "Botswana Weighs Lifting Hunting Ban, With Eye on Reducing Elephant Population," *NPR–WBEZ*. February 22, 2019. Accessed from https://www.npr.org/2019/02/22/696992009/botswana-weighs-lifting-hunting-ban-with-eye-on-diminishing-elephant-population

V.L. Hendrickson. "New Zealand Locks the Doors From the Inside," *The New York Times*. February 22, 2019. Accessed from https://www.nytimes.com/2019/02/22/realestate/new-zealand-locks-the-doors-from-the-inside.html

The Heritage Foundation. *2018 Index of Economic Freedom*. 2018. Washington, DC: Author. Accessed from https://www.heritage.org/index/pdf/2018/book/index_2018.pdf

The Heritage Foundation. *2018 Index of Economic Freedom: Canada*. 2017. Washington, DC: Author. Accessed from https://www.heritage.org/index/country/canada

The Heritage Foundation. "2018 Index of Economic Freedom," *Commentary: International Economies*. 2018. Washington, DC: Author. Accessed from https://www.heritage.org/international-economies/commentary/2018-index-economic-freedom

The Heritage Foundation. *2019 Index of Economic Freedom*. 2019. Washington, DC: Author. Accessed from https://www.heritage.org/index/

The Heritage Foundation. *2019 Index of Economic Freedom: Belize*. 2016. Washington, DC: Author, p. 118. Accessed from https://www.heritage.org/index/pdf/2019/countries/belize.pdf

The Heritage Foundation. *Belize: Economic Freedom Score.* 2016. Washington, DC: Author. Accessed from https://www.heritage.org/index/pdf/2016/countries/belize.pdf

The Heritage Foundation. *Chile: Economic Freedom Score.* 2018. Washington, DC: Author. Accessed from https://www.heritage.org/index/pdf/2018/countries/chile.pdf

The Heritage Foundation. *Colombia: Economic Freedom Score.* 2020. Washington, DC: Author. Accessed from https://www.heritage.org/index/country/colombia

The Heritage Foundation. *Malaysia: Economic Freedom Score.* 2019. Washington, DC: Author. Accessed from https://www.heritage.org/index/country/malaysia

The Heritage Foundation. *New Zealand: Economic Freedom Score.* 2016. Washington, DC: Author. Accessed from https://www.heritage.org/index/pdf/2016/countries/newzealand.pdf

The Heritage Foundation. *Peru: Economic Freedom Score.* 2016. Washington, DC: Author. Accessed from https://www.heritage.org/index/pdf/2017/countries/peru.pdf

The Heritage Foundation. *United States: Economic Freedom Score.* 2016. Washington, DC: Author. Accessed from https://www.heritage.org/index/pdf/2016/countries/unitedstates.pdf

David Hirschmann, Meir Pugatch, David Torstensson, et al. *Infinite Possibilities: U.S. Chamber International IP Index (Fourth Edition).* February 2016. Washington, DC: Global Intellectual Property Center. Accessed from https://www.theglobalipcenter.com/wp-content/uploads/2017/04/GIPC_Index_Report_2016.pdf

Liz Hoffman and Aruna Viswanatha. "Goldman Sachs in Talks to Admit Guilt, Pay $2 Billion Fine to Settle 1MDB Probe," *The Wall Street Journal*. Updated December 19, 2019. Accessed from https://www.wsj.com/articles/goldman-sachs-in-talks-to-admit-guilt-pay-2-billion-fine-to-settle-1mdb-probe-11576760406

Eustance Huang. "Sales of Video Games Soar As the Coronavirus Leaves Millions Trapped in Their Homes," *CNBC*. April 2, 2020. Accessed from https://www.cnbc.com/2020/04/03/video-games-sales-soar-as-coronavirus-leaves-millions-trapped-at-home.html

Craig Hudson. "Why Diversity Is Key for New Zealand's Technology Industry to Flourish," *IdeaLog*. May 30, 2017. Accessed from https://idealog.co.nz/tech/2017/05/why-diversity-key-new-zealands-technology-industry-flourish

Murray Hunter. "Malaysia's Massive Foreign Worker Dependency," *Malaysia Today*. Last updated November 27, 2019. Accessed from https://www.malaysia-today.net/2019/11/27/malaysias-massive-foreign-worker-dependency-murray-hunter/

Gareth Hutchens. "Economy Is Growing Faster Than Expected at 3.1%, But News Is Not All Good," *The Guardian*. May 31, 2016. Accessed from https://www.theguardian.com/business/2016/jun/01/australias-gdp-growth-rises-by-11-in-march-quarter-taking-annual-rate-to-31

Icelandic Film Centre. *Industry & Funding* (Website). n.d. Accessed from http://www.icelandicfilmcentre.is/support-schemes/25-reimbursement/

.id. "Australia: Language Spoken at Home," *Community Profile: Australia* (Website). n.d. Accessed from https://profile.id.com.au/australia/language

IHS Towers. *MTN Announces Exchange of Shares in INT Towers Limited* (Press Release). February 1, 2017. Accessed from https://www. ihstowers.com/news/mtn-group-announces-exchange-shares-int-towers-limited/

The Independent in Business. "Covid-19: Zim in Throes of Unprecedented Recession," *Zimbabwe Independent*. April 10, 2020. Accessed from https://www.theindependent.co.zw/2020/04/10/covid-19-zim-in-throes-of-unprecedented-recession/

Innovation Media Consulting. "The Role of Print in a Digital World," *Innovation in News Media 2019–2020 World Report*. April 15, 2019. Accessed from https://innovation.media/newswheel/the-role-of-print-in-a-digital-world

International Air Transport Association. *Air Passenger Market Analysis*. May 2018. Montreal, Canada: Author. Accessed from https://www. iata.org/publications/economics/Reports/pax-monthly-analysis/passenger-analysis-may-2018.pdf

International Airport Review. "The Top 20 Busiest Airports in the World By Passenger Number," *IAR*. October 2, 2019. Accessed from https://www.internationalairportreview.com/article/32311/top-20-largest-airports-world-passenger-number/

International Bank for Reconstruction and Development/The World Bank. *Doing Business 2019: Training for Reform—A World Bank Group Flagship Report, 16th Edition*. 2019. Washington, DC: Author. Accessed from https://www.doingbusiness.org/en/reports/global-reports/doing-business-2019

International Monetary Fund. "Belize: 2017 Article IV Consultation—Press Release; Staff Report; Informational Annex; Statement by the Executive Director for Belize," *IMF Country Report No. 17/286*. September 2017. Washington, DC: Author.

International Monetary Fund. "Belize's 2016–17 Sovereign Debt Restructuring—Third Time Lucky?" *IMF Working Paper WP/18/121.* May 2018. Washington, DC: Author

International Monetary Fund. *Policy Responses to COVID-19* (website). n.d. Washington, DC: Author. Accessed from https://www.imf.org/en/Topics/imf-and-covid19/Policy-Responses-to-COVID-19#I

Michael Janda. "Australia's Banks Are Too Big for the Nation's Good," *ABC News.* August 30, 2016. Accessed from https://www.abc.net.au/news/2018-08-31/janda-aus-banks-are-too-big/7789830

Francisco Jara and Luis Jaime Cisneros. "Shaken by Corruption, Peruvians Back Major Government Overhaul," *Yahoo! News.* December 10, 2018. Accessed from https://www.yahoo.com/news/shaken-corruption-peruvians-back-major-government-overhaul-155359083.html

Megan Jerrard. "9 Best Things to Do in Iceland," *International Expeditions.* December 11, 2017. Accessed from https://www.ietravel.com/blog/9-best-things-do-iceland

John J. Johnson, César N. Caviedes, Paul W. Drake, and Marcello A. Carmagnani. "Chile," *Encyclopædia Britannica.* Last updated March 10, 2020. Accessed from https://www.britannica.com/place/Chile

Scott Johnson. "A Visit to Robben Island, the Brutal Prison That Held Mandela, Is Haunting and Inspiring," *Smithsonian Magazine.* May 2012. Accessed from https://www.smithsonianmag.com/travel/robben-island-a-monument-to-courage-62697703/

Steven Johnson. "Australian Home Prices Tipped to Plunge 40 Per Cent As Coronavirus Hits Economy," *The Daily Mail UK).* April 1, 2020. Accessed from https://www.dailymail.co.uk/news/article-8174539/Australian-house-prices-tipped-plunge-40-cent-coronavirus-hits-economy.html

Joint United Nations Programme on HIV/AIDS (UNAIDS). *Global Report: UNAIDS Report on the Global AIDS Epidemic.* 2012. Geneva, Switzerland: Author. ISBN 978-92-9173-592-1 (digital version). Accessed from https://www.unaids.org/sites/default/files/media_asset/20121120_UNAIDS_Global_Report_2012_with_annexes_en_1.pdf

Alexandra Jolly. "President Wants Colombia to Be Most Educated Latin American Country by 2025," *Colombia Reports.* February 13, 2014. Accessed from https://colombiareports.com/new-colombian-initiative-educated-latin-american-country-2025/

Anna Junker. "Calgary Among Least Affordable Places in Alberta to Live: Report," *Calgary Herald.* August 29, 2018. Accessed from https://calgaryherald.com/news/local-news/calgary-third-least-affordable-place-to-live-in-alberta-report-says

Nazuin Zulaikha Kamarulzaman. "Employers Lament Unclear Boundaries As Malaysia's RM1,200 Minimum Wage Looms," *The Edge Markets.* December 27, 2019. Accessed from https://www.theedgemarkets.com/article/employers-lament-unclear-boundaries-malaysias-rm1200-minimum-wage-looms

Ted Karasote. "They Shoot Elephants, Don't They?" *Salon.* December 14, 2004. Accessed from https://www.salon.com/2004/12/13/elephants/

Madhura Karnik. "India's Diamond Industry Is Already Weak, and Demonetisation Could Push It Into Critical Care," *Quartz India.* December 7, 2016. Accessed from https://qz.com/india/854224/indias-diamond-industry-is-already-weak-and-demonetization-could-push-it-into-critical-care/

Safaa Kasraoui. "Tourism's Contribution to Morocco's GDP Increased by 5% in 2016: HCP," *Morocco World News.* October 21, 2017. Accessed from https://www.moroccoworldnews.com/2017/10/231762/tourism-morocco-gdp-hcp/

Eman Katem. "Canada's Higher Education System Continues to Rank Among the Top in the World," *Canada Study News*. May 17, 2018. Accessed from https://www.canadastudynews.com/2018/05/17/canadas-higher-education-system-continues-to-rank-among-the-top-in-the-world/

Robin Kawakami. "A Walk on New Zealand's Wild Side: Hiking the Routeburn Track," *The Wall Street Journal*. January 30, 2015. Accessed from https://www.wsj.com/articles/a-walk-on-new-zealands-wild-side-hiking-the-routeburn-track-1422641118

Christopher Kent. *The Limits of Interest-Only Lending*. Address to the Housing Industry Association Breakfast. Sydney, Australia. April 24, 2018. Accessed from https://www.rba.gov.au/speeches/2018/sp-ag-2018-04-24.html

Will Kenton. "Exchange Controls," *Investopedia: Laws & Regulations*. April 30, 2019. Accessed from https://www.investopedia.com/terms/e/exchangecontrol.asp

Simon Khalaf and Lali Kesiraju. "U.S. Consumers Time-Spent on Mobile Crosses 5 Hours a Day," *Flurry Analytics Blog*. March 2, 2017. Accessed from https://www.flurry.com/post/157921590345/us-consumers-time-spent-on-mobile-crosses-5

Kiddle. "Economy of New Zealand Facts for Kids," *Kiddle Encyclopedia*. Last modified November 21, 2019. Accessed from https://kids.kiddle.co/Economy_of_New_Zealand

Joseph Kiprop. "The 10 Most Populated Cities in Victoria, Australia," *World Atlas*. Last updated March 27, 2018. Accessed from https://www.

worldatlas.com/articles/the-10-most-populated-cities-in-victoria-australia.html

Knoema. "Australia—Urban Population As a Share of Total Population," *World Data Atlas* (Website). n.d. Accessed from https://knoema.com/atlas/Australia/Urban-population

Jacqueline Kochak. *South African Chaos Could Impact Country's Food Supply*. August 21, 2018. Auburn, AL: Auburn University Food Systems Institute. Accessed from https://aufsi.auburn.edu/blog/2018/08/21/south-african-chaos-could-impact-countrys-food-supply/

Oleg Komlik. "Fed With Credit: Financial 'Liberalization,' Deregulation and the Role of Credit in Iceland's Collapse," *Economic Sociology and Political Economy*. August 19, 2015. Accessed from https://economicsociology.org/2015/08/19/fed-with-credit-financial-liberalization-deregulation-and-the-role-of-credit-in-icelands-collapse/

KPMG. *Evolve—Intelligent Insurance: The South African Insurance Industry Survey 2017*. August 2017. Cape Town: KPMG South Africa. Accessed from https://home.kpmg/content/dam/kpmg/za/pdf/2018/October/16436MC%20INSURANCE%20SURVEY%20low%20res%20RR.pdf and https://assets.kpmg/content/dam/kpmg/za/pdf/2017/08/reinsurance-tables.pdf

KPMG. *Icelandic Tax Facts 2015: In-depth Information on the Icelandic Tax System*. 2016. Reykjavík: KPMG Iceland. Accessed from https://assets.kpmg/content/dam/kpmg/pdf/2016/05/tnf-iceland-mar29-2016.pdf

Alda Krevec. "Iceland Tightens Restrictions on Foreign Property Rights," *The Reykjavík Grapevine*. May 3, 2013. Accessed from https://grapevine.is/news/2013/05/03/iceland-foreign-property-rights/

Raksha Kumar. "India Has Lots of Newspapers and Lots of Readers and One Big Journalism Problem," *Columbia Journalism Review*. June 10, 2019. Accessed from https://www.cjr.org/business_of_news/india-has-lots-of-newspapers-and-lots-of-readers-and-one-big-journalism-problem.php

Katya Kupelian and Abby Narishkin. "Look Inside the New $1.3 Billion Complex at Singapore's Changi Airport, With a 130-Foot Indoor Waterfall," *Business Insider*. April 17, 2019. Accessed from https://www.businessinsider.com/singapore-airport-complex-changi-airport-indoor-waterfall-mall-2019-4

Aung San Suu Kyi and Michel Sidibé. *UNAIDS World AIDS Day Report 2012*. 2012. Switzerland: USAIDS. ISBN 978-92-9253-000. Accessed from https://www.unaids.org/sites/default/files/media_asset/JC2434_WorldAIDSday_results_en_1.pdf

Raoul Leering and Timme Spakman. *Countries Hit Most by the Coronavirus Value Chain Shock*. April 2, 2020. Amsterdam: ING Bank N.V. Accessed from https://think.ing.com/downloads/pdf/article/countries-hurt-most-by-covid-19-global-value-chain-shock

Glenn Leibowitz. "Iceland Celebrates Christmas Unlike Any Other Country in the World," *Inc*. December 20, 2017. Accessed from https://www.inc.com/glenn-leibowitz/why-worlds-coolest-christmas-tradition-can-be-found-in-iceland.html

Little India Desk. "India to Be World's Third Largest Travel and Tourism Economy in a Decade: Report," *Little India*. March 23, 2018. Accessed from https://littleindia.com/india-to-be-worlds-third-largest-travel-and-tourism-economy-in-a-decade-report/

Los Angeles Almanac. *Air Distances Between Los Angeles & Foreign Cities* (Website). n.d. Accessed from http://www.laalmanac.com/transport/tr52.php

Lumen Learning. "Art of New Zealand," *Boundless Art History* (Website). n.d. Accessed from https://courses.lumenlearning.com/boundless-arthistory/chapter/art-of-new-zealand/

Amanda Macias. "10 Facts Reveal the Absurdity of Pablo Escobar's Wealth," *The Independent*. December 29, 2017. Accessed from https://www.independent.co.uk/news/people/pablo-escobar-worth-wealth-money-how-much-a8133141.html

Amanda Macias. "Trump Gives $717 Billion Defense Bill a Green Light. Here's What the Pentagon Is Poised to Get," *CNBC*. August 13, 2018; updated August 14, 2018. Accessed from https://www.cnbc.com/2018/08/13/trump-signs-717-billion-defense-bill.html

Hilary MacGregor. "The Nazca Lines of Peru: An Ancient Riddle Etched in the Earth Makes for a Perfect Family Adventure," *The Los Angeles Times*. October 31, 2015. Accessed from https://www.latimes.com/travel/la-tr-d-nazca-lines-main-20151101-story.html

Howard Marks. *Growing the Pie*. Los Angeles: Oaktree Capital Management, LLP. 2019. Accessed from https://www.oaktreecapital.com/docs/default-source/memos/growing-the-pie.pdf

Shula E. Marks. "Southern Africa," *Encyclopædia Britannica*. n.d. Accessed from https://www.britannica.com/place/Southern-Africa

Dina Fine Maron. "How Strong Is Africa's Last Elephant Stronghold," *National Geographic*. June 13, 2019. Accessed from https://www.nationalgeographic.com/animals/2019/06/elephants-poached-in-botswana/

Timothy W. Martin and Andrew Jeong. "Military-Spending Spat Stirs Worry Over U.S. Forces in Korea," *The Wall Street Journal*. Updated February 3, 2019. Accessed from https://www.wsj.com/

articles/military-spending-spat-stirs-worry-over-u-s-forces-in-korea-11549195200

Zareer Masani. "English or Hinglish—Which Will India Choose?" *BBC*. November 27, 2012. Accessed from https://www.bbc.com/news/magazine-20500312

Fumi Matsumoto. "Coal Expected to Be Australia's Most Valuable Export in 2018–19," *Nikkei Asian Review*. January 13, 2019. Accessed from https://asia.nikkei.com/Business/Markets/Commodities/Coal-expected-to-be-Australia-s-most-valuable-export-in-2018-19

Miklos Mattyasovszky. "The Largest Countries in the World," *World Atlas*. Last updated December 16, 2019. Accessed from https://www.worldatlas.com/articles/the-largest-countries-in-the-world-the-biggest-nations-as-determined-by-total-land-area.html

Alfonce Mbizwo. "UPDATE 2-Zimbabwe Has Potential to Meet 20 Pct of Global Lithium Demand," *Reuters*. February 28, 2018. Accessed from https://www.reuters.com/article/zimbabwe-mining/update-2-zimbabwe-has-potential-to-meet-20-pct-of-global-lithium-demand-idUSL8N1QI2ID

Julie McCarthy. "Why Do So Few People Pay Income Tax In India?" *NPR*. March 22, 2017. Accessed from https://www.npr.org/sections/parallels/2017/03/22/517965630/why-do-so-few-people-pay-income-tax-in-india

Henry McDonald. "Ireland's Age of Affluence Comes to an End," *The Guardian*. April 5, 2009. Accessed from https://www.theguardian.com/world/2009/apr/05/ireland-economy-vat-unemployment

Kristen McTighe. "The World's Food Supply Depends on Morocco. Here's Why," *Public Radio International*. November 21, 2013. Accessed from https://www.pri.org/stories/2013-11-21/worlds-food-supply-depends-morocco-heres-why

Beryl Menezes. "Indian IT Services Exports Seen Growing 12–14% in Year Ahead," *LiveMint*. February 11, 2015. Accessed from https://www.livemint.com/Industry/bCLOgyaLGiIi6TuhmN0S7J/Indian-IT-services-exports-seen-growing-1214-in-year-ahead.html

Christopher D. Merwin, Masaru Sugiyama, et al. *The World of Games: eSports—From Wild West to Mainstream*. New York: The Goldman Sachs Group, 2018. Accessed from https://www.goldmansachs.com/insights/pages/infographics/e-sports/report.pdf

Chris Michael. "Has Tokyo Reached 'Peak City'?" *The Guardian*. June 14, 2019. Accessed from https://www.theguardian.com/cities/2019/jun/14/has-tokyo-reached-peak-city

Ben Midgley. "The Six Reasons the Fitness Industry Is Booming," *Forbes*. September 26, 2018. Accessed from https://www.forbes.com/sites/benmidgley/2018/09/26/the-six-reasons-the-fitness-industry-is-booming/#194e8b84506d

Geoffry Migiro. "Which Country Has the Most Donut Shops Per Capita?" *World Atlas*. Last updated May 9, 2019. Accessed from https://www.worldatlas.com/articles/which-country-has-the-most-donut-shops-per-capita.html

Migration Policy Institute. *The Top Sending Countries of Immigrants in Australia, Canada, and the United States*. n.d. Washington, DC: Author. Accessed from https://www.migrationpolicy.org/programs/data-hub/top-sending-countries-immigrants-australia-canada-and-united-states

Andrea Miller. "Australia Has Gone 27 Years Without a Recession—Here's What's Behind the Country's Economic Run," *CNBC*. February 8,

2019. Accessed from https://www.cnbc.com/2019/02/08/australia-has-gone-27-years-without-a-recession.html

Terry Miller, Anthony B. Kim, and James M. Roberts, with Patrick Tyrrell and Tori K. Whiting (Foreword by Steve Forbes). *2018 Index of Economic Freedom*. 2018. Washington, DC: The Heritage Foundation. Accessed from https://www.heritage.org/index/pdf/2018/book/index_2018.pdf

Daniel J. Mitchell. "New Zealand's Remarkable Economic Transformation," *Fee.org* (Foundation for Economic Education). September 21, 2016. Accessed from https://fee.org/articles/new-zealands-remarkable-economic-transformation/

Anjali Karol Mohan. "Bengaluru, *Sans* a City Plan," *Deccan Herald*. October 13, 2019. Accessed from https://www.deccanherald.com/opinion/in-perspective/bengaluru-sans-a-city-plan-768173.html

Renee Montagne. "Bacardi Biography Details the 'Fight for Cuba,'" *NPR Morning Edition*. September 8, 2008. Accessed from https://www.npr.org/templates/story/story.php?storyId=94320922

Motley Fool Staff. "Starbucks (SBUX) Q2 2018 Earnings Conference Call Transcript," *The Motley Fool*. April 26, 2018. Accessed from https://www.fool.com/earnings/call-transcripts/2018/04/28/starbucks-sbux-q2-2018-earnings-conference-call-tr.aspx

Myasha Mudukuti. "We May Starve, but at Least We'll Be GMO-Free," *The Wall Street Journal*. March 10, 2016. Accessed from https://www.wsj.com/articles/we-may-starve-but-at-least-well-be-gmo-free-1457653915

Ralph Mupita. *MTN Group Limited: Integrated Report for the Year Ended 31 December 2018*. 2018. Fairland, South Africa: Author. Accessed from https://www.mtn.com/wp-content/uploads/2019/03/MTN-AR-2019_LORES.pdf

Chris Muronzi. "How Zimbabwe Caught the World Off Guard With Another New Currency," *Quartz Africa*. February 26, 2019. Accessed from https://qz.com/africa/1559982/zimbabwe-new-currency-rtgs-dollar-replaces-bond-notes/

Mako Muzenda. "Zimbabwe: Sweeping Changes Threaten Education System," *Daily Maverick*. February 21, 2017. Accessed from https://www.dailymaverick.co.za/article/2017-02-21-zimbabwe-sweeping-changes-threaten-education-system/

Gay Nagle Myers. "A Record Year for Cuba Tourism Numbers," *Travel Weekly*. January 7, 2019. Accessed from https://www.travelweekly.com/Caribbean-Travel/A-record-year-for-Cuba-tourism-numbers

Oishimaya Sen Nag. "Countries With the Longest Coastline," *World Atlas*. Last updated June 18, 2018. Accessed from https://www.worldatlas.com/articles/countries-with-the-most-coastline.html

Oishimaya Sen Nag. "The Seven Natural Wonders of Africa," *World Atlas*. Last updated August 20, 2019. Accessed from https://www.worldatlas.com/articles/the-seven-natural-wonders-of-africa-unique-and-mesmerizing-travel-destinations.html

Oishimaya Sen Nag. "The Tallest Peaks in New Zealand," *World Atlas*. Last updated February 13, 2018. Accessed from https://www.worldatlas.com/articles/the-tallest-peaks-in-new-zealand.html

Oishimaya Sen Nag. "Where Does the Kalahari Desert Lie?" *World Atlas*. Last updated April 25, 2017. Accessed from https://www.wordlatlas.com/articles/where-does-the-kalahari-desert-lie.html

Ashley Nagaoka. "90% of Singapore's Residents Own a Home. What's Their Secret?" *Hawaii News Now*. June 4, 2019; updated June 5, 2019. Accessed from https://www.hawaiinewsnow.com/2019/06/05/help-solve-hawaiis-housing-crisis-some-leaders-are-looking-singapore/

National Oceanic and Atmospheric Association. *What Is the Great Barrier Reef?* (Website). Washington, DC: Author. Last updated January 7, 2020. Accessed from https://oceanservice.noaa.gov/facts/gbrlargeststructure.html

Natural Resources Canada. "Canada Has the Third-Largest Proven Oil Reserve In the World, Most of Which Is in the Oil Sands," *Oil Resources* (Website). Date modified December 16, 2019. Accessed from https://www.nrcan.gc.ca/energy/energy-sources-distribution/crude-oil/oil-resources/18085

NetAdmin. "The 10 Richest Countries in Africa," *IT News Africa*. February 5, 2015. Accessed from https://www.itnewsafrica.com/2015/02/top-10-richest-countries-in-africa-rated/

Scott Neuman. "South Africa Reports First COVID-19 Deaths; Goes Into 3-Week Lockdown," *NPR*. March 27, 2020. Accessed from https://www.npr.org/sections/coronavirus-live-updates/2020/03/27/822363982/south-africa-reports-first-covid-19-deaths-goes-into-3-week-lockdown

New World Encyclopedia Contributors. "Belize," *New World Encyclopedia*. Last updated December 13, 2019. Accessed from https://www.newworldencyclopedia.org/p/index.php?title=Belize&oldid=1027520

New World Encyclopedia Contributors. "Botswana," *New World Encyclopedia*. November 17, 2019. Accessed from https://www.newworldencyclopedia.org/entry/Botswana

New World Encyclopedia Contributors. "Cusco," *New World Encyclopedia.* Last updated November 22, 2017. Accessed from https://www.newworldencyclopedia.org/entry/Special:Cite?page=Cusco

Tim Neville et al. "52 Places to Go in 2017," *The New York Times.* January 4, 2017. Accessed from https://www.nytimes.com/interactive/2017/travel/places-to-visit.html

New Zealand Government. *Economic and Financial Overview 2016.* Wellington, New Zealand: The Treasury. n.d. ISSN: 1173-2334 (Print); ISSN: 1178-749X (Online). Accessed from https://treasury.govt.nz/sites/default/files/2010-04/nzefo-16.pdf

Newsroom. "Nasdaq Iceland," *InvestoPress Today.* July 22, 2019. Accessed from https://investopress.com/nasdaq-iceland

News24 Correspondent. "Air Zimbabwe Banned From Europe … So Is It Safe for Mugabe to Use?" *News24.* May 17, 2017. Accessed from https://www.news24.com/Africa/Zimbabwe/air-zimbabwe-banned-from-europe-so-is-it-safe-for-mugabe-to-use-20170517

Steven Nickolas. "What Is the Minimum Capital Adequacy Ratio Under Basel III?" *Investopedia.* Updated July 20, 2019. Accessed from https://www.investopedia.com/ask/answers/062515/what-minimum-capital-adequacy-ratio-must-be-attained-under-basel-iii.asp

Tefo Nombolo. "Tourist Arrivals Surpass 2 Million in 2016," *Botswana Guardian.* December 5, 2016. Accessed from http://www.botswanaguardian.co.bw/news/item/2289-tourists-arrivals-surpass-2-million-in-2016.html

Rosalba O'Brien. "Chilean Presidential Hopeful Piñera Pledges Infrastructure Spending," *Reuters.* May 5, 2017. Accessed from https://www.reuters.com/article/us-chile-politics/chilean-presidential-hopeful-pinera-pledges-infrastructure-spending-idUSKBN1811HD

Josy O'Donnell. "9 Interesting Facts About the Sahara Desert," *Conservation Institute*. June 12, 2013. Accessed from https://www. conservationinstitute.org/interesting-sahara-desert-facts/

Barry O'Halloran. "Ryanair Plans to Carry 200M Passengers Annually by 2024," *The Irish Times*. November 7, 2016. Accessed from https://www. irishtimes.com/business/transport-and-tourism/ryanair-plans-to-carry-200m-passengers-annually-by-2024-1.2857501

Patricia O'Toole. "Opinion—Theodore Roosevelt Cared Deeply About the Sick. Who Knew?" *The New York Times*. June 1, 2019. Accessed from https://www.nytimes.com/2019/01/06/opinion/theodore-roosevelt-health-care-progressive.html

Jefte Ochaeta. "Belize's Economic Growth Slows Substantially," *Amandala*. April 2, 2016. Accessed from https://amandala.com.bz/news/belizes-economic-growth-slows-substantially/

OECD/WTO. *Aid for Trade at a Glance 2017: Promoting Trade, Inclusiveness, and Connectivity for Sustainable Development*. 2017. Geneva: WTO and Paris: OECD Publishing, p. 338. Accessed from http://dx.doi.org/10.1787/aid_glance-2017-en

Elijah Oliveros-Rosen. "Economic Research: For Latin America, the Path to Economic Recovery From COVID-19 Remains Uncertain," *S&P Global—Ratings*. March 31, 2020. Accessed from https://www. spglobal.com/ratings/en/research/articles/200331-economic-research-for-latin-america-the-path-to-economic-recovery-from-covid-19-remains-uncertain-11414665

Sharon Omondi. "What Are the Biggest Industries in Peru?" *World Atlas*. April 11, 2019. Accessed from https://www.worldatlas.com/articles/what-are-the-biggest-industries-in-peru.html

Organisation for Economic Cooperation and Development. *OECD Economic Surveys—Iceland*. September 2015. Paris: Author. Accessed from http://www.oecd.org/economy/surveys/Iceland-2015-overview.pdf

Organisation for Economic Cooperation and Development. *OECD Economic Survey of Indonesia* (Website). 2019. Paris: Author. Accessed from http://www.oecd.org/economy/indonesia-economic-snapshot/

Organisation for Economic Cooperation and Development. "PISA Worldwide Ranking: Average Score of Math, Science and Reading," *FactsMaps* (Website). 2015–16. Accessed from http://factsmaps.com/pisa-worldwide-ranking-average-score-of-math-science-reading/

Organisation for Economic Cooperation and Development. *Revenue Statistics 2019—Australia*. 2019. Paris: Author. Accessed from https://www.oecd.org/tax/revenue-statistics-australia.pdf

Andrey Ostroukh and José de Córdoba. "Russia Writes Off Cuban Debt," *The Wall Street Journal*. July 12, 2014. Accessed from https://www.wsj.com/articles/russia-writes-off-cuba-debt-1405083869

Olumide Oyekunle. "The Largest Economies in Africa by GDP, 2019," *The African Exponent*. February 20, 2019. Accessed from https://www.africanexponent.com/post/9786-top-six-countries-with-the-biggest-gdp-in-africa

Thomas Page. "By Foot or Helicopter, the High Atlas Is One of the World's Hidden Ski Gems," *CNN Travel*. November 14, 2016. Accessed from https://www.cnn.com/travel/article/morocco-atlas-mountain-ski-trek/index.html

S.C. Pallin, O. Meekers, K. Lupu. *South Africa: A Total Market Approach for Male Condoms—PSI/UNFPA Joint Studies on the Total Market for Male Condoms in Six African Countries*. November 2013. Washington,

DC: PSI and New York: United Nations Population Fund. Accessed from https://www.unfpa.org/sites/default/files/pub-pdf/PSI_SouthAfrica_Dec5final%5Bsmallpdf.com%5D.pdf

Rupert Parker. "Hiking to the Lost City in Colombia," *Travel Magazine*. April 1, 2019. Accessed from https://www.thetravelmagazine.net/hiking-to-the-lost-city-in-colombia.html

Beena Parmar. "Mumbai's Dabbawalas Up Delivery Charges by ₹100," *The Hindu Business Line*. July 2, 2014; updated March 12, 2018. Accessed from https://www.thehindubusinessline.com/news/mumbais-dabbawalas-up-delivery-charges-by-100/article20810873.ece

Sienna Parulis-Cook. "Banff & Lake Louise Ready for Surge in Chinese Tourism With Digital and Industry Marketing Strategy," *Dragon Tail Interactive*. April 26, 2017. Accessed from https://dragontrail.com/resources/blog/banff-lake-louise-ready-for-surge-in-chinese-tourism-with-digital-and-industry-marketing-strategy

Gonzalo Pastor. *Peru: Monetary and Exchange Rate Policies, 1930–1980* (IMF Working Paper WP/12/166). June 2012. Washington, DC: International Monetary Fund. Accessed from https://www.imf.org/external/pubs/ft/wp/2012/wp12166.pdf

Doris Peručić. *Analysis of the World Cruise Industry* (White Paper). October 31, 2019. Zagreb, Croatia: Edward Bernays University College. Accessed from https://hrcak.srce.hr/file/343878

Phama. "Medicines Price Control Will Have Negative Repercussions," *Malaysiakini*. October 3, 2019. Accessed from https://www.malaysiakini.com/letters/494410

Kenneth Pletcher. "Uluru/Ayers Rock," *Encyclopædia Britannica*. n.d. Accessed from https://www.britannica.com/place/Uluru-Ayers-Rock

Kelvin M. Pollard, Linda A. Jacobsen, and Mark Mather. *The U.S. Population Is Growing at the Slowest Rate Since the 1930s* (Website). February 18, 2020. Washington, DC: Population Research Bureau. Accessed from https://www.prb.org/the-u-s-population-is-growing-at-the-slowest-rate-since-the-1930s/

Colin Post. "Lima Metro's Third Line Planned," *Peru Reports.* July 10, 2015. Accessed from https://perureports.com/lima-metros-third-line-planned/1743/

Fanny Potkin. "Exclusive: WhatsApp in Talks to Launch Mobile Payments in Indonesia—Sources," *Reuters.* August 20, 2019. Accessed from https://www.reuters.com/article/us-whatsapp-payments-indonesia-exclusive/exclusive-whatsapp-in-talks-to-launch-mobile-payments-in-indonesia-sources-idUSKCN1VA0KG

Anita Powell. "Botswana Again Wins Title As Africa's Least Corrupt Nation," *VOA News.* December 4, 2012. Accessed from https://www.voanews.com/africa/botswana-again-wins- title-africas-least-corrupt-nation

Praxi5 Advisory Group Ltd. *Dangriga Tourism Destination Development Plan.* January 2019. Belize City: Belize Tourism Board. Accessed from https://belizetourismboard.org/wp-content/uploads/2019/10/Dangriga-TDDP-Final-.pdf

Press Trust of India (PTI). "775 Per Cent Jump in Passenger Car Ownership in 24 Years: Report," *Economic Times.* June 28, 2016. Accessed from https://economictimes.indiatimes.com/775-per-cent-jump-in-passenger-car-ownership-in-24-years-report/articleshow/52958430.cms

Press Trust of India (PTI). "India Has the Cheapest Mobile Data in World: Study," *Economic Times.* March 6, 2019. Accessed from https://economictimes.indiatimes.com/tech/internet/india-has-the-cheapest-mobile-data-in-world-study/articleshow/68285820.cms

Press Trust of India (PTI). "Mid-Air Collision Averted Between Two Indigo Planes Over Bengaluru Airspace," *The Economic Times*. Last updated July 12, 2018. Accessed from https://economictimes.indiatimes.com/industry/transportation/airlines-/-aviation/mid-air-collision-averted-between-two-indigo-planes-over-bengaluru-airspace/articleshow/64958633.cms

Press Trust of India (PTI). "Mumbai 12th Richest City Globally; Total Wealth at USD 950 Billion," *The Economic Times*. February 12, 2018. Accessed from https://economictimes.indiatimes.com/news/economy/indicators/mumbai-12th-richest-city-globally-total-wealth-at-usd-950-billion/articleshow/62870741.cms?from=mdr

Press Trust of India (PTI). "On Track: Railways' Safety Record in 2017–2018 Best in 57 Years, Shows Official Data," *The Economic Times*. April 14, 2018. Accessed from https://economictimes.indiatimes.com/industry/transportation/railways/on-track-railways-safety-record-in-2017-2018-best-in-57-years-shows-official-data/articleshow/63757894.cms?from=mdr

Press Trust of India (PTI). "Textile Sector Growing Exponentially, Has More Potential: Smriti Irani," *Economic Times*. September 21, 2017. Accessed from https://economictimes.indiatimes.com/industry/cons-products/garments-/-textiles/textile-sector-growing-exponentially-has-more-potential-smriti-irani/articleshow/60782956.cms

Press Trust of India (PTI). "World Bank Sees FY21 India Growth at 1.5–2.8%; Slowest Since Economic Reforms Three Decades Back," *The Economic Times*. Last updated April 13, 2020. Accessed from https://economictimes.indiatimes.com/news/economy/finance/covid-19-causes-severe-disruption-to-indian-economy-says-world-bank/

articleshow/75104474.cms?utm_source=contentofinterest&utm_medium=text&utm_campaign=cppst

PricewaterhouseCoopers International Limited, The World Bank/IFC. *Paying Taxes 2013: The Global Picture.* 2012. United Kingdom: Author. Accessed from www.pwc.com/payingtaxes

Shwweta Punj. "Left High and Dry," *India Today.* April 8, 2017 (issue date April 17, 2017). Accessed from https://www.indiatoday.in/magazine/the-big-story/story/20170417-liquor-ban-supreme-court-verdict-national-state-highways-986139-2017-04-08

Norie Quintos. "Banff: Escape to the Rugged Beauty of Canada's First National Park," *National Geographic Traveler.* November 17, 2016. Accessed from https://www.nationalgeographic.com/travel/destinations/north-america/canada/banff/best-trips-2017-banff-canada/

Anuradha Raghu. "Can Palm Oil Demand Be Met Without Ruining Rainforests?" *Bloomberg Business Week.* December 12, 2019 (updated December 16, 2019). Accessed from https://www.bloomberg.com/news/articles/2019-12-12/can-palm-oil-demand-be-met-without-rainforest-ruin-quicktake

Suresh Ranjarajan. "Does India Need Foreign Universities to Improve the Quality of Education in India," *Entrepreneur.* March 31, 2017. Accessed from https://www.entrepreneur.com/article/292181

Mark Rao. "When the Grass Is Greener In Australia for Local Tech Start-Ups," *The Malaysian Reserve.* October 15, 2019. Accessed from https://themalaysianreserve.com/2019/10/15/when-the-grass-is-greener-in-australia-for-local-tech-start-ups/

Reporters Without Borders. *2019 World Press Freedom Index—A Cycle of Fear*. 2019. Paris: Author. Accessed from https://rsf.org/en/2019-world-press-freedom-index-cycle-fear

Research and Markets. *Singaporean Defense Market—Attractiveness, Competitive Landscape and Forecasts to 2024* (Press Release). August 2019. ID: 4850684. Accessed from https://www.researchandmarkets.com/reports/4850684/singaporean-defense-market-attractiveness

Reserve Bank of New Zealand. *Regulatory Impact Assessment of Basel III Capital Requirements in New Zealand*. September 2012. Wellington, New Zealand: Author. Accessed from https://www.rbnz.govt.nz/-/media/ReserveBank/Files/regulation-and-supervision/banks/policy/4932427.pdf?la=en

Restaurant Association of South Africa. *South Africa's Top 100: Award-Winning Restaurants 2017*. November 2016. Douglasdale, South Africa: A RASA Management Services Publication. Accessed from http://restaurant.org.za.dedi279.nur4.host-h.net/wp-content/uploads/2016/11/Book-single-page-with-covers-v2.compressed.pdf

Charles Riley. "Bitcoin Hits $13,000 on Zimbabwe Exchange," *CNN Business*. November 16, 2017. Accessed from https://money.cnn.com/2017/11/16/investing/bitcoin-zimbabwe-price/index.html

Barry Ritholtz. "Iceland Found Another Way to Clean Up a Financial Crisis," *Bloomberg*. September 25, 2018. Accessed from https://www.bloomberg.com/opinion/articles/2018-09-25/iceland-found-another-way-to-clean-up-a-financial-crisis

Mark Roberts, Frederico Gil Sander, and Sailesh Tiwari (Eds.) *Time to Act: Realizing Indonesia's Urban Potential*. 2019. Washington, DC: International Bank for Reconstruction and Development/The World Bank. Accessed from https://openknowledge.worldbank.org/bitstream/handle/10986/31304/9781464813894.pdf

Larry Rohter. "Divorce Ties Chile in Knots," *The New York Times*. January 30, 2005. Accessed from https://www.nytimes.com/2005/01/30/weekinreview/divorce-ties-chile-in-knots.html

Eric Rosen. "As Billions More Fly, Here's How Aviation Could Evolve," *National Geographic*. June 20, 2017. Accessed from https://www.nationalgeographic.com/environment/urban-expeditions/transportation/air-travel-fuel-emissions-environment/

Nandita Roy and Elena Karaban. *Doing Business Report: With Strong Reform Agenda, India Is a Top Improver for 2nd Consecutive Year* (Press Release). October 31, 2018. Accessed from https://www.worldbank.org/en/news/press-release/2018/10/31/doing-business-report-with-strong-reform-agenda-india-is-a-top-improver-for-2nd-consecutive-year

Michael Safi. "Demonetisation Drive That Cost India 1.5M Jobs Fails to Uncover 'Black Money,'" *The Guardian*. August 30, 2018. Accessed from https://www.theguardian.com/world/2018/aug/30/india-demonetisation-drive-fails-uncover-black-money

P.R. Sanjai. "400 Deaths a Day Are Forcing India to Take Car Safety Seriously," *Economic Times*. January 10, 2018. Accessed from https://economictimes.indiatimes.com/news/politics-and-nation/400-deaths-a-day-are-forcing-india-to-take-car-safety-seriously/articleshow/62439700.cms?from=mdr

Santander. "Chile: Economic and Political Outline," *TradePortal* (Website). Last updated October 2019. Madrid, Spain: Export Enterprises, S.A. and Banco Santander, S.A. Accessed from https://en.portal.santandertrade.com/analyse-markets/chile/economic-political-outline

Heidi Sarna. "How to Go 'Tiger Trekking' in India's Ranthambore National Park," *CNBC*. Last updated October 29, 2019. Accessed from https://

www.cnbc.com/2019/10/28/tiger-treks-india-ranthambore-national-park.html

Dato' Sri Akhbar Satar. *Transparency International's 2018 Corruption Perceptions Index: Malaysia* (Press Release). January 29, 2018. Selangor, Malaysia: Transparency International Malaysia. Accessed from https://transparency.org.my/pages/news-and-events/press-releases/transparency-international-s-2018-corruption-perceptions-index-malaysia-1

Benjamin Elisha Sawe. "The Biggest Industries in New Zealand," *World Atlas*. Last updated February 21, 2018. Accessed from https://www.worldatlas.com/articles/the-biggest-industries-in-new-zealand.html

Benjamin Elisha Sawe. "Ethnic Groups of Malaysia," *World Atlas*. Last updated July 18, 2018. Accessed from https://www.worldatlas.com/articles/ethnic-groups-of-malaysia.html

Benjamin Elisha Sawe. "Religious Beliefs in Colombia," *World Atlas*. Last updated July 27, 2018. Accessed from https://www.worldatlas.com/articles/religious-beliefs-in-colombia.html

Courtney Schiessl. "Here's Everything You Need to Know About Chilean Wine," *Vinepair*. August 28, 2018. Accessed from https://vinepair.com/articles/chile-wine-guide/

Joseph E. Schwartzberg, Sanjay Subrahmanyam, T.G. Percival Spear, and Philip B. Calkins, et al. "India," *Encyclopædia Britannica*. Last updated March 18, 2020. Accessed from https://www.britannica.com/place/India

S.P. Sharma. *India's Rank Slips to 133rd in 2018 From 122nd in 2017 on World Happiness Index 2018: World Happiness Report 2018.* March 2018. New Delhi, India: PHD Chamber of Commerce and Industry. Accessed from http://phdcci.in/image/data/Research%20

Bureau-2014/Economic%20Developments/Economic-2018/March/
India%27s%20rank%20slips.pdf

Shantanu Nandan Sharma. "Delhi Could Be the World's Most Populous
City by 2028. But Is It Really Prepared?" *The Economic Times*. Last
updated February 17, 2019. Accessed from https://economictimes.
indiatimes.com/news/politics-and-nation/delhi-could-be-the-
worlds-most-populous-city-by-2028-but-is-it-really-prepared/
articleshow/68027790.cms?utm_source=contentofinterest&utm_
medium=text&utm_campaign=cppst

Tom Shaw, Michelle Burns, Kevin Johnson, et al. *Starbucks Corp. Investor
Day 2018* (Corrected Transcript). December 13, 2018. Seattle, WA:
Starbucks. Accessed from https://s22.q4cdn.com/869488222/files/
doc_downloads/2018/12/18/Starbucks-2018-NYC-Investor-Day_
Corrected-Transcript.pdf

Daniel Sheehy. "An Eyewitness Account of Pinochet's Coup 45 Years Ago,"
Smithsonian.com. September 10, 2018. Accessed from https://www.
smithsonianmag.com/smithsonian_institution/eyewitness-account-
pinochets-coup-45-years-ago-180970241/

Michael Sheetz. "Corona Beer Maker Constellation Ups Bet on Cannabis
With $4 Billion Investment in Canopy Growth," *CNBC*. August 15,
2018. Accessed from https://www.cnbc.com/2018/08/15/corona-
maker-constellation-ups-bet-on-cannabis-with-4-billion-investm.
html

Ragnhildur Sigurdardottir. "Icelanders in Shock As Tourism Collapse
Halts Economic Miracle," *Bloomberg*. June 19, 2019. Accessed from
https://www.bloomberg.com/news/articles/2019-06-20/icelanders-
in-shock-as-tourism-collapse-halts-economic-miracle

Caleb Silver. "Top 20 Economies in the World: Ranking the Richest
Countries in the World," *Investopedia*. Updated November 19, 2019.

Accessed from https://www.investopedia.com/insights/worlds-top-economies/

Laura Silver and Courtney Johnson. "Internet Connectivity Seen As Having Positive Impact on Life in Sub-Saharan Africa," *Global Attitudes and Trends*, Pew Research Center. October 9, 2018. Accessed from https://www.pewresearch.org/global/2018/10/09/internet-connectivity-seen-as-having-positive-impact-on-life-in-sub-saharan-africa/

Saurabh Sinha. "India Fastest Growing Domestic Aviation Market for 4th Year," *The Times of India*. Updated February 8, 2019. Accessed from https://timesofindia.indiatimes.com/business/india-business/india-fastest-growing-domestic-aviation-market-globally-for-four-years-in-a-row-says-iata/articleshow/67888272.cms

Sue Slaght. "Hike Huayna Picchu—One of the World's Most Dangerous Climbs," *Travel Tales of Life*. June 24, 2015. Accessed from https://traveltalesoflife.com/huayna-picchu-one-of-worlds-most-dangerous-hikes/

Carin Smith and Matthew le Cordeur. "Confusion Over Ban on Foreign Land Ownership," *Fin24*. February 13, 2015. Accessed from https://www.fin24.com/Economy/Confusion-over-ban-on-foreign-land-ownership-20150213

David Smith. "Internet Use on Mobile Phones in Africa Predicted to Increase 20-Fold," *The Guardian*. June 5, 2014. Accessed from https://www.theguardian.com/world/2014/jun/05/internet-use-mobile-phones-africa-predicted-increase-20-fold

Mike Snider. "Facebook Reportedly Looks to Link Messenger, WhatsApp, and Instagram Messaging," *USA Today*. January 25, 2019. Accessed from https://www.usatoday.com/story/tech/talkingtech/2019/01/25/

facebook-instagram-whatsapp-linked-messaging-reportedly-works/2676662002/

Spanish Gurus. "Why Colombia Deserves Your Visit," *Medium*. November 20, 2016. Accessed from https://medium.com/@google_82078/why-colombia-deserves-your-visit-50524f1b8ae7

Kiran Stacey and James Kynge. "India Regains Title of World's Fastest-Growing Major Economy," *Financial Times*. February 28, 2018. Accessed from https://www.ft.com/content/cb5a4668-1c84-11e8-956a-43db76e69936

Staff Writer. "The Biggest Economies in Africa," *BusinessTech*. July 10, 2018. Accessed from https://businesstech.co.za/news/finance/257337/the-biggest-economies-in-africa/

Staff Writer. "World Bank Cuts South Africa's GDP Growth for 2019," *BusinessTech*. January 9, 2019. Accessed from https://businesstech.co.za/news/business/292774/world-bank-cuts-south-africas-gdp-growth-for-2019/

Swiss Chamber of Commerce in Peru. *Peru: Major Business Sectors*. April 2018. Lima: Switzerland Global Enterprise. Accessed from https://www.s-ge.com/sites/default/files/publication/free/major-business-sectors-peru-s-ge-2018-04.pdf

László Szerb, Gábor Márkus, Esteban Lafuente, and Zoltan J. Acs. *Global Entrepreneurship Index 2019: Technical Report*. DOI: 10.13140/RG.2.2.17692.64641. January 2020. Washington, DC: The Global Entrepreneurship and Development Institute (and The Regional Innovation and Entrepreneurship Research Center). Accessed from https://www.researchgate.net/publication/338547954_Global_Entrepreneurship_Index_2019/link/5e20a855a6fdcc10156f76d8/download

Alexandra Talty. "The 16 Best Destinations for Cheap Flights in 2020," *Forbes*. November 27, 2019. Accessed from https://www.forbes.com/sites/alexandratalty/2019/11/27/the-16-best-destinations-for-cheap-flights-in-2020/#6dd5cfde1d62

Weizhen Tan. "Indonesia Plans to Move Its Capital From Jakarta. Here's Why," *CNBC*. May 1, 2019. Accessed from https://www.cnbc.com/2019/05/02/indonesias-joko-widodo-decides-to-move-capital-from-jakarta.html

Chris Taylor. "Smartphone Users Check Facebook 14 Times a Day," *CNN Business*. Updated March 28, 2013. Accessed from https://www.cnn.com/2013/03/28/tech/mobile/survey-phones-facebook/index.html

Romila Thapar, K.R. Dikshit, Philip B. Calkins, and Joseph E. Schwartzberg, et al. "India: The British, 1600–1740," *Encyclopædia Britannica*. Last updated March 18, 2020. Accessed from https://www.britannica.com/place/India/The-British-1600-1740

Shashi Tharoor. "Newspapers Thrive, in India," *The Japan Times*. May 22, 2017. Accessed from https://www.japantimes.co.jp/opinion/2017/05/22/commentary/world-commentary/newspapers-thrive-india/#.XrG6x5p7mJt

Peter Theodosiou and Jason Thomas. "More People Are Moving From Australia to New Zealand Than Vice Versa for the First Time in 25 Years, NZ Government Statistics Reveal," *SBS News*. February 2, 2016. Accessed from https://www.sbs.com.au/news/more-people-moving-to-new-zealand-from-australia-than-vice-versa

Amy Tikkanen and the Editors of Encyclopædia Britannica. "Cook Strait—Strait, New Zealand," *Encyclopædia Britannica*. n.d. Accessed from https://www.britannica.com/place/Cook-Strait

Amy Tikkanen and the Editors of Encyclopædia Britannica. "Pablo Escobar—Colombian Criminal," *Encyclopædia Britannica*. n.d. Accessed from https://www.britannica.com/biography/Pablo-Escobar

Craig Tindale. "Australia's Economy Is a House of Cards," *Steve Keen's Debtwatch*. November 14, 2017. Accessed from https://www.debtdeflation.com/blogs/2017/11/14/australias-economy-is-a-house-of-cards/

TNN. "Richest 1% Own 58% of Total Wealth in India," *The Times of India*. January 16, 2017. Accessed from https://timesofindia.indiatimes.com/business/india-business/richest-1-own-58-of-total-wealth-in-india/articleshow/56591274.cms

Tourism New Zealand. *Annual Report 2016/2017*. Auckland, New Zealand: Author. Accessed from https://www.tourismnewzealand.com/media/3231/tourism-new-zealand-annual-report-2016-17.pdf

Mfuneko Toyana and Nomvelo Chalumbira. "UPDATE 3-South Africa in Recession for First Time Since 2009; Rand Slumps," *Reuters*. September 4, 2018. Accessed from https://www.reuters.com/article/safrica-economy-gdp/update-2-south-africa-in-recession-for-first-time-since-2009-rand-slumps-idUSL8N1VQ25G

The Treasury of the New Zealand Government. *New Zealand Economic and Financial Overview 2016*. April 6, 2016. Wellington, New Zealand: Author. Accessed from https://treasury.govt.nz/publications/economic-overview/new-zealand-economic-and-financial-overview-2016#formats

Daniel Trotta. "Bacardi Demands U.S. Explain Giving Havana Club Brand to Cuba," *Reuters*. February 1, 2016. Accessed from https://www.reuters.com/article/cuba-bacardi-havana-club/bacardi-demands-u-s-explain-giving-havana-club-brand-to-cuba-idUSL2N15G2NB

Zeke Turner. "Iceland Takes Hard Look at Tech Boom Sparked by Its Cheap, Bountiful Power," *The Wall Street Journal*. April 19, 2018. Accessed from https://www.wsj.com/articles/iceland-takes-hard-look-at-tech-boom-sparked-by-its-cheap-bountiful-power-1524130201

Louise Twining-Ward et al. *Sub Saharan Africa Tourism Industry Research*. November 18, 2009. Washington, DC: World Bank, Africa Region's Finance and Private Sector Development Department. Accessed from http://siteresources.worldbank.org/INTAFRSUMAFTPS/Resources/2049902-1327506860777/FinalSSATourismRpt1118.pdf

UNESCO. *World Heritage List: Tikal National Park* (Website). n.d. Accessed from http://whc.unesco.org/en/list/64

Batya Ungar-Sargon. "Is Chile's Troubled Past the Reason Its Wines' Future Is So Bright?" *Vinepair*. August 2, 2017. Accessed from https://vinepair.com/articles/chile-wine-past-present-future/

Shanidy Vasquez. "COVID-19 to Belize's Economy," *Breaking Belize News*. April 20, 2020. Accessed from https://www.breakingbelizenews.com/2020/04/20/covid-19-to-belizes-economy/

Adam Veitch. "Comuna 13: How a Medellin Community Turned a War Zone Into a Tourist Attraction," *Colombia Reports*. June 14, 2019. Accessed from https://colombiareports.com/comuna-13-how-a-medellin-community-turned-a-war-zone-into-a-tourist-attraction/

Ed Vulliamy. "Medellín, Colombia: Reinventing the World's Most Dangerous City," *The Guardian*. June 9, 2013. Accessed from https://www.theguardian.com/world/2013/jun/09/medellin-colombia-worlds-most-dangerous-city

Nora Walsh. "How to Travel to Patagonia," *Travel + Leisure*. December 4, 2016. Accessed from https://www.travelandleisure.com/trip-ideas/how-to-travel-to-patagonia

Andy Wang. "The Digital Desert: Opportunities and Challenges in Sub-Saharan Africa," *Harvard International Review*. January 11, 2020. Accessed from https://hir.harvard.edu/the-digital-desert-opportunities-and-challenges-in-sub-saharan-africa/

Yue Wang. "How People Are Earning Millions From Tencent's WeChat—But Not Everyone's Happy," *Forbes*. January 23, 2018. Accessed from https://www.forbes.com/sites/ywang/2018/01/23/how-people-are-earning-millions-from-tencents-wechat-but-not-everyones-happy/#715cf3d25563

Amanda Williams. "3 Reasons to Suck Up the Cost and Visit Churchill, Manitoba," *A Dangerous Business Travel Blog*. May 4, 2019. Accessed from https://www.dangerous-business.com/3-reasons-to-suck-up-the-cost-and-visit-churchill-manitoba/

The World Bank. *Doing Business 2015: Going Beyond Efficiency* (12th Edition). 2014. International Bank for Reconstruction and Development/The World Bank. Accessed from https://www.doingbusiness.org/content/dam/doingBusiness/media/Annual-Reports/English/DB15-Full-Report.pdf

The World Bank. *Doing Business 2017: Equal Opportunity for All*. 2017. Washington, DC: International Bank for Reconstruction and Development/The World Bank. Accessed from https://www.doingbusiness.org/content/dam/doingBusiness/media/Annual-Reports/English/DB2018-Full-Report.pdf

The World Bank. *Doing Business 2018: Reforming to Create Jobs*. 2018. Washington, DC: Author. Accessed from https://www.doingbusiness.org/content/dam/doingBusiness/media/Annual-Reports/English/DB2018-Full-Report.pdf

The World Bank. *Doing Business 2020: Economic Profile—Peru*. Washington, DC: Author. n.d. ISBN 978-1-4648-1440-2. Accessed from https://www.doingbusiness.org/content/dam/doingBusiness/country/p/peru/PER.pdf

The World Bank. "Ease of Doing Business in India," *Doing Business* (website.) n.d. Accessed from https://www.doingbusiness.org/en/data/exploreeconomies/libya#

The World Bank. "Ease of Doing Business Rankings," *Doing Business* (Website). n.d. Accessed from https://www.doingbusiness.org/en/rankings

The World Bank. "Economy Profile: Belize," *Doing Business 2019: Training for Reform* (a World Bank Group Flagship Report). Washington, DC: Author. Accessed from https://www.doingbusiness.org/content/dam/doingBusiness/country/b/belize/BLZ.pdf

The World Bank. "Economy Profile: Peru," *Doing Business 2019: Training for Reform* (a World Bank Group Flagship Report). Washington, DC: Author. Accessed from https://www.doingbusiness.org/content/dam/doingBusiness/country/p/peru/PER.pdf

The World Bank. *GDP Growth (Annual %)—Tunisia, Morocco, Algeria* (Website). 2019. Washington, DC: Author. Accessed from https://data.worldbank.org/indicator/NY.GDP.MKTP.KD.ZG?end=2018&locations=TN-MA-DZ&start=1999

The World Bank. *The World Bank in Chile* (Website). 2019. Washington, DC: Author. Accessed from https://www.worldbank.org/en/country/chile

The World Bank. *The World Bank in Malaysia* (Website). Last updated March 2019. Washington, DC: Author. Accessed from https://www.worldbank.org/en/country/malaysia/overview

World Economic Forum. *The Global Human Capital Report, 2017: Preparing People for the Future of Work* (Insight Report). 2017. Switzerland: Author. ISBN 978-1-944835-10-1. Accessed from http://www3.weforum.org/docs/WEF_Global_Human_Capital_Report_2017.pdf

Worldometer. *Botswana Population Live* (Website). Shanghai: Dadax. Accessed from https://www.worldometers.info/world-population/botswana-population/

Timothy Worstall. "Congratulations to Robert Mugabe—Zimbabwe's Unemployment Rate Now 95%," *Forbes*. March 5, 2017. Accessed from https://www.forbes.com/sites/timworstall/2017/03/05/congratulations-to-robert-mugabe-zimbabwes-unemployment-rate-now-95/#1c40286c244c

Timothy Worstall. "With 95% Unemployment Rate, Robert Mugabe Insists Zimbabwe Is Not Fragile," *Forbes*. May 5, 2017. Accessed from https://www.forbes.com/sites/timworstall/2017/05/05/with-95-unemployment-rate-robert-mugabe-insists-zimbabwe-is-not-fragile/#644d94a568e8

Tim Wyatt. "Cuba to Finally Give Citizens Internet Access on Their Phones As Government Launches 3G Service," *The Independent*. December 6, 2018. Accessed from https://www.independent.co.uk/news/world/americas/cuba-internet-access-mobile-cell-phones-wifi-3g-connection-telecoms-a8667771.html

Yale School of Environmental Studies. "Forest Governance—Colombia," *Global Forest Atlas*. n.d. Accessed from https://globalforestatlas.yale.edu/amazon-forest/forest-governance/forest-governance-colombia

Li Yuan. "Private Businesses Built Modern China. Now the Government Is Pushing Back," *The New York Times*. October 3, 2018. Accessed from https://www.nytimes.com/2018/10/03/business/china-economy-private-enterprise.html

Wendy Zeldin. "Zimbabwe: Indigenization and Empowerment Act," *Library of Congress: Global Legal Monitor.* April 2, 2008. Accessed from https://www.loc.gov/law/foreign-news/article/zimbabwe-indigenization-and-empowerment-act/